Electric Power Industry Outlook and Atlas
1997 TO 2001

Electric Power Industry Outlook and Atlas

1997 TO 2001

PennWell Power Group

Magazine Editors

and Contributors

PennWell Books

PennWell Publishing Company
Tulsa, Oklahoma

Electric Power Industry Outlook and Atlas

1 9 9 7 T O 2 0 0 1

Publication Data
This special report was published in November 1996.

Publisher
Published by the Information Products Group of PennWell Publishing Company, publishers of *Power Engineering, Power Engineering International, Electric Light & Power, Independent Energy, Utility Automation,* and *Energy Marketing.*

For Ordering Copies
If you would like additional information about our publications, or if you would like to order a copy on a 15-day inspection, just write to: PennWell Books, Box 21288, Tulsa, OK 74121. Phone (800) 752-9764.

Editorial Staff
Sponsoring Editor: James A. Ferrier
Copy Editor: Barbara Clarke
Designer: Suzanne Crolley/Designs by Suzanne
Maps: Michael Kerr and Brent Church

Cover Photograph
Kevin G. Buesing
Green Bay, WI

Copyright © 1996 by
PennWell Publishing Company
1421 South Sheridan/P.O. Box 1260
Tulsa, Oklahoma 74101

ISBN 0-87814-652-0

Printed in the United States of America

1 2 3 4 5 00 99 98 97 96

Contents

Worldwide Electricity Supply Outlook

Fuels Outlook

Technology Outlook

——— Regulatory Issues Outlook ———

——————— Atlas ———————

Figures

Figures

Tables

Tables

Electric Power Industry Outlook and Atlas

1997 TO 2001

Introduction

BOB SMOCK
PUBLISHER
POWER GROUP MAGAZINES

The global electric power industry is entering an exciting new era in its second century. The tightly regulated, state-controlled, monopolistic industry of the past hundred years is giving way to a vital, competitive, market-driven, customer-oriented, fast-growing industry. Developing nations around the globe are seeing unprecedented economic growth which requires massive and rapid growth in infrastructure industries such as electric power.

In response to these exciting industry developments we are publishing the first edition of PennWell Publishing Company's *Electric Power Industry Outlook*. This power industry outlook has been written by editors from and contributors to our power industry magazines, including *Power Engineering*, *Power Engineering International*, *Electric Light & Power*, *Independent Energy*, and *Utility Automation*. They bring many years of insight and expertise to this first edition of *Electric Power Industry Outlook*.

Our goal in this publication is to provide you some guidance on where the global electric power industry is headed.

WORLDWIDE ELECTRICITY DEMAND

The first section covers the outlook for worldwide electricity demand. The global electric power industry is enjoying a huge surge in demand, particularly in emerging nations. The cause of this rise in demand is the widespread adoption of market economies and the resulting surge in economic growth following the collapse of communism. Electric power generation and delivery are primary infrastructure needs of rapidly growing economies in developing nations. At least half the population of the developing nations still do not have access to electric power.

Average annual electricity generation per person in developing countries is 660 kilowatt-hours, compared to 10,500 in the United States, and 6,000 in Western Europe and Japan. That is changing rapidly.

Electrification of the world economy is another driver of this growth surge. Electricity is the favored form of energy consumption. Electricity is expected to be the fastest-growing form of end-use energy worldwide through the year 2010, according to the U.S. Department of Energy. From 1990 to 1992, electricity consumption worldwide grew six times as fast as total end-use energy consumption.

Freeing electric production and delivery from the shackles of government control also has fueled this worldwide surge. Electric power traditionally has been considered a state monopoly in most countries. Central planners stifled electric power and economic development in too many nations. That is coming to an end and electric power industries are among the leading beneficiaries.

During the past few years many state electricity monopolies have been privatized or have provided an opportunity for private investors to develop new electric generation and delivery capacity. Developing countries whose economic growth is limited by shortages of electric power, such as China and India, have turned to private power development to help them catch up. A key feature of this trend is permitting outside private investment, which requires improved understanding of the role profit and risk management play in attracting private investment.

The size of the electric power market in developing countries has been estimated to be as high as one trillion dollars over the next 20 years. The most rapid growth right now is occurring in Asia. Next growth markets to take off are expected to be Latin America, the Middle East, and Eastern Europe.

Demand growth in the developed nations is at a lower rate but even moderate growth in these large electric systems generates a need for massive construction of new facilities. Worldwide,

Figure I–1. World electricity consumption, 1970-2010

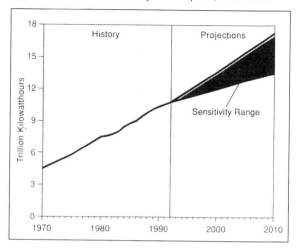

electricity growth is expected to average 2% per year through the year 2010 as shown in Figure I–1.

This publication focuses on the demand outlook for North America, South and Central America, Europe, Russia, the Middle East, Africa, Asia, and the Pacific Rim countries.

WORLDWIDE ELECTRICITY SUPPLY

The next section of our outlook reviews electricity supply. Most forecasts of the world power generation market estimate that an average of 100 GW of new capacity per year will be added for at least the next 10 or 15 years.

In the developing countries, supply has been unable to keep up with demand, chiefly due to institutional obstacles.

In the United States, generating capacity has been growing at the rate of about one-half percent a year while power demand is growing at the rate of about 2.5% a year. A few gas turbines are going on-line each year, but that new capacity is barely offsetting power plant retirements.

As a result, power generation reserve margins in the United States are falling at the rate of about two percentage points a year.

Table I–1
U.S. utility generating capacity reserve margin

	1990	1991	1992	1993	1994	1995
Generating Capacity (GW)	691	693	695	700	703	705
SUMMER PEAK (GW)	546	551	549	581	586	605
MARGIN %	21%	20%	21%	17%	17%	14%

As shown in Table I–1, the U.S. utility reserve margin has dropped from 21% at the beginning of the decade to less than 15% in 1995. A hot summer in 1996 will drive it even lower. In the past a reserve margin of 15% was the trigger level for a new round of capacity construction. That is obviously no longer the case, but as the margin drops U.S. power generators must respond and begin constructing new generating plants at a much faster pace than that of the past few years.

A key role in meeting the demand for new electrical capacity worldwide is played by the independent power producers (IPPs). Independent, nonutility power production was born in the United States in the mid-1980s. By 1990, IPPs were building one-half the new generating capacity in the United States. The IPP trend, led by independent developers based in the United States, moved to other countries such as the United Kingdom which privatized its state-owned utility in 1990. IPPs are now playing a major role in electric power expansion in many Asian countries. IPPs also will play a major role in developing markets in other parts of the world.

In the following pages is an analysis of the electricity supply side in each of the major regions of the world.

FUELS OUTLOOK

The changing fuels pattern for world electricity production is shown in Figure I–2. The use of all fuels increases but the "market shares" change. The most rapidly growing fuel is natural gas whose share of electricity generation rises from 13% in 1990 to 17% in 2010.

Figure I–2. World electricity consumption by generating fuel type, 1990 and 2010

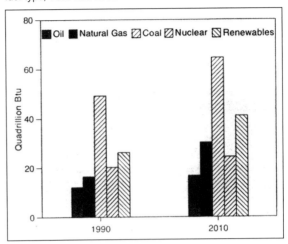

Hydroelectricity, the dominant form of renewable energy, also increases its share of electricity production over the 20-year period, particularly in the developing countries. Hydroelectricity is the most efficient method for generating electric power but it is almost completely developed in the industrialized nations.

Use of coal and oil for electricity production rises but their shares of the total declines slightly. Coal is the major fuel for world electricity production with a share of about 35%.

Nuclear power, the remaining major energy source for electricity production, grows slightly but its market share declines the most, from 17% in 1990 to 14% in 2010. Nuclear power is popular in Asia and is enjoying rapid growth there, but that growth is being offset largely by premature retirements of operating nuclear plants in the industrialized countries.

Environmental concerns, particularly over carbon dioxide emissions, could change the fuel mix. The fossil fuels, particularly coal, add to carbon dioxide emissions. Hydroelectricity and nuclear power do not. A worldwide crackdown on carbon dioxide could improve the prospects for nuclear power and decrease the prospects for coal.

TECHNOLOGY OUTLOOK

You can find a review of the major power technologies in the following pages, including fossil steam power generation, nuclear, combined-cycle, gasification, renewables, and automation technology.

The most significant new technology in recent years has been the combined-cycle, actually the gas turbine. Rapid advances in gas turbine efficiency and unit size in the past six or seven years have driven combined-cycle thermal efficiencies to almost 60%, by far the best among the thermal generation systems.

This technology development explains much of the growth in natural gas noted above. Natural gas is the best fuel for gas turbines because they require clean fuels.

The desire to match coal and other solid fuels, our most abundant and low-cost fuels, with gas turbines explains the rise of gasification technology. This technology converts relatively dirty solid fuels into clean fuel gas. After decades of development it is finally catching on commercially, particularly in the petroleum industry where they can gasify residual solid hydrocarbons such as petroleum coke.

Other new technologies such as pressurized fluidized-bed combustion and fuel cells also are showing promise as commercial technologies for use after the year 2000.

REGULATORY ISSUES

Finally, we cover world developments in regulations which is the most rapidly changing and significant of all the subjects covered in this outlook. As mentioned earlier, there is a worldwide trend toward deregulation, privatization, and power industry restructuring. It is probably the most significant institutional change in the world power industry since it began.

However, understanding these global institutional changes poses great problems. Each nation approaches power industry regulation in a different manner. Attempts to regionalize power industry regulation such as the European Community's energy policy program have not succeeded . . . at least not yet. That leaves us with a crazy quilt of regulations and approaches to power industry structure. Many countries, such as the United States, have highly fragmented power industry regulatory structures with much autonomy delegated to individual states or provinces.

The common theme around the world is the increasing level of competition in national power industries. The United Kingdom is one of the pioneers. The United Kingdom privatized their state-owned electric power monopoly almost overnight in 1990. They created two large, privately owned generating companies, a privately owned electric transmission system, privately owned electricity distribution companies, and, most significantly, they created a wholesale bulk power pool linking the generating and power delivery companies.

Both buyers and sellers can bid into this pool. Supply is open to all and the lowest cost generators prevail. There is also a method for direct links between buyers and sellers. Electricity prices have fallen and the U.K. system appears to be working fairly well.

The U.K. model is spreading. Former members of the British empire such as New Zealand and parts of Australia are adopting it. Several states and regions of the United States also are adopting pool systems similar to the United Kingdom's.

In the United States a major step toward a more competitive power industry was taken in April 1996 when the Federal Energy Regulatory Commission published rules for opening up access to the nation's electric transmission system. A new, competitive, wholesale electricity market is now developing, similar to the national wholesale natural gas market that developed after that industry was deregulated a few years ago. In fact, many of the natural gas marketing firms have opened businesses in this new electricity market.

Electric utility distribution franchises in the United States are no longer restricted by transmission access to their own company's vertically integrated generation system or to a nearby utility's generation system. Any utility in the United States can buy or sell wholesale power to or from any other utility, as long as it can find an available transmission path with available capacity. Low-cost producers have much broader access to utility customers now. Transmission owners must make their transmission systems available to everyone on an equal basis.

While competition is definitely spreading throughout the world power industry, many countries are still tightly regulated and opportunities for competition in the power industry are still quite limited.

The environmental trend is much less clear. Several years ago there was growing concern over global warming and rising pressure to limit emissions of gases such as carbon dioxide thought to contribute to global warming. Some European countries even adopted emission limits. The United States adopted a program that does not restrict emissions but seeks to limit the growth of carbon dioxide through voluntary programs.

The developing countries have been much less receptive to concern over global warming, arguing that the developed countries account for most carbon dioxide emissions but want to restrict further growth in those emissions. This action limits the ability of developing countries to take equal advantage of fossil fuels to drive their power system growth.

This debate has blunted the global effort to restrict carbon dioxide. More convincing scientific evidence that carbon dioxide does directly contribute to global warming, or that global warming is actually occurring, could change this global environmental issue.

We hope you find our *Electric Power Industry Outlook* useful and informative. Please tell us what you think.

Robert Smock, publisher, PennWell power industry magazines, 1421 S. Sheridan Ave., Tulsa, OK, 74112.

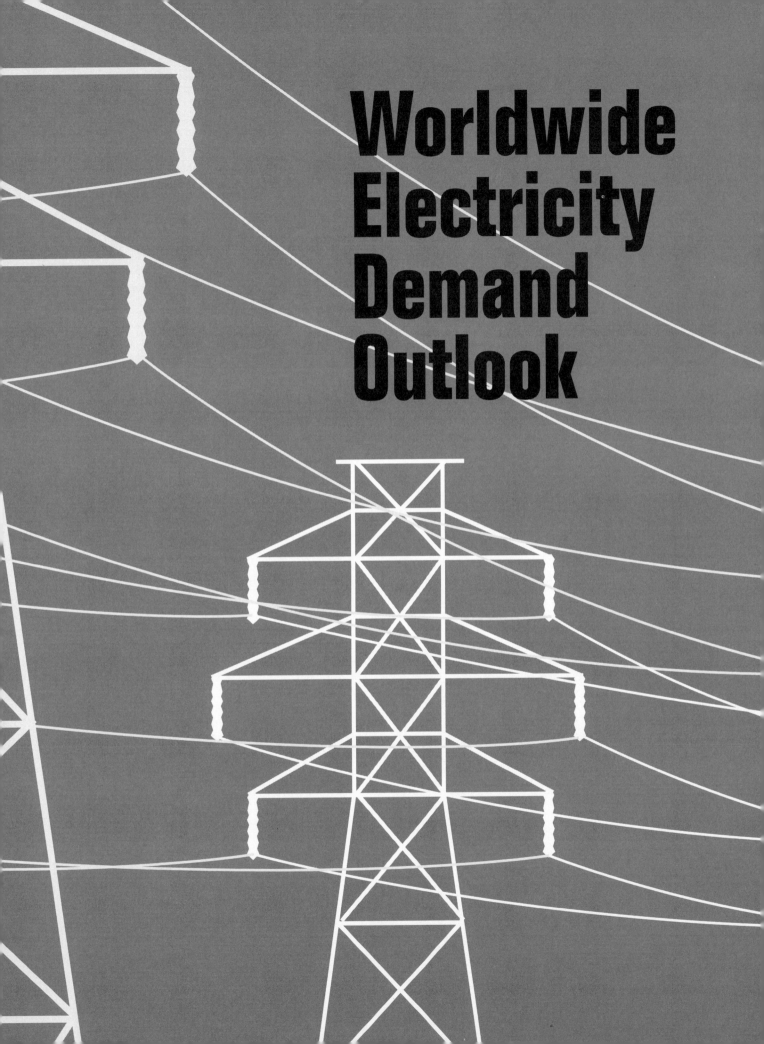

Worldwide Electricity Demand Outlook

Chapter 1
North America Electricity Demand

DENISE WARKENTIN
NEWS EDITOR, *ELECTRIC LIGHT & POWER*
EDITOR, *ENERGY MARKETING*

OVERVIEW

More efficient generation technologies will offset the projected increase in per capita demand for electricity that will amount to an average annual rate of 0.5% from 1994 to 2015.

According to the Energy Information Administration's (EIA) publication, *Annual Energy Outlook 1996 with Projections to 2015*, this will be a continuation of a trend that occurred in the first half of the 1990s. Then increases in appliance efficiency and insulation standards, along with industrial awareness of the impacts of energy costs on production costs, dampened the growth of electricity consumption, with demand lagging behind economic growth. According to EIA, this trend, with electricity demand growing more slowly than the economy, is expected to continue over the next two decades.

EIA also pointed out that rather than looking for a significant reduction in individual energy consumption, the energy savings that result from higher efficiencies can be expected to be used for new products and services and for new features that will be added to traditional products.

AGGREGATED DEMAND

According to the North American Electric Reliability Council (NERC), aggregated summer peak demand for 1995 to 2004 for the United States is projected to increase by an average annual growth rate of 1.7%, as shown in Table 1–1. For Canada, the aggregated summer peak demand for the forecast period is projected to have an annual average growth rate of 1.9%, while, for Mexico, 1.8%. Refer to Table 1–1 for more detail on both Canada and Mexico and to the Latin American chapters in this book for more information on demand in Mexico. Table 1–2 is NERC's projected summer capacity and demand for the years 1995 to 2004.

Table 1–1
Peak electricity demand (summer MW)

			Actual 1994	Projected 1995	1996	1997	1998	1999	2000	2001	2002	2003	2004	AAGR (%)
ECAR		U.S.	87,165	87,165	88,636	90,446	91,493	93,257	94,270	95,676	97,032	98,715	100,159	1.6
ERCOT		U.S.	44,162	45,440	46,249	47,130	48,282	49,328	50,478	51,475	52,557	53,655	54,690	2.1
MAAC		U.S.	46,019	44,571	45,099	45,733	46,365	46,964	47,632	48,324	49,020	49,710	50,078	1.3
MAIN		U.S.	42,562	43,958	44,716	45,515	46,358	47,109	47,772	48,497	49,104	49,874	50,696	1.6
MAIN	EM	U.S.	7,288	7,388	7,484	7,579	7,665	7,750	7,836	7,921	8,007	8,093	8,178	1.1
MAIN	NI	U.S.	17,928	18,600	18,950	19,350	19,750	20,100	20,450	20,800	21,150	21,500	21,900	1.8
MAIN	SCI	U.S.	7,772	8,081	8,201	8,299	8,417	8,546	8,646	8,734	8,715	8,839	8,954	1.1
MAIN	WUM	U.S.	9,574	9,889	10,081	10,287	10,526	10,713	10,840	11,042	11,232	11,442	11,664	1.9
MAPP		U.S.	27,000	28,736	29,486	30,109	30,462	30,918	31,387	32,142	32,721	33,047	33,636	1.8
NPCC		U.S.	47,581	47,495	47,990	48,444	48,909	49,356	49,911	50,299	50,804	51,273	51,673	0.9
NPCC	NE	U.S.	20,519	20,425	20,650	20,814	20,979	21,146	21,471	21,639	21,974	22,243	22,463	1.1
NPCC	NY	U.S.	27,062	27,070	27,340	27,630	27,930	28,210	28,440	28,660	28,830	29,030	29,210	0.8
SERC		U.S.	132,584	140,227	144,099	147,397	150,962	154,341	157,486	160,834	164,085	167,393	170,794	2.2
SERC	FL	U.S.	32,904	32,662	33,438	34,159	34,972	35,577	36,213	36,883	37,496	38,128	38,834	1.9
SERC	SOU	U.S.	32,596	35,457	36,843	37,420	38,298	39,082	39,879	40,654	41,482	42,291	43,149	2.2
SERC	TVA	U.S.	23,398	24,521	25,136	25,766	26,415	27,084	27,763	28,452	29,140	29,825	30,514	2.5
SERC	VAC	U.S.	43,686	47,587	48,682	50,052	51,277	52,598	53,631	54,845	55,967	57,149	58,297	2.3
SPP		U.S.	56,035	59,001	60,200	61,120	62,170	63,247	63,820	64,712	65,787	67,016	68,559	1.7
SPP	N	U.S.	13,354	14,534	14,837	15,121	15,420	15,714	15,965	16,223	16,488	16,839	17,148	1.9
SPP	SE	U.S.	23,300	24,490	24,952	25,255	25,655	26,081	26,111	26,378	26,818	27,315	27,785	1.4
SPP	WC	U.S.	19,381	19,977	20,411	20,744	21,095	21,452	21,744	22,111	22,481	22,862	23,626	1.9
WSCC		U.S.	102,212	103,821	106,251	108,281	109,987	111,723	113,395	115,123	116,963	118,835	120,696	1.7
WSCC	AZN	U.S.	13,985	13,839	14,107	14,442	14,765	15,088	15,391	15,715	16,047	16,381	16,717	2.1
WSCC	CNV	U.S.	51,634	52,990	53,943	54,840	55,595	56,413	57,171	57,956	58,827	59,716	60,545	1.5
WSCC	NWP	U.S.	31,277	30,101	31,196	31,710	32,281	32,736	33,198	33,688	34,215	34,770	35,286	1.8
WSCC	RMP	U.S.	6,955	7,146	7,252	7,520	7,624	7,762	7,901	8,038	8,165	8,280	8,424	1.8
TOTAL		**U.S.**	**585,320**	**600,414**	**612,726**	**624,175**	**634,988**	**646,243**	**656,151**	**667,082**	**678,073**	**689,518**	**700,981**	**1.7**
MAPP		Canada	4,772	4,978	5,040	5,031	5,114	5,159	5,273	5,321	5,366	5,414	5,465	1.0
NPCC		Canada	41,448	41,584	42,825	43,870	45,147	45,905	46,551	47,247	47,987	48,663	49,284	1.9
NPCC	NB	Canada	1,594	1,767	1,804	1,834	1,870	1,907	1,943	1,978	2,014	2,051	2,089	1.9
NPCC	NS	Canada	1,247	1,303	1,312	1,322	1,339	1,358	1,380	1,405	1,433	1,463	1,495	1.5
NPCC	ONT	Canada	20,918	20,214	20,767	21,399	21,811	22,170	22,485	22,818	23,121	23,437	23,775	1.8
NPCC	PEI	Canada	127	130	132	135	137	140	143	146	149	152	155	2.0
PNCC	QUE	Canada	17,562	18,170	18,810	19,180	19,990	20,330	20,600	20,900	21,270	21,560	21,770	2.0
WSCC		Canada	12,878	12,556	13,105	13,442	13,721	13,942	14,210	14,563	14,725	14,980	15,292	2.2
TOTAL		**Canada**	**59,098**	**59,118**	**60,970**	**62,343**	**63,982**	**65,006**	**66,034**	**67,131**	**68,078**	**69,057**	**70,041**	**1.9**
WSCC		Mexico	1,034	1,123	1,210	1,276	1,392	1,488	1,593	1,708	1,831	1,961	2,100	7.2
TOTAL		**NERC**	**645,452**	**660,655**	**674,906**	**687,794**	**700,362**	**712,737**	**723,778**	**735,921**	**747,982**	**760,536**	**773,122**	**1.8**
ASCC		Alaska	524	531	534	545	579	602	607	613	619	625	632	2.0

Notes: NPCC New England's Peak Demand has Direct Control Load Management and Interruptible Demand already subtracted out.
MACC's Peak Demand has Control Load Management and Interruptible Demand already subtracted out.

[Courtesy North American Electric Reliability Council]

The EIA stated that information in its report should be taken together with other sources of information since during the year new and different information becomes available that will change EIA observations and projections about demand.

According to the EIA, all energy forecasts in past years have overestimated the future prices of

Table 1–2
Projected capacity and demand (summer MW)

	Projected 1995	1996	1997	1998	1999	2000	2001	2002	2003	2004
Internal Demand	661,980	676,325	689,250	701,869	714,282	725,368	737,578	749,703	762,323	774,995
Standby Demand	707	755	806	850	883	910	941	975	1,008	1,023
Total Internal Demand	662,687	677,080	690,056	702,719	715,165	726,278	738,519	750,678	763,331	776,018
Direct Control Load Management	6,923	7,498	8,160	8,747	9,462	10,318	11,010	11,419	11,759	12,140
Interruptible Demand	20,787	22,096	23,082	23,450	24,232	23,727	24,006	24,186	24,763	24,830
Net Internal Demand	634,977	647,486	658,814	670,522	681,471	692,233	703,503	715,073	726,809	739,048
Total Owned Capacity	773,936	781,791	785,112	791,867	798,530	807,810	817,219	827,616	836,661	846,083
Inoperable Capacity	7,851	6,672	6,570	6,221	6,151	6,723	6,723	6,228	6,228	6,228
Net Operable Capacity	766,085	775,119	778,542	785,646	792,379	801,087	810,496	821,388	830,433	839,855
IPPs	33,906	36,374	39,245	41,204	42,440	43,990	44,670	45,428	46,452	46,629
Capacity Purchases	25,510	25,160	26,006	25,731	26,238	23,176	21,362	20,848	21,145	21,518
Full Respons Purchases	9,786	9,704	10,412	10,087	10,487	9,654	7,610	7,351	7,888	7,883
Capacity Sales	16,893	16,613	16,803	16,354	15,306	12,933	12,360	12,228	12,432	12,145
Full Respons Sales	7,013	6,974	7,143	6,923	7,095	6,873	6,558	6,603	6,842	6,616
Adjustments	12	12	12	12	12	12	12	12	12	12
Planned Capacity Res	808,596	820,028	826,978	836,215	845,739	855,308	864,156	875,424	885,586	895,845
Planned Outages	20,430	17,029	15,237	18,101	16,854	17,336	15,390	17,275	18,258	15,749
Net Capacity Less Outage	788,167	802,999	811,741	818,114	828,885	837,972	848,766	858,149	867,328	880,096

Notes: Planned Capacity Resource Sum of the subregional capacity resources may not equal the WSCC U.S. totals because: (1) subregional peak demands on which resources are based may occur in different months than the coincident WSCC U.S.

[Courtesy North American Electric Reliability Council]

fossil fuels. This tendency was the most notable in the 1970s and early 1980s. Predictions of energy prices made during those years have been proven by history to be dramatically overstated. According to EIA, the major factors that were underestimated and which now produce sharply lower price forecasts include:

- increased competition among suppliers,

- significant penetration of new exploration and drilling technologies that reduce costs and increase the size of the U.S. petroleum resource base, and

- decreased energy demand as a market response to high prices and as a result of policy initiatives to constrain energy usage.

In recent years, energy forecasters, including EIA, have projected lower estimates of future fuel prices than actually materialized. At present, there is no guarantee that new factors will not cause prices to rise slower or faster than current projections, or even to fall from current levels.

Energy prices in EIA's 1996 report are lower than those contained in the agency's 1995 report. However, EIA pointed out that total consumption in 2010 is expected to be about the same—105 quadrillion British thermal units. Residential and commercial demand is higher in the 1996 report due to lower prices and higher projected growth for new electricity uses. With slower growth in energy-intensive industries, industrial demand is lower. Transportation demand is about the same.

NATURAL GAS, COAL INCREASE SHARE IN ELECTRICITY GENERATION SOURCES

Electricity generation from natural gas and coal through 2015 is projected to increase significantly in order to meet increased electricity demand and to compensate for the decline in nuclear generation (see Figure 1–1).

Figure 1–1. Electricity generation by fuel, 1970-2015 (billion kWhr)

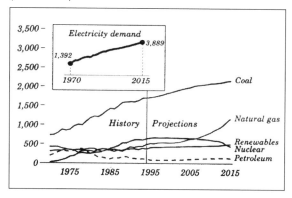

With lower capital requirements, natural gas increases its share of generation. Because fossil fuel prices are lower in EIA's 1996 projections, renewable energy sources penetrate more slowly than in the agency's 1995 projections.

EIA pointed out that one nuclear unit, Watts Bar 1, is assumed to be completed in 1996. No other new nuclear units are projected by 2015. Nuclear generation rises slightly early in the projections, with this new unit and increased utilization; however, with about 40% of the nuclear capacity scheduled to retire by 2015, nuclear generation declines from 2000 and beyond.

The 1996 EIA report shows higher expectations for oil production, while oil prices are projected to be slightly lower than in the agency's 1995 report. In 2010, the average price is $23.70 per barrel (in 1994 dollars), nearly $1 a barrel lower than last year's projection. The 2015 price is $25.43 a barrel.

The average wellhead price of natural gas in the 1996 report is significantly lower than in the 1995 report. The 1996 report projects average wellhead prices in 2010 at $2.15 per thousand cubic feet (compared with almost $3.50 in 1995 projections), rising to $2.57 per thousand cubic feet in 2015. Higher assessments of domestic resources, due in part to technology gains, contribute to reduced price projections. In addition, EIA pointed out that industry competition reduces the costs of transmission and distribution so that delivered prices of gas rise at a slower rate than the wellhead price.

Coal minemouth prices are projected to decline slightly over the forecast period, due to increasing productivity, flat real wage increases, and competitive pressures on long-term contracts. In 2010, the minemouth price is projected to be $17.43 per ton, compared with $23.30 in the 1995 projections. Average electricity prices, which are expected to remain essentially flat throughout the forecast period, are slightly lower than in 1995 projections because the projected fossil fuel prices are lower.

Although projected world oil prices in the 1996 report are almost $1 a barrel lower in 2010 than they were in the 1995 report, the projection for crude oil production is similar to 1995 projections. Overall, U.S. oil production declines over the projection period and the share of petroleum consumption met by net imports reaches 57% in 2005 and remains at about that level through 2015 (as compared with 45% in 1994).

GAS PRODUCTION INCREASES 1.3% ANNUALLY FROM 1994 TO 2015

Driven primarily by growth in consumption, natural gas production increases at an average annual rate of 1.3% from 1994 to 2015. Imports of gas, mostly from Canada, satisfy the remaining increase in demand. Coal production also increases by 0.8% a year through 2015 to meet increasing demands for electricity generation, industrial uses, and exports.

With lower prices projected for fossil fuels, renewable energy production (including hydropower) is 0.8 quadrillion Btu lower in the 1996 forecast than it was in the 1995 forecast. Lower prices, particularly for natural gas, delay the penetration of some renewable technologies. In the EIA 1996 forecast, renewable energy production is 7.8 quadrillion Btu in 2010, rising to 8.5 quadrillion Btu in 2015.

NATURAL GAS CONSUMPTION TO INCREASE

As Figure 1–2 illustrates, natural gas consumption increases by an average of 1.6% per year as gas-fired electricity generation more than doubles from 1994 to 2015. Industrial use of natural gas for boiler fuel and chemical feedstocks also grows. Coal remains the primary fuel for electricity generation. Total coal consumption grows at an average annual rate of 0.8%, with 90% of the coal used for generation.

Petroleum consumption grows at an average rate of 0.9% a year. About two-thirds of the petroleum is used for transportation, as increases in vehicle-miles traveled offset increases in vehicle efficiency throughout the projection period.

Consumption of renewable fuels increases at an average annual rate of 1.5%. Most renewable fuels are used for electricity generation, including cogeneration, with the remainder for dispersed heating and cooling and for blending into vehicle fuels. Hydropower, the main renewable source used for generation, increases only slightly through 2015 because of a shortage of new, large sites and because regulatory actions limit capacity at existing sites.

ELECTRICITY CONSUMPTION EXPECTED TO RISE

Electricity consumption is expected to grow at an average annual rate of 1.4% through 2015. With efficiency gains partially offsetting the penetration of new electricity-using equipment, this growth rate is slower than the 2% average annual growth in gross domestic product (GDP).

Electricity consumption is expected to grow at an average annual rate of 1.4% through 2015.

As shown in Figure 1–3, energy use per dollar of GDP (referred to as energy intensity) has declined since 1970, especially during times of rapid energy price increases.

In the 1970s and early 1980s, energy intensity declined at an average rate of nearly 2% annually as the economy shifted to less energy-intensive industries and increasingly efficient technologies. In the late 1980s and into the projection period, moderate price increases, and the projected growth of more energy-intensive industries, lead to a slower projected decline—at an average annual rate of 1.1% from 1994 to 2015.

Figure 1–2. Energy consumption by source, 1970-2015 (quadrillion Btu)

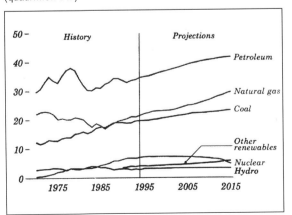

Figure 1–3. Energy use per capita and per dollar of gross domestic product, 1970-2015

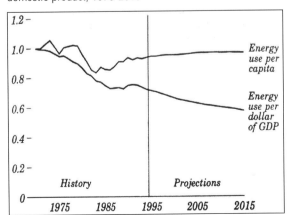

Energy use per person, which also declined from 1970 through the early 1980s, increased in the mid-1980s as energy prices dropped. Per capita energy use is expected to remain nearly stable through 2015 and well below the record highs of the early 1970s, as increasingly efficient technologies offset growing demand for energy services. Per capita demand for electricity increases at an average annual rate of 0.5% through 2015, but per capita demand for other energy sources remains flat.

EIA predicts that as energy prices increase, additional efficiency improvements are likely beyond the standards set out by the Energy Policy Act of 1992 and the National Appliance Energy Conservation Act of 1987.

Carbon emissions from energy use are projected to increase by 1.1% a year through 2010, reaching 1,660 million metric tons. In comparison, EIA's 1995 report projected 1,621 million metric tons in 2010. The 1996 forecast report of total energy consumption in 2010 is about the same as that projected in 1995, but emissions are higher due to a shift from renewable energy to fossil fuels, particularly for electricity generation. Beyond 2010, with slower growth demand, emissions grow at a slower rate, reaching 1,735 million metric tons in 2015.

In EIA's 1996 report, lower energy prices result in more consumption, which is coupled with higher projected growth for new electricity uses, so that residential and commercial sector emissions are higher than those projected in the 1995 report. Both industrial and transportation sector emissions are nearly the same as projected in 1995.

ENERGY CONSUMPTION

Energy delivered to final consumers only represents a part of the elements that affects total primary energy consumption. EIA defines the difference between primary energy consumption and delivered energy consumption as the sum of losses associated with the generation, transmission, and distribution of electricity. The losses are allocated to the end-use sectors (residential, commercial, and industrial) in proportion to each sector's share of electricity use.

How energy consumption is measured has become more important over time as reliance on electricity has expanded. In 1970, electricity accounted for only 12% of delivered energy to the nontransportation end-use sectors. Since that time, growth in electricity use in applications such as space conditioning, consumer appliances, telecommunications equipment, and industrial machinery has resulted in a far greater divergence between total and delivered energy consumption estimates.

At the end-use sectorial level, tracking primary energy consumption is necessary to link specific policies with overall goals. Since carbon emissions, for example, are closely correlated with total energy consumption, analyzing growth rates by end-use sector may be more important in developing carbon stabilization policies than analyzing growth rates for delivered energy consumption.

ENERGY CONSUMPTION VERSUS DELIVERED ENERGY

In 1994, primary energy consumption was one-third greater than delivered energy. This relationship, according to EIA, is expected to be stable throughout the forecast period (to 2015) as more efficient generation technologies offset increased demand for electricity.

The greater the share of electricity in the delivered energy basket, the more important efficiency gains in electricity-using equipment and the electricity delivery system become in reducing energy requirements and total carbon emissions. Choices made at the consumer level remain a key element of such forecasts.

Consumption to Reach 108 Quadrillion Btu

Primary energy consumption is projected to reach 108 quadrillion Btu by 2015. This is 21% higher than the 1994 level. Between 1975 and 1985 as energy prices grew, sectorial energy consumption grew relatively little as shown in Figure 1–4.

Between 1985 and 1994, however, stable energy prices contributed to a marked increase in sectorial energy consumption.

Energy prices and economic growth assumptions are key inputs in developing energy consumption forecasts. To help bracket the uncertainty inherent in any long-term forecast, alternative oil prices and economic growth assumptions were used to highlight the sensitivity of the 1996 forecast to different oil price and economic growth paths.

The different oil price cases are particularly important because of past market volatility. The primary effects of alternative oil price paths are on the demand for transportation fuels. Oil use for transportation in the high world oil price case is 4% lower than in the low world oil price case in 2015. Higher oil prices result in consumer choices that favor the purchase of more fuel-efficient vehicles and a slightly reduced demand for travel services.

Varying economic growth affects overall energy demand in each of the end-use sectors to a greater degree. By 2015, high economic growth assumptions result in a 14% increase in total annual energy consumption, as compared with the low-growth case.

RESIDENTIAL ELECTRICITY USAGE

Energy consumption in the residential sector is projected to rise by 3.6 quadrillion Btu or 20% from 1994 to 2015. In 2015, out of a total of 22 quadrillion Btu of energy use, 14.2 quadrillion Btu will be consumed to provide electricity for homes. Most (87%) of the growth in this sector is

Figure 1–4. Energy use by sector, 1970-2015 (quadrillion Btu)

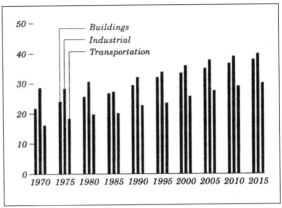

Figure 1–5. Residential primary energy consumption by fuel, 1970-2015 (% of total)

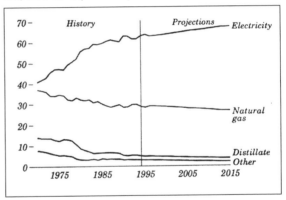

associated with increased use of electricity, as shown in Figure 1–5.

The trend toward electrification is longstanding. It is expected to continue, based on sustained growth in housing in the South, where almost all new homes use central air conditioning, and on the use of new electrical devices that continue to penetrate the market.

While its share declines slightly, natural gas consumption in the residential sector is projected to grow by more than one-half percent a year through the forecast period. Gas prices during this period are stable and relatively low in comparison to other fuels. Natural gas heat pumps capture an increasing share of the home heating market, and an increase of 16.7 million in the number of homes heated by natural gas by 2015 is higher than the increase in the number of homes heated with electricity and oil.

Space Heating

Space heating in the residential sector is by far the most energy-intensive end-use. This is depicted in Figure 1–6.

Over the past seven years (1987 to 1994), space heating consumption has grown by more than 2% a year; however, increases in equipment efficiency and tighter building codes would moderate future growth. Building shell efficiency gains are projected to cut space heating demand in new homes by nearly 25% per square foot in 2015 relative to 1994.

Residential energy use for refrigeration, which has the toughest efficiency standards to date, has declined by more than 2% annually over the past seven years. Energy requirements for this end use are projected to decline at almost the same rate through 2015 as older, less-efficient refrigerators are replaced by newer models.

"Other uses" include smaller appliances, such as personal computers, dishwashers, and clothes dryers. These uses have grown by 6% a year over the past seven years, as shown in Figure 1–6. These uses now account for 27% of total residential energy use, and they are projected to account for 39% in 2015 as small electric appliances continue to penetrate the market. The promotion of voluntary standards, both within and outside the appliance industry, is expected to forestall even larger increases.

Technology Improvements

The reference case forecast offered in EIA's 1996 projections includes the projected effects of several different policies aimed at increasing residential end-use efficiency. Examples include:

- minimum efficiency standards for equipment;
- building efficiency standards; and
- voluntary energy savings programs designed to promote enhanced efficiency.

The 1995 technology case projects residential energy consumption by assuming no further increases in efficiency of equipment or building shells beyond that available in 1995. Compared with the reference case, 6% more energy would be required in 2015.

The high technology case projects residential energy consumption by assuming that the most energy-efficient technology considered is always chosen. Energy use in this case is 14% below the reference case forecast in 2015. Household energy use in 2015 would be 19% lower in this case than in the 1995 technology case.

In the reference case, space heating provides the largest energy savings relative to the 1995 technology case, as shown in Figure 1–7. As shown in Table 1–3, this is due in part to a projected 21% increase in the stock efficiency of natural gas furnaces.

Figure 1–6. Residential primary energy consumption by end use, 1987, 1994, and 2015 (quadrillion Btu)

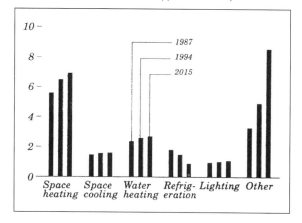

Figure 1–7. Residential energy savings from improved technology, 1995-2015 (quadrillion Btu)

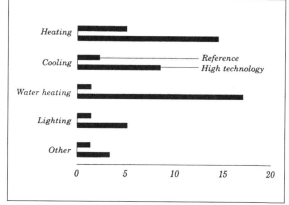

Table 1–3
Residential appliance stock average efficiencies, 1994 and 2015

Equipment Type	1994: Stock Average	1994: New Purchases	2015: Reference Case	2015: 1995 Technology	2015: High Technology
Natural Gas Furnace	1.00	1.17	1.21	1.14	1.29
Air Source Heat Pump	1.00	1.16	1.50	1.17	1.86
Electric Water Heater	1.00	1.02	1.04	1.01	2.85
Natural Gas Water Heater	1.00	1.05	1.15	1.06	1.67
Refrigerator	1.00	1.39	1.48	1.39	1.52
Building Shell Integrity	1.00	1.10	1.09	1.03	1.17

Building shell integrity is projected to increase by 9% over the forecast period, as new homes constructed to tighter building codes are added to housing stock. Water heating, which has historically exhibited slower efficiency gains, is projected to continue that trend, with only a 4% projected increase in electric water heater stock efficiency by 2015.

In the high technology case, however, water heating demonstrates the largest potential for energy savings. This can be seen in Figure 1–7. The use of electric heat pump water heaters in place of conventional resistance technology can substantially cut the amount of energy needed to provide the same amount of hot water. Gas water heaters can also provide substantial energy savings over 1994 levels.

COMMERCIAL DEMAND

Energy use projections for the commercial sector, as shown in Figure 1–8, depict growth slowing overall, with shares for all fuels remaining stable over the forecast period.

Primary energy use is expected to equal 16 quadrillion Btu in 2015—nearly three-fourths of which is attributed to electricity use.

Slow growth in the commercial sector (0.8% per year) is expected for two reasons:

(1) Commercial floor space growth increases by only 1.1% a year over the forecast period, compared with an average increase of 1.5% a year over the past two decades.

(2) Energy consumption per square foot declines by 0.3% per year over the forecast horizon.

Overall, efficiency standards, voluntary government programs aimed at improving efficiency, other technology improvements, and efficiency gains in electricity generation all contribute to a decline in commercial energy intensity.

The Role of Fuels

Electricity, including associated production and distribution losses, is projected to account for about 73% of the energy supplied to the commercial sector throughout the forecast period. All-electric end-uses, such as lighting and office

Figure 1–8. Commercial nonrenewable primary energy consumption by fuel, 1970-2015 (% of total)

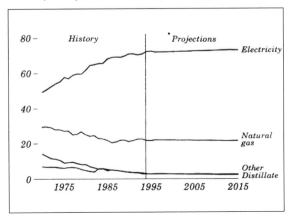

equipment, allow this fuel to keep the share gained over the past 25 years.

Natural gas is projected to contribute just over 21% of commercial energy use from 1994 to 2015. Projected stable fuel prices inhibit any appreciable growth in renewable energy's share of energy consumption in the commercial sector.

New Office Equipment Leads Energy Demand Increases

Primary energy consumption for commercial lighting—the single most important end use in the sector—is projected to increase by 0.5% a year over the forecast period. The adoption of more energy-efficient equipment is key to slowing growth in commercial sector energy demand for lighting, as well as for space heating, space cooling, and water heating end uses, as shown in Figure 1–9. In addition, increasing building shell efficiency is another cause of slow growth.

The highest growth rates are expected for end uses that have not yet saturated the commercial market. Energy use for personal computers and other office equipment grows by slightly over 2% a year throughout the forecast. New telecommunications technologies and medical imaging equipment increase the demand for electricity in the "all other" end-use category. Moreover, the commercial activities that use more equipment from the "all other" category are

projected to grow faster than the average growth rate for commercial floor space as a whole.

EIA's 1996 reference case incorporates the selection of improved equipment in the commercial sector, and significant efficiency improvements are expected for building shells, including roofing, insulation, and windows.

The projected improvements contribute to a decline in commercial energy intensity of 0.3% a year over the forecast. The 1995 technology case assumes that equipment will become no more efficient than what was available in 1995, and that no improvements will be made to the shells of existing buildings. In comparison, the high technology case assumes that only technologies with the highest efficiency considered in the EIA's 1996 outlook report will be chosen, and that existing building shells will be improved so that, by 2015, they will be as efficient as current new construction.

Energy use in the 1995 technology case is expected to be just 2.4% higher than in the reference case by the end of the forecast, as shown in Figure 1–10, with energy use per square foot of commercial floorspace declining by 0.2% a year. Projections for stable fuel prices slow the penetration of more efficient technologies in the reference case. The exclusion of higher equipment cost considerations in the high technology case provides the opportunity for an additional 2.0 quadrillion Btu (12%) of primary energy savings in 2015, with energy intensity falling by 0.9% a year from 1994 to 2015.

Technology Improvements

Figure 1–11 compares cumulative total energy savings expected over the forecast due to the use of improved technologies in the reference and high technology cases relative to the 1995 technology case.

Cumulative energy use is projected to be 3.7 quadrillion Btu lower in the reference case and 27.6 quadrillion Btu lower in the high technology case than in the 1995 technology case.

Figure 1–9. Commercial primary energy consumption by end use, 1994 and 2015 (quadrillion Btu)

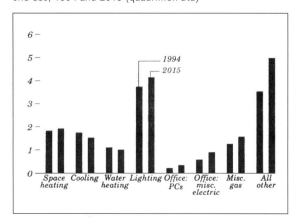

Table 1–4
Increase in efficiency of highest efficiency equipment considered, relative to 1992 stock (%)

Equipment	1995	2005	2015
Electric Heat Pumps	75.9	89.5	107.1
Centrifugal Chillers	73.3	75.7	78.2
Fluorescent Lighting	45.5	45.5	71.8
Lighting With Controls	61.6	61.6	90.9
Gas Furnaces	23.1	47.7	47.7
Gas Chillers	89.5	100.0	131.6
Gas Water Heaters	61.8	61.8	61.8
Distillate Boilers	37.5	44.6	44.6

Electric technologies afford the greatest opportunity for savings in the high technology case, yielding over 83% of the total. Table 1–4 shows some of the equipment responsible for the energy savings.

Efficiency advances are shown in Table 1–4 relative to stock average equipment in 1992, the base year for commercial equipment in EIA's 1996 forecast report. Efficiency gains in commercial lighting, space heating, and cooling provide electricity savings.

INDUSTRIAL DEMAND

Primary energy use in the industrial sector is projected to increase by 18% over the forecast period as shown in Figure 1–12.

Electricity and natural gas are the dominant energy sources in the industrial sector, due to large machine drive requirements and ease of fuel handling. Electricity demand is projected to increase 14% by 2015, whereas natural gas consumption is 27% higher in 2015, primarily because of the relatively low price projected for gas. Industrial petroleum consumption grows by 16% over the forecast, mostly due to increasing demand for feedstock. Coal consumption declines by 0.1% a year, as new steelmaking technologies reduce the demand for metallurgical coal.

From 1970 to 1986, changes in the fuel shares of industrial energy consumption reflected the developments in energy markets. Electricity's share increased from 23% to 35%, natural gas fell from 33% to 25%, and coal fell from 16% to 10%.

Figure 1–10. Variation from reference case primary commercial sector energy use in two alternative cases, 1994-2015 (quadrillion Btu)

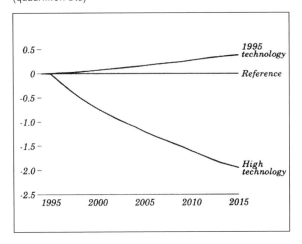

Figure 1–11. Cumulative commercial energy savings from improved technology, 1994-2015 (quadrillion Btu)

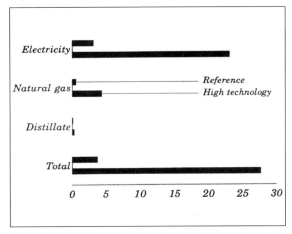

Figure 1–12. Industrial primary energy consumption by fuel, 1970-2015 (quadrillion Btu/year)

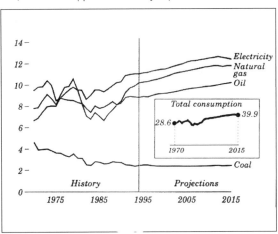

During those years, natural gas was widely perceived to be in short supply and coal was less desirable because of its environmental effects. As a result, industry began to adopt more electricity-intensive processes. After 1986, electricity's share stabilized, and natural gas began to recover its share of the industrial energy market. Natural gas continues to gain some ground in the forecast, as gas supplies are projected to be ample and prices stable.

Industrial Energy Consumption

More than two-thirds of all the energy consumed in the industrial sector is used to provide heat and power for manufacturing; 16% is consumed for nonmanufacturing heat and power; and 15% is consumed in feedstocks (raw materials) and in other miscellaneous uses.

In the manufacturing sector, the three largest end-use consumers of energy for heat and power are petroleum refining, chemicals, and pulp and paper. In 1994, the refining industry consumed 2.9 quadrillion Btu of energy; the chemical industry, 2.8 quadrillion Btu; and the pulp and paper industry, 2.7 quadrillion Btu.

Industrial Energy Intensity

Changes in manufacturing energy intensity (consumption per unit of output) can be separated into two effects. One component reflects underlying increases in equipment efficiency; the other arises from structural changes in the composition of manufacturing output.

Since 1970, the use of more energy-efficient technologies, combined with relatively low growth in energy-intensive industries, has contributed to moderate industrial energy consumption. These factors have offset higher industrial output levels; therefore, total energy consumption has been virtually unchanged for the past 20 years. These basic trends are expected to continue.

Between 1994 and 2015, the U.S. manufacturing output mix is expected to shift from more energy-intensive industries, such as primary metals, toward less energy-intensive industries, such as electronics. The share of total manufacturing output attributed to the energy-intensive industries falls from 32% to 26% in the forecast period. Thus, even if no specific industry experienced a decline in intensity, aggregate manufacturing intensity would decline. Overall, about half of the change in primary energy intensity in the manufacturing sector is due to structural shifts within the sector away from energy-intensive industries.

The balance of improvement in energy intensity relates primarily to expected efficiency gains in both energy-intensive and nonenergy-intensive industries. The relative growth in machinery and equipment production is a key factor: these industries grow almost 50% faster than the manufacturing average (2.6% versus 1.9% annually).

In the high technology case, which assumes that future changes in industrial energy intensity will approximate the decline between 1970 and 1990, almost 7 quadrillion Btu less energy is used in 2015 than for the same level of output in the reference case. Over the forecast period, industrial energy intensity declines at a rate of 1.8% a year in the high technology case—almost double the rate of decline in the reference case (0.9%).

In the 1995 technology case, industry consumes almost 3 quadrillion Btu more energy in 2015 than in the reference case. The reference case includes cost and market penetration estimates for new technologies, as well as continued improvements in energy efficiency.

In the 1995 technology case, energy efficiency remains at the level achieved in 1995 new plants, but average efficiency still improves as old technology is retired and new 1995 technology is brought on-line. It is important to note that these efficiency cases are based solely on the industrial sector and do not incorporate any feedback effects on other energy markets.

THE FUTURE AND COMPARATIVE FORECASTS

The nation's current reliance on technologies which did not exist two decades ago should serve as a reminder that technologies not considered today could play an important, although currently unforeseen role, in energy markets through 2015.

One factor with an enormous potential to affect energy use within the forecast horizon is the aging of the population. After many decades of stability, the proportion of the population over age 55 will increase at a striking rate after 2000. By 2015, it is expected that there will be one-third more 55-year-olds than there are now.

The EIA's 1996 forecast through 2015 shows far less volatility than has occurred historically. Between 1974 and 1984, volatile world oil markets dampened domestic oil consumption. Consumers switched to electricity-based technologies in the buildings sector, while in the transportation sector, new car fuel efficiency nearly doubled.

Natural gas use declined as a result of high prices and limitations on new gas hookups. Between 1984 and 1994, both petroleum and natural gas consumption rebounded, bolstered by plentiful supplies and declining real energy prices.

Three other organizations—Data Resources, Inc. (DRI), Gas Research Institute (GRI), and the WEFA Group—develop comprehensive energy projections within time frames similar to EIA. Given their potentially disparate assumptions about, for example, the effects of government policies and technological developments over the next 20 years, the forecasts have remarkable similarities.

Electricity is expected to remain the fastest growing source of delivered energy, as shown in Table 1–5.

The rate of growth is down sharply from historical rates in each of the forecasts because many traditional uses of electricity approach

Table 1–5

Alternative forecasts of average annual growth rates in energy consumption (%)

	History		Projections			
Energy use	1974-1984	1984-1994	AEO96 (1994-2015)	DRI (1994-2015)	GRI (1994-2015)	WEFA (1994-2013)
Petroleum*	-0.1	1.2	0.9	1.0	0.7	0.9
Natural gas*	-1.7	1.7	1.0	1.0	1.1	0.7
Coal*	-3.0	-1.4	-0.1	1.0	-0.8	0.1
Electricity	3.0	2.5	1.4	1.6	1.9	1.7
Delivered energy	-0.4	1.9	1.0	1.1	1.0	0.9
Electricity losses	2.5	1.4	0.7	0.7	1.4	1.2
Primary energy	0.2	1.8	0.9	1.0	1.1	1.0

*Excludes consumption by electric utilities.

saturation while efficiency standards rise. Growth in petroleum and natural gas consumption also generally slows as overall population growth declines, the population ages, and economic expansion slows.

Residential and Commercial Sectors

Growth rates in energy demand for the residential and commercial sectors are expected to decrease by 50% from the rates between 1984 and 1994, largely because of projected lower growth in population, housing starts, and commercial floorspace additions. Other contributing factors include: increasing energy efficiency due to technical innovations and legislated standards; voluntary government efficiency programs; and reduced opportunities for additional market penetration of end uses like residential air conditioning and personal computers in the commercial sector, where they are already being used extensively.

Differences among forecasts relate importantly to differing views on the growth of new uses for energy, which tends to affect electricity particularly. By fuel, electricity (excluding generation and transmission losses) remains the fastest growing energy source for both sectors across all forecasts, as shown in Table 1–6.

Table 1–6
Forecasts of average annual growth in residential and commercial energy demand (%)

Forecast	History 1984-1994	Projections			
		AEO96 (1994-2015)	DRI (1994-2015)	GRI (1994-2015)	WEFA (1994-2013)
Residential					
Petroleum	0.1	-0.6	-1.1	-1.1	-0.3
Natural gas	0.7	0.5	0.5	0.5	0.1
Electricity	2.6	1.7	1.2	1.6	1.9
Delivered energy	1.7	0.8	0.5	0.7	0.7
Electricity losses	2.1	1.0	0.9	1.0	1.9
Primary energy	1.9	0.9	0.7	0.9	1.3
Commercial					
Petroleum	-4.8	-0.1	-0.6	-0.6	-0.5
Natural gas	1.5	0.7	1.1	0.7	0.2
Electricity	3.3	1.2	1.9	2.0	1.9
Delivered energy	1.2	0.9	1.3	1.1	0.9
Electricity losses	2.8	0.6	1.6	1.5	1.9
Primary energy	2.0	0.8	1.4	1.3	1.4

Natural gas use also grows, but at lower rates, and petroleum use continues to fall but not as rapidly as during the historical period.

Industrial Sector

The industrial sector in all the forecasts shows slower growth in primary energy consumption than it did between 1984 and 1994, as shown in Table 1–7.

Table 1–7
Forecasts of average annual growth in industrial energy demand (%)

Forecast	History 1984-1994	Projections			
		AEO96 (1994-2015)	DRI (1994-2015)	GRI (1994-2015)	WEFA (1994-2013)
Petroleum	0.1	0.7	1.1	1.4	0.7
Natural gas	2.3	1.1	1.0	1.2	1.3
Coal	-1.1	-0.1	1.2	-0.6	0.1
Electricity	1.7	1.1	1.6	2.1	1.4
Delivered energy	2.2	0.9	1.2	1.3	1.3
Electricity losses	1.2	0.4	0.7	1.6	0.9
Primary energy	2.0	0.8	1.1	1.3	1.2

The decline is attributable to lower growth for gross domestic product and manufacturing output. In addition, there has been a continuing shift in the industrial output mix toward less energy-intensive products. The growth rates in the industrial sector for different fuels between 1984 and 1994 reflect a shift from petroleum products and coal to a greater reliance on natural gas and electricity.

Natural gas use grows more slowly than in recent history across the forecasts, because much of the potential for fuel switching was realized during the 1980s. Growth for electricity in EIA's 1996 report is lower than in the other forecasts, because the introduction of new electricity-based processes is assumed to proceed more slowly in the coming decades. Coal forecasts vary according to alternative views of its potential as an environmentally acceptable boiler fuel, as well as expected developments in domestic steel production and processes.

ELECTRICITY CONSUMPTION TO INCREASE

For the future, electricity is expected to continue its role as an economical and convenient energy source for North American consumers. The national consumption of electricity has increased nearly 12-fold since 1950, and electrical appliances have become familiar components of nearly every household.

New appliances, such as personal computers, facsimile machines, and home multimedia centers, are increasing the demand for electricity even further, and new, unforeseen uses for electricity are certain to appear in the future. Nevertheless, although electricity consumption is expected to increase, its rate of growth is expected to decline relative to historic levels.

Historically, electricity demand has been associated with economic growth, as depicted in Figure 1–13.

Figure 1–13. Electricity sales, GDP, and population growth, 1970-2015

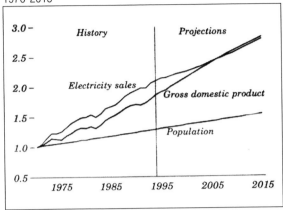

Before the 1970s, households and industry embraced electrical appliances and machinery as efficient work-saving devices and growth in electricity consumption surpassed the economic growth rate by nearly a factor of two. During the 1970s and 1980s, however, escalating fossil fuel prices and the costs of new construction increased the price of electricity production. Consequently, the growth in demand for electricity accelerated.

SLOW DEMAND GROWTH EXPECTED

Even though energy prices remained relatively stable in the first half of the 1990s, increases in appliance efficiency and insulation standards, along with industrial awareness of the impacts of energy costs on production costs, dampened the growth of electricity consumption, and demand growth lagged behind economic growth. This trend is expected to continue, with electricity demand growing more slowly than the economy over the next two decades.

Despite slower demand growth, 252 gigawatts of new generation capacity will be needed between 1994 and 2015 to satisfy electricity demand growth and to replace retiring units. Between 1994 and 2015, 84 gigawatts, or 12% of current generating capacity, is expected to retire, including 36 gigawatts of nuclear capacity; 30 gigawatts of this nuclear capacity is assumed to be retired after 2010, almost one-third will be needed to replace the loss of nuclear capacity.

The reduction in baseload nuclear capacity has a significant impact on the electricity outlook after 2010. Although 2010 to 2015 represents only 25% of the projection period, 49% of the new combined-cycle and 26% of the new coal capacity projected over the entire forecast are expected to be brought on-line during this time frame.

The increase in baseload construction is expected to put upward pressure on coal and natural gas prices. Between 1994 and 2010, coal prices to electricity suppliers decline by 0.5% a year, and natural gas prices increase by only 0.7% a year. After 2010, coal and gas prices rise by 0.3% and 3.9% a year, respectively. As a result, electricity prices are projected to remain relatively stable throughout the forecast period. If the operating lives of many nuclear plants were extended beyond their scheduled retirement dates, the need for new capacity and the demand for coal and natural gas would decline. Such extensions also would moderate the price increases that are projected for both coal and gas.

RESIDENTIAL DEMAND TO INCREASE 1.7%

With the number of U.S. households expected to rise by 25% over the forecast period, residential demand for electricity will grow by 1.7% annually, as shown in Figure 1–14.

Residential electricity demand changes as a function of the time of day, week, or year. During summer in hot climates, residential demand peaks in the late afternoon and evening, when household cooling and lighting needs are highest. This periodicity increases the peak-to-average load ratio for local utilities, which rely on quick-starting gas turbines or internal combustion engines to satisfy peak demand.

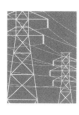

Figure 1–14. Annual electricity sales by sector, 1970-2015 (billion kWhr)

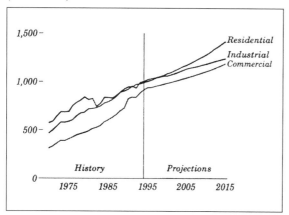

Although many regions have surplus baseload capacity, strong growth in the residential sector will result in a need for more "peaking" capacity. Between 1994 and 2015, generating capacity from gas turbines and internal combustion engines is expected to more than double.

Over the forecast period, electricity demand in the commercial and industrial sectors grows by 1.2% and 1.1% per year, respectively. Annual commercial floorspace growth of 1.1% and industrial output growth of 1.7% drive the increase.

In addition to sectorial sales, nonutilities and cogenerators in 1994 produced 156 billion kilowatt-hours for their own use in industrial and commercial processes. By 2015, these producers are expected to maintain about the same share of total generation, increasing their own-use generation to 218 billion kilowatt-hours as demand for manufactured products increases.

Three broadly defined categories of suppliers satisfy the demand for electricity. They are: utilities, cogenerators, and nonutilities other than cogenerators. In 1994, utilities accounted for 91.3% of total capacity, cogenerators 5.8%, and other nonutilities 2.4%.

In the forecast, utilities continue to dominate the electric power industry in terms of capacity ownership, which increases from 700 gigawatts in 1994 to 756 gigawatts in 2015 (82% of the total). Utilities account for 57% of the new capacity constructed during the forecast period. Cogenerators and other nonutilities significantly increase their share of the market, accounting for 43% of new capacity construction and capturing 18% of total capacity by 2015.

Chapter 2
Latin America Electricity Demand

ANN CHAMBERS
ASSOCIATE EDITOR
POWER ENGINEERING INTERNATIONAL AND
POWER ENGINEERING

OVERVIEW

In the 1950s, only 30% of the population of Central and South America was served by electricity. The region experienced strong economic growth during the 1960s and 1970s, which was matched by rapid expansion of the electrical infrastructure. (Table 2–1) Today, approximately 70% of the population has access to electricity as a result of large investments in generation, transmission, and distribution facilities in the 1960s and 1970s. Consumption per capita has also increased dramatically in the past decade, from 1.0 to 1.4 MWh, placing it above many other developing regions, but still below the 6.6 MWh average in developed countries. (Table 2–2)

With a 628-GW hydroelectric potential, Latin America is expected to be second only to China in new hydroelectric capacity. Over the next 15 years, this region is projected to install 121 GW of new capacity. Of this total, hydropower will account for 58 GW, costing $52 billion(US). (Table

Table 2–1
Per capita electricity consumption, history and projection

| | Megawatthours per Person | | |
	1980	1993	2015
Central and South America	0.9	1.3	1.7

Table 2–2
Latin American demand basics

Country	Population (millions)	GDP(US)$ (billions)	GDP Growth Rate	Inflation Rate	Generation Capacity		Total Generation
Argentina	34.3	$270.8	-4.4%	3.7%	18	GW	62,800 GWh
Bolivia	7.9	$7.2	3.5%	12.5%	.75	GW	2,400 GWh
Brazil	160.7	$886.3	4.5%	23.2%	56	GW	255,000 GWh
Chile	14.2	$98	7.8%	8.2%	4.8	GW	24,400 GWh
Colombia	36.2	$172.4	n/a	n/a	10	GW	n/a
Ecuador	11.5	$17.9	2.4%	23%	2.3	GW	n/a
Mexico	94	$728.7	3.5%	7.1%	3.3	GW	130 GWh

2–3) Gas will provide 37 GW, at a cost of $23 billion(US); and coal will fire 15 GW, for $22 billion(US). Coal costs are lower in Latin America than in Africa because of varying levels of retrofits and repowering of existing plants. Capital needs will vary widely with the local situation.

Table 2–3
Hydro/renewable energy consumption, history and projections

| | Quadrillion Btu | | | | | | |
| | History | | | Projections | | | |
Region	1990	1993	1995	2000	2005	2010	2015
Central/South America	3.9	4.2	4.4	4.5	4.7	4.9	5.0
World Total	26.3	28.1	30.0	34.0	38.3	43.4	49.7

Table 2–4
Net nuclear energy consumption, history and projections

| | Billion kilowatthours | | | | | | |
| | History | | | Projections | | | |
Region	1990	1993	1995	2000	2005	2010	2015
Central/South America	9	8	9	9	18	18	1
World Total	1,894	2,080	2,161	2,292	2,300	2,290	2,026

Over the next 20 years, electricity demand in Central and South America is expected to grow fairly steadily, at around 2.6% annually. (Table 2–4) Demand is expected to increase to accommodate an expected 2.2% annual population growth rate, to expand the percentage of the population served by electricity, and to keep pace with economic growth. Increased demand will be met by new generating capacity and by greater use of existing capacity. There is currently surplus capacity in some Central and South American countries where demand growth has been lower than expected. (Table 2–5) For example, Venezuela is selling surplus to Brazil and Colombia.

The electric power industry in Central and South America is undergoing significant change. The overall economic climate and the need of governments to focus their limited resources on social infrastructures, have led to a shortage of public financing for the region's capital-intensive electricity industry. (Table 2–6) Concurrently, international lending institutions face severe competition for their resources and are focusing their emphasis on sectors that cannot find financing from the private sector. (Table 2–7) There is also a general perception of large inefficiencies in the region's electricity production and consumption, which is moving many governments toward deregulation and privatization of electric power industries. (Table 2–8)

Chile, Argentina, and Peru have followed the lead of the United Kingdom in restructuring their

Table 2–5
Net electricity consumption, history and projections

| | Billion kilowatthours | | | | | | |
| | History | | | Projections | | | |
Region	1990	1993	1995	2000	2005	2010	2015
Central/South America	448	390	527	608	690	776	863
World Total	10,382	10,761	11,355	13,090	14,922	16,877	19,087

Table 2–6
Changes in generation and capacity, 1995-2010, cumulative

Region	Solid Fuel	Oil	Gas	Hydro/ Renewable	Nuclear	Total
Generation change (TWh)						
Latin America	34	53	100	240	10	438
World Total	2,845	53	2,550	1,188	445	7,081
Capacity change (GW)						
Latin America	15	11	37	58	2	121
World Total	426	41	463	261	73	1,190

[Courtesy International Energy Agency]

Table 2–7
Private investment in Latin America

| | In billions of nominal U.S. dollars | | | | | | | |
Source	1987	1988	1989	1990	1991	1992	1993	1994
International Private Debt	1.8	(0.3)	(6.5)	2.5	4.1	7.0	16.7	10.2
Intl. Portfolio Equity	0.1	0.2	0.4	1.1	6.2	8.2	25.2	10.5
Foreign Direct Investment	5.8	8.0	8.2	7.9	12.3	13.6	16.2	18.8
Subtotal International	7.7	7.6	2.1	11.5	22.6	28.9	58.0	39.5
Domestic	94.2	115.7	145.4	140.8	124.1	143.4	161.9	194.2
Total	101.9	123.3	147.5	152.3	146.7	172.3	219.9	233.7

Table 2–8
Investment in electric power in Latin America, 1995-2010

| | In billions of 1993 U.S. dollars | | | | |
| | Electric Power Investment | | | | |
Region	Official	Private	Total	Total Private	Power %
Latin America	80	122	202	4,800	2.5
World Total	315	1,233	1,548	16,200	7.6

[Courtesy International Energy Agency]

power industries, including the separation of generation, transmission, and distribution activities. The restructuring is being followed by strong efforts to ensure competition and privatization. In Argentina, unbundling of the industry has entailed the sale of state-owned companies and the formation of private

companies. Privatization is allowing more and more players into the field, and as construction continues and the infrastructure expands and diversifies, more of the population will have access to electricity, and demand growth will surely be only one step behind the spreading transmission lines. (Table 2–9)

Table 2–9
Annual gross domestic product growth rates by region

	Percent per year			
	History		Projections	
Region	**1970-80**	**1980-90**	**1990-2000**	**2000-15**
Central/South America	5.8	1.1	3.9	3.8
World Total	3.5	2.8	2.2	3.1

Argentina. After four strong years of economic growth and low inflation, Argentina's economy contracted in 1994, in the wake of the Mexican peso crises, which started in December 1994. Electricity demand is generally strongly tied to the gross domestic product and other general economic indicators. Argentina has a well-developed electricity sector, recently privatized and deregulated, with separate markets for generation, transmission, and distribution. (Table 2–10)

Table 2–10
Argentina's energy demand

Industrial	42.9%
Residential	32.0%
Commercial	9.9%
Other	15.2%

Recent capacity additions have been hydro-electric plants. Argentina boasts approximately 6,500 MW in hydroelectric facilities, 1,000 MW of nuclear power, and 7,000 MW of conventional thermal plants, including some combined-cycle plants. There is also a significant amount of self-generation in this country. Peak demand, which occurs in the summer months of July and August, soars to nearly 11,000 MW.

Demand is growing in Argentina, but with an electric generating capacity of 18 GW, Argentina is a net exporter of electricity, and it will probably continue to have excess electricity in coming years. In 1994, Argentina generated 62.8 billion

kWh, of which hydroelectricity and nuclear power account for more than one-half, and conventional thermal generation fills in the remainder.

Recent economic difficulties are largely attributed to reduced investor confidence throughout Latin America in the aftermath of Mexico's peso crisis. Argentina's response to investor concerns was an economic package, announced in the spring of 1995, combining tax increases and spending decreases totaling $3.3 billion(US). In addition, Argentina implemented measures to strengthen its financial system, tightened its fiscal policies, and arranged an external support package with the International Monetary Fund. These steps should help ensure Argentina's economy will be one of the more stable ones in Latin America, and therefore one of the higher demand growth nations.

Argentina is attempting to exploit the benefits of its low-cost hydroelectric power by constructing a series of plants to provide more than 70% of the nation's electricity by 2000. the largest of those now in operation is the 4 x 350-MW Piedra del Aguila station in the southern province of Neuquen. Designed and constructed by the state, the plant has since been privatized, providing some unusual challenges to increase operating efficiency. Piedra del Aguila is one of five hydro plants either completed or under construction along the Limay River.

Approximately 1,800 kilometers of high-voltage transmission lines link the five hydro stations with metropolitan Buenos Aires. Hydroelectric plants currently provide approximately 60% of Argentina's electric generating capacity, with nearly one-third of that capacity coming from the Rio Limay facilities. By the turn of the century, analysts expect hydro to increase its share to 70% of the nation's estimated 80 million GWh annual demand.

Transmission is a strength of the power system in Argentina. Most of the system is interconnected or in the process of becoming interconnected through the Argentine System of Interconnection. Argentina has nine power regions: Greater Buenos Aires, the Coast, Comahue, Buenos Aires Province, the Center, Cuyo, the Argentine

Northeast, the Argentine Northwest, and the Patagonian System.

Brazil generated 243.3 TWh in 1995, up 7.6% from 1994. The leap was higher than the average annual growth, which had been 3.8% between 1990 and 1994. The gross domestic product jumped 4.2% in 1995. Approximately 90% of the country has electricity services, up from only about one-half the population in 1970. (Table 2–11)

Table 2–11
Brazil's power consumption, 1994

Brazil	Totals	% of total
Population	150 million	100
Consumption	235,420 GWh	100
Gross National Product	$500 billion	100
Northern Region		
Population	10 million	7
Consumption	11,506 GWh	5
GNP	$22 billion	4
Northeastern Region		
Population	44 million	29
Consumption	36,900 GWh	16
GNP	$68 billion	14
Center-West Region		
Population	10 million	6
Consumption	10,854 GWh	5
GNP	$31 billion	6
Southeastern Region		
Population	64 million	43
Consumption	141,561 GWh	60
GNP	$291 billion	58
Southern Region		
Population	23 million	15
Consumption	34,599 GWh	15
GNP	$88 billion	18

[Courtesy Banco de Investimentos Granantia S.A.]

Brazil's total electric power capacity as of 1994 was 56 GW, of which about 94% came from hydroelectric plants, and the remaining 7% from diesel oil, charcoal and wood, natural gas, and nuclear power plants. With a rapidly growing population, an estimated four million rural households currently are without access to electricity. With an expanding industrial base, Brazil is planning for 4–5% annual increases in electric power demand for the foreseeable future. Eletrobras, Brazil's national electric holding company which accounts for about two-thirds of Brazil's genera-

tion, has estimated that Brazil will need 2,500 to 3,000 MW per year of new electric generating capacity through 2004 to meet this increased demand, at an annual cost of $6 to $8 billion(US).

Hydroelectricity will account for much of the increased capacity, with the remainder coming largely from coal and nuclear plants.

Eletropaulo, one of Sao Paulo state's three electricity companies, reported a 3.8% increase in use in 1995 with 54.7 TWh generated as compared to 52.7 TWh in 1994. Residential use rocketed a record 11.7%, but industrial use fell 1.4 %.

The industrial slip was attributed primarily to a crisis in the textiles sector, which saw energy sales dip more than 11%. Other utilities reported similar trends for the year. (Table 2–12) Most of Brazil's territory is still not covered by an integrated electric grid, so much of the country must make do with inadequate supply from local generators, most of which are thermal, burning diesel and fuel oil. The local generators also tend to be expensive and unreliable.

Table 2–12
Brazil's energy consumption

Sector	Percentage
Industrial	39
Transportation	19
Residential	16
Energy	8
Commercial	5
Public Service	3
Other	10

[Courtesy Banco de Investimentos Granantia S.A.]

There is no serious imbalance in the supply of electric energy, but some potential problems are noted by experts. Conservative planning with a growth rate of 3.5–4% annually could lead to deficits in electricity generating capacity as early as 1998. But growth of electricity demand actually is running higher than 7%.

From 1973 to 1979, electricity use averaged 12% growth annually. This growth rate is attributed at least partially to the development of basic industry and infrastructure. Since 1980, the country's economy has teetered on the edge of a recession, and growth rates have declined. The economy is now stabilizing and a surge of economic

development is expected, and with it, a surge in electricity use and demand.

Brazil is facing a need to expand electric generation capacity by 25 GW through 2004. The situation is particularly serious in the populous South and Southeastern regions. As a result, the government is taking measures to attract private power developers and to accelerate privatization.

Demand has been rising for the past two decades, and conservative estimates project 5–6% annual growth through 2004. As a result, Brazil will need 13.5 to 36 GW of new capacity in the coming decade, totaling $20 billion(US) to $54 billion(US) in investment. CEMIG, one of the largest state utilities in Brazil, estimates that the state of Minas Gerais needs about 1,700 MW of new capacity with a total investment of $2.8 billion(US) in the next two years. CEMIG's calculations predict power rationing in the region if there is no new capacity. The utility is adding 1.5 million new hookups per year.

Brazil is working to privatize generation at the state and federal levels, unbundling and selling utilities. Also, Brazil's utilities are selling off about 8.4 GW of power projects that are stalled in various stages of construction. (Table 2–13)

Table 2-13
Distributing companies in Brazil

Total Consumption—235,420 GWh in 1994		
Company and State	GWh	Percentage
Eletropaulo - Sao Paulo	53,002	22
Cemig - Minas Gerais	31,646	13
Light - Rio de Janeiro	21,975	9
CPFL - Interior of SP	13,042	6
CEEE - Rio Grande do Sul	13,900	6
Cesp - Sao Paulo State	13,558	6
Copel - Parana State	11,147	5
Celpe - Pernambuco	8,094	3
Celsec - Santa Catarina	7,565	3
Coelba - Bahia	6,622	3
Cerj - Rio State	5,796	2
Celg - Goias	4,741	2
Escelsa - Espirito Santo	4,514	2
Cataguases - Minas Gerais	2,500	1
Ceb - Brasilia	2,355	1
Enersul - Mato Grosso do Sul	1,847	1
Cemat - Mato Grosso	1,446	1
Others	38,026	16

[Courtesy Banco de Investimentos Ganantia S.A.]

Despite the progressive attitude surrounding power issues in Brazil, the nation is having difficulty attracting international investors. One problem is the utilities themselves. Many are not creditworthy, which makes project financing difficult. Subsidies and cross-subsidization also blur the picture. The uncertain regulatory future is another tripping point. Domination of hydropower coupled with subsidized electricity rates protect the market against new, thermal power plants. The dynamics of hydropower minimize the need for peaking capacity, so rates on the margin of such a system tend to be low. Politics, as with all of the Latin American countries, is viewed as stormy and uncertain. This picture can frighten timid investors, although Brazil has instituted a solid legal system to provide a foundation for investment.

Dominican Republic. The government of the Dominican Republic is working to begin privatization of all or part of its Compania Dominicana de Electricidad (CDE), and to draw private power companies into its electricity industry. This area is experiencing an electricity crisis which is becoming progressively worse, with blackouts lasting up to 20 hours per day. CDE has an installed capacity of 800 MW, but demand has reached 1,150 MW. This crisis is driving plans for privatization.

Trinidad is expected to see growth of 4–5% annually in electricity demand through 2000. A majority of the demand increase is expected to come from industrial customers, which currently consume about 63%, or 2,210 MWh, of the total 3,490 MWh of electricity sold. Residential demand accounts for 25% of the electricity sold and commercial demands 10%.

The Andean Region. The Andean nations, consisting of Bolivia, Colombia, Ecuador, Peru, and Venezuela, have a population nearing 100 million people, accounting for approximately 20% of the Latin American population. This region has more than one-half of Latin America's oil, natural gas, and coal reserves, and approximately 40% of its hydroelectric potential.

The Andean nations generated 153,207 GWh of electricity in 1994, of which 80% was hydroelectric and 20% thermoelectric. These countries have 22% of Latin America's total installed generating capacity. It is estimated that they will need a 15% increase in capacity to meet forecast demand by 2000. Installed capacity was 37,013 MW in 1994, and projections indicate these nations will need 42,500 MW to meet demand in 2000.

Bolivia has a long history of political and economic instability and it ranks among the poorest countries in South America. However, it has seen significant economic gain in recent years due to free market policies of the government. Inflation has fallen from nearly 12,000% in 1985 to 9.3% at the close of 1993. Bolivia is pursuing aggressively the expanding markets of East Asia and Europe and the promotion of free trade throughout the western hemisphere.

Bolivia faces great challenges in providing its growing population with adequate electricity, domestic gas, potable water, and telecommunications. In order to attract enough capital to improve and enhance basic infrastructure, the government has undertaken an ambitious program of capitalization—a form of privatization in which only 50% of state companies are sold off to private investors. The remaining half is distributed in shares to all citizens over 18 years of age through a special government pension fund. The government hopes to raise between $1 and $2 billion(US) in new, direct investment in key economic sectors through this program. It is selling six major state monopolies, including the state utility, ENDE.

If the capitalization program continues smoothly, and the economic gains of the past few years are an indication of future gains, electric demand in Bolivia should grow strongly through the coming decade as infrastructure and basic services are expanded and the economy grows.

Installed capacity in 1994 was 780 MW and the nation's utilities generated 2,879 GWh of electricity during the year, recording 2,260 GWh of electricity sales. Approximately two-thirds of the population has access to electricity and per capita

consumption was 320 kWh. During 1994, electricity consumption grew by 9% and forecasts indicate continuing growth averaging 7% annually.

Privatization has been spurred by a variety of factors, principally predictions indicating strong demand combined with opportunities to export electricity due to the country's strategic geographic site. The electricity sector is made up of an interconnected system and three main isolated systems. The interconnected system accounts for nearly 90% of the country's consumption and approximately 77% of installed capacity. Of the electricity generated in Bolivia, 60% is thermal and 40% is hydro. Total electricity generation in 1994 was 2.4 billion kWh.

Colombia reports a 5.3% economic growth in 1995, but national unemployment also rose, from 7.1% to 7.9%. Colombia's economy generated about 225,000 new jobs in 1995, but it was not enough to offset the population increase.

The Colombian government plans to invest $27 billion in the next four years to improve its infrastructure. Insurgency operations in Colombia continue to affect the energy infrastructure and operating costs are 10% higher in Colombia than other countries due to security reasons alone, although there has been a general decrease in guerrilla activity since 1992.

Colombia's electricity demand has been growing by 5.9% annually since 1992. The electric sector will need more than $2 billion(US) in private capital over the next four years to build enough new capacity to avoid electricity rationing. Despite its substantial oil, coal, and natural gas resources, Colombia has a severe shortage of generating capacity. About 78% of Colombia's current capacity is based on hydroelectric generation, which is scarce in time of drought.

Colombia has an installed capacity of 9,811 MW and it generated 45,230 GWh in 1994—78% from hydroelectric sources and 22% thermoelectric. The transmission grid has nearly 14,000 kilometers of 500-, 230- and 115-kV lines.

Colombia's electricity industry expansion plan, set in 1992, predicts that investment of approximately $7 billion(US) will be needed between 1997 and 2007, with 80% of that going to power generation needs and 20% to transmission. Generation opportunities are open to private-sector participation.

Ecuador had a very difficult year in 1995. There was high-ranking political scandal and a border war with Peru. The conflict was resolved in August 1995, after several months of negotiation in Brazil. The war cost around $10 million(US) per day, partly because trade between the two countries was suspended. Ecuador's economy was adversely affected by both the political strife and the expensive war. Gross domestic product grew only 2.4% in 1995, well below the government's original target of 5%. Gross domestic product rates are expected to stay under 3% through 1997.

However, high interest rates have helped to contain inflation, which fell from 45% in 1994 to 23% in 1995. Inflation is expected to continue its decline through 1996. Following the war with Peru, the government passed a $500 million(US) war-tax bill to reduce the increased public debt. Another step was an increase in residential electricity prices by 140%.

Ecuador has an installed capacity of 2,295 MW and in 1994 generated 3,324 GWh of electricity— 65% from hydroelectric sources and 35% thermoelectric. Approximately three-fourths of the population has access to electricity services and the nation's per capita annual consumption is around 540 kWh. In 1994, consumption grew slightly more than 5%. A number of electricity capacity projects are under consideration, including hydroelectric and natural gas-fired generation.

A serious drought in 1995 affected the country's hydroelectric generating capacity, resulting in blackouts for six to 13 hours per day.

Peru has an installed capacity of 4,195 MW and in 1994 generated 15,181 GWh of electricity. Electricity services are available to approximately 57% of the population and per capita consumption is around 550 kWh annually.

Demand in Peru has grown at about 10% annually for the past several years and projections forecast growth of around 7% annually through 2000, dropping to around 5.5% after the turn of the century.

The economy in Peru is expanding, and demand for electricity is anticipated to grow hand-in-hand with the economy. In 1990, only 45% of the population had electricity, but in early 1996 more than 60% had electricity, and the figure is rising. Mini-hydroelectric facilities of around 2 MW are now scattered throughout the Andes and the government is also working to provide solar panels to people who live in the mountains without electricity. But the infrastructure in Peru is lagging behind as almost no money was spent between 1975 and 1990 for new capacity, or even maintenance of installed capacity.

More than 75% of the nation's electricity comes from facilities sited on the rivers which flow swiftly down through the mountains, and these rivers promise almost unlimited electric power capacity. But, in times of drought, as many of Peru's neighboring countries have discovered the hard way, too much reliance on hydroelectric power can lead to brownouts, blackouts and rationing.

The government is working to attract private investment for the costly infrastructure needs of the industry, but response has been slow. The government liberalized the industry in late 1992 and the effort is finally starting to pay off. The government auctioned Edegel, Lima's 700-MW hydroelectric generating system in the fall of 1995, bringing in $500 million(US) for a 60% stake to Endesa of Chile. Etvensa, a 200-MW thermal backup facility, was sold in December 1995. The new owners of these facilities, and others which are being sold, are required to invest in their assets. Edegel's operators are increasing capacity by 100 MW this year as a step toward their 200 MW increase commitment for the site. The government is also starting construction on more capacity and hoping to sell the plants later.

Gas-fired generation is being considered, and built, near Peru's extensive gas fields. Industry experts contend that the natural gas reserves offer the only lasting answer to the electricity shortage in Peru. With the economy primed to grow 5% annually in the coming years, industry analysts calculate that the nation must add generation capacity at the rate of 8.5–10% annually to keep up.

Venezuela

Venezuela has installed capacity of 19,932 MW, generating 67,632 GWh in 1992 and selling 52,000 GWh. Approximately 90% of the population has access to electricity services. Demand grew at 5% during 1994 and a demand growth rate of 3–3.5% is anticipated throughout the next decade. Much of the growth is expected to be supplied through natural gas-fired thermoelectric generation.

Chile

Chile. After years of political isolation, Chile is now widely viewed as a successful example of how free trade policies and protection for foreign investment can help fuel economic growth in South America. Over the last decade, the country has had one of the region's most successful economies, registering 11 consecutive years of economic expansion. Chile's economy had an excellent year in 1995, growing about 7.8% in real terms, up from 4% in 1994. The rapid growth was fueled by two main factors: high prices for copper and continued domestic political and social stability. Chile's economy is expected to grow strongly in the next couple of years with low inflation and low unemployment rates.

Electricity production in Chile increased from 7.3 billion kWh in 1970 to 24.4 billion kWh in 1994. According to the National Energy Commission, electricity generation grew another 9.2% in 1995. Hydroelectric facilities account for about 75% of this, with the remainder coming from thermal stations. Much of Chile's electricity is produced by industry directly for its own consumption.

Chile's electric utility companies are thriving. Strong domestic energy demand, a stable regulatory environment, and solid management have made Chile the strongest country in Latin America. In addition to addressing domestic power needs, Chilean utility firms have ventured heavily into foreign markets. They are purchasing stakes in the newly privatized sectors in Argentina and Peru, and likely will become involved in Bolivia, Ecuador, and Colombia once the regulatory environment in those countries improves.

Although Chile is not endowed with abundant indigenous hydrocarbon sources, the country's energy sector is seeing a great deal of activity as domestic energy demand rises rapidly. Chile has become one of the most outward looking nations for new energy sources in Latin America. Major energy projects under way include several natural gas pipelines, construction of new natural gas-fired power stations, several hydroelectric plants, refinery upgrade, and cogeneration projects and oil exploration joint-ventures.

It is estimated that Chile will have to invest more than $3 billion(US) in the next decade in new power-generating plants and transmission equipment. In order to meet the need for increased generating capacity in the country, Chile's power companies have initiated several electricity projects. Electricity generation in 1994 topped 24.4 billion kWh from 4.81 GW of installed capacity.

Guatemala

Guatemala, the northernmost country in Central America, is bordered by Mexico on the north. It has a population of around 10 million, two million of whom live in the capital, Guatemala City. Guatemala's market for electrical infrastructure and equipment shrank in 1993, but has been growing by about 6% annually since. This nation has a long history of prudent fiscal and monetary policymaking which adds stability to the economy.

Generating capacity comes from three types of plants: hydroelectric, contributing about 58% of the power generated; thermal, contributing approximately 38%; and cogeneration, adding about 22%. State entities supply 78% of the power generated and the private sector contributes the

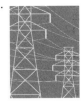

remaining 22%. Guatemala currently generates around 700 MW of electric power, of which 427 MW are generated by hydroelectric facilities. These plants are sometimes low in dependability and efficiency, which is driving up costs. Forecast demand for 1997 will exceed 1,000 MW and by the end of 1996, 200 additional MW will be generated. Electricity costs have increased by about 575% in the last 12 years. Monthly energy sales are grouped as industrial, 33%; commercial, 28%; residential, 30%; municipal, 7%; and others, 2%.

The government is planning a handful of electric capacity construction projects in the coming decade, including hydro, geothermal, and gas facilities. Known private sector projects are mainly hydro-based.

To meet increasing demand, the government is turning to the private sector. According to the Ministry of Energy and Mines, more than $2.6 billion(US) will be needed to expand the electrical capacity in Guatemala before the year 2000, more than in any other Central American country, according to the United Nations Economic Commission on Latin America and the Caribbean. Contracts already signed will bring an additional 650 MW by 2000.

Panama is projected to have electricity demand growth of 5.6–7.2% annually in the next year or so. The state-owned energy utility, IRHE, has outlined plans to meet the demand, including new plants, greater efficiency, conservation, plant maintenance, and purchasing excess supply from private sector sources both in country and out. IRHE's installed capacity in 1995 was 921 MW. The available capacity, however, was only about 636 MW due to maintenance downtime and low water levels, which adversely affected hydroelectric output. (Table 2–14) Average demand was 467 MW, but peak demand soared to 619 MW, only slightly lower than available capacity. After subtracting losses in transmission and adding upcoming demand growth, IRHE obviously needs to boost capacity quickly to avoid electricity rationing or brownouts.

Table 2–14
Panama's hydroelectric generation

Hydro Station	1996	1997
Los Valles	273 GWh	280 GWh
La Estrella	245 GWh	267 GWh
Bayano	651 GWh	525 GWh
Fortuna	1,360 GWh	1,446 GWh
Total	2,529 GWh	2,518 GWh

IRHE is selecting from 38 bidders to build and operate a new 100 MW cogeneration plant, to be operational by January 1998. IRHE is also taking bids for a 120 MW hydroelectric plant on the Esti River to be owned and operated by IRHE and forecast to be operational in 1999. The utility has also undertaken an extensive public education campaign to decrease energy waste, and is cutting transmission losses through an aggressive maintenance program. The utility plants are to bring losses down to 19% by 1997.

Cost of electricity in Panama continues to be very high. Average cost in the residential sector is $12 per kWh(US), double that of Honduras or El Salvador. Electricity cost for the commercial sector is only slightly less. IRHE explains the high costs by noting that other Central American governments subsidize electricity costs.

Mexico. This economy is experiencing difficulties since the massive depreciation of the peso in December 1994, which brought on a financial crisis and exposed vulnerabilities in the economy. Inflation and interest rates soared following the crisis. The problems in Mexico have raised concern for other Latin American economies and slowed international investment, extending the impact of the crisis. Mexico is laboring to turn the economy around with a National Development Plan announced in May 1995, setting a goal of 5% annual economic growth through 2000. Official projections for 1996 are relatively optimistic at 3% economic growth and 20% inflation.

For the past four decades, the electric power industry in Mexico has experienced uninterrupted growth with an annual average growth rate of 4.9% from 1988 to 1994. This rate exceeded that of the entire economy, 2.8%, partially due to the

industry's ability to provide for industrial, commercial, and consumer growth as well as maintain low rates. Between 1984 and 1993, electric power sales experienced an annual growth rate of 5.2%. By December 1994, installed capacity totaled 31,000 MW. By 2003, an additional 12,000 to 14,000 MW will be needed. Of this, approximately 1,650 MW will be generated by the Mexican government and the rest by the private sector.

Approximately 1,000 to 1,500 MW will be needed annually over the next seven years to accommodate demand, estimated to increase at an annual growth rate of 4–5%. Inflation is nipping at the heels of the industry sector, as the 1995 electricity rate increase of 30% will not be sufficient to cover the projected 50% inflation.

Energy savings programs are also being implemented to accommodate growing demand, and they are expected to produce significant benefits. The standardization of refrigerators could generate savings of 2,278 GWh by 2003. In order to include other electric apparatus and expand the savings, the program is being expanded to air conditioning, three-phase motors, pumping systems, home pumps, washers, and residential lamps.

There are also corporate incentives which reduce operational costs through participation in cogeneration projects. This program seems to be aiding the electricity sector in meeting demand, as 28 self-supply and cogeneration projects, representing an investment of $363 million(US) and 675 MW have been approved by the government since 1992. The projects include 10 cogeneration plants operated by steam or other thermal fuel with a capacity of 400 MW and six plants for self-supply projects. Given their use of gas in the production process, industries such as steel, cement, sugar, chemicals, petrochemicals, paper, fertilizers, ceramics, and textiles are expected to add to the list of cogeneration plants.

Chapter 3
Europe Electricity Demand

ANN CHAMBERS
ASSOCIATE EDITOR
POWER ENGINEERING INTERNATIONAL AND
POWER ENGINEERING

OVERVIEW

The Eastern Europe and former Soviet Union region is projected to have relatively slow demand growth in the next decade or so, largely attributed to reduced economic growth rates and the slowdown of production in the industrial sector, particularly in the former Soviet Union. (Table 3–1) Economic recovery is anticipated in the late 1990s, which could spur growth in electricity consumption. More rapid increases are expected in Eastern Europe before 2000, because market reforms have been introduced more quickly there than in many of the Soviet nations.

Table 3–1
Net electricity consumption, history and projections

Region	Billion kilowatthours						
	History			Projections			
	1990	**1993**	**1995**	**2000**	**2005**	**2010**	**2015**
Western Europe	2,116	2,196	2,374	2,708	3,022	3,343	3,680
Eastern Europe	418	357	375	439	506	577	653
Former Soviet Union	1,488	1,300	1,148	1,250	1,344	1,445	1,553
World Total	10,382	10,761	11,355	13,090	14,922	16,877	19,087

Table 3–2
Per capita electricity consumption, history and projection

Region	Megawatthours per Person		
	1980	**1993**	**2015**
Western Europe	4.0	5.0	7.8
Eastern Europe and Former Soviet Union	4.0	4.0	5.1

Total electricity consumption in Eastern Europe and the former Soviet Union is projected to grow by less than 0.3% annually through 2000, due to slow economic growth of 0.6% annually. (Table 3–2) After 2000, as the region's economy recovers and grows by 3.7% annually, electricity use is projected to grow at an average annual rate of 1.8% through 2015, according to U.S. Department of Energy statistics. Demand for electricity is expected to lag behind gross domestic product growth, because economic growth in the region is being driven by corrections of past economic distortions brought about by the centrally planned, rather than market-driven, economies. At the same time, the demand for electricity is expected to outpace population growth, resulting

29

Table 3–3
Electric power investments by region, 1995-2010

Type	Western Europe	Central and Eastern Europe	Newly Independent States	World Totals
Generation				
Solid fuel	102	19	24	734
Natural gas	89	10	33	298
Oil	1	7	2	29
Nuclear	85	3	26	129
Hydro/renewables	15	5	13	235
Subtotal	**215**	**44**	**98**	**1,426**
Transmission	20	3	14	200
Distribution	78	11	30	480
General	20	6	14	173
Subtotal	**118**	**19**	**58**	**854**
Total	**333**	**63**	**156**	**2,279**
Annual Average	22	4	10	152

Table 3–4
Projected worldwide changes in generation and capacity, 1995-2010

Region	Solid Fuel	Oil	Gas	Hydro/ Renewable	Nuclear	Total
Generation change (TWh)						
Western Europe	295	(38)	569	99	5	931
Central & Eastern Europe	62	26	57	14	3	162
Newly Independent States	9	(16)	234	67	108	402
World Total	2,845	53	2,550	1,188	445	7,081
Capacity change (GW)						
Western Europe	51	1	132	17	5	200
Central & Eastern Europe	8	10	15	5	2	39
Newly Independent States	10	2	53	14	15	80
World Total	426	41	463	261	73	1,190

in increased consumption per person. Per capita consumption is projected to increase by 24% between 1993 and 2015. (Table 3–3)

Little construction of new generating capacity is expected in Eastern Europe and the former Soviet Union in the next few years, since many countries have excess capacity, with capacity exceeding demand by 20–100% in some nations. (Table 3–4) This period of surplus capacity is being used by some nations to develop new legislative and regulatory reforms, and some countries are undergoing a restructuring of the electric power industry similar to those under way in other parts of the world. In 1990, Poland began a major

restructuring of its electric power system, creating three independent sectors for generation, transmission, and distribution. The Polish Power Grid Co., which is fully owned by the state, maintains the transmission system. Distribution, which has the option to privatize in the near future, is provided by 33 joint stock companies owned by the state. Generation is provided by 32 independent generating companies.

Hungary is also privatizing its electricity supply sector and is in the process of selling six electricity distribution companies and seven fossil-fueled power plants. The capacity for sale is more than 5 GWs.

In the early 1990s, the Council of Mutual Economic Assistance (CMEA) coordinated large quantities of electricity flows between many of these nations, but with the political changes that have so drastically altered this region, electricity trade is also undergoing change. Most Eastern European countries are determined to shift their trade toward the European Union at the expense of their former trading partners in the East. In 1992, the Czech Republic, Hungary, Poland, and Slovakia created a new institution, Centrel, to interconnect their electric power systems as a first step toward full integration with Western Europe's system.

The economies of the countries in Central and Eastern Europe and the Newly Independent States (NIS) declined during the early 1990s. (Table 3–5) Most of the countries have older, coal-fired plants with little or no environmental controls. Over the next 15 years, roughly 18 GW of coal- and oil-fired capacity will be decommissioned in Central and Eastern Europe and the NIS. Other coal and nuclear plants will be upgraded and equipped with environmental and safety controls. The NIS nations are seeking foreign capital to upgrade the older, coal-fired plants. The need for capital investment in these regions is estimated at $142 billion(US), with much of it for retrofits and plant upgrades. (Table 3–6)

In the long term, strong growth is anticipated in both gas-fired capacity, with 15 GW in Central and Eastern Europe and 53 GW in the NIS, and coal-fired capacity, 8 GW in Central and Eastern

Table 3–5
Annual gross domestic product growth by region

	Percent per year			
	History		Projections	
Region	1970-80	1980-90	1990-2000	2000-15
Western Europe	3.0	2.6	2.1	2.6
Eastern Europe	3.5	1.8	-1.1	4.2
Former Soviet Union	3.2	2.1	-4.4	3.7
World Total	3.5	2.8	2.2	3.1

Table 3–6
Investment in coal by type of technology, 1995-2010

	(In billions of US dollars)			
	Type of Coal Technology			
Region	Conventional	New CCT	Retrofit/power	Total
Western Europe	0	86	16	102
Central & Eastern Europe	4	7	9	19
Newly Independent States	5	9	10	24
World Total	218	389	129	734

Table 3–7
Hydro/renewable energy consumption, history and projections

	Quadrillion Btu						
	History			Projections			
Region	1990	1993	1995	2000	2005	2010	2015
Western Europe	4.6	5.1	5.3	5.8	6.3	6.9	7.6
Eastern Europe	0.4	0.4	0.5	0.3	0.5	1.0	1.5
Former Soviet Union	2.4	2.4	2.5	2.6	2.8	2.9	3.1
World Total	26.3	28.1	30.0	34.0	38.3	43.4	49.7

Table 3–8
Net nuclear energy consumption, history and projections

	Billion kilowatthours						
	History			Projections			
Region	1990	1993	1995	2000	2005	2010	2015
Western Europe	703	774	783	813	786	768	722
Eastern Europe	54	54	45	55	558	59	58
Former Soviet Union	201	205	194	234	212	206	161
World Total	1,894	2,080	2,161	2,292	2,300	2,290	2,026

Europe and 10 GW in the NIS. The NIS is also expected to add 14 GW of hydroelectric capacity. (Table 3–7) Across this vast region, a number of older nuclear reactors are still operating. It is estimated that approximately $26 billion will be devoted to adding new and upgrading older nuclear reactors. (Table 3–8)

Western Europe is expected to invest $215 billion(US) in power generation over the next 15 years. It will spend $89 billion(US) for 132 GW of new gas-fired plants—more than any other region in the world—and will generate 22% of its total power needs with gas in 2010. By contrast, only 6% of the total power needs were gas-generated in 1991. Much of this new capacity will be combined-cycle used for base load generation. In addition, $102 billion(US) will be invested in 51 GW of new, coal-fired, power generation, much of it after the turn of the century. Nuclear will add 5 GW and hydropower will add 17 GW to Western European generating capacity.

EUROPE

Electricity demand in Europe is expected to increase at approximately 2.5% annually in the future, primarily spurred by economic growth. Electricity demand growth is less than the expected gross domestic product growth of 2.6% due to the saturation of the electricity markets in this region, according to the U.S. Department of Energy's Energy Information Administration (EIA) statistics. Gas-fired units are expected to supply the majority of future demand, with 93 gigawatts of gas-fired capacity projected by 2010, including 71 gigawatts of combined-cycle capacity. Another 33 gigawatts of hydroelectric capacity is also projected.

The electricity industry in Europe is undergoing massive changes due to privatization efforts, changing regulations, restructuring of the industry, and increasing competition. Plans are under way to create an international electricity market, but politics have slowed these efforts. Norway and the United Kingdom have been the most aggressive nations in the privatization arena. Both have unbundled generation, transmission, and distribution while introducing competition and establishing electricity spot markets. Finland enacted legislation in 1995 which removed licensing requirements and allowed power sales to customers and importing and exporting of electricity. Mandatory transmission access was also included. Portugal recently split its state utility into

three companies for generation, transmission, and distribution, with plans to introduce independent power producers to the mix in the future. Spain has opened its electricity market to the private producers.

Legislation allows independent power producers to build facilities and sell power, including all of the 10 GWs of new capacity the nation needs by 2000. In Italy, the state utility owns more than one-half of the country's generating capacity. Italy began work to privatize its utility in 1995. The remainder of the capacity is owned by municipal utilities, small companies, and self generators. The state utility has 47.5 GWs of capacity and likely will be divided into several companies before privatization. After 10 years of negotiations, Turkey recently signed its first build-operate-transfer agreement with an international consortium. Demand for electricity in Turkey is projected to grow by 246% in the next 15 years due to rapid economic growth, according to EIA figures.

The European community is also taking steps to coordinate grids and generation between its nations, while facilitating exports and imports of power to accommodate local demands.

International Integration of Generation and Transmission

Europe is looking increasingly to international integration of generation and transmission to answer rising supply and demand issues. Historically, the electric sector has evolved and has been operated in an integrated manner, within a national framework. The electric industry in industrialized countries has had a stable operating mode around integrated systems integrated over large areas and regulation in a national or regional framework and controlled by national equity. This national control often was extended in these countries to include fuel suppliers and manufacturers who benefited from a protected national market. This policy was often sought by the government to limit risks in fuel supplies.

Trans-border electricity trade was little developed and international relationships were often limited to technical cooperation and aid programs.

However, in the past decade, this traditional approach to power generation has been questioned as technological developments reached saturation levels and increases in power demand became insignificant, thus draining productivity factor gains. More questions have been raised in countries where the power generation sector is or was excessively fragmented, where regulations failed, or where effectiveness of traditional operators became doubtful.

Like many other branches of industry, the electric sector has been drawn into a worldwide economy, characterized by the globalization of the financial sphere and by equity mobility.

The process takes many forms, including deregulation, de-integration, competition, shift to downstream, and new definitions of relationships. Opening of capital and privatization of public utilities have led to foreign shareholding possibilities and to new international alliances between electric utilities. Deregulation, de-integration, and development of competition allow upstream players, downstream players, and even sideline players such as bankers, to enter the playing field.

International development has taken hold in Europe as German utilities look toward Northern and Eastern Europe, British electricians concentrate on the Asia-Pacific region, Spanish electricians concentrate on Latin America, and the French go global with deals in Africa, Latin America, Asia, and Europe.

Power projects in Central and Eastern Europe are expected to require as much as $90 billion(US) through 2004, according to projections from the European Privatization & Investment Corp. As yet, there are few independent power projects in Eastern Europe, but in Central European countries, particularly the Czech Republic, Poland, and Hungary, they are becoming more viable as these nations continue efforts toward privatization. (Table 3-9)

Table 3-9
Central and Eastern Europe power profiles

Country	Capacity (MW)	Thermal (%)	Nuclear (%)	Hydro (%)	Demand (TWh)
Bulgaria	12,074	53	31	16	38.2
Czech Rep.	10,655	72	17	11	58.9
Hungary	7,200	74	26	<1	34.4
Latvia	2,021	26	0	74	6.4
Lithuania	5,929	44	44	12	14.7
Poland	32,700	94	0	6	133
Romania	22,365	n/a	n/a	n/a	54.1
Slovakia	6,800	43	27	30	23.4
Estonia	3,268	100	0	0	7*
Macedonia	1,380	72	0	28	6.4

*Estonia produced 9 TWh in 1993, consuming 7 TWh and exporting 2 TWh.

[Courtesy United States Energy Association]

Table 3–10
Electric and commercial electricity prices, April 1995

Country	Price (US cents/kWh)
Germany	16.99
Spain	10.51
Austria	10.35
Belgium	9.79
Italy	8.60
Netherlands	8.18
France	7.85
Ireland	7.58
United States	7.11
United Kingdom	6.68
Finland	6.03
Norway	5.44
Australia	4.55
Sweden	4.26
Canada	4.12
South Africa	4.08

[Courtesy National Utility Service Inc.]

Impressive Growth of General Economic Picture

The general economic picture shows continued impressive growth throughout Eastern Europe and the Baltic States and continued but slower reductions in the former Soviet Union. Sharp declines in inflation rates throughout the former Soviet Union and regionwide progress in economic stabilization and market-oriented reform are expected to improve the overall economic outlook there. Electricity prices are moving toward market levels and some countries have made significant strides. (Table 3–10) In the Ukraine, for example, average prices for

households were raised in October 1995 to 70–75% of cost recovery levels, followed by another rise in January 1996.

Domestic prices for oil products in Russia and Uzbekistan were estimated to have reached world market levels at the close of 1995, and in the second half of 1995, Uzbekistan also phased out state subsidies to electricity and gas companies. In Hungary, electricity and gas laws require that prices cover costs by January 1, 1997. As a result, prices were increased significantly in 1995 with another 18–25% hike early in 1996.

Throughout Central Europe, needs are pressing for plant refurbishment and environmental upgrading. In the Central European countries of Poland, the Czech Republic, and Hungary, progress toward realistic market conditions and development of an effective financial market are enabling international lenders and equity partners to operate much as they would in Western Europe. Growth in power consumption and in gross domestic product often are aligned closely and real gross domestic product growth remains well below 1989 levels in most of the region. Even in countries where the decline of the early 1990s largely has been offset, existing total generating capacity will be sufficient in the short term because of more efficient energy use today than under the old centrally planned regime. There are, however, opportunities for plant refurbishment and upgrading, environmental protection, and replacement of capacity. There also may be opportunities for plants tied to hard-currency industries, or where commodities can be bartered against the cost of the power plant.

Poland. Around 96% of Poland's electricity is generated by coal-fired power plants, with the remainder hydropower-based. Of the 96%, 53% burn hard coal and 41% lignite. In recent years, electricity generation has remained level at around 133 TWh annually. There is a downward trend in emissions of fly ash, SO_2 and NO_x which resulted from a year-on-year decline in the amount of power generated, down from 136.36 TWh in 1990 to 133.66 TWh in 1993, coupled with the use of

higher quality coal, the introduction of flue-gas treatment, and improved electrostatic precipitators.

Hungary has an installed capacity of 7,200 MW, with 74% of its power coming from thermal sources, 26% originating at nuclear facilities, and less than 1% contributed from hydroelectric sites. Electricity demand in 1993 was 34.4 TWh, with 31.9 TWh produced domestically and 2.5 TWh imported.

Development plans foresee investments of around $7 billion(US) through 2005 in the power sector, to be financed partially by government utility and partially by outside sources through export credits, international bank loans, and private investors.

Italy. In 1992 and 1993 Italy suffered a significant slowdown in its economic growth, reflected by moderate gross national product growth of 2.2% in 1994. Italy's electric power demand, however, has increased steadily, as a result of a marked economic recovery in 1994 and 1995. To meet this slow but constant growth, a boost in electric generation capacity is expected in the next few years as older power plants will be refurbished and upgraded with newer and higher efficiency equipment. At the same time, new power plants are planned to enter the mix in the next several years.

Italy is showing a renewed interest in nuclear energy as the importance of clean and renewable energy sources is continuously growing.

In 1994, the Italian market demand for electrical energy-related products, equipment, and systems reached $5,260 million(US). In 1995, the market increased by approximately 5.3% in local currency terms, totaling $5,415 million(US). In 1996, the market was estimated at $5,640 million(US) at an expected growth rate of 4.1%. Through 1997 and 1998 the yearly rate of growth is expected to increase approximately 5% in current terms.

The moderate increase is due mainly to Italy's past economic difficulties and to the slow recovery in following with its National Energy Plan, which includes energy source diversification, energy conservation technology, and renewable energy. Investments are expected in the fields of gas generation, distribution, and use to meet at least 25% of Italy's total energy demand. Multi-fuel power plants and clean-coal technologies are also being favored for planned construction.

Sweden. After a 1980 referendum, the Parliament decided to phase out nuclear power, which produces one-half the country's electricity, by 2010. The Energy Commission now has backed down from that commitment. The date has been considered unrealistic, but Sweden still plans to phase out its nuclear stations. The country is working to bring alternative power sources on-line and to develop energy savings programs, but no detailed plan has been worked out to explain how Sweden can compensate for the loss of nuclear power.

Price is also a factor, as the energy commission projected closing the reactors by the original date would cost approximately $10-13 billion(US), pushing electricity prices up by 50%. Sweden is working to have a free market for electricity with all customers free to choose their suppliers in the near future.

End use of energy totaled 384 TWh in 1994, of which 141 TWh was used in industry, 157 TWh in housing, services, and district heating, and 86 TWh in the transport system. The eight largest production companies generate 90% of the electricity in Sweden and the state and municipalities together control most of the production.

Denmark. According to the Danish Ministry of Energy, a major goal of the Danish energy policy is to reduce overall energy consumption by 15% and carbon dioxide emissions by 20% by the year 2005.

Germany. Energy consumption and production differs markedly among the western and eastern German states. In western Germany, demand has increased slowly but steadily from year to year. In eastern Germany, by contrast, demand decreased in the early 1990s and only recently has begun to increase again.

In western Germany, current power-generating capacity is expected to meet the demand for electricity in the foreseeable future. Energy demand is expected to grow by 1–1.5% in the coming decade. Local industry projections predict that a new cycle of investment and modernization in power-generating plants will occur around the year 2005. These changes will be implemented to meet the growing demand for electricity driven by industrial innovation and increased automation in telecommunications and information processing.

Energy use in Germany totaled 528 billion kWh in 1994, up 0.2% from 1993. Electric power generation remained constant at 526 billion kWh, of which 87% was generated by public utilities, 11% by private industry, and 1% by the railroad industry. Power generation by public utilities increased by 0.5% in 1994 to 455 kWh.

Belgium.
In 1994, Belgium registered an increase in electricity consumption to 67,719 GWh, a rise of 4.8%, compared with a 1.2% rise in 1993. This growth was mainly the result of economic recovery, with high voltage consumption rising by 6.5%. The industrial sector accounted for 50% of electricity consumption and services accounted for 10%. Low voltage consumption, for households and similar uses, increased 1.5% in 1993, held down by mild climatic conditions. Low voltage electricity represented about 33% of consumption. Average consumption growth over the past five years was about 3.4%, well above the European Union average of 1.2%.

Over the past 20 years, electricity consumption has increased at a faster annual rate than that of the gross domestic product. Electricity consumption grew at 3.4%, significantly higher than the GDP growth average of 2%. Also, electricity consumption has continued to grow while primary energy consumption remains unchanged. Compared to other countries in the European Union, electricity's share of final energy consumption in Belgium, at 16.8%, is lower than the European Union average of 18.1%. The continued improvement in the economic outlook forecasts an increase in electricity consumption of about 3.5% in 1995 and a return to the annual growth pattern of 2.5% thereafter.

The former Soviet Union.
Eastern Europe and the former Soviet Union are expected to have relatively slow electricity demand growth in the coming years, with the EIA projecting annual demand growth of only 1.3%. Political and economic difficulties contribute to this region's low growth rates. If the economies of the Eastern European and former Soviet Union nations fulfill their potential of economic recovery near the turn of the century, electricity demand growth rates in these suffering regions could skyrocket into the next century. The EIA hopes for growth rates in these regions to rise to 1.8% after 2000, if the economy can attain a 3.7% growth rate. Per capita consumption in these regions is expected to jump by 24% by 2015.

Little construction is expected to occur in Eastern Europe as many of these nations already have excess generating capacity of 20–100%. Many of the countries with generating excesses are taking advantage of this slow growth period as an opportunity to institute reforms and restructuring, including privatization.

Poland's generation is provided by 32 independent companies and distribution may privatize in the near future. Hungary is also working to privatize its supply, attempting to sell six distribution companies and seven fossil-powered generation facilities. The state-owned utility is divesting all of its generation assets except the Paks Nuclear Power Plant, which provides 45% of the nation's electricity. For now the state utility will retain ownership of the national grid.

In 1992, the Czech Republic, Hungary, Poland, and Slovakia created Centrel, a new institution, to connect their electric power grids, as a step toward electricity trade with their European

neighbors. To trade power with Europe, the Soviet nations must invest heavily in their grids to meet the standards of the European nations.

Problems in NIS Power Sector

The NIS power sector covers one-sixth of the world's land surface and has the largest combined proven energy reserves of any region in the world, but it has problems. There is an energy crisis, there has been a decline in energy production, an increase in nonpayment for fuels, and energy is skyrocketing. Many of the power sectors are bankrupt and inadequate electricity rates do not cover the cost of producing the power.

A variety of factors have contributed to the crisis, including destruction of economic links between the republics, a slump in the production of energy resources, and a lack of adequate investment in the industry. There is not enough funding to pay for the essential components of the energy sector—fuel, maintenance, repairs, and capital investments. Development of the NIS energy sector has the potential to make a significant contribution in meeting the world's energy needs. Efficient development of these resources will require unprecedented cooperation within the international energy industry, and therefore will provide enormous opportunities.

Now the republics are working to overcome these many crippling difficulties, working to modernize their existing energy systems with life extension programs and modifications to the transmission systems, controls, and instrumentation. They would like to add pollution controls. The utilities are learning many aspects of running a business in a market economy, including ways to raise foreign capital and implement acceptable bookkeeping methods.

The NIS and the countries of Central and Eastern Europe are making ambitious plans to expand their electric power infrastructure, with an estimated 136 GW of installed capacity to be in place by 2010, according to U.S. Trade and Development Agency statistics.

Russia. The economy in the Far East is expected to stabilize soon, leading to an increase in electricity demand. Expansions are planned at Bureyskaya Hydroelectric Power Plant, plus a variety of upgrades and modifications to other existing power plants. Major demand increases are expected in the south of the region with up to 3 million MWh of electricity imports projects.

Major projects scheduled by the turn of the century include:

- complete construction of 2,000-MW Burey Hydroelectric Power Plant,

- start construction of Urgal 1 Hydroelectric Power Plant in Khabarovsk Territory,

- start construction of Nishne-Burey Hydroelectric Power Plant in Amursk Territory, and

- complete construction of Vilyuy Hydroelectric Power Plant Unit 3, Yakut Central Fossil Power Plant, Magadan Heat and Power Plant, and Ust-Srednekan Hydroelectric Power Plant.

The decade of 2000 to 2010 is expected to be a turning point in the national economy with positive growth in the industrial and economic markets. New hydroelectric facilities are being contemplated in Khabarovsk and Amursk territories in this era, along with one or two nuclear power plants in Khabarovsk and Primorsk territories.

Ukraine. Total installed capacity in Ukraine is 54,200 MW, with fossil-fueled plants providing 67.6% and nuclear plants providing 25% of that total. There are 104 fossil-fueled plants, ranging from 150 MW to 800 MW, with a combined capacity of 28,700 MW. However, 82% of all operating units already have reached their designed service-life limit of 100,000 hours, and 48% already have exceeded maximum allowed service-life limits of 170,000 hours. Twenty units have been in operation for 200,000 hours.

Armenia can produce only an average of 12 million kWh of electricity daily toward meeting a demand approaching 30 million kWh daily. Before 1988, the installed capacity of power plants in Armenia was about 3,500 MW, with 1,750 MW from fossil-fueled power plants, 800 MW from one nuclear plant, and 950 MW from hydroelectric power plants.

Development of the energy sector is a high priority for the government, and is supported by the United States and other foreign nations, along with international organizations in the country, but the government lacks financing for many of the potential projects.

Kazakhstan. Production and consumption of electricity in Kazakhstan decreased 24% from 1990 to 1994, from production of 104.7 million MWh to 79.5 million MWh, and was projected to fall to 75.2 MWh for 1995. The generation drop is caused by the physical and technological deterioration of the power plants combined with economic difficulties.

By 2010 electricity consumption could increase to 115–125 million MWh. There is an existing deficit of approximately 12 million MWh, so the country needs to add 38–48 million MWh of additional capacity. This will require new generating units with total capacity of 4,400-5,300 MW by 2010. (Table 3–11)

Table 3–11
Kazakhstan proposed new power plants

Name	Rating
Ekibastus Hydroelectric Plant	1,000 MW
South Kazakhstan Hydro Plant	1,000 MW
Aktubinsk Power Plant	954 MW
Atyrausk Power Plant	150 to 300 MW
Uralsky Power Plant 2	100 to 380 MW
Aktubinsk Power Plant	100 to 280 MW
Shimkentsk Power Plant 3	80 to 160 MW
Karagandinsk Power Plant 2	185 MW
Karagandinsk Power Plant 3	110 MW
Zhezkazgansk Power Plant 2	220 to 330 MW
Balhash Power Plant	110 MW
Tselinograd Power Plant 2	185 MW
Ust-Kamenogorsk Plant 1 & 2	180 to 360 MW

*Predictions indicate Kazakhstan will need to add
4,400 to 5,300 MW of generating capacity by 2010.*

[Courtesy Kazakhstanenergo]

Kyrgyzstan. Energy production is shifting increasingly from coal to hydroelectric and the demand for residential heating is declining because electricity is more convenient and can be purchased on credit.

Heating plant consumption is declining because the plants are not generating enough revenue to pay their fuel expenses and they are being taken out of service when steam production is not essential.

To meet demands, construction of the hydroelectric facilities and associated transmission and distribution lines needs to be accelerated dramatically.

Slovak Republic. The Slovak electrical power plants of Bratislava generated 22,861 GWh of electricity in 1995. Of that, approximately 50% is credited to the nuclear power plant in Bohunice, which produced 11,437 GWh. Coal and gas plants produced 6,269 GWh or 27.4%. Hydroelectric power accounted for 22.5% at 5,155 GWh.

Forecasts predict electricity sales to increase by 1,700 GWh in 1996. Total production is 23,400 GWh with a total installed capacity of 6,829 MW. Annual electricity consumption per capita is 4,390 kWh. Industry consumes 53.5% of the total generation, residential consumption accounts for 43.6%, and transportation uses 2.9%.

Estonia is a small country on the southern Gulf of Finland coast of the Baltic Sea with a total area of 45,226 square kilometers and a population of 1.56 million. Installed capacity of the state utility, Eesti Energia, is 3,268 MW and the thermal capacity is 4,199 MW. The energy system produces 99% electrical and 35% thermal energy in the republic, exporting 35% of the electricity to the neighbor states of Estonia—Latvia and Russia. All of the nation's power is produced by thermal power plants.

Latvia has struggled with its transition to independence. Latvia has had to compete with a new economic system and an electrical separation

from the old unified Soviet system. Demand for electricity has declined substantially over the last three years. Latvia has an installed capacity of 2,021 MW, with 74% of its power coming from hydroelectric sources and the other 26% from thermal sources. Electricity demand is 6.4 TWh.

Electricity is an urgent problem in Latvia because it does not have its own significant energy resources to supply its needs. The economy is fully dependent on foreign energy resources, so the energy crisis in Russia has caused a crisis in supply to Latvia. Of the Baltic States, only Latvia has an unfavorable electricity balance, as domestic generation covers only about one-half the total demand.

Lithuania has an installed capacity of 5,929 MW. Electricity production in 1993 was 14.7 TWh and Lithuania exported approximately 20% of that electricity. Lithuanian officials are interested in increasing energy efficiency through price reforms and demand-side management programs.

Bulgaria has an installed capacity of 12,074 and an available capacity of 8,700 MW. Electricity demand, as of 1993, was 38.2 TWh. Bulgaria is working to implement a market-oriented economy and to improve industrial sector performance and to tighten environmental protections. However, unlike most nations, power demand in Bulgaria has been dropping. The decrease in demand started in 1990 and total consumption of primary energy has decreased by 40% compared to 1989. After several years of decline, the recession seems to have abated. After a decline in gross domestic production and electricity demand of nearly 20%, the country is showing a turnaround and a small increase.

Romania. At the close of 1993, installed capacity of the Romanian Power System was 22,365 MW. Consumption jumped 2.87 in 1993 from 1992. Despite the country's large generating capacity, poor conditions of the thermal power plants, combined with fuel shortages and a lack of hard currency to buy fuel, have created problems. In the past, these led to a need for a fuel rationing system. The future looks brighter, however, as state utility Renel recently commissioned a large nuclear plant, a significant stride toward better accommodating demand.

Czech Republic. The republic exported 2.0 TWh of electricity in 1994, mostly to Italy and Switzerland, with supply well exceeding demand. A downturn in the economy has led to decreasing electricity demand by about 15% between 1990 and 1993. In 1993, the electricity consumption demand reached its lowest point. It began growing again in 1994, with a 2.6% increase and grew again in 1995.

Macedonia has an installed electric capacity of 1,380 MW. Electricity demand in 1993 was 6.4 TWh.

Albania has 20 electric power plants with an installed capacity of 1,670 MW.

Chapter 4

Middle East and Africa Electricity Demand

ANN CHAMBERS
ASSOCIATE EDITOR
POWER ENGINEERING INTERNATIONAL AND
POWER ENGINEERING

THE MIDDLE EAST

The Middle East is expected to experience strong growth in electricity demand prior to 2000, almost 6% annually, with demand growth tapering off to 2.5% after 2000. The growth in demand, particularly before 2000, will be spurred by moderate economic growth, which is projected at 3.4% annually through 2015, and further electrification and infrastructure improvements in some areas. Saudi Arabia alone plans to invest $2.84 billion(US) over the next six years in various electric power projects in the country. The projects will be partially funded by an electricity consumption tax, which was imposed in January 1996. In January 1995, the government also increased electricity rates by 63% for individuals and companies that consume more than two MWh per month. The Middle East is expected to have a fuel mix shift in power production as the region moves to substitute gas for oil to release more oil for export. (Table 4–1)

Table 4–1

Projected worldwide changes in generation and capacity, 1995-2010

Region	Solid Fuel	Oil	Gas	Hydro/ Renewable	Nuclear	Total
Generation change (TWh)						
Middle East	5	13	233	13	0	265
Africa	163	36	159	38	3	399
World Total	2,845	53	2,550	1,188	445	7,081
Capacity change (GW)						
Middle East	1	3	44	3	0	52
Africa	15	8	26	6	0	55
World Total	426	41	463	261	73	1,190

Increased international cooperation and trade are also planned among a number of nations in the Middle East and in neighboring regions. Currently, five countries—Egypt, Jordan, Iraq, Syria, and Turkey—are interconnecting their systems and discussing agreements for electricity transfers. Trade agreements are expected to be approved by the five countries by the close of 1996. The first phase of the project is expected to include electricity trades of: 400 MW between Turkey-Syria and Syria-Iraq, 300 MW between Syria and Jordan, 400 MW from Jordan to Egypt,

and 300 MW from Egypt to Jordan. Transfers of up to 750 MW are expected in the next phase of the project between Turkey and Iraq, Turkey and Syria, and Syria and Iraq.

Power consumption increases in the Middle East have been running 10–15% annually and the power authorities are planning major investment programs in generation and distribution. The need for generation, transmission, and distribution construction is expected to remain high although regional cooperation and interconnection programs are expected to ease growing demand needs. (Table 4–2)

Table 4–2
Net electricity consumption, history and projections

	Billion kilowatthours						
	History			Projections			
Region	**1990**	**1993**	**1995**	**2000**	**2005**	**2010**	**2015**
Middle East	190	196	245	293	339	381	426
Africa	285	299	304	362	430	507	593
World Total	10,382	10,761	11,355	13,090	14,922	16,877	19,087

The United States Department of Energy's Energy Information Administration predicts growth of approximately 6% annually through the turn of the century, with growth slipping to around 2.5% thereafter. Regional agencies place the expected demand growth closer in line with recent demand, at 10–15% annually. (Table 4–3)

Table 4–3
Per capita electricity consumption, history and projection

	Megawatthours per Person		
	1980	**1993**	**2015**
Middle East	0.9	1.3	1.6
Africa	0.4	0.4	0.5

Electricity demand growth is spurred by economic growth, projected to hover near 3.5% annually in the next two decades, and by scattered electrification and infrastructure improvements. Saudi Arabia plans to invest $2.84 billion(US) in the next six years for electricity availability improvements and capacity expansions. Saudi Arabia instituted an electricity consumption tax in January 1996 to partially fund the planned improvements. Electricity rates have also been significantly increased. As capacity expands

throughout the Middle East, gas is expected to pick up an increased share of the market, allowing the nations to free more oil for export.

Iran hopes to raise its electrical generating capacity from 21 GW at present to 35 GW by 1998. A $1.4 billion(US) 2,090-MW plant under construction in southern Iran is one major project. However, U.S. sanctions may affect further progress on this project. China has agreed to provide four 325-MW generators for a new $700 million(US) plant in Arak. This project is expected to come on-line by 2000. In mid-1995, Iranian officials stated their intent to build 10 nuclear power plants by 2015. The goal of the program is the use of nuclear power to provide about 20% of the country's power needs. Iran's current installed capacity is 20.9 GW with production of 70 billion kWh.

Iraq. Approximately 90% of Iraq's national power grid was destroyed during the Gulf War. Existing generating capacity of 9,000 MW in December 1990 was reduced to only 340 MW by March 1991. Roughly 85% of Iraq's 20 power stations were damaged or destroyed in the Gulf War. In early 1991, transmission and distribution infrastructure was also destroyed, including the 10 substations serving Baghdad and about 30% of the country's 400-kV transmission network. Generation capacity is now estimated at 5,000 MW with a total production of 25.7 billion kWh annually. Total energy consumption is 0.9 quadrillion Btu, or 46.7 million Btus per capita.

Israel. Driven by rapid economic growth in increased immigration, Israel's electric power demand is growing by 9–10% annually. The Israel Electric Co. (IEC), Israel's national utility, estimates that electric power demand will grow at an average rate of about 5% through 2002, and that a doubling of production capacity, to more than 12 GW, will be necessary by that year. To meet this increased demand, IEC is aiming to raise between $1.2 and 1.3 billion(US) annually in financing for generation, transmission, and distribution systems.

As part of an effort to increase privatization of the Israel electric power sector, the Ministry of Energy has directed IEC to purchase at least 900 MW of power from independent power producers by the year 2005, with up to 150 MW of that expected to come from solar and wind facilities. In 1994, the Israeli government made a strategic decision to have 20% of the country's power demands met by independent power producers. This should help the country keep pace with rising demand.

One area of potential regional cooperation involves integration of individual national power transmission grids into a regional power network. Such a network would, among other benefits, allow power companies to take advantage of differences in peak demand periods, reduce the need for installation and maintenance of reserve generating capacity, and provide outlets for surplus generating capacity. Israel's installed capacity is around 4.3 GW with an annual production of 25 billion kWh. Total energy consumption is 0.55 quadrillion Btu and per capita consumption or 105 million Btus.

Syria. In September 1993, President Asad declared that a secure supply of electricity was the right of every Syrian. Following this declaration, contracts were awarded for the construction of several new, gas-turbine power stations. Demand in the country will likely climb as power generation and availability increase. Syria has an installed capacity of 4 GW with annual generation of 5.7 billion kWh, predominantly fueled by oil and gas, with about 25% hydroelectric.

Turkey has announced plans to spend $715 million(US) on electric power projects in 1996, and energy officials are working to revive plans for the country's first nuclear power plant. Demand for electric power is escalating at more than 8% annually in Turkey and is projected to reach 94 million MWh by the end of 1996. Capacity stood at 20,951 MW at the close of 1995, and the government hopes to increase capacity to 21,217 MW by the end of 1996. Turkey's electricity demand in 1995 was almost 72,000 GWh, and it is expected to soar to 308,000 GWh by 2010.

In 1993, Turkey's energy production was 48.4% hydroelectric, 27% lignite, 1.7% hard coal, 13.2% natural gas, 7.6% petroleum, and 0.02% geothermal. Turkey must add 1,000 MW annually to meet demand.

According to reports from the Turkish government, 187 more power plant units are needed by 2010. Per capita consumption in the country is expected to increase from 1,200 kWh to 3,300 kWh by 2010. The government acknowledges the importance of adequate electricity supply and is placing importance on build-operate-transfer and build-operate-own type generation projects.

Turkey is hampered by its limited energy reserves. Estimates are that by 2010, 69% of the country's coal reserves and 66% of its hydroelectric potential will have been developed. In 1994, Turkey imported more than 50% of its primary energy, and imports are expected to surpass 60% by 2010. Efforts are being made to expand the natural gas-fired capacity. Natural gas was first used for power generation there in 1985, but by 1993, gas was contributing 15% to the mix. (Table 4–4)

Table 4–4
Current and projected energy sources for Turkey

Fuel	1995	2000	2010
Coal	36%	37%	42%
Gas	17%	26%	25%
Hydroelectric	38%	31%	26%
Nuclear	0%	0%	4%
Oil	9%	6%	3%

[Courtesy TEAS]

The largest utility in Turkey is the state-owned Turkish Power Generation and Transmission Company (TEAS), which has a market share of more than 90%. The grid operator, Turkish Electricity Distribution Company (TEDAS), is also state owned. Except for Greece and Syria, the grid is interconnected with its bordering neighbors.

Turkey has been enacting legislation to protect its environment since 1983, and flue-gas desulfurization systems are being installed on numerous existing coal-fired facilities. Other

environmental protection technologies, such as electrostatic precipitators and upgrades to waste disposal equipment, have also found a market there.

AFRICA

Africa's electricity demand is projected to grow at an average of 3.2% annually over the next two decades, with electricity infrastructure growth ongoing, bringing electric power to more of the extensive poor rural areas and to serve electricity-starved industries in many African nations.

Africa is a massive area of land, and there are broad ranges of available natural resources and economic development levels. Southern Africa accounts for approximately 50% of the continent's electricity consumption, while North Africa consumes approximately 30% and sub-Saharan Africa uses 20%.

According to Energy Information Administration figures, per capita consumption is dramatically different. South Africa consumes 4.2 MWh per capita; North Africa, including Morocco, Algeria, Libya, Tunisia, and Egypt, consumes 0.8 MWh per capita; and sub-Saharan Africa only 0.14 MWh per capita. Average consumption in developed nations is around 6.6 MWh per capita.

The nations of Africa are pursuing a variety of plans to meet demand increases, including working with private developers, restructuring, and partial privatizations.

South Africa has undertaken a program to electrify 1.75 million homes by 2000, in an attempt to even out its distribution. Currently, many poor areas have no access to electricity, but urban areas are almost fully electrified. About 40% of the population has access to electricity, but the government is striving to increase that figure to 72% by the turn of the century. Lack of access is generally due to transmission infrastructure shortfalls, not to a shortage of generating capacity. Eskom, the national electric utility, has excess generating capacity. South Africa is also entertaining

plans to develop its international connections to expand trade with utilities in neighboring regions as part of the Southern Africa Power Pool.

In Africa, only 18 million rural people have been connected to electricity in the past 20 years, while the continent's rural population has increased by 188 million. Given prevailing trends, it is unlikely that people living in rural areas or poor urban neighborhoods will soon enjoy the benefits of electricity. Recognizing that many traditional, grid electrification programs have failed, energy planners and donors have begun to advocate a decentralized, dispersed, renewable energy approach using photovoltaics or solar home systems. Although home systems have an important role to play, this single option cannot fill the wide gap between those who enjoy the advantages of electricity and those who do not. To bring the advantages of modern civilization to the rural world requires a market-driven approach that can make a wide menu of energy products available at an affordable cost. (Tables 4–5 and 4–6)

Table 4–5

Net nuclear energy consumption, history and projections

| | Billion kilowatthours | | | | | |
| | History | | | Projections | | |
Region	1990	1993	1995	2000	2005	2010
Middle East	0	0	0	0	0	4
Africa	8	7	9	9	9	9
World Total	1,894	2,080	2,161	2,292	2,300	2,290

Table 4–6

Hydro/renewable energy consumption, history and projections

| | Quadrillion Btu | | | | | | |
| | History | | | Projections | | | |
Region	1990	1993	1995	2000	2005	2010	2015
Middle East	0.1	0.2	0.2	0.3	0.4	0.5	0.5
Africa	0.6	0.6	0.5	0.7	0.8	0.9	1.0
World Total	26.3	28.1	30.0	34.0	38.3	43.4	49.7

While centralized grid electrification has an important long-term role to play, a decentralized approach may be more appropriate in the short- to medium-term given the current low electricity demands of widely dispersed people in rural areas. Energy services needed most in rural households are cooking, water, and space heating.

These are provided mainly through wood and agricultural residues, not through electricity or solar energy, which may be the most appropriate available energy forms. The top 1–2% of the population demands full electricity services; and without access to the grid, this group is likely to have a small generator set, fueled either by kerosene, petrol, diesel, or photovoltaics. The next 3–5% of the population demands lighting, a radio, television, and video. This is a prime group for 40- to 60-watt solar home systems. The next group, about 15% of population, needs lighting, a radio, and possibly a small television set. People in this group often have a car battery that they take into town when it needs recharging. This group needs a 20- to 40-watt solar home system and 10- to 15-watt solar lanterns.

Some 80% of the rural population uses candles, kerosene, and sometimes a flashlight for lighting. They may also own a small radio operated on dry cell batteries. It is unlikely that this group will be electrified by either grid or individual solar systems in the next 20 years. Solar lanterns or portable fluorescent lights, such as people in industrialized countries use for camping, are prime lighting sources for these people. Small solar panels are also being considered for rural electrification. (Table 4–7)

Table 4–7
Annual gross domestic product growth rates by region

| Region | Percent per year | | | |
| | History | | Projections | |
	1970-80	1980-90	1990-2000	2000-15
Middle East	4.8	1.5	3.3	3.4
Africa	4.2	1.4	2.3	3.5
World Total	3.5	2.8	2.2	3.1

Botswana currently has an installed capacity of 197 MW. Approximately 75% of the total electricity in this country is used by the copper and diamond mining industries. The country is developing an extended rural-electrification strategy, with ongoing projects being extended to serve the needs of farmers in the Tuli Block on the Limpopo River. The government is in the midst of a major housing project and land-serving program to provide 23,000 housing units in the next few years. This program is expected to have a major impact on energy demand in the coming years.

Kenya. A 1993 World Bank study showed that more rural and urban households in Kenya enjoy electricity through small solar home systems than through the grid. In 1993, 20,000 households used a solar system, compared to 17,000 connected to the grid. Many households, uncertain whether grid electrification would ever reach their area, have purchased solar home systems, despite the absence of projects or programs to promote the systems. The systems cost $700(US), and only the wealthiest of the rural population can afford such a system. Nevertheless, the solar systems sold provide enough business for the private sector to build an infrastructure in rural areas. As a result, solar outlets are now found in most major and many smaller towns in Kenya. Total installed capacity of solar installations in 1993 was estimated at more than 1 MW, mainly supplying electricity to households.

Kenya's government reduced the import tax on solar panels in 1986, which helped accelerate the market. It is likely that more than 5,000 households have purchased solar systems since 1993, possibly as many as 15,000. Trends indicated by the World Bank in 1993 appear to have continued, and are recognized by the Rural Electrification Program of the Kenya Power and Lighting Co. The program's master plan specifically includes solar and other decentralized options. The government continues to subsidize grid connection and energy services while taxing solar systems at high rates.

Population growth in Kenya far exceeds the growth rate of urban and rural grid connections and solar home systems combined. In 1996, urban growth is estimated at 240,000 people or 40,000 to 60,000 households. New grid connections will number approximately 10,000 to 15,000 in urban areas and 4,000 to 8,000 in rural areas. If another 4,000 to 8,000 solar home systems are added, the total number of households benefiting will total 20,000 to 30,000. This compares to the incremental

growth of homes of about 100,000 to 150,000. The growth of the potential market is significant, and if the public sector tries to keep up, it may result in too heavy a burden for scarce public financial resources. The traditional grid electrification approach is unlikely to produce timely or cost-effective results. While solar home systems can fill market niches, they cannot function as the sole answer to rural electrification needs.

Malawi. All baseload electricity in Malawi comes from hydroelectric plants operated by Eskom, the electrical supply commission. Its gas turbines and diesel units are for standby use only. In 1991, Malawi's hydro capacity was 146 MW. Thermal units added another 23 MW. Another 2 MW of diesel are sited in the northern tip of the country, and self-generators are estimated to have 24 MW of capacity from steam plants, diesels, and two small hydro stations. Current demand for electricity is 130 MW at peak, but it is expected to jump to 250 MW by 1999.

Morocco. Rural Morocco is almost totally without electricity, but the Office National de L'Electricity (ONE) is working to extend service to 2,000 villages. ONE is exploring a variety of resources in an effort to meet an estimated 7% growth in demand. A four-unit, 1,200-MW steam station is being constructed and will enter service by 1999. Three 100-MW combustion turbines are being completed, and an expansion of eight 330-MW units is being planned for the Jorf Lasfar station. The government has announced plans to spend $1 billion(US) on the power sector in 1996 in an attempt to meet coming demand, and has invited the private sector for equity-participation.

Tanzania. Tanzania's electricity is primarily hydroelectric power, and the country is experiencing generation shortfalls in drought or dry weather conditions. Some diesel-powered units are available, but they are expensive to operate and drain the country's foreign exchange reserves. The government is exploring plans to use its indigenous coal to generate electricity. Tanzania is a light electrical consumer with an installed capacity of 482 MW, of which 445 MW is in the interconnected grid system and 37 MW in isolated generating stations.

This country implemented an economic reform program almost a decade ago; and between 1986 and 1991, demand for electricity grew at an annual average of 10.2%, with peak demand rising at 7.85%. The national economy is sustaining recovery, and the government is assuming that electricity demand growth will maintain this trend. Demand is projected at 650 MW by 2000, rising to 825 MW by 2005.

Zanzibar is currently part of Tanzania, receiving power through undersea high-voltage transmission lines to Mtoni receiving station. The transmission lines are more than 10 years old, and Tanzania has a power shortage during its dry season.

Power shortages in Tanzania have caused severe power interruptions in Zanzibar. Zanzibar has a peak electricity demand of 14 MW. It is seeking large capacity and small modular generators using fossil fuels. The African Development Bank is funding the upgrade of the country's distribution system and is considering funds for installing additional capacity projects. The World Bank is also considering funding these projects. Zanzibar's peak requirement is expected to escalate to around 24 MW by 2003.

Zambia is looking to expand its hydroelectric capacity through Kafue Gorge Lower Hydroelectric Plant. Hydroelectricity is the leading source of power in Zambia. It has seven hydroelectric facilities, totaling more than 1,670 MW, and these have made the Zambia Electricity Supply Corporation an exporter of electrical power.

Zimbabwe. ZESA has determined that two 220-MW units are needed to meet the growing demand on the generation system and to reduce dependence on imported power. Zimbabwe is importing nearly 10% of its power from Zambia, but Zambia plans to decrease its power exports. ZESA has an installed capacity of 1,930 MW.

Chapter 5
Asia and Pacific Electricity Demand

MICHAEL T. BURR
SENIOR EDITOR
INDEPENDENT ENERGY

OVERVIEW

Asia is host to the most dramatic economic boom in recent times. While the people of these countries still rank near the bottom of the scale in earnings and production per capita, gross national product (GNP) growth figures in the high single digits over the past several years have begun to narrow the gap between the region's developing countries and the industrialized nations of the world.

Asia is home to several of the world's most populous nations—China (1.2 billion), India (913 million), Indonesia (190 million), Pakistan (126 million), Bangladesh (122 million), and Vietnam (73 million). These large populations are also among the world's poorest, with annual individual incomes as low as $190 (Vietnam). The effects for the electric power industry have been minimal generating capacity, sparse power grids, and low per-capita electricity consumption rates.

In the past several years, however, the economies of developing Asia have been growing at rates ranging from 5–11% annually. Such growth is expected to continue in the future, albeit at a slightly slower pace than the recent past. (Table 5–1) The Asian Development Bank (ADB) estimates gross domestic product (GDP) growth across much of Asia will average 6–9% through 1997. In the longer term, growth is anticipated to continue at a strong pace. Developing Asian economies are projected to grow an average of 6% a year through the year 2000, with similar growth expected in the following decade.

Such economic growth is accompanied by expanding manufacturing and commercial sectors, increasing family incomes, and rising power consumption. Additionally, as nations pursue ambitious rural development and electrification programs, large populations are beginning to have access to electricity for the first time. Numerous transmission and distribution projects in various stages of development are expected to extend power grids in Asia substantially.

Table 5-1
Macro factors in Asian energy markets

	Real Growth (% Annual Change in GDP/Capita, 1985-1994)	Energy Use Growth (1980-1992)	Installed Capacity (MW, 1994)	Power Use (kWh/capita)	Projected GDP Growth (Est. Avg. % through 2000)	Projected New MW (Through 2000)	Projected New MW (Through 2005)
Bangladesh	2.1	8.5	2500	80	5	1000	2250
China	6.9	5.1	200000	692	5.5	90,000	215000
India	2.9	6.8	81000	310	6	13500	145000
Indonesia	6	7.2	21000	200	7	9000	15000
Korea	7.8	9.2	36000	238	6	4600	24000
Laos	2.1	NA	260	44	NA	1,500	2,500
Malaysia	5.7	NA	8,000	1,610	7	7,000	9200
Myanmar	NA	NA	1100	55	NA	220	500
Nepal	2.2	8.4	1100	41	2.5	250	500
Pakistan	1.6	6.9	13,000	350	6	5000	13000
Philippines	1.8	3.1	10500	420	7.2	4200	13,000
Sri Lanka	2.7	1.3	2000	168	5	1,800	2000
Thailand	8.2	10.1	13,000	965	7.5	4500	11000
Vietnam	NA	NA	4400	125	8	8000	12000
Average	4.17	6.05		378.43	6.61		
Total			Total Capacity 393860			Total 150570	Total 464950

With economic growth, as well as development efforts by governments and multilateral agencies, per-capita consumption of electricity has more than doubled since 1980. Continued economic growth, development, and electrification are expected to increase per-capita consumption by 5.3% per year, or by more than 50% by the year 2015. (Figure 5-1) This will result in a total of 3,250 billion kilowatt hours of new electricity consumption by 2015, according to the U.S. Energy Information Administration. PennWell's

estimates call for electric power demands in the Asian region to rise by more than 375 GW through the year 2005. Through the year 2010, Asia's power infrastructure demands could nearly double, from a current installed capacity of about 500 GW. Details about the power demands in several Asian countries are included.

Australia, with 17.8 million people, has a gross domestic product (GDP) over $320 billion. The country's economy has grown by an average of 1.2% annually since 1985—slightly lower than the United States' 1.3% growth rate during the same period.

New electricity demands in Australia are expected to be nominal through the year 2000, as existing capacity appears adequate to meet demands in most places, and efficiency is improving at many plants. Australia has a very competitive electricity market. As in all truly competitive markets, there will be a move to greater differentiation among suppliers as each targets the different energy service needs of specific customer groups. This differentiation and niche marketing will see a range of different suppliers. In the generation sector, there is a potential market among the five eastern and

Figure 5-1. Electricity consumption per capita

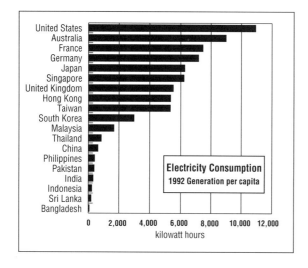

southern states for eight major generators, each with capacities of 1,000 MW or more. In addition there are several small generators, either operating or planned, with outputs greater than 30 MW.

Australia is expected to be a mixed market with many new participants. One market will provide physical energy such as generators, transmission and distribution (T&D) authorities, and retail business. The second market is quite different and new to the industry—the financial intermediaries. There will be new players such as banks and other financial institutions, bringing the expertise to operate various exchange mechanisms.

As utilities move into energy service businesses there will be greater involvement in developing end-use technology, especially in the industrial area, where new technologies can provide a competitive edge for manufacturers. Demand for new technology, investment, telecommunications, and financial services could prove high during the next several years.

Bangladesh. With about 118 million people, Bangladesh ranks ninth in the world in population. With current GDP growth rates estimated at 5.3%, and projections calling for continued 5% annual growth through the end of the decade, Bangladesh is expected to have 1,000–1,500 MW of new electric power demand by the year 2000, and 2250 MW of new demand by 2005.

Bangladesh is working to overcome capacity shortfalls that are projected to persist through 1999. Also, Bangladesh has been plagued with transmission losses as high as 41% in 1990.

The government of Bangladesh is inviting bids for private power projects, after the World Bank applied its policy of withholding aid for countries with no government commitment to reform. The country went without multilateral development funding for two years.

China leads Asia in terms of size, economic growth rate, and power demands. Real economic growth for the past 10 years has averaged nearly 7% in China, with GDP growth projected to

continue from 5.5–6.5% through the year 2000. Energy demands are expanding rapidly in China, with at least 45,000 MW of new capacity expected to be required by the year 2000, and 120,000 MW needed by 2005.

This power demand is driven by strong economic growth—too strong, in fact, to be manageable. The country's economy grew by nearly 10% through the 1980s, with growth in the industrial sector reaching 20%. In the early 1990s growth reached 12% and higher, but the government seems to be succeeding at limiting the economy.

The central government is taking steps to increase generation capacity to match economic growth. Growth of the electricity sector has not kept pace with overall economic growth in the past 10 years, resulting in power shortfalls now that are expected to continue and worsen over the next several years. Additionally, the government expects to increase electrification from less than 90% in 1993 to 95% by the year 2000.

Power demands are most concentrated in the industrial northeastern and coastal provinces, including Shandong, Liaoning, Jilin, and Heilongjiang. Shandong alone calls for 7,500 MW of new capacity to be added by the year 2000. Additionally, Guangdong Province, adjacent to Hong Kong, and Shanxi Province in central China have large load-growth expectations.

Despite growth in the power sector, severe problems persist. First is the lack of electricity in various areas. Second is a shortage of peaking power supply. Third, coal has been in short supply for power generation in many areas. This shortage is caused by limits in coal transportation and varieties, declining coal quality, and skyrocketing coal prices. Fourth, utilities are having increasing difficulty in collecting payment for electricity and heat. Finally, there was a sharp decrease in the scale of installations last year. This likely will cause a severe lag effect on power construction and power supply in the next two to three years. The Power Ministry plans to install 10,000 MW of large and medium power units in

1996, increasing the power capacity to 220 GW by the end of this year.

The Ninth Five-Year Plan (1996-2000) projects that the country's capacity, 210 GW at the end of last year, should be increased to 300 GW by the turn of the century and 550–600 GW by 2010. Last year China generated 1 million GWh of electricity. In the year 2000, 1.4 million GWh are expected to be generated, representing an annual growth of 7%.

Expected growth in power generation through 2000 differs by region. The coastal areas remain the focus of attention to most foreign developers and investors, although some inland provinces have become more aggressive in soliciting foreign investment.

Provinces are busy finalizing their plans for power growth according to different power demand estimates and economic growth rates. For example, in the northeastern provinces of Liaoning, Jilin, and Heilongjiang, where 132 GWh was generated last year, a moderate increase to 175 GWh by 2000 is planned. This represents a 6.2% annual increase, lower than the power generating growth rate projected for the whole country. In Shanxi Province, where 60% of China's coal is produced, a 4,200 MW increase is planned for the Ninth Five-Year Plan.

India.
Energy demands have been increasing substantially in India, averaging 6.8% growth per year for the past decade. Power demands are expected to continue increasing by 7.6% per year through the year 2000, and 4.6% a year thereafter. India has experienced real economic growth averaging 2.9% in the past decade, and GDP growth is expected to continue at about 6% through the end of the decade. Investment during the next 10 years is projected at nearly $140 billion, with conservative estimates projecting that 13,500 MW of new capacity will be required by the year 2000, and 48,000 MW required by 2005. Some estimates call for up to 145,000 MW of new capacity requirements by 2005.

A wide range of conflicting forecasts of India's power requirements suggests that the magnitude

of the crisis is yet to be accurately determined. Without a reliable demand forecast, planning for the power industry cannot be conducted optimally. One demand forecast suggests that 142,000 MW of additional capacity will be required, including peak demand, in the next 10 years only under certain conditions. One such set of conditions is that new projects are operated at 75% peak load factor, T&D losses continue at 22%, no further captive or cogeneration capacity is added, and no installed base plants are repowered. However, all of these are untenable as most power purchase agreements (PPAs) are signed for 85–90% offtake. T&D losses are likely to decrease with privatization in the medium future, captive and cogeneration capacity will increase rapidly in the near future, and there are extensive plans for installed base repowering.

Under these conditions the demand for additional capacity in the next 10 years could fall below 100,000 MW. This figure may be further reduced with wheeling of power from surplus areas to deficit areas and in the long run through demand side management (DSM). These aspects can have an enormous effect on capacity planning and particularly PPAs that will be signed in the next five years, especially since there has been about 250,000 MW of new capacity addition activity recorded to date.

Government figures from several ministries show there are important links between key sectors. For instance, 66.5% of India's installed capacity is coal-based, almost 65% of coal is transported by rail—coal accounts for 45% of goods transported by rail. A forecasted shortage in coal will lead to substantial imports, affecting the country's balance of payments. A similar situation exists with other fuel areas, too. It is not clear whether the forecasted increase in fuel imports is sustainable from the finance ministry's view.

Indonesia.
With over 180 million people, Indonesia ranks among the world's most populous countries. The country is comprised of more than 3,000 islands, extending from peninsular Malaysia to New Guinea. Indonesia has a diverse energy

base, with domestic natural gas, low-sulfur coal, hydropower potential, geothermal resources, and biomass.

Most of Indonesia's people live on the islands of Java and Sumatra (Bali), and therefore most new capacity will be located there. A significant amount of this power—around one-third—is expected to be built by the private sector.

During the past decade, Indonesia has had real economic growth of 6% per year, and energy use has been growing at an estimated 7.2% per year. GDP growth, at 7.5% in 1995, is expected to continue at about 7% through the rest of the decade. Steady increases in GDP per capita, combined with accelerated development in industrial and commercial sectors, are resulting in increasing power demands. In the past five years, power demands are estimated to have risen by an average of 14.5% annually. Demands are expected to continue rising at a similar rate as the country's population becomes more prosperous. Indonesia is expected to require 9,000 MW of new capacity by the year 2000, and 15,000 MW by 2005.

Although Perusahaan Listrik Negara (PLN) is an increasingly strong utility, a large share of Indonesian industrial, commercial, and residential energy users rely on captive power systems. About 7,000 MW of power capacity is estimated to be supplied by captive power plants. This situation is due largely to the fact that the PLN distribution network is inadequate to meet the power requirements of a widely scattered island population. PLN is increasing electrification, and hopes to supply power to 81% of Indonesia's population by 1999.

The island of Java represents by far the largest share of Indonesia's power market, with 20,000 MW of demand. About 70% of Java's population is served with electricity. About 1,000 MW of demand is spread among the other islands. This demand is expected to increase to 5,000 MW by 2000, as economic growth continues and electrification programs proceed.

South Korea is among Asia's most successful developing nations, with a booming industrial

sector and strong financial and commercial sectors. The country's economy has experienced real growth of 7.8% annually during the past decade. This economic development has resulted in a strong demand for electric power. Energy use has grown by 9.2% during the same time period. Investment in electric power generation, transmission, and distribution facilities has been massive over the last two decades, and installed capacity currently stands at 36,000 MW. Korea's per-capita electricity use—238 kilowatt hours—is low compared to developed nations, but is just above the average for Asia's developing economies.

The country's gross domestic product is projected to continue growing at a rate of 6% during the next several years, with power demands increasing accordingly. The country expects to install at least 4,600 MW of new capacity by the year 2000, and 24,000 MW of new plants by 2005. With anticipated industrial growth, additional investment will be required to improve the quality and efficiency of power supplies. The average annual growth rate of electric power demand is expected to be 5.5% per year through 2006. Electricity consumption per capita is expected to double by that time, as Korea Electric Power Co. (KEPCO) expands the reach and capacity of the country's distribution system.

Korea's Ministry of Trade, Industry, and Energy (MOTIE) recently announced plans to add 72 new generating units totaling 37.5 GW of capacity through the year 2006. Additionally, MOTIE's new power plan calls for a reduction in peak demand through DSM and system reliability improvements. MOTIE's long-term development plan calls for advancing the country's power sector to match the level of quality of power in developed countries by the year 2001. MOTIE expects to invest 9.3 trillion won (about $12.2 billion(US)) in power generation and T&D facilities, and technology development.

Malaysia plans to increase its electric capacity from 8,000 MW in 1996 to 15,000 MW by the year 2000, with demands requiring 9,200 MW of new

capacity by 2005. The country's demand for electricity could reach 25,000–30,000 MW by 2020, if economic growth projections are borne out.

Malaysia's recent growth has been driven by increases in industrial production and infrastructure development, as well as increased domestic spending. The country's current GDP growth of nearly 8% per year is expected to slow somewhat through the year 2000, with continued strong growth in the 5–6% range projected in subsequent years.

Of Asia's developing economies, Malaysia is one of the more prosperous and economically advanced. This applies to the country's power market as well, which is well enough developed that it offers few prospects for new private power development in the near term. With projects currently in the pipeline, installed capacity should be adequate to satisfy the more than 9% growth demand that is expected annually through the end of the decade. As growth continues, however, solicitations for additional projects may be announced. The government has halted review of additional proposals until after 1996, when the country's future supply needs are expected to be more clearly understood.

Myanmar's installed generating capacity totals 1,100 MW, with demand growth resulting in a future need for an estimated additional 220 MW by the year 2000, and 500 MW by the year 2005.

Myanmar has significant gas reserves and potential hydropower capacity, but a small domestic market. A private sector consortium is developing the country's gas reserves, and agreements have been signed for a pipeline and gas-fired power plant project and a hydropower project.

Philippines. The economy is growing steadily—with GDP growth rates around 5% in 1994 and 1995, and projected growth to accelerate to 5.5% or higher in 1996. The government projects long-term growth at about 7% annually. According to the Department of Energy (DOE), electric power consumption is expected to

outpace economic growth in the future. Power demands are expected to grow by about 12% per year over the next decade, with more than 1,000 MW of new capacity required each year for the next 10 years. Long-term projections call for 92,000 MW of capacity to be added between 1996 and 2025.

Sri Lanka consumed nearly 4,400 GWh of electricity during 1994, of which 39% represents industrial energy use. Growth in demand has at times increased faster than growth in GDP. The country has experienced real economic growth of 2.7% in the past decade, with current expansion of GDP estimated at 5%. Electricity demand, however, grew from 1993 to 1994 by 9.7%, and annual growth in demand is projected to continue in the 9–10% range for the next five years. The country anticipates that it needs to install new capacity totaling 780 MW, and to invest some $1.8 billion in transmission and distribution systems, by the year 2001.

In Sri Lanka, the Ceylon Electricity Board (CEB) is expected to require between 600 MW and 780 MW of new generating capacity by the end of the decade, along with $400 million in T&D investments.

Taiwan's economy is expected to grow by about 6.5% for the next several years. Taiwan, facing expanding brownouts, is moving to build some 15 GW of new capacity through the rest of the decade. Taiwan hopes to add nearly 24,000 MW of new generating capacity by the year 2006. About 20% of the new capacity planned between now and 2010 (about 7,260 megawatts) is expected to be built by independent power producers.

Thailand needs to add 1,000 MW of new capacity each year for the next decade to keep pace with the country's 6–9% per-year demand growth rate. Electricity demand is expected to triple to more than 30,000 MW during the next 15 years. In the future, Thailand is likely to increase imported electricity from neighboring Laos, Malaysia, and Vietnam.

Demand for electricity in Thailand totaled about 12,000 MW in 1995, very close to the Electricity Generating Authority of Thailand's (EGAT) 13,000 MW of generating capacity. State utility EGAT is seeking 2,000–3,000 MW from IPPs.

Vietnam. Facing the need to double its installed power generation capacity by the year 2000, Vietnam is pursuing a range of development alternatives to add an estimated 3,000 MW of new power plants. As part of the country's progress toward a market economy, Vietnam has relaxed its rules regarding investment in power plants. The country enacted a new electricity law early in 1995, paving the way for private participation in the power sector.

Vietnam has a long way to go, however, before its energy development goals are met. The government estimates some $7.7 billion of investment is required for projects from pipelines to power plants before the year 2000. While multilateral agencies have begun lending money for projects in Vietnam, fundamental problems make development difficult. For example, state-owned utilities in Vietnam are not creditworthy, although they have made progress in the right direction by raising electricity tariffs to levels that more closely match the utilities' costs.

Another challenge is that the country's power transmission infrastructure is not well developed, making it difficult to plan power projects. T&D systems financed with multilateral funds will provide additional confidence in the private sector

that the country's system will work right. Vietnam has been slow to begin opening to private power, but progress is expected to advance quickly in the next few years. A combination of multilateral support and the participation of international oil and gas companies, who will provide fuel and develop gas transportation and power facilities, is likely to boost development of Vietnam's power sector.

The World Bank last year approved a $165 million(US) loan for rehabilitation and expansion of the power systems in southern and central Vietnam, under the jurisdictions of Power Companies No. 2 & 3. The project includes refurbishment of the distribution systems in Ho Chi Minh City, Hue, and Nhatrang, conversion of three open-cycle turbines to a combined-cycle unit, and construction and expansion of transmission lines and substation facilities. Additionally, the project provides funds for training, resettlement, and system efficiency improvement.

In northern Vietnam, the Asian Development Bank (ADB) approved financing for the first phase of a long-term program of rehabilitation and expansion of T&D facilities.

The program will rehabilitate distribution systems in Hanoi, Hai Phong, and Nam Dinh, which together use about 40% of the power distributed in northern Vietnam. The project will cost about $115 million, with $80 million in foreign exchange funds from the ADB, and $35 million to come from Vietnam.

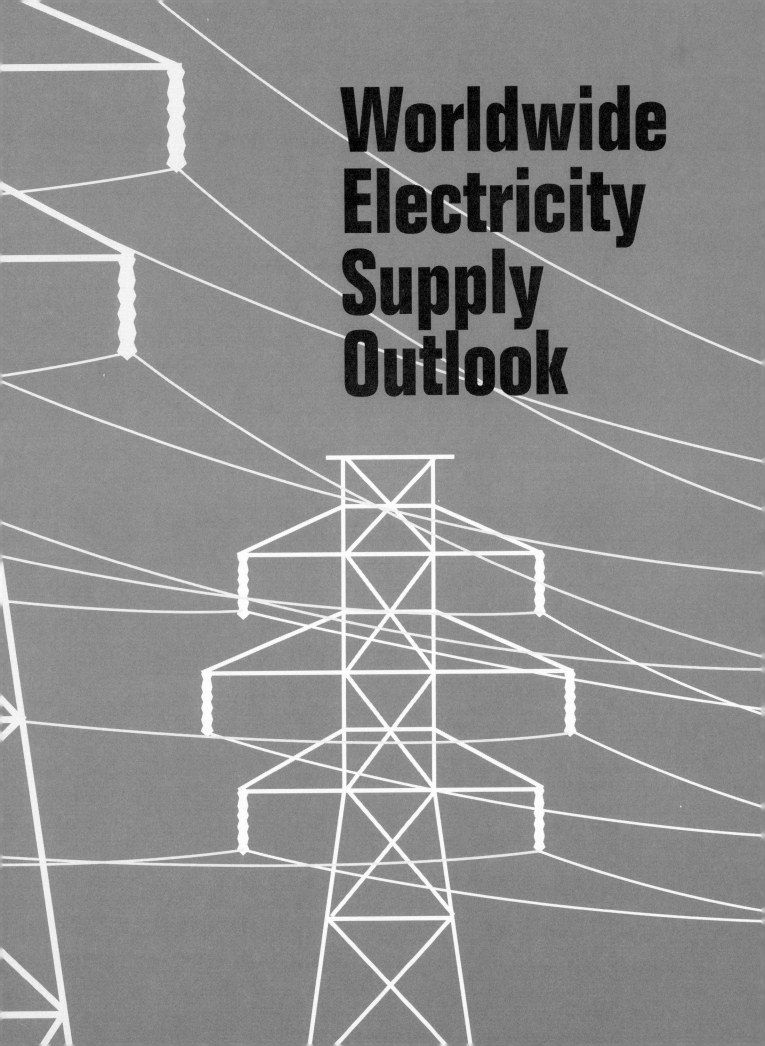

Worldwide Electricity Supply Outlook

Chapter 6
North America Electricity Supply

DENISE WARKENTIN
NEWS EDITOR, *ELECTRIC LIGHT & POWER*
EDITOR, *ENERGY MARKETING*

Natural gas prices to electricity suppliers are projected to rise by 1.4% a year over the 1994 to 2015 period, according to the Energy Information Administration's (EIA) *Annual Energy Outlook 1996*. This means that gas prices will rise from $2.24 per thousand cubic feet in 1994 to $3.02 in 2015. At the same time, EIA projects that gas-fired electricity generation will increase by 143%, from 474 to 1,153 billion kilowatt-hours. Offsetting these increases will be:

- stable coal prices,

- declining revenue requirements for capital expenditures (largely due to deregulation of the electric utility industry), and

- improved efficiencies for new plants.

OVERVIEW AND ELECTRICITY INDUSTRY RESTRUCTURING

Both suppliers and consumers are grappling with ongoing changes in the structure of electricity markets in the United States. In the past, electricity suppliers had secure, franchised service territories and were essentially guaranteed recovery of expenditures made to provide service to customers. Consumers, in turn, had to purchase their electricity from suppliers that controlled their areas. Today, the situation is changing.

Electric utilities, nonutility power producers, and power brokers are positioning themselves to meet the needs of customers, and consumers—especially large industrial ones—now look beyond the utilities serving their areas to alternative suppliers for their power needs.

Many questions remain about the evolving market structure. Some of these questions follow:

- Will all consumers eventually be able to choose their electricity suppliers?

- How will the major sectors of the electricity supply business evolve?

- How long will the transition to the new structure take?

- Who will bear the transition costs, and how large will they be?

- How will more competitive electricity prices be set?

- What will be the impact on new generating capacity construction?

- What efficiency improvements will be seen in the supply and demand sectors of the market?

These questions and many others are being debated by utilities, nonutilities, consumers, and state and federal policymakers. The answers to questions about industry restructuring are likely to involve both legislative changes and new market institutions. Such issues have not yet been resolved. A preliminary analysis of the impact of electricity market restructuring on capacity choice decisions by plant type and on the near-term future of electricity prices is discussed in this chapter.

New power generators are expected to face greater business risk in a competitive market. At the same time, there will be greater opportunities for profit and greater chances of loss in the absence of regulatory assurances, such as

established rates of return on investment and fuel adjustment clauses. In order to raise capital, power generators must compensate shareholders for bearing that greater risk by providing higher returns on equity.

Figure 6–1 shows the sensitivity of capacity expansion decisions in the National Energy Modeling System to changes in the cost of capital for electric power generators.

The North American Reliability Council's (NERC) projections for total electricity generating capacity through 2004 is shown in Table 6–1. Total generating capacity in 1995, according to NERC, is at 807,730 MW. By 2004, total generating capacity will have increased to 892,712 MW. Table 6–2 shows NERC's projections (through 2004) of capacity margins by NERC region. More detailed information about Mexico can be found in the Latin American chapters in this book.

In a competitive market, generating technologies that require high initial capital costs and relatively low operating costs are less attractive

Table 6–1

Electricity generating capacity

	Actual 1994	Projected 1995	1996	1997	1998	1999	2000	2001	2002	2003	2004
Nuclear	114,593	113,634	116,066	116,129	116,172	116,181	116,128	116,128	116,128	116,128	116,128
Hydro	119,041	119,327	119,464	119,963	120,107	120,208	120,534	120,577	121,695	122,415	123,540
Pumped Storage	17,563	18,244	18,599	18,604	18,584	18,604	18,853	18,849	18,841	19,041	19,052
Geothermal	2,256	2,256	2,256	2,373	2,413	2,473	2,503	2,503	2,503	2,503	2,503
Coal	309,193	310,147	311,175	311,983	312,340	312,329	312,263	312,182	312,767	313,065	313,806
ST - Oil	30,520	30,163	30,240	30,408	30,597	30,628	31,255	31,255	31,619	31,170	31,130
ST - Gas	47,374	47,012	47,100	46,954	46,912	46,967	46,946	46,645	46,604	46,653	46,690
ST - Dual Fuel	68,042	67,889	67,919	67,789	67,830	67,475	66,912	66,891	66,937	67,300	67,161
CT - Oil	24,816	24,932	26,047	26,075	26,253	26,278	27,095	27,894	28,594	29,441	29,759
CT - Gas	9,861	11,557	12,512	12,905	14,779	16,643	18,525	20,456	22,451	24,068	25,958
CT - Dual Fuel	15,096	16,037	16,169	16,912	17,714	19,537	21,821	23,436	25,113	26,572	28,322
CC - Oil	253	568	570	570	570	570	570	570	570	599	599
CC - Gas	4,352	4,683	4,849	4,919	5,254	6,347	8,297	11,265	13,383	15,351	16,831
CC - Dual Fuel	5,595	6,298	6,797	6,797	7,552	8,283	8,533	9,074	9,099	9,099	9,640
Other	683	1,079	2,061	2,731	4,823	6,007	7,551	9,527	11,345	13,256	14,964
IPPs	33,006	33,904	36,375	39,245	41,205	42,440	43,991	44,671	45,429	46,452	46,629
Total Capacity	802,244	807,730	818,199	824,357	833,105	840,970	851,777	861,923	873,078	883,113	892,712

Notes: General Note Sum of the subregional capacity resources may not equal the WSCC U.S. total because subregional peak demands on which resources are based may occur in different months than the coincident WSCC U.S. peak.

Combustion Turbine Oil Includes diesel capacity
Combustion Turbine Gas Includes diesel capacity
Combustion Turbine Dual Includes diesel capacity
Nonutility Generating Reflects projected expiration of NUG contracts in ERCOT.

[Courtesy North American Electric Reliability Council]

Table 6–2
Electricity planned capacity resources

Capacity Margins - S			(% of Planned Capacity Resources) Projected									
			1995	1996	1997	1998	1999	2000	2001	2002	2003	2004
ECAR		U.S.	16.4	15.8	15.2	14.8	14.3	14.9	15.0	15.1	15.1	14.8
ERCOT		U.S.	19.5	18.4	17.1	15.7	14.6	14.2	14.2	14.7	14.7	13.9
MAAC		U.S.	20.8	21.1	20.4	20.1	20.0	19.5	19.5	19.0	18.9	19.2
MAIN		U.S.	16.4	16.3	16.5	16.3	16.3	16.3	16.6	16.9	16.8	16.7
MAIN	EM	U.S.	13.6	15.5	15.4	15.3	15.2	15.3	15.5	15.8	15.3	15.5
MAIN	NI	U.S.	16.9	15.5	15.3	15.1	15.3	15.8	16.3	16.5	16.6	16.7
MAIN	SCI	U.S.	19.1	19.7	19.4	17.8	18.4	17.9	17.7	18.3	18.1	17.3
MAIN	WUM	U.S.	15.1	15.8	17.0	18.0	17.3	16.9	17.1	17.0	17.2	17.0
MAPP		U.S.	16.8	15.9	14.6	13.6	12.6	12.6	12.1	10.4	9.1	7.6
NPCC		U.S.	23.3	23.4	22.7	22.2	21.1	20.4	17.2	16.6	15.8	15.6
NPCC	NE	U.S.	22.7	22.8	22.4	21.9	21.2	19.2	13.7	13.1	11.8	10.9
NPCC	NY	U.S.	23.8	23.8	23.0	22.5	20.9	21.2	19.7	19.1	18.6	18.9
SERC		U.S.	16.0	16.9	15.9	15.6	15.8	15.5	15.5	15.3	15.2	15.2
SERC	FL	U.S.	18.7	17.7	17.9	16.5	17.4	16.8	16.3	16.1	15.2	15.1
SERC	SOU	U.S.	15.3	14.7	14.1	14.2	14.0	14.0	14.3	14.2	14.6	14.1
SERC	TVA	U.S.	11.2	16.2	14.1	14.1	14.1	13.9	13.7	13.5	13.2	13.6
SERC	VAC	U.S.	16.8	18.4	16.7	16.7	16.8	16.5	16.8	16.6	16.6	16.8
SPP		U.S.	18.5	16.1	15.3	15.1	14.5	15.3	15.2	14.9	14.3	13.4
SPP	N	U.S.	20.9	20.0	19.3	17.9	16.9	16.1	16.9	16.8	15.9	16.3
SPP	SE	U.S.	20.5	16.4	15.6	15.7	15.5	18.5	18.7	17.8	17.0	15.9
SPP	WC	U.S.	14.1	12.8	11.8	12.2	11.2	10.6	9.6	9.7	9.7	8.0
WSCC		U.S.	21.8	21.1	20.4	20.5	19.9	19.1	18.3	17.3	16.4	15.6
WSCC	AZN	U.S.	19.5	19.1	17.6	16.8	16.3	15.5	14.9	14.2	13.0	12.3
WSCC	CNV	U.S.	18.7	17.7	17.2	17.4	16.4	15.8	15.3	14.2	13.4	12.4
WSCC	NWP	U.S.	32.8	29.7	32.8	32.8	31.9	31.2	30.4	29.8	28.9	27.8
WSCC	RMP	U.S.	24.3	24.4	21.9	22.6	23.6	22.3	23.0	22.4	23.0	24.2
TOTAL		**U.S.**	**18.7**	**18.4**	**17.6**	**17.2**	**16.8**	**16.6**	**16.2**	**15.8**	**15.5**	**15.1**
MAPP		Canada	39.8	38.2	38.3	37.4	35.7	34.3	33.7	33.2	32.6	34.0
NPCC		Canada	44.1	43.2	42.6	40.9	40.9	39.5	38.5	38.8	38.3	38.1
NPCC	NB	Canada	41.1	50.6	49.9	48.9	49.3	48.2	47.7	47.1	47.5	46.5
NPCC	NS	Canada	50.7	51.0	50.7	50.1	49.4	48.6	47.8	46.8	45.8	44.9
NPCC	ONT	Canada	32.4	30.9	29.8	28.6	27.9	25.0	23.9	24.2	23.1	21.5
NPCC	PEI	Canada	18.3	22.4	22.9	21.7	22.2	22.8	21.0	21.5	20.7	21.2
NPCC	QUE	Canada	53.8	52.4	52.2	50.0	50.3	49.8	49.0	49.4	49.1	49.7
WSCC		Canada	37.7	35.7	35.6	34.6	34.9	34.1	32.6	33.0	33.7	32.2
TOTAL		**Canada**	**42.4**	**41.3**	**40.8**	**39.3**	**39.2**	**37.9**	**36.9**	**37.2**	**36.9**	**36.5**
WSCC		Mexico	1.2	0.0	19.1	16.4	15.7	19.0	17.3	11.4	5.1	1.6
TOTAL		**NERC**	**21.5**	**21.0**	**20.3**	**19.8**	**19.4**	**19.1**	**18.6**	**18.3**	**17.9**	**17.5**
ASCC		Alaska	54.9	54.7	54.0	53.2	52.5	52.1	51.6	51.1	50.6	50.1

[Courtesy North American Electric Reliability Council]

than technologies that require smaller initial capital outlays but have higher downstream operating costs. For example, as shown in Figure 6–1, increasing the cost of capital by four percentage points relative to the reference case leads to 4.9 gigawatts more gas-fired combustion turbine and combined-cycle capacity among newly-built plants and 2.8 gigawatts less coal-fired capacity. Total capacity additions decline slightly as the cost of capital rises, because fewer plants are built to displace existing plants whose operating costs are rising.

Figure 6–1. Changes in unplanned capacity additions (GW), 1994-2015, as a function of changes in discount rates (basis points)

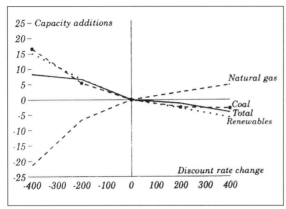

Figure 6–2. Electricity prices in two cases, 1995-2000

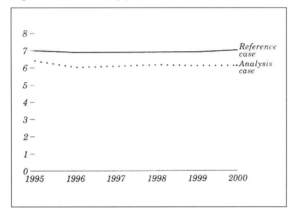

In addition to providing incentive to build plants with lower capital costs, growing competition will put downward pressure on electricity prices. The costs of power plants, power purchase contracts, and fuel supply contracts that are uneconomical will be difficult to recover in a competitive market. The treatment of such unrecoverable, or stranded costs (or assets) is among the most important issues in the restructuring debate.

Figure 6–2 shows the potential price impact in the near-term.

The upper line represents the regulated prices in the reference case, where all operating costs and embedded costs are recovered from ratepayers. The lower line represents the price when generation is priced at the marginal operating cost. In other words, during a given time frame, generators are paid the operating cost of the most expensive unit running (the marginal unit). The analysis assumes that the transmission and distribution system will continue under cost-of-service regulation.

The difference between the two lines is an indication of the change in prices that could occur if the market were free to value generation at its short-run marginal cost. The gap between the two represents the portion of fixed costs that would not be recoverable in a competitive market.

Many factors will affect the actual outcome of the restructuring process. Fuel prices and the energy efficiency and capital costs of various generating technologies will play a major role in determining which types of plants are built to meet the demand for electricity.

Similarly, while competition is expected to lead to lower electricity prices, the treatment of stranded costs, efficiency gains that producers are able to make, and any additional costs introduced (such as higher metering and billing costs to accommodate real-time pricing) will influence the prices paid by various consumers. In addition, while the results shown depict average national results, consumers in different regions of the country may see dramatically different results.

HYDROPOWER REGULATORY ISSUES

Recognizing the lack of available large sites for new hydroelectric dams, reduced public investment, and environmental constraints, EIA projects minimal growth for conventional hydropower; however, recent rulings, especially to protect fish, could result in capacity declines.

In June 1994, the U.S. Supreme Court ruled that states may regulate water under the standards of the Clean Water Act, shifting licensing authority from the Federal Energy Regulatory Commission (FERC). In September 1994, the U.S. Court of

Appeals directed that more weight be given to state fishery and Indian Tribe recommendations. In March 1995, the National Marine Fisheries Services (NMFS) and the U.S. Fish and Wildlife Service (FWS) proposed increased flows and changes in water priorities on the Northwest's Columbia River.

Breaching and removal of dams is also being discussed. In December 1994, the FERC stated its authority to order dam removal. The FWS has proposed removal of Washington's Wanapum and Priest Rapids dams, and the Columbia River Inter-Tribal Fish Commission has urged breaching for lower dams on the Snake River and the John Day Dam on the Columbia.

Hydroelectric dams could be affected nationwide. In July 1995, the NMFS proposed listing coho salmon as a threatened species from the Northwest to central California. In the Southwest, flow restrictions could cut peaking generation at Glen Canyon Dam, with similar changes required in Colorado, Utah, Wyoming, and Montana. In the Midwest, the U.S. Army Corps of Engineers may reduce power generation on the Missouri River for fish protection. Operational changes also could be required at Hudson River dams to protect fish.

Each of these decisions generally is viewed as reducing hydroelectric power output. The value of hydropower will be reduced if water use is switched to less valuable off-peak, rather than peaking, generation.

NATURAL GAS GAINS GROUND

Fossil fuels, which in 1994 accounted for 70% of electricity generation, are projected to account for 79% in 2015. Much of the increase is in the use of natural gas, which currently fuels 14% of total generation, but grows to 27% by 2015, supplanting nuclear energy as the nation's second-largest electricity source, as shown in Figure 6–3.

Figure 6–3. Electricity generation by fuel, 1994 and 2015 (billion kWhr)

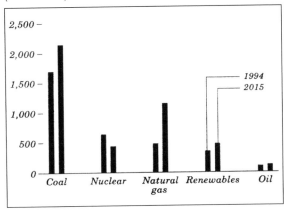

Three factors explain the trend toward the increased use of natural gas:

(1) Although the utilization of existing nuclear power plants is increasing, 37 gigawatts of nuclear capacity are assumed to be retired by 2015, with no new nuclear orders on the horizon.

(2) Combined-cycle technologies are demonstrating efficiencies up to 60%, compared with 35% for coal-steam technologies. Combined-cycle units also have short construction times (1 to 3 years) and relatively low capital investment costs, making them attractive to nonutilities.

(3) Between 1994 and 2015, gas prices to utilities should increase by only 1.4% annually (as compared with 2.8% from 1994 to 2010, as forecasted by EIA in 1995).

The electricity sector currently consumes 80% of U.S. coal production, which is used to produce 52% of the nation's electricity. In EIA's 1996 forecast report, average capacity factors for coal-fired power plants increase from 62% to 74%, and utilities have already reported plans to construct 16 gigawatts of new coal-fired capacity. Nevertheless, slower growth in demand for electricity, long construction times for coal-fired plants, and 19

gigawatts of coal-fired retirements are expected to decrease coal's share of generation to about 50% in 2015.

ADVANCED GENERATION TECHNOLOGY

Technology types for new electric-generating capacity are chosen on the basis of cost while meeting local and federal emissions constraints. The leveled cost of electricity production includes the time-discounted cost of construction, fixed and variable operating and maintenance costs, and fuel costs. Figure 6–4 shows electricity generation costs for conventional and advanced technologies for 2000 and 2015.

The choice of technologies for capacity additions can be decided by changes in these components of the leveled cost.

In the EIA's 1996 forecast report, the capital costs of conventional technologies are assumed to be constant. For advanced technologies, after an initial downward adjustment to account for technological optimism, capital costs decline as a function of market penetration. Heat rates for both advanced and conventional fossil-fired technologies decline annually from 2000 until 2010. In 2015, the last year of the EIA forecast period, leveled costs for combined-cycle capacity

are 8% lower than for coal. Table 6–3 depicts the costs of producing electricity for the years 2000 and 2015.

Table 6–3
Costs of producing electricity, 2000 and 2015

Item	2000		2015	
	Conventional pulverized coal	Advanced combined cycle	Conventional pulverized coal	Advanced combined cycle
	1994 mills per kilowatthour			
Capital	26.41	11.24	26.18	7.00
O&M	10.72	4.82	10.72	4.82
Fuel	13.58	23.35	7.42	24.38
Total	50.72	39.41	44.32	36.20
	Btu per kilowatthour			
Heat rate	9,840	7,300	8,142	5,687

ELECTRICITY PRICES TO REMAIN STABLE

Between 1994 and 2015, the average price of electricity is projected to remain relatively stable, declining by 0.1% a year. Figure 6–5 charts utility fossil fuel prices and electricity prices for the years 1994 to 2015.

As a result, average electricity expenditures for residential consumers are expected to be $11 a month (1994 dollars) lower in 2015 than they were in 1994.

Figure 6–4. Electricity generation costs for conventional and advanced technologies, 2000 and 2015

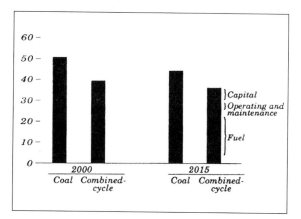

Figure 6–5. Utility fossil fuel prices and electricity prices, 1994-2015

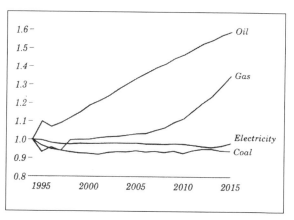

The cost of producing electricity, and ultimately the price paid by consumers, is a function of fuel costs, operating and maintenance costs, and the cost of capital. For existing plants, fuel costs typically represent $23 million annually or 50% of the total operational costs (fuel, wholesale power, and operating and maintenance costs) for a 300-megawatt coal-fired plant and $40 million annually or 85% of the total operational costs for a gas-fired combined-cycle plant of the same size in 1994.

As stated earlier, natural gas prices to electricity suppliers are expected to rise by 1.4% a year in the forecast period, while gas-fired generating capacity will increase by 143%. These increases will be offset in due course by a variety of factors, which are listed at the beginning of this chapter.

Although oil prices to utilities are expected to increase by 59%, greater utilization of plants for which oil is the primary fuel is expected to lead to a 19% increase in oil-fired generation by 2015. However, oil currently accounts for only 3.1% of total generation, and that share is expected to decline to 2.8% by 2015.

CAPITAL COSTS EXPECTED TO DECLINE

Capital costs associated with the recovery of investments in power plants and transmission and distribution facilities are expected to decline by 0.6% annually from 1994 to 2015, as shown in Figure 6–6.

The decline in capital costs is made possible by increased utility reliance on:

- wholesale power purchases,

- lower construction costs for new combustion turbine and combined-cycle generating technologies, and

- the availability of adequate capacity for current generation needs.

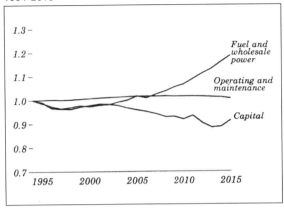

Figure 6–6. Utility and nonutility revenue requirements, 1994-2015

A yearly 0.2% decline in operating and maintenance costs is also expected, as more turbine-based capacity is installed and operated.

For a typical 300-megawatt plant, operating and maintenance costs for advanced gas turbines are about one-half those for conventional coal-fired generators. Typically, turbine-based generators are removed from service an average of 15 days a year for planned maintenance, compared with 30 days for coal-steam generators.

Fuel costs increase only slightly in the forecast, by an average of 0.1% annually, as coal prices decline by 0.3% and gas prices rise by 1.4% between 1994 and 2015. In contrast, wholesale power purchases (electricity sales from nonutilities to utilities) more than triple, increasing from 204 to 637 billion kilowatt-hours between 1994 and 2015. By purchasing power, utilities avoid capital-intensive construction and financing costs.

ENERGY PRODUCTION AND THE ENVIRONMENT

Electricity generators currently produce 36% of national carbon emissions from energy production. Their share is expected to increase to 38% by 2015. Currently, coal accounts for 52% of total electricity generation, but produces 87% of

electricity-related carbon emissions, as shown in Figure 6–7.

Figure 6–7. Carbon emissions from electricity generation by fuel, 1994-2015 (million metric tons)

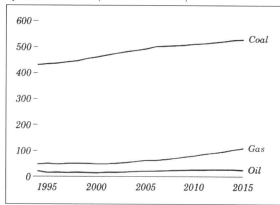

In contrast, gas-fired generators account for 15% of generation and produce only 9% of electricity-related carbon emissions. As a fuel, coal releases nearly twice as much carbon per Btu as natural gas does. While oil accounts for 3% of electricity generated, carbon emissions from oil-fired generators make up about 4% of total electricity emissions.

Between 1994 and 2015, 37 gigawatts of nuclear capacity are expected to be retired, resulting in a decline of 207 billion kilowatt-hours per year, or 32%, from current nuclear generation. To compensate for the loss of baseload capacity and to meet rising demand, 230 gigawatts of new fossil-fueled capacity will be needed. The resulting increase in generation from fossil fuels will increase carbon emissions by 160 million metric tons, or 32%, over current levels.

Although renewable capacity (discussed later in this chapter) increases from 94 gigawatts in 1994 to 115 gigawatts in 2015 reducing the impact of nuclear retirements on total carbon emissions, the intermittent nature of renewable technologies prevents them from compensating completely for the losses in nuclear capacity.

More than 95% of the sulfur dioxide (SO_2) produced by utility boilers comes from the combustion of coal, with sulfur-bearing residual

oils contributing the remainder. By 2000, as a result of the Clean Air Act Amendments of 1990, electricity producers are required to reduce SO_2 emissions by 10 million tons from 1990 levels in two phases: Phase 1 in 1995 and Phase 2, which takes effect in 2000.

During Phase 1, 261 generating units at 110 utility plants were issued emissions allowances that permit SO_2 emissions up to a fixed amount per year. Because the amount allowed generally is less than a plant's historical emissions, most utilities instituted additional emissions reduction strategies.

Switching to lower-sulfur, subbituminous coal was the option chosen by more than half of the Phase 1 generators. In Phase 2, emissions constraints on Phase 1 plants will be tightened, and restrictions will be set for the remaining 2,500 boilers at 1,000 plants, reducing SO_2 emissions by another two million tons, as shown in Figure 6–8.

Because allowance prices are expected to increase significantly after 2000, it is expected that almost 32 gigawatts of capacity will be retrofitted with scrubbers to achieve the Phase 2 goal.

NUCLEAR GENERATION

The EIA's 1996 forecast report assumes that all nuclear units will operate to the end of their current license terms, with 49 units (37 gigawatts)

Figure 6–8. Sulfur dioxide emissions from utility generation, 1990-2015 (million metric tons)

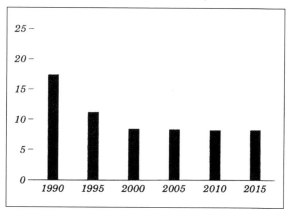

retiring through 2015. Just over 80% of these retirements occur in the last five years of the forecast. One unit under construction, Watts Bar 1, is assumed to begin operation in 1996, and no new orders are assumed.

Given these assumptions, 61 nuclear units are projected to provide 10% of total electricity generation in 2015. This is down from a projected high of 20% in 1996. Although the forecast does not project explicitly new nuclear units to become operable by 2015, an alternative interpretation could be that new reactors replace existing capacity that is retired ahead of schedule.

Nuclear generation forecasts depend on both operating capacity and assumed capacity factors. The national average capacity factor, which was below 60% in the 1970s and 1980s, has surpassed 70% since 1991, as shown in Figure 6–9.

Improvements have been gained through long refueling cycles and a decrease in the mandated shutdowns that were prevalent after the accident at Three Mile Island. EIA's projections assume that individual reactor performance improves for the first 20 or 25 years of operation, after which it declines as units age. As a result, the national average stays near 74%, with a slight decline from 2007 through 2012 due to reactor aging, after which retirements of older reactors bring the average capacity factor back up.

Two alternative EIA analyses (the high and low nuclear cases) show how changing assumptions about the operating lifetimes of nuclear plants affect the reference case forecast of nuclear capacity. See Figure 6–10.

The low nuclear case assumes that all units are retired 10 years before their license expiration dates (90 units by 2015). Early shutdowns could be caused by unfavorable economics, waste disposal problems, or physical degradation of the units.

The high nuclear case assumes 10 additional years of operation for each unit (only two units retired by 2015), suggesting that license renewals would be permitted. Conditions favoring such an outcome could include continued performance improvements, a solution to the waste disposal

Figure 6–9. Nuclear power plant capacity factors, 1973-2015 (%)

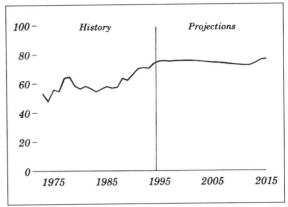

Figure 6–10. Operable nuclear capacity in three cases, 1994-2015 (GW)

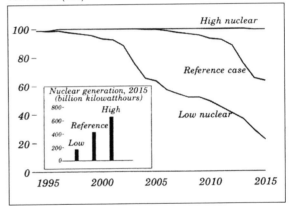

problem, or stricter limits on emissions from fossil-fired generating facilities.

The low nuclear case forecasts approximately 100 new fossil-fueled units (assuming an average unit size of 300 megawatts) to replace the retiring nuclear units, split between coal-fired (12%) and combined-cycle (69%) capacity. The additional fossil-fueled capacity produces 23 million metric tons of carbon emissions above the EIA's 1996 reference case. Also, eight gigawatts of additional, new, renewable and fuel cell capacity is built. In the high nuclear case, 35 gigawatts of new capacity additions (mostly fossil-fueled plants) are avoided, as compared with the 1996 reference case, and carbon emissions are reduced by 25 million metric tons (4% of total emissions by electricity generators).

RENEWABLE ENERGY RESOURCES

Geothermal electricity generation grows from 17 billion kilowatt-hours in 1994 to 24 billion in 2015, as shown in Figure 6–11. Geothermal resources are limited to steam and hot water in the western United States in the EIA's 1996 projection report.

Projected expansion of flashed steam and binary cycle units is offset by an expected decline at The Geysers site, where reservoir water is being depleted. Growth in geothermal electricity is expected in international markets.

Biomass

Generation from biomass (wood, grasses, and residues) grows from 47 billion kilowatt-hours in 1994 to 67 billion in 2015. Cogeneration, mostly in the paper and wood industries, is about 80% of the total. The projections combine current direct-fired units and additions of new, integrated, gasification combined-cycle units. A portion of the fuel for the new units, first available in 2000, is expected to be produced by dedicated energy crops. Municipal solid waste (MSW) generation increases from 19 to 36 billion kilowatt-hours.

Because MSW combustion is primarily a waste disposal method, it is limited by the availability of waste streams. Recycling, composting, and landfills provide ample options for disposition of the waste, while environmental concerns keep costs high for MSW units. Moreover, the ability of local jurisdictions to direct waste flows to MSW plants has been restricted by the courts, making use of the technology more uncertain. The share of MSW generation from low-Btu gas extracted from landfills is projected to grow from 14% in 1994 to nearly 18% in 2015.

Wind Power

Although wind energy currently is one of the most economical renewable energy technologies, its market penetration is sensitive to cost projections for competing fuels. Current projects of low-fuel costs (especially for natural gas) increase the uncertainty of wind power's future.

Wind capacity is expected to increase to about five gigawatts nationally by 2010 and to about 12 gigawatts by 2015. Penetration is expected primarily in the West, where resources are favorable, with most of the growth coming after 2010, when gas prices rise and the demand for new capacity is greater.

Relative to other technologies, the amount of wind capacity that needs to be in place to deliver a given amount of effective capacity is high because capacity factors for wind power are relatively low. Nevertheless, the amount of electricity generated from wind turbines is expected to grow from three billion kilowatt-hours in 1994 to 33 billion kilowatt-hours in 2015 (an average increase of more than 11% a year).

In 1995, the Federal Energy Regulatory Commission overturned California's Biennial Resource Planning Update, because it set higher prices for electricity from renewable than from traditional sources. This decision eliminates 927 megawatts of wind capacity that was included in previous EIA forecasts from the agency's 1996 forecast. In addition, some members of Congress have proposed repeal of the tax credit for wind power (1.5 cents per

Figure 6–11. Electricity generation from grid-connected renewables, 1994-2015 (billion kWhr)

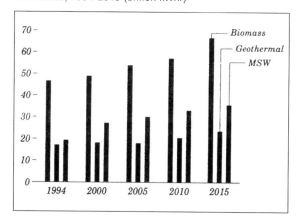

kilowatt-hour), introducing further uncertainty into the market.

Solar Generation

EIA projects expansion of grid-connected solar electricity generation (mostly late in the forecast period) from less than one billion kilowatt-hours in 1994 to more than six billion in 2015 primarily for peak-load requirements, as shown in Figure 6–12.

Still, solar will continue to account for less than 2% of all renewable electricity generation, and its share of the overall grid-connected U.S. electric power supply will remain small.

Solar-thermal generating capacity, primarily dish stirling or central receiver technologies, is more than 1.7 gigawatts in 2015, assuming that existing parabolic trough capacity remains in place. Grid-connected photovoltaics continue to expand, as does U.S. manufacture of cells and modules. Electric utilities are investing in photovoltaics to create demand and spur improvements, and state incentives make the technology attractive. Nevertheless, most new photovoltaic applications will be on a small scale.

The EIA's projections do not include off-grid photovoltaic applications, such as for isolated vacation homes, lights and signals, and consumer devices. Off-grid generation from photovoltaics probably will grow by 5 to 10 megawatts a year

Figure 6–12. Solar thermal and photovoltaic electricity generation, 1994-2015 (billion kWhr)

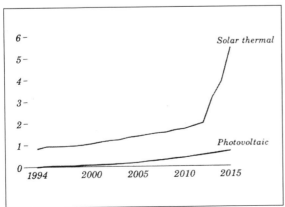

through 2000 and increasingly thereafter. World markets for cells and models produced in the United States are also expected to grow substantially. The economics of off-grid generation are particularly beneficial in developing countries, where new generating technologies are needed to supply electricity to rural areas not served by grid-connected utilities.

TECHNOLOGICAL OPTIMISM

In the EIA 1996 forecast report's reference case, capital costs for construction of new, advanced generating facilities are assumed to decline as a function of market penetration. Higher costs are assumed to account for both technological optimism and inexperience in constructing new designs. These factors account for the difference between costs based on engineering estimates before a plant is built and the actual costs.

To examine the impacts of these assumptions, high and low technology cases were developed. In the high case, learning effects were assumed to decrease by four percentage points (relative to the reference case value of 10%) for each doubling of capacity, and an increase of four percentage points was assumed in the low technology case. In addition, factors that increase the cost of the earliest units constructed were halved and doubled from their reference case values in the high and low case, respectively.

Between 1994 and 2015, advanced coal-fired capacity additions are two gigawatts higher in the high technology case than in the low case. Advanced gas-fired capacity additions are 10 gigawatts higher, as shown in Figure 6–13, due to a 35% difference in the capital costs for first-of-a-kind units across the two cases.

Conversely, capacity additions for conventional coal- and gas-fired technologies are 5 and 15 gigawatts lower, respectively, in the high than in the low case. The capital costs for first-of-a-kind

units using renewable technologies are 42% lower in the high case than in the low case, and renewable capacity additions are 16 gigawatts higher.

TURBINES, COMBINED-CYCLE PLANTS CLAIM MAJOR ADDITIONS

In the reference case, electricity suppliers are expected to add 252 gigawatts of new capacity, equivalent to 840 new 300-megawatt power plants. Of the new capacity, the following percentages of plants are expected:

- 12%, coal-steam

- 78%, gas-turbine

- 9%, renewable technologies

- 1%, fuel cells

In addition, between 1994 and 2015, utilities are expected to repower or life-extend 268 gigawatts or 38% of current capacity. Figure 6–14 shows the new generating capacity by fuel type in three cases over the forecast period.

Depending on the generating technology chosen, current construction costs for a typical 300-megawatt plant range from $400 per kilowatt

for combined-cycle technologies to $1,500 per kilowatt for coal-steam technologies. These costs, combined with the difficulty of obtaining permits and developing new generating sites, make refurbishment of existing power plants at $260 per kilowatt an attractive option for utility resource planners. Between 1994 and 2015, utilities are expected to refurbish 770 coal-, 172 gas-, and 74 oil-fired generators.

From 1994 to 2015, the annual average growth rate for gross domestic product ranges between 2.5 and 1.5% in the high and low economic growth cases, respectively. The difference of a percentage point in the economic growth rate leads to a 0.7% change in electricity demand, with a corresponding difference of 140 gigawatts of new capacity required across the high and low economic growth cases. Regardless of economic conditions, utilities are expected to retire 12% of current capacity, or 1,221 generating plants, by 2015.

GENERATING CAPACITY, CARBON EMISSIONS ON THE RISE

Electricity consumption grows in the forecast, but the rate of increase lags behind historical

Figure 6–13. New electricity generation capacity in three cases, 1994-2015 (GW)

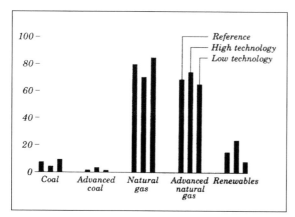

Figure 6–14. New generating capacity by fuel type in three cases, 1994-2015 (GW)

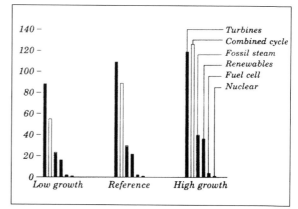

levels as a result of efficiency improvements and demand-side management programs. The following demographic projections for the 1994 to 2015 period are major determinants of sectoral electricity consumption:

- the annual growth rate for the population over age 16 is 0.1 percentage points lower than the 1.1% growth rate from 1963 through 1993,

- the annual growth rate for commercial floor space is 0.8 percentage points lower than the 1.9% growth rate from 1989 through 1993, and

- efficiency improvements in industrial processes and equipment continue at least at recent levels.

A significant deviation from these assumptions would result in substantial changes in electricity demand.

To analyze the effects of changes in the assumptions, a high demand case was prepared assuming that growth in demand for electricity would be 0.4 percentage points higher than in the reference case, or 1.8% a year. In this case, 109 gigawatts more new generating capacity is needed than in the reference case between 1994 and 2015. This is equivalent to 363 new 300-megawatt generating plants. Figure 6–15 shows new generating capacity by fuel type in two cases.

The additional capacity results in a 6% increase in coal consumption and a 9% increase in natural gas consumption relative to the reference case in 2015; carbon emissions are 38 million metric tons, or 2%, higher. The additional capacity in the high demand case includes 19 gigawatts, or 18%, more renewable capacity equivalent to 380 new 50-megawatt power plants.

THE FUTURE AND COMPARATIVE FORECASTS

The electric power industry is currently undergoing a metamorphosis from traditional, rate base/rate-of-return regulation to a market-driven, competitive structure. Although the ultimate outcome of the transformation is unclear, sufficient pressure from consumer and business organizations increases the likelihood that some sort of change will occur.

At a minimum, utilities and regulators need to respond to consumer demands for competitive pricing and flexibility in choosing local suppliers. At a maximum, a complete divestiture of transmission facilities by investor-owned utilities, coupled with retail wheeling (which gives residential customers the ability to select their electricity suppliers) may well prevail.

According to EIA, the reality will, most likely, fall somewhere between these two extremes. In addition to market-driven uncertainties, recent and future legislation affecting demand-side management (DSM) programs, emissions control strategies, transmission access, and the uncertain future of the nuclear industry could also influence utility decisions.

The stringent efficiency standards for new appliances mandated by EPAct could displace the current market for DSM programs and cause resources to be refocused on policies designed to cut operating costs. In 1993, utilities reduced their overall actual peak load by 23 gigawatts, with energy savings in excess of 44 billion

Figure 6–15. New generating capacity by fuel type in two cases, 1994-2015 (GW)

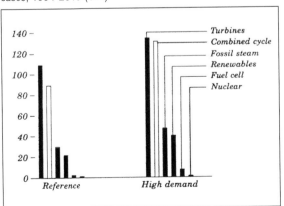

kilowatt-hours or 1.5% of total U.S. generation. Although the future of DSM programs is uncertain, utilities report that by 1998 they expect to reduce their potential peak load by a total of 33 gigawatts, with energy savings of 90 billion kilowatt-hours, or 3% of total U.S. generation. In 1993, utilities spent $2.8 billion on DSM; they currently plan to increase that amount to $3.9 billion by 1998.

EPAct also created a class of generators, called exempt wholesale generators or EWGs, which have the potential to transform the role of new nonutility suppliers and to affect electricity trade. These non-rate-based generators are exempt from traditional utility regulation and can market their power to utilities through access to utility transmission systems as ordered by the FERC. This could expand into the formation of regional transmission groups or RTGs, which are power pools dedicated to the efficient and equitable use of regional transmission facilities. It could also lead to the shared ownership of the transmission facilities, where suppliers share transmission costs on the basis of resource utilization. By severing the current binding of local generation to local distribution, these agreements could significantly affect the amounts and types of new generating capacity and lead to the retirement of uneconomical generating facilities.

Although utilities have responded to the reductions in sulfur dioxide and nitrogen oxide emission mandated by the Clean Air Act Amendments of 1990, new environmental regulations and advances in low-pollution generating sources also could alter the future mix of generating capacity. Voluntary programs such as the Climate Change Action Plan could be replaced by emissions reduction mandates similar to the Clean Air Act of 1963, which established the federal government's role in regulating air quality, and increase the cost of fossil-fuel generation technologies relative to renewable technologies.

Conversely, by providing alternates to large-scale, central-site, coal-steam units, distributed generation, including fuel cell and solar technologies, could preempt future emissions

control mandates and decrease coal's dominant position as a generating fuel. Furthermore, advances in gas-turbine technologies could dampen the effect of rising gas prices by providing more output per unit of fuel.

Progress has continued on new nuclear designs. Four advanced designs are being developed jointly by the U.S. Department of Energy and private industry, and two have received final design approval from the Nuclear Regulatory Commission. Due to high technological optimism and learning factors, EIA does not project new nuclear units to become operable by 2015. However, a significant decrease in nuclear construction costs or greater experience in the implementation of new nuclear designs could accelerate penetration with new orders before 2015.

Comparison across forecasts shows considerable variation in the commercial and residential sectors. Electricity sales projections for 2010 range from 1,220 billion kilowatt-hours (Data Resources, Inc.) to 1,346 billion kilowatt-hours (The WEFA Group) for the residential sector. EIA's projection is 1,282, and from 1,105 to 1,262 billion kilowatt-hours for the commercial sector. Figure 6–16 shows electricity sales projections across the different forecasts.

The forecasts for total electricity sales in 2010 range from 3,958 billion kilowatt-hours (Gas Research Institute) to 3,604 billion (EIA). Different assumptions governing the expected economic activity in each sector, coupled with diversity in the estimation of penetration rates of energy-efficient technologies, are the primary reasons for the variation among forecasts.

For example, by assuming slow growth in housing stocks but more powerful growth in commercial floor space, DRI projects weaker residential sales but stronger commercial and industrial sales than the EIA's 1996 projection report. Similarly, because GRI projects stronger industrial output, its industrial sales projections are higher than the other forecasts.

According to EIA, all the forecasts compared agree that stable coal prices and slow growth in

Figure 6–16. Electricity sales projections, 2010 (billion kWhr)

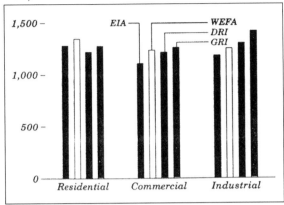

Figure 6–17. Electricity generating capacity projections, 2010 (GW)

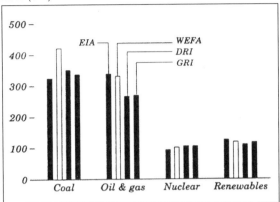

electricity demand relative to gross domestic product will tend to keep the price of electricity stable (or declining in real terms) until 2010.

Because the other forecasters project higher total electricity sales than EIA, their projections of the total capacity needed by 2010 are also proportionally higher. Although sensitive to the mix of technologies chosen, typically, an increase of 0.1 percentage points in sales results in an average capacity increase of about 20 gigawatts. For example, EIA's projections of capacity in 2010 is 92 gigawatts lower than the WEFA forecast—reflecting the difference between consumption growth rates of 1.3% and 1.7% a year, respectively.

The distribution of sales among sectors affects the mix of capacity types needed to satisfy sectoral demand. Although EIA's mix of capacity among fuels is similar to the other forecasts, small differences in sectoral demands across the forecasts lead to significant changes in capacity mix.

For example, growth in the residential sector coupled with an oversupply of baseload capacity results in a need for more peaking and intermediate capacity than baseload. Consequently, utilities would be expected to plan for more combustion-turbine and fuel-cell technologies than coal, oil, or gas steam capacity for the future.

With a higher projection of residential demand growth than the other forecasts, EIA expects more oil and gas capacity in 2010, as shown in Figure 6–17.

Chapter 7
Latin America Electricity Supply

ANN CHAMBERS
ASSOCIATE EDITOR
POWER ENGINEERING INTERNATIONAL AND
POWER ENGINEERING

OVERVIEW

The Latin American region, including Mexico, the Caribbean, and Central and South America, expects to add up to 82 GW of generation capacity in the coming decade, with a growth rate exceeding the worldwide average of 3% annually. Brazil expects to be the biggest player in the region, accounting for more than 30% of the new capacity, a projected 25 GW. Mexico is next with around 12 GW of capacity additions; Colombia, more than 8 GW; Venezuela, more than 7 GW. Argentina and Chile also expect to have aggressive growth and construction.

SOUTH AMERICA

With electrical demand forecast to grow by as much as 6% in several Latin American countries, energy ministers and secretaries in countries such as Colombia and Peru have redoubled their marketing efforts to attract prospective international investors and developers to their energy sector privatizations.

Colombia's attempt to improve investor perceptions of domestic electricity market stability, transparency, and regulatory regime robustness has created a market structure similar to England and Wales, with a competitive generating pool which determines the price daily. In Peru, the Special Commission for Privatization (CEPRI) recently prequalified eight consortia in bidding to own and expand the 200-MW Ventanilla power station. The selections are the second solicitation in the continuing privatization of Empressa Publica de Electricidad del Peru S.A. (ElectroPeru), the country's largest utility.

As Latin American countries travel down the road toward a final privatization destination, at least two key themes are clear: (1) investors need to know they can compete for creditworthy customers and (2) new power stations can be built according to competitive tender.

Table 7–1
Latin American statistics

| Country | Latin American Statistics | | | |
	Electricity Consumption (GWh)	Per Capita Consumption (kWh)	Installed Capacity (MW)	Total Generation (GWh)
Argentina	48,176	1,438	17,801	61,668
Bolivia	2,325	301	756	2,646
Brazil	232,967	1,463	55,401	251,484
Chile	22,479	1,627	5,149	26,137
Colombia	31,618	906	9,599	40,348
Costa Rica	3,901	1,206	1,009	4,431
Dominican Rep.	4,155	545	2,451	5,874
Ecuador	5,524	498	2,295	7,447
El Salvador	2,413	427	769	2,858
Guatemala	2,640	263	769	3,094
Honduras	1,807	321	541	2,486
Mexico	101,063	1,072	30,044	126,464
Nicaragua	1,141	267	447	1,634
Panama	2,581	1,007	956	3,216
Paraguay	2,751	647	6,529	31,449
Peru	12,441	543	4,152	14,326
Puerto Rico	n/a	n/a	4,200	n/a
Uruguay	4,658	1,479	2,041	7,989
Venezuela	57,347	2,761	19,600	71,388

[Courtesy OLADE]

Table 7–2
Electric power investments by region, 1995-2010

| (in billions of US dollars) | | |
Type	Latin America	World Totals
Generation		
Solid fuel	22	734
Natural gas	23	298
Oil	8	29
Nuclear	3	129
Hydro/renewables	52	235
Subtotal	**108**	**1,426**
Transmission	42	200
Distribution	36	480
General	17	173
Subtotal	**94**	**854**
Total	**202**	**2,279**
Annual Average	13	152

The electric power industry in Central and South America is undergoing significant change. (Table 7–1) The overall economic climate and the need of the governments to focus their limited resources on social infrastructures, have led to a shortage of public financing for the region's capital-intensive electricity industry. Concurrently, international lending institutions face severe competition for their resources and are focusing their emphasis on sectors that cannot find financing from the private sources. (Table 7–2) There is also a general perception of large inefficiencies in the region's electricity production and consumption, helping to move the governments toward deregulation and privatization.

Latin America continues to make progress in privatizing state-owned assets while fostering a new round of independent power development. As countries around the region forge ahead in opening their power sectors to additional private participation, companies that offer a broad range of energy development and operational services will find steadily improving business opportunities.

Wind energy appears a promising technology for this region, with an estimated market of $250 million(US) according to some estimates. In addition to small wind plants, there is a steady stream of rural electrification projects using small hybrid wind and solar systems. There is currently more talk than action regarding wind and solar, but some projects are moving ahead. Developers are looking at 20 to 30 MW of wind projects for Chile's northern regions, and in Ecuador the government is committed to wind but still working out its plans. The American Wind Energy Association estimates that 10 to 20 MW of wind power could be developed in Ecuador.

Natural gas is a big contender in this area for the future. The natural gas industry in the region is in a position to become an important force in the development of power generation across the continent. Natural gas projects are being spurred by the more stable political environment which allows the financing of these expensive projects. Location of gas reserves in relation to markets is slowing some development of the large reserves.

The general preference for hydroelectric power plants slowed entry of natural gas-fired power plants. The hydro preference was driven also by the tendency of the region's governments to construct large infrastructure projects regardless of their economic viability. South America has large proven reserves, up to 272 trillion cubic feet (TCF), plenty to supply regional demand and to produce gas for export. In 1991,

gas consumption in Latin America was less than 3.1 TCF, very low when compared with the 18.9 TCF consumed in the United States or the 11.3 TCF consumed in Western Europe. Only Argentina uses natural gas at levels comparable with the United States, as this nation counts natural gas for 40% of its primary energy. Argentina, Bolivia, Brazil, Chile, and Peru are the most promising markets for natural gas development. Since hydroelectric facilities provide most of the electricity in many of these nations, power supply is heavily dependent on rainfall, and as the nations are looking to other sources of electricity, they are turning increasingly to natural gas. Natural gas-fired facilities can be placed into operation more quickly than hydroelectric plants, and natural gas is less expensive to burn than other fossil fuels. Natural gas also burns cleaner, making it easier to fit into the stringent environmental regulations of the region.

CENTRAL AMERICA

The Central American countries are working to interconnect their utilities by a transmission line of 500 kV with an approximate length of 1,678 km called the Central American Electrical Interconnection System. The system will link stations in countries from Guatemala through Panama. The project was planned by technicians to permit transport of all possible energy to reinforce and stabilize the distribution systems in the area. According to local officials, the electrical power systems in the region are partially interconnected by about 230 km of transmission lines, but the connection does not permit complete power exchanges among the countries.

The project will be developed over a 10-year period with the first stage set in 1997, interconnecting 230 km between El Salvador and Honduras. The complete main transmission line will have a capacity of 500 kV, but will be energized only with 230 kV in the first stage. The

second stage, between the year 2003 and 2004, includes energizing of the other 500 kV, including additional power generation projects to be developed in the region. The Central American interconnection project will require an investment of $500 million(US) and will be financed by the Inter American Development Bank.

Brazil. After a three-year delay, the government of Brazil made substantial progress in 1995 to privatize state-owned utility assets and establish a framework for independent power development. In June 1995, the Brazilian Congress enacted legislation to restructure the country's power industry and lay the groundwork for private power. Brazil privatized the federal power distributor ESCELSA, and announced plans to privatize its four major regional generating utilities.

The state governments in Brazil are working to unbundle and privatize their electricity utilities as well. Existing facilities and facilities currently under construction are all being considered for sale and privatization. (Table 7–3)

Table 7–3
Generating companies in Brazil

Company	MW	Market Share
Total installed capacity 60,400 in 1994		
Itaipu (including Paraguay stake)	12,600	21%
Eletrobras	23,747	39%
Furnas - Southern region	8,511	14%
Chesf - Northeastern	8,360	14%
Eletronorte - Northern	3,666	6%
Eletrosul - Southern	3,210	5%
Cesp - Sao Paulo	9,434	16%
Cemig - Minas Gerais	4,600	8%
Copel - Parana	3,337	6%
Others	6,467	11%
Eletropaulo - S. Paulo	1,390	2%
CEEE - Rio Grande do Sul	1,367	2%
Light - Rio de Janeiro	802	1%
Celg - Goias	464	1%
Escelsa - Espirito Santo	174	0%
CPFL - Sao Paulo	126	0%
Celesc - Santa Catarina	70	0%
Cerj - Rio de Janeiro	66	0%
Cataguazes - Minas Gerais and RJ	55	0%
Enersul - Mato Grosso do Sul	46	0%
Ceb - Brasilia	36	0%
Cemat-Mato Grosso	23	0%
45 other smaller	1,850	3%

[Courtesy Banco de Investimentos Ganantia S.A.]

Brazil's total electric power capacity in 1994 was 56 GW, of which about 94% came from hydroelectric plants, and the remaining 7% from diesel oil, charcoal and wood, natural gas, and nuclear power plants. (Table 7–4)

Table 7–4
Brazil's energy supply

Source	Percentage
Electricity	38
Petroleum	33
Wood	8
Bagasse	7
Natural gas	2
Other	12

Brazil generated 243.3 TWh in 1995, up 7.6% from 1994. The leap was higher than the average annual growth, which had been 3.8% between 1990 and 1994. The gross domestic product jumped 4.2% in 1995. Approximately 90% of the country has electricity services. Only about one-half the population had residential electricity in 1970.

Estimates predict that infrastructure investment for electricity could need up to $30 billion(US) in the next decade. Estimates indicate that more than 70 hydroelectric and thermal projects may be made available to private investors as the government looks for ways to open up the sector.

The country has enormous untapped hydro-electric power potential, with enough rivers for three times its current 55,000 MW of hydroelectric capacity. Also, about 80 hydroelectric power stations have been started, but not completed, due to lack of funds.

Privatization legislation passed in February 1995 aims to address the problem. Two new large plants—a 210-MW plant at Igarapava, on the Rio Grande river between Sao Paulo and Minas Gerais, and a 1,293-MW facility at Serra da Mesa on the Tocantins River 155 miles north of Brasilia—are scheduled to come on-line in 1998.

Brazil currently has one operable nuclear unit, the 626-MW Angra 1 unit. This unit has been shut down for about two years due to technical problems. Two other nuclear plants, Angra 2 & 3, are in the construction pipeline. Work on these

plants began in 1977, but was halted in 1988 due to lack of funds. In July 1992, $1.5 billion(US) in financing was arranged to complete Angra 2, with a 1,245-MW capacity, by 1998. Angra 3, 1,229 MW, is not expected to be finished until 2010.

Eletropaulo, one of Sao Paulo state's three electricity companies, reported a 3.8% increase in use in 1995 with 54.7 TWh generated as compared to 52.7 TWh in 1994. Residential use rocketed a record 11.7%, but industrial use fell 1.4%. The industrial slip was attributed primarily to a crisis in the textiles sector, which saw energy sales dip more than 11%. Other utilities reported similar trends for the year.

Eletrobras reports that Brazilian energy distributors are losing more than $1 billion(US) annually to power theft, lack of controls, and lack of maintenance to lines and equipment. Approximately 16% of the state's energy produced and transmitted in 1995 was not paid for—approximately 40 TWh. The Ministry of Mines and Energy reports that it views losses of up to 10% as acceptable. Eletrobras estimates that as many as 400,000 illegal connections to the grid are made annually and many low income users are charged the minimum 30 kWh a month although their use may be significantly higher because utilities cannot afford to install meters for accurate billing.

The Ministry of Mines and Energy is planning a trans-Brazil transmission line project, expected to cost approximately $532 million(US), to be financed with both public and private capital. The 500-kV line would be 1,500 km long, and according to current estimates, could be completed in 1997. The line would connect the northern side of the country, which has a generating excess, to the southern region, which is expected to pass its generating limits in the next few years at current growth rates. Plans are also under way to add a 700-kilometer transmission link through the Lower Amazon region, with completion expected in 1998. (Table 7–5)

In Brazil, there are concessions for new power generation projects of 6,000 MW, valued at about $15 billion(US), and another 20 projects are under consideration. Brazil's government is pushing for

Table 7–5
Brazil transmission lines

Total circuit length - 138 kV to 750 kV - 110,115 km, 1994		
Company	Length	Market Share
Eletrobras	23,747	39%
Furnas - Southern region	8,511	4%
Chesf - Northeastern	8,360	16%
Eletronorte - Northern	3,666	3%
Eletrosul - Southern	3,210	15%
CESP - Sao Paulo	9,434	16%
Cemig - Minas Gerais	4,600	15%
Copel - Parana	3,337	4%
Others	83,811	26%

[Courtesy Banco de Investimentos Granantia S.A.]

Table 7-6
Argentina's capacity and production

Distribution of installed capacity	Percent
Hydro	42.8
Steam	31.6
Gas turbines	14.5
Nuclear	6.6
Diesel	4.4
Distribution of electricity production	
Hydro	33.0
Steam	38.9
Nuclear	15.4
Gas turbines	11.7
Diesel	1.0

many of these projects to be on-line by 2000 or 2005.

Argentina.

In Argentina, the government is making strong progress in its attempt to privatize power, under way since 1991, and it is instituting a market-based system to allow easier market entry for power generation companies. The government has privatized more than 6,000 MW of generation and plans to privatize another 7,000 MW in the next several years. Around 60% of the distribution grids are under private control.

A substantial wholesale power market has emerged, including the sale of electricity by self-generators and cogenerators to the national or local grid. About 80% of Argentina's electrical infrastructure and many of its existing generation assets have been privatized. It has adopted a competitive generator market with light regulatory intervention at the distribution and transmission arenas. Other countries in the region are looking to Argentina as a model for privatizing and drawing international participation in to their electricity sectors.

Electricity generation in Argentina leapt by 3.9% in 1995, despite the overall economy, which was hit by the 1994 devaluation in Mexico and shrank by 2.5%. (Table 7–6)

Buenos Aires province, with an economy the size of Chile's and Colombia's combined, was the last of Argentina's 24 provinces to authorize privatization of its electricity generation, transmission, and distribution. The privatization is still in its early stages, but could raise several hundred mil-

lion dollars. Several Argentine provinces which were near bankruptcy have been selling off their electric utilities, but Buenos Aires resisted the trend. The privatization in this province seems to be politically motivated.

Installed generating capacity was 18 GW in 1994, and more hydroelectric generation is being developed. Demand for electricity in Argentina is increasing, with the energy ministry estimating growth of 6.6% in 1994 and 5.2% for 1995. Supply should increase slightly in the next few years as new projects come on-line, and demand is expected to continue to grow with the gross domestic product.

Natural gas has a strong share of the electricity market in Argentina when compared with the other Latin American nations, and there should continue to be opportunities for natural gas facility construction, adding to the versatility of supply. The largest current project is the Yacyreta plant, 3,000 MW, on the Parana River. It is jointly owned by Argentina and Paraguay. The first unit began generating electricity in 1994 and the plant is expected to be fully operational in 1998. The Yacyreta and other hydroelectric projects are slated for privatization. Argentina also is building a nuclear power plant, Atucha 2, which it plans to privatize along with its two operating nuclear plants—Atucha 1, 335 MW, and Embalse, 600 MW.

In April 1996, Argentina sold its remaining stake in distribution company Empresa Distribuidora La Plata. Government shares in two distributors serving the Buenos Aires area, Edenor

and Edesor, were sold in December 1995. The government retains a 19.5% share in Edenor, since the winning bidder declined to purchase the full 39% offered. The government also chose to retain its 25% share in transmission company Transener, after receiving only one bid in December 1995.

Chile is expected to invest around $5 billion(US) in new generation and related areas in the next few years. Chile led the region when it implemented marginal cost pricing in 1981. The dual principles of demand-driven supply and electricity priced at margin, with the least efficient plant in the system defining the hourly spot price, have been accepted in the United Kingdom, Argentina, Peru, and Bolivia. The tariffs are calculated on a marginal cost basis and system dispatch is ordered by efficiency. In some countries capacity tariffs are more traditional, with a private investor guaranteed a fixed return for making capacity available to the grid, but these have been pared to the bone, putting inefficient or costly new construction at risk.

Peru's marginal cost regulatory regime pays a capacity tariff of $72.46(US) per kWh, which translates to approximately $350(US) per kWh of new construction, adjusted for a 12% pre-tax annuity rate of return over 20 years. In marginal cost pricing, the most efficient generators profit from the arbitrage margin available from inefficient producers and a calculated risk assessment of future supply and demand. In Chile, electricity is no longer priced on a cost-plus basis, but is subject to the cyclical upturns and downturns of a commodity-based industry.

Electricity production in Chile increased from 7.3 billion kWh in 1970 to 24.4 billion kWh in 1994, and generation grew by another 9.2% in 1995. Hydroelectric generation accounts for about 75% of this, with the remainder coming from thermal power stations. Much of Chile's electricity is produced by industry directly for its own consumption. A small amount also comes from geothermal sources.

Estimates predict that Chile must invest $3.3 billion(US) in the next decade for new power

generating plants and transmission equipment to meet increasing demand.

Dominican Republic. The government of the Dominican Republic is working to begin privatization of all or part of its Compania Dominicana de Electricidad (CDE), and to draw private power companies into its electricity industry. This area is experiencing an electricity crisis which is becoming progressively worse, with blackouts lasting up to 20 hours per day. CDE has an installed capacity of 800 MW, but demand has reached 1,150 MW. This crisis is driving plans for privatization.

The utility is also experiencing problems generating enough electricity to meet escalating demand due to deteriorating equipment. Outages are also caused by private companies which have ceased supplying power to the grid due to non-payment. The CDE is somewhat insolvent and had to be assisted with a $52 million(US) government subsidy in November 1995 to pay its bills.

Trinidad currently has electricity sales of approximately 3,490 MWh of electricity annually. A 4–5% growth in demand is expected through 2000, with a majority of that coming from industrial customers. Outages are low and the system carries a substation reliability factor of 99.92%.

Bolivia. The Bolivian government is undergoing a capitalization program to encourage private-sector participation in its electricity sector. In this program, a strategic partner must contribute capital equal to the value of the participating utility, setting up a new company with double the value of the original one, then the strategic partner takes over management control.

Bolivia's power sector is divided into several stand-alone systems with both vertically integrated and non-vertically integrated companies. Installed capacity in 1994 was 780 MW and the nation's utilities generated 2,879 GWh of electricity during the year, recording 2,260 GWh of electricity sales. Approximately two-thirds of the population has access to electricity and per capita consumption is 320 kWh annually. During 1994, electricity consumption grew by 9% and forecasts indicate continuing growth averaging 7% annually.

The regulatory framework for the electricity sector was laid out in the Power Sector Regulatory System Legislation, separating standard-setting and regulatory issues. A new Electricity Law regulates disaggregating generation, transmission, and distribution in the National Interconnected System, and establishes a new tariff-setting mechanism. Specific functions still are being defined and will be established in upcoming Power Sector Deregulation and Market Organization legislation.

Under the Electricity Law, Campania Boliviana de Electricidad (COBEE), the Bolivian electricity company and main distributor, and the three electricity generating companies which resulted from the breakup of Empressa Nacional de Electricidad (ENDE) have exclusive access to the national transmission grid until 1999. After 1999, all new generators will have free access to the grid. The generating companies operate the grid under licenses and are subject to the National Load-Dispatching Committee.

The generators can contract with other generators, distributors, and nonregulated firms. The integrated companies and distributors in isolated systems are allowed to operate under concessions with a maximum duration of 40 years.

The sector is composed of an interconnected system and three main isolated systems. The interconnected system represents 89%, or 2,225 GWh, of the national consumption and 77%, 600 MW, of the installed capacity. (Table 7–7) Generation in the interconnected system, which accounts for nearly 90% of the country's consumption and approximately 77% of installed capacity, comes from four companies: Empresa Corani, 126 MW; Empresa Guaracachi, 183 MW; Empresa Valle Hermoso, 149 MW; and COBEE, the national power company, 142 MW. Approximately 60% of the electricity in Bolivia is thermoelectric and 40% is hydroelectric. (Table 7–8)

Bolivia has three major distribution companies, COBEE, CRE, and ELFEC, which serve 80% of the

Table 7–7
The Andean Region

Total generation 1994	153,207 GWh
hydroelectric	80%
thermoelectric	20%
Installed capacity	37,013
% of Latin America's installed capacity	22
Andean needed capacity, 2000	42,500
% increase needed by 2000	15
Population	100 million
% of Latin America's population	20

The Andean nations are Bolivia, Colombia, Ecuador, Peru, and Venezuela.

Table 7-8
Andean Region capacity and generation statistics

Installed Capacity (MW)			
Country	Hydro	Thermal	Total
Bolivia	332	448	780
Colombia	7,659	2,152	9,811
Ecuador	1,471	824	2,295
Peru	2,454	1,741	4,195
Venezuela	10,675	8,925	19,932
Andean Total	22,591	14,090	37,013
Latin America Total	101,111	66,098	170,448

Power Generation (GWh)			
Bolivia	1,749	1,318	3,067
Colombia	42,860	4,190	47,050
Ecuador	1,828	1,047	2,875
Peru	12,634	2,547	15,181
Venezuela	44,975	22,657	67,632
Andean Region Total	104,046	31,759	135,805
Latin American Total	465,291	206,673	692,854

[Courtesy OLADE]

market. Privatization is going on for the distribution companies as well as the generators. Distributors are obligated to satisfy electricity demand in their concession area and the tariff system sets maximum prices for the market along with market prices for fixed-term contracts and spot prices for the bulk market. Electricity demand is expected to grow by approximately 7% in the future.

Colombia has an installed capacity of 9,811 MW and it generated 45,230 GWh in 1994—78% from hydroelectric sources and 22% thermoelectric. The transmission grid has nearly 14,000 kilometers of 500-, 230- and 115-kV lines.

Colombia passed Law 143 in 1994, providing for essential power sector activities. Private firms can organize, operate, maintain, or manage any of

the public-service power activities under temporary concession which cannot exceed 30 years. Twenty-year extensions of these concessions can be granted. At the end of a private concession, all property reverts to the grantor, who will pay salvage value to the concession holder.

Expansion planning and tariff-setting criteria and methods for the electricity sector are handled by the Ministry of Energy and Mines' Mining-Energy Planning Unit and the Energy and Gas Regulating Commission. Interconexion Electrica, S.A., a public-private firm, is responsible for the National Interconnected System and the National Dispatching Center. The National Operations Council sets the technical aspects of the system and ensures compliance with operating regulations. Firms owning generating plants can use the grids under either a free-access or a regulated mode.

Colombia's electricity industry expansion plan, set in 1992, predicts that investment of approximately $7 billion(US) will be needed between 1997 and 2007, with 80% of that going to power generation needs and 20% to transmission. Generation opportunities are open to private-sector participation.

Trade regulations in the Colombian energy sector changed substantially as 1995 drew to a close. Private sector participation in generation as well as distribution became much easier for developers and investors working to close projects within the country. Government officials announced plans to sell off more than 3,000 MW of state-owned capacity to the private sector; participating investors could either undertake new construction projects or buy plants which are already in use. The latest announcement calls for a 10-plant sale of coal, gas-fired, and hydropower assets. (Table 7–9)

Table 7-9
Investment in coal by type of technology, 1995-2010

Region	Conventional	Clean Coal	Retrofit CCT	Total
	In billions of 1993 dollars			
Latin America	8	13	1	22
World Total	218	389	129	734

Consortium activity within the country met a milestone in the fall of 1995 when the $750 million Termobarranquilla S.A. (TEBSA) project in northern Colombia reached financial closure after an 18-month development period. An international slate of companies led by ABB Energy Ventures of Princeton, N.J., U.S.; Energy Initiatives Inc., A U.S.-based subsidiary of General Public Utilities Corp.; and Colombia-based Lancaster Distral Group completed financing October 20, 1995, to fund acquisition of the existing 240-MW Termobarranquilla power station and begin construction of a new 750-MW, gas-fired, combined-cycle facility next to the existing plant.

Electrical capacity generated by the joint facilities was scheduled for availability to part-owner Corporacion Electrica de la Costa Atlantica (CORELCA) in 1996 under a 20.5-year power purchase agreement. Full combined-cycle operation of the finished plant is expected within 36 months.

Colombia's Reference Expansion Plan calls for a move from an almost 70% hydropower/30% thermal mix to 60%/40% mix. The Termobarranquilla project is expected to be a major participant for new thermal capacity and demand in the country, since its 90% load factor will be capable of supplying 10% of national demand.

Ecuador

Ecuador has an installed capacity of 2,295 MW and in 1994 generated 3,324 GWh of electricity— 65% from hydroelectric sources and 35% thermoelectric. Approximately three-fourths of the population has access to electricity services.

Ecuador is experiencing serious crises in supply and has been undergoing electricity rationing for several years. Privatization is needed badly, but there is no consensus in Ecuador regarding the proper way to undertake such a vast project.

The National Interconnected System is owned by the Instituto Ecuatoriano de Electrification (INECEL), the Ecuadorian Electrification Institute. INECEL holds three main hydroelectric plants— 1,075-MW Paute, 150-MW Agoyan, and 70-MW Pisayambo. The main thermoelectric plants are 140-MW Guayaquil, 125-MW Esmeraldas, 54-MW Santa Rosa, and 31-MW Guangopolo.

Ecuador's main transmission grid is 820-kilometers long with 1,170 kilometers in branches. There are 18 power companies connected to this grid, plus two smaller stand-alone systems.

Ecuador is experiencing a crisis in electricity supply, but with the political instability and regulatory stumbling blocks, private-sector participation is extremely limited. Following the next elections, the electricity sector hopefully can be successfully privatized. Without substantial changes and progress, the electricity supply crisis in this nation is expected to remain or, in all likelihood, worsen.

Peru has an installed capacity of 4,195 MW and in 1994 generated 15,181 GWh of electricity. Electricity services are available to approximately 57% of the population and per capita consumption is around 550 kWh annually. Peak electricity demand growth exceeded 11% in 1993 and 1994, as real gross domestic product growth jumped 12% annually.

Peru's Electricity Concessions Law of 1992 set up a system of concessions to promote private-sector participation in the development of power-sector activities. The Ministry of Energy and Mines and the Electricity Tariffs Commission have responsibility for setting policies, standards, and tariffs in the power industry. These two agencies have the power to allow involvement from the domestic and foreign private sectors in development and to require transmission companies to allow access to the country's grids to promote competition in the generation side.

The 1992 law was supplemented in 1993 with a decree defining the principles of competition, efficiency, and tariff-setting for electricity-sector activities.

To improve supply in the short term, the government is working to privatize a variety of projects and facilities either through sale of current facilities, straight privatization, or build-own-operate arrangements.

The government has announced plans to invest $1.2 billion(US) in generation and transmission projects in the next three years, with the government only temporarily owning any projects built in this period. The government also expects the private sector to make a similar investment in the sector during the same time frame.

Investment opportunities in Peru are expected to continue expanding since the nation has the legal and regulatory frameworks in place. Evolution and expansion of the economy is expected to drive up demand for electricity, and supply is projected to increase incrementally to expand with demand.

More than 2,100 MW of plant and system sell-offs were planned for 1996. Peru is counting on $1.2 billion(US) in private-sector investment in the country's power industry through 2000. Meeting these goals will be difficult for Peru, as the entire region is plagued by a lack of creditworthiness in the utility market, which makes it difficult to finance power projects that rely on long-term power sales agreements.

Venezuela has an installed capacity of 19,932 MW, generating 67,632 GWh in 1992 and selling 52,000 GWh. Approximately 90% of the population has access to electricity services. Demand grew at 5% during 1994, and a demand growth rate of 3–3.5% is anticipated throughout the next decade. Much of the growth is expected to be supplied through natural gas-fired thermoelectric generation.

The national transmission grid includes more than 10,000 kilometers of 765-, 400-, and 230-kilovolt lines. In 1992, Venezuela created the Comision Regulatoria de Energia Electrica (CREE), the Electric Power Regulating Commission, and the Fondo Para el Desarrollo del Servicio Electrico (Fundelec) the Electricity Service Development Fund. These formed the groundwork for the new regulatory framework for the electric power sector. CREE has authority over rates of return, tariffs, expansion plans, and investment coordination, and Fundelec has responsibility for monitoring the electricity-sector's cost structures and for reviewing technical aspects of regulation.

In May 1995, Fundelec submitted a proposed regulatory framework which will evolve into a

totally free-market system. Fundelec's stated intention is achieving complete privatization of the sector in the next five to six years.

Currently, the electricity sector is comprised of four publicly-owned and four privately-owned companies. Four companies are integrated, two are exclusively distributors, and the other four are mixed. Despite this nation's progressive work toward privatization, economic and political uncertainties have been hindering private-sector participation to date.

Guatemala.

The electrical power generation and distribution industry in Guatemala is dominated by two entities, one totally government owned, the National Electrification Institute (INDE), and one which is majority government owned, the Guatemalan Electric Co. (EEGSA). INDE is responsible for most of the generation and distribution, and EEGSA for some distribution, residential, commercial, and instructional installation, maintenance, and administrative operations.

The effective demand in Guatemala is estimated at 775,000 users, divided into three main groups: residential, 84%; commercial and industrial, 14%; and others, 2%. Hydroelectric facilities generate approximately 58% of the power, thermal contributes approximately 38%, and cogeneration provides about 22%. State entities supply 78% of the power and the private sector the remaining 22%.

Currently Guatemala generates nearly 700 MW of electricity, 427 of that through hydroelectric plants. Forecast demand for 1997 will exceed 1,000 MW, so there is a strong need for additional capacity and efficiency improvements in this country. Electricity costs have increased by about 575% n the last 12 years. The government is working to bring a variety of projects on-line in the coming decade, including geothermal facilities, gas-fired, and hydroelectric plants. These are predominantly smaller facilities of under 100 MW, but a few more ambitious plants ranging up to 330 MW are also on the schedule. A few private-sector projects are also planned, but these are mostly very small facilities of around 10 MW. They are primarily hydroelectric facilities.

Panama.

This nation is projected to have 5.6–7.2% annual growth in electricity consumption, and the state-owned utility, IRHE, is scrambling to meet this demand with new plants, greater efficiency, conservation, plant maintenance, and purchasing supply from private-sector sources. IRHE's installed capacity in 1995 was 921 MW, but available capacity was only about 636 MW due to downtime of plants for maintenance and variability in water levels, which affect hydroelectric output. Average demand was 467 MW, but peak demand was 619 MW, barely below available capacity. IRHE needs to expand capacity, and quickly, to avoid electricity rationing or brownouts. In the first half of 1996, Panama experienced an unusually long rainy season, resulting in record water levels that will translate into greater production at the country's four hydroelectric plants.

Electricity is very expensive in Panama, more than $12(US) per kWh, double the cost in neighboring states. Panama explains the high cost by pointing out that the other Central American governments subsidize electricity costs.

IRHE is buying excess energy from private power producers such as Petroterminales de Panama, the U.S.-owned oil pipeline across Panama which owns a 20-MW plant. The Panama Canal Commission owns several plants with a combined capacity of 151 MW, the excess of which is sold to IRHE. If the military bases in Panama are reverted by the end of 1999 as scheduled, IRHE will have the opportunity to obtain more power from the Canal Commission plants. Panama also is working to purchase up to 30 MW daily from Honduras.

Mexico

has an installed capacity of 35,381 MW, with the state-owned Federal Electricity Commission (CFE) and Central Light and Energy owning about 90%. The public-sector capacity is 61% thermoelectric, 29% hydroelectric, 6% carboelectric, 2% geothermal, and 2% nuclear.

(Table 7–10) Several projects which are under way will increase capacity by 3,706 MW in the next three years. About half of the country's current generating capacity relies on fuel oil. Hydroelectric plants account for nearly 30%, and natural gas about 13%. Coal, nuclear, geothermal, and other energy sources make up the remaining 10%.

Table 7–10
Mexican power statistics

Installed Capacity	MW
Hydro	8,008
Thermal	20,641
Geothermal	720
Nuclear	675
Total	30,044
Generation by Type of Plant	GWh
Hydro	25,799
Thermal	89,284
Geothermal	6,576
Nuclear	4,806
Total	126,464
Total energy consumption	101,063 GWh
Per capita consumption	1,072 kWh

[Courtesy OLADE]

CFE estimates that Mexico will require $23 billion(US) for electric generation, transmission, and distribution projects between 1995 and 2004, with about one-half the investment coming from the private sector. New generation capacity needs are estimated to exceed 13,000 MW.

Four projects were completed in 1995: oil-fired Topolobampo II, hydroelectric Ziamapan and Huites, and a new nuclear unit at Laguna Verde— the nation's only nuclear power plant. Projects scheduled for completion in 1996 include hydroelectric facilities San Rafael and Temascal, coal-fired Carbon II, and oil-fired Tuxpan. Most of the remaining needed capacity, which exceeds 9,000 MW, is expected to be provided by independent power producers.

The 1993 Law of Public Service of Electrical Energy established the CFE as a decentralized public organization in charge of granting concessions for electricity. Under the law, only this commission can sell electricity for public use. Private individuals may generate electricity for independent production, autogeneration, cogeneration or small production, export, or for emergency supply.

Mexico is working to privatize and create electric markets with long-term goals of allowing companies to participate in any of the production process phases as well as supplying basic raw materials. Privatization could also permit private-sector ownership of existing plants. In the short term, privatization should create a competitive market in the industry to allow the private sector to participate as builder or provider of electricity. Separating the stages of production should help facilitate investment. The build-transfer-lease option has been used in seven projects to generate 3,840 MW of capacity.

According to estimates, an investment of $14.5 billion(US) will be needed to assure supply through 2003, with additions of approximately 12,000 to 14,000 MW. Of that, $8.5 billion would be needed to finance plant construction and $6 billion would support electric power transmission and distribution.

The economy is in a serious recession with the Finance Ministry reporting a 6.9% drop in gross domestic product in 1995. Mexico's problems began with the massive depreciation of the peso in December 1994, which brought on a financial crisis and exposed vulnerabilities in the economy. Mexico's financial problems raised concerns for other Latin American economies and discouraged international investors, which are so badly needed.

The National Development Plan, announced in May 1995, set a goal of 5% annual economic growth for 1995–2000. Official economic projections for 1996 are relatively optimistic, calling for 3% economic growth and 20% inflation.

Chapter 8
Europe Electricity Supply

ANN CHAMBERS
ASSOCIATE EDITOR
POWER ENGINEERING INTERNATIONAL AND
POWER ENGINEERING

EUROPE

Western Europe generates much of its electricity through nuclear power. France obtains 75% of its electricity via nuclear plants and Belgium, 56%. But much of Europe is moving away from nuclear power, at least in new construction.

According to forecasts from the U.S. Department of Energy's Energy Information Administration (EIA), only France and Turkey are expected to have net increases in nuclear capacity in the coming decade or longer. Seven other West European nations are expected to have net decreases in nuclear capacity due to retirement of currently generating facilities. Political opposition is slowing or halting nuclear additions in Finland, Sweden, and Germany. In the United Kingdom, privatization of advanced gas-cooled and PWR nuclear reactors is underway. This privatization will exclude new nuclear construction from government assistance, pushing the price out of the competitive range and halting nuclear construction there. France is pro-nuclear, but demand is not expected to grow significantly in the coming decade or so, and therefore no new nuclear sites are expected to be built there until well past 2000.

The development of cogeneration is an important challenge for both the policy-makers and the power industry in Europe. Economic and efficient generation is available through cogeneration and worldwide technological developments of gas turbines and gas engines have introduced new prime movers for electricity production. Cogeneration also fits in nicely with environmental consciousness and the international regulatory push for greenhouse gas reduction to reduce global warming through lowered emissions.

Cogeneration demands a different approach to power production in that it requires changing structures among public utilities. In the changing market, utilities are generally looking for

cooperation and partnerships, and a utility serving heat needs is as important as one serving electricity needs. These two needs can be combined or partnered through cogeneration, because cogeneration is power production based on heat demand. In the Netherlands, Germany, United Kingdom, and Scandinavia a large portion of energy is used for the production of heat in many industries with a high heat demand, like refineries and chemical plants, paper mills, greenhouse horticulture, and the dairy industry.

Historically, electricity production and distribution has been a public service with a strong government involvement, and its rapid development over the past 40 years required high investments with long-term commitments. Investments were influenced by politics, and one of the consequences was the development of monopoly structures within the electricity sector.

Now there is a major trend toward the introduction of market influences in the electricity sector, and a wave of liberalization can be observed in Europe. Liberalization and the development of international energy markets are considered essential objectives for the future development of energy policies, and one which will unlock the potential of today's new, more efficient technologies.

Throughout Europe, environmental emissions are falling steadily. Governmental regulations, current and forthcoming, are one impetus, but efficiency and economy are also driving factors. Environmental concerns in Europe are applying pressure for renewables programs, but hydroelectric generation is not expected to gain much ground in popularity as exploitation of hydroelectric resources is creating other environmental concerns, such as flooding of floodplains, dislocation of various populations, and disruption of fisheries. Much of the hydroelectric potential of this region is already developed.

Efforts are under way to decrease the costs of such fuels as wood waste, landfill methane, geothermal, wind, and solar energy. Efficiency rates and performance are on the rise. Wind power especially is coming to the forefront of the renewables race, with turbines available which are capable of generating electricity in winds of 9 to 13 miles per hour. Scientists project that by 2003 research could lower the cost of wind-generated electricity to four cents per kWh.

The European market for wind energy generators had exceptional growth in the past few years, although it stalled somewhat in 1996. (Table 8–1) The market activity was stimulated by a preferential pricing law for selling wind-generated electricity to utilities, government subsidies, and support from environmentalists. By the end of 1993, the European Union had installed wind generating capacity of 1,673 MW, with Germany and Denmark the main players. Although Germany was the largest producer of wind energy in the European Union by the end of 1993, much of its capacity was supplied by Denmark with only about half of the capacity installed coming from German producers. Growth continued through 1995, as installed capacity in Germany alone reached 836 MW.

Table 8–1
European installed wind capacity

Country	Capacity (MW)
Germany	643.1
Denmark	539.1
Netherlands	153.7
Great Britain	150.0
Spain	72.5
Other EU countries	114.6

Denmark generates 2% of its power via wind, of which approximately 70% of the turbines are owned by local cooperatives providing free electricity locally and selling excess to the national grid. The government intends to generate 10% of the nation's power via wind by 2000. The government in the United Kingdom has pledged to generate 3% of its electricity by wind power by 2000. There are already 25 clusters of wind turbines in England and Wales, with future construction planned in Ireland and Scotland. The United Kingdom has announced a goal of 1.5 GW of wind capacity by 2000.

Solar energy is seen as having a potentially strong future, but it is currently a very small

percentage of the electricity generating capacity of Europe—with hydroelectricity, biomass, and geothermal being more common and generally less expensive.

Throughout Central Europe, needs are pressing for plant refurbishment and environmental upgrading. In the Central European countries of Poland, the Czech Republic, and Hungary, progress toward realistic market conditions and development of an effective financial market are enabling international lenders and equity partners to operate much as they would in Western Europe. Growth in power consumption and in gross domestic product are often closely aligned and real gross domestic product growth remains well below the 1989 levels in most of the region.

Even in countries where the decline of the early 1990s has been largely offset, existing total generating capacity will be sufficient in the short term because of more efficient energy use today than under the old centrally planned regime. There are, however, opportunities for plant refurbishment and upgrading, environmental protection, and replacement of capacity that has reached the end of its useful life. There also may be opportunities for plants tied to hard-currency industries, or where commodities can be bartered against the cost of the power plant. (Table 8–2) Although enormous difficulties remain associated

with Central and Eastern Europe and the former Soviet Union, the market is gradually opening and a wealth of valuable experience is available to strategic investors who want to be involved in the region.

Poland. Around 96% of Poland's electricity is generated by coal-fired power plants, with the remainder hydropower-based. (Table 8–3) Of the 96%, 53% burns hard coal, and 41%, lignite. In recent years, electricity generation has remained level at around 133 TWh annually. Total installed capacity is 32,700 MW. The power industry, including both electricity and heat production, is widely regarded as the main cause of atmospheric pollution.

Table 8–3
Poland's electrical sector

Coal	96%
hard coal	53%
lignite	41%
Hydroelectric	4%
Total generation	133 TWh
Installed capacity	32,750 MW

In 1990 Poland began a major restructuring process in its electric utility system, creating three independent sectors for generation, transmission, and distribution. The process is now well advanced but not yet complete. The Polish Power Grid Co., PPGC, a joint-stock company fully owned by the state, maintains the transmission system. Generation of power is handled by 32 independent generating companies. The distribution sector is represented by 33 joint-stock companies owned by the state, but with the option to privatize in the near future. PPGC has participated in the development of a wholesale electricity market. The company also has been able to sign long-term power contracts to allow financing of improvement projects within the utility.

There is a downward trend in emissions of fly ash, SO_2, and NO_x which resulted from a year-on-year decline in the amount of power generated, down from 136.36 TWh in 1990 to 133.66 TWh in 1993, coupled with the use of

Table 8–2
European maintenance projects planned through June 1997

Country	Number of projects	Total value
Austria	9	$25,691,000
Belgium	4	$18,060,000
Czech Republic	5	$8,606,000
Denmark	6	$6,649,000
Estonia	5	$21,890,000
Finland	9	$4,046,000
Germany	37	$122,930,000
Norway	2	$1,736,000
Russia	2	$7,000,000
Slovenia	2	$700,000
Spain	14	$14,558,000
Sweden	1	$3,000,000
Switzerland	34	$81,435,000
Ukraine	2	$800,000
United Kingdom	20	$45,419,000
Total	162	$362,520,000

Data is for 2.5 year period preceding June 1, 1997

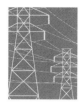
higher quality coal, the introduction of flue-gas treatment and improved electrostatic precipitators. The quality of hard coal used has improved significantly, while the parameters for lignite have remained relatively constant.

The methods being used for emission reduction in Poland can be divided into four main groups:

(1) pre-combustion measures,

(2) measures used during combustion,

(3) post-combustion measures, and

(4) improved energy utilization.

In the area of pre-combustion treatment, a number of Polish coal mines have started to install coal cleaning facilities, as power plants seek lower-sulfur fuels. The sulfur content of Polish hard coal ranges from 0.4–2%, and of lignite from 0.25–1.2%, and estimates predict that the coal cleaning technologies being introduced could reduce SO_2 emissions by 340,000 t/a by the end of 1997. However, there are doubts regarding the extent to which pre-combustion coal cleaning will be used because of its impact on the fuel price.

To reduce emissions during combustions, several approaches are being used. These include fluidized bed combustion, dry desulfurization, and low-NOx burners. Fluidized beds have been chosen for refurbishment of the 10 × 200 MW Turow lignite-fired power plant and the Zeran cogeneration facility, as well as for a number of newly built cogeneration plants, including Lublin, Rzeszow, and Kielce. Also there are plans to install pressurized fluidized bed (PFBC) boilers at the Krakow and Pruszkow cogeneration plants.

Polish power plants have achieved NO_x emissions reductions of around 40% by using low-NO_x burners and probably they will be the primary method of NO_x reduction. One exception is the Opole power plant, where an ammonia flue-gas treatment system is likely needed in addition to low-NO_x burners.

Post-combustion emission reduction measures cover the control of SO_2 and fly ash. Wet desulfurization is planned or is under construction at many Polish power plants, including:

- Belchatow, 4 × 360 MW;

- Opole, 6 × 360 MW;

- Siersza, 2 × 130 MW and 4 × 120 MW;

- Polaniec, 8 × 200 MW;

- Kokienice, 2 × 500 MW and 8 × 200 MW;

- Jaworzno, III 6 × 200 MW;

- Krakow, 4 × 120 MW and 1,457 MW; and

- Skawina, 100 MW.

Apart from its high efficiency, the main advantage of wet desulfurization technology in the Polish context is that the country has abundant limestone resources. Some semi-dry installations are also planned.

Fly ash emissions have been reduced significantly in recent years. Lower overall power production and the use of higher quality coal have contributed to the reduction, but the main reasons have been that Poland has focused considerable attention in this area for many years. All new installations now have precipitators of around 99.6–99.9% efficiency, and older units are being upgraded. This is helped by the fact that electrostatic precipitators are produced in Poland, so considerable local expertise is available.

The final emission reduction method being employed is the encouragement of improved energy utilization. Measures include revised pricing structures, demand side management (DSM), and incentives for consumers.

The most powerful incentive is pricing, as can be seen from recent trends. During the period from December 1989 to June 1994, the price of industrial hard coal rose by a factor of 62.1 in local currency (equivalent to a factor of 14.3 in US$), the price of electric power for industry rose by a factor of 17.4 (4.1 in US$), and of gas for industry by 14.1 (3.3 in US$). At the same time, the price of electricity for domestic consumers climbed by a factor of 57.7 (13.3 in US$) and for gas by 158.6 (36.6 in US$).

Hungary has an installed capacity of 7,200 MW, with 74% of its power coming from thermal sources; 26%, nuclear facilities; and less than 1%, hydroelectric sites. Electricity demand in 1993 was 34.4 TWh, with 31.9 TWh produced domestically and 2.5 TWh imported. (Table 8–4)

Table 8–4
Hungarian power companies

	1990	1993
Installed capacity (MW)	7,184	7,235
Peak load (MW)	6,534	5,612
Electricity demand (TWh)	39.2	35
Net Imports (TWh)	11.1	2.5
National utility generation (TWh)	28.1	31.8
nuclear	13.7	13.8
coal	8.6	9.0
oil and gas	5.0	8.3
auto producers	0.8	0.7

Hungary underwent a change in economic and social structure in 1989 and 1990, bringing the electricity generation, supply, and distribution under control of a two-tiered corporate structure group. The Hungarian power companies and subsidiaries, power plants, and regional distribution companies came into being on January 1, 1992. The main goal of these changes was to establish appropriate conditions for privatization, but the sector was not privatized in this period.

The current regulatory framework, established by the Electricity Law of 1994, has the objective of generating electric power at the least cost as well as assuring stable supply of electricity to the consumers at reasonable prices and assuring the profitability of the sector in the same time. The Hungarian Energy Office takes the responsibility to prepare price proposals in accordance with the pricing policy set out in the law. The prices are subject to the Ministers for Industry and Trade agreement. The law also declares responsibilities for licensing of new units in the energy sector.

Another government decree requires environmental assessment studies for power generation units of capacities higher than 50 MW and transmission lines higher than 120 kV. Units of capacities exceeding 600 MW are licensed by the Parliament. Governmental approval is needed to have a license for a plant with a capacity between 200 and 600 MW. For units less than 200 MW the Minister for Industry and Trade has to approve the choice of fuel. The Hungarian Energy Office issues licenses for the production, transmission, distribution, and supply of energy.

New, stricter emissions standards will have a significant effect on the power sector. A grace period will be allowed for existing plants to meet the new standards. This will be a key financial issue since none of the coal- and oil-fired plants can meet the limits without flue-gas desulfurization and other equipment. Regional Environmental Protection Inspectorates are taking the responsibility for issuing environmental licenses.

Hungary's coal- and oil-fired plants are the major sources of air pollution and sulfur dioxide. In 1992 power plants accounted for 50% of national sulfur dioxide and about 20% of nitrogen oxide emissions. The more than 30% decrease of sulfur dioxide emissions between 1980 and the present was partially due to the commissioning of a nuclear plant at Paks. After finishing the electrostatic precipitator program in 1990, all coal-fired units were furnished with precipitators and a very low particulate emission level was achieved.

The power plant development strategy calls for smaller units for flexibility. Existing plants are being retrofit and upgraded to combined-cycle with gas and steam. A new, 150-MW, coal-fired, circulating, fluidized-bed unit is planned for the Inota Plant and more units are being considered to replace decommissioned plants at Borsod and Matra. In a longer view, the government is expecting to install larger units to use indigenous lignite resources. After 2005, large power plants are being planned for greenfield sites. Coal-fired plants burning imported hard coal or nuclear units are being considered. Development plans foresee investments of around $7 billion(US) through 2005 in the power sector, to be financed partially by the government utility and partially by outside sources through export credits, international bank loans, and private investors.

Italy. The government of Italy has committed to privatizing its electricity sector, starting with sale of 16–24% of ENI, the parastatal energy and chemical giant. The sale is scheduled for

Table 8–5
Data on Italy's electrical power systems

Figures are in millions of US dollars			
	1994	**1995**	**1996**	**Ave. Growth**
Import market	$1,355	$1,565	$1,710	9%
Local production	$5,575	$5,590	$5,720	
Exports	$1,670	$1,740	$1,790	
Total market	$5,260	$5,415	$5,640	5%

Estimated future inflation rate: 5%

1995 import market share: Germany 28%, US 17%, Switzerland 13%, France 11%, UK 10%

November 1996, and will be open to international investors. (Table 8–5)

Early in 1995, ENEL, the national electric power company, announced a five-year $30 million(US) investment program. Approximately 40% of the expenditures will go to southern Italy and the other 60% to central and northern Italy. The plan earmarks $12.5 million for power plant refurbishing and updating, and $12 million for distribution systems. New power plants are not included in the plan, but expenditures of approximately $5.7 million(US) will be needed to complete the plants already planned or under construction. ENEL is implementing the investment program to avoid the projected power deficit of 3,700 MW by the year 2002, if there is no new power plant construction.

On the environmental control side, ENEL started a testing program in the early 1980s to acquire direct experience of desulfurization technologies and to investigate the problems associated with their application in the Italian context. Because of the lack of suitable disposal sites in Italy for flue-gas desulfurization wastes, ENEL concentrated its development effort on standard non-regenerable, advanced-type and regenerable-type processes for new plants and for retrofits. The fact that ENEL plants are equipped to burn different fuels led to the elimination of some newer control technologies such as spray dryers, whose efficiency with high sulfur fuels is not well proven.

The United Kingdom. Pre-privatization,

responsibility for generation and transmission in England and Wales lay with the Central Electricity Generating Board (CEGB), while 12 area boards undertook distribution and supply to end customers in their regions. All boards were owned by the state, and the government had substantial influence. The CEGB sold electricity to the area boards on a bulk supply tariff, set annually on a cost-plus basis.

In 1990's privatization, the CEGB was split into three generation companies, of which National Power was the largest, with responsibility for transmission and system operations. A wholesale market was established, based on an electricity pool, into which generators bid on prices for each of their generating sets every day. Electricité de France and two Scottish companies also bid into the pool, to supply electricity through international interconnectors.

New generating companies are allowed to enter the market, and many are doing so. The area boards have been turned into regional electricity companies, operating distribution systems and buying electricity from the pool to sell to end customers. Supply also is becoming a competitive activity for large customers initially, with all customers gaining choice in supplier by 1998.

CO_2, SO_2, and NO_x emissions from United Kingdom power stations have all taken a steep drop in the last few years. The Electricity Association, the trade body which represents all the major electricity generation, transmission, distribution, and supply companies in the United Kingdom, comments, "Action by the United Kingdom electricity industry is delivering significant reductions in emissions."

The industry's own forecasts suggest that annual CO_2 emissions will be 42 million tons of carbon (MtC) in 2000, 12 MtC lower than in 1990. This reduction is greater than the total national savings target of 10 MtC per year by 2000 set by the UK's commitments under the Climate Change Convention. The government has updated its own emissions forecasts, and now expects not just stabilization, but a fall in U.K. emissions by 2000.

The government has set the electricity industry annual target reductions for SO_2 up to 2003 and for NO_x up to 1998, under the European Large Combustion Plants Directive.

Spain. The Spanish power market is dominated by 14 power generating and distributing companies. Eight of these companies are private corporations owned by the government. Electricity rates are fixed by the government on an annual basis. The electricity grid is managed by a government-owned company independent of the utilities. In the last decade, the government has promoted investment in natural gas to replace other fossil fuels as a primary energy source. Investments have been directed toward creating a national gas grid.

Large investments have been earmarked toward replacing coal power plants with natural gas. The Spanish government also subsidized local lignite and hard coal production to maintain employment because of the industry's strong political influence.

In 1991, the government drafted the National Energy Plan establishing guidelines for energy development through 2000. The plan promotes energy efficiency and allocates investment to diversify Spain's energy sources. It specifically promotes cogeneration and renewable development. It also allowed independent producers to enter the market and gain importance in the power generating business—currently holding 5.7% of total electricity production. Since 1992, power produced through cogeneration has more than doubled and renewable energy has grown considerably.

Spanish utility Endesa is focusing on CO_2 reduction as part of its overall environmental plan. Three areas have been identified for further attention:

(1) Improvement of power generation efficiency. Specific actions have included conversion of the As Pontes thermal power plant to use a mixture of lignite and subbituminous coal. Endesa is also investigating the use of PFBC and inte-

grated coal gasification combined-cycle technologies.

(2) Fuel quality improvement. Lower-ash imported coals are being used, as well as subbituminous coal and natural gas.

(3) Substitution to non-CO_2-producing generation methods. Efforts are under way to increase the use of wind, sun, biomass, and mini-hydro technologies.

Progress has been made in reducing CO_2 emissions from Endesa's power plants. This improvement has been achieved mainly by the use of better quality fuels, resulting in an upward trend in Higher Heating Value (HHV), and an associated fall in heat rate. The average net heat rate fell by 138 kcal/kWh during the period from 1988 to 1994, leading to a 5% reduction in specific emissions.

Baltic States. The close cooperation between the Nordic countries in the field of electricity exchange is expanding. During the summer of 1995, the energy ministers of Sweden, Norway, Denmark, and Finland agreed in principle to create a joint electricity market.

Norway and Sweden removed their border tariffs for electricity on January 1, 1996, creating an international electricity exchange. The exchange allows both generators and consumers to trade across the border. The pool is viewed as a beginning for a much larger market, to include Finland, Denmark, and mainland Europe. Germany receives electricity from Denmark already and will begin importing electricity from Norway in 1998.

Norway boasts the world's only complete power exchange for trading and clearing standardized electricity contracts. Electricity is being treated as a "normal commodity" traded on the stock exchange. In 1994 the domestic stock exchange, Statnett Marked A/S, traded 25% of the Norwegian electricity consumption, or 28 TWh. Trade for 1996 is projected to top one-third of total consumption. The new, wider electricity market is expected to increase competition and stabilize

prices from the sharp peaks and troughs that had been seen on the market.

As the European market moves further toward liberalization, electricity futures, derivatives, brokers, and short-term power trading will become more commonplace as customers press for lower energy prices. Already Norway's experience shows benefits to retail wheeling and industry restructuring. Norway's electricity prices have fallen approximately 20% for all customer classes since the introduction of competition two years ago. Norway is the most advanced of these four countries at the moment, but Finland and Sweden are closing the gap because their hydropower base has made it easier for them to meet electrical demands. The combination of the Norwegian and Swedish exchanges has gone smoothly and is functioning on a day-to-day basis. The coming Nordic energy exchange will further consolidate the mix of market players.

Eleven of the states on the Baltic Rim have a large electricity surplus that would be available for trade. But according to a recent market analysis released by NUTEK, Sweden's National Board for Industrial and Technical Development and the country's central public authority for matters concerning the long-term development of energy, it is uncertain whether any of the region's excess capacity can be exported effectively until political and other market conditions become more transparent.

NUTEK predicts:

- trade increases between the Nordic countries in general,

- trade increases between Sweden and Germany in the next few years,

- demand increases in Poland and Russia which will be associated with a more attractive economic environment, and

- electricity imports to Sweden replace some of the its nuclear power production capacity.

The markets in this region differ widely but all share a common feature: domestic energy markets that are being transformed by new laws and fundamental regulatory policies which are still developing. Priorities lie in the sculpting of a price structure which would enable utilities to achieve cost coverage, but there are regulations and structures which are impeding progress in some nations.

Sweden.

Oil, hydroelectric, and nuclear power are the main sources of energy in Sweden. The country has plentiful hydropower resources but no oil or coal reserves. Oil demand has been almost halved since 1970 by energy conservation efforts and the substitution of nuclear-generated electricity for oil. The nuclear plants are powered by imported fuel. (Table 8–6)

Table 8–6
Data on Sweden's electrical power systems

	Figures are in millions of US dollars			
	1994	1995	1996	Ave. Growth
Import market	$1,696	$1,730	$1,730	2%
Local production	$1,678	$1,762	$1,762	
Exports	$1,732	$1,819	$1,819	
Total market	$1,642	$1,673	$1,673	4%

Estimated future inflation rate: 3%

1994 import market share: Germany 24%, US 16%, France 8%, Finland 7%, UK 6%

Sweden is very dependent on imports of raw materials for energy, importing nearly 70%. An extension of the existing natural gas network has been discussed, along with construction of pipelines from Norway and Russia, but no decision has been made to date.

Sweden's first nuclear power reactor entered operation in 1972, and the 12th and last reactor in 1985. The reactors are sited at four power stations in the southern part of the country. Barseback has two reactors totaling 1,200 MW, Ringhals has four for 3,475 MW, Oskarshamn has three for 2,200 MW, and Forsmark has three for 3,090 MW. After a 1980 referendum, the Parliament decided to phase out nuclear power, which produces one-half the country's electricity, by 2010. The Energy Commission has now backed down from that commitment. The date has been considered unrealistic, but Sweden still plans to phase out its nuclear stations.

The country is working to bring alternative power sources on-line and to develop energy savings programs, but no detailed plan has been worked out to explain how Sweden can compensate for the loss of the nuclear power. Price is also a factor, as the energy commission projected closing the reactors by the original date would cost approximately $10–$13 billion(US), pushing electricity prices up by 50%. Sweden is working to have a free market for electricity with all customers free to choose their suppliers in the near future.

The Parliament has limited the nation's ability to expand hydropower assets by declaring that the four remaining undammed rivers in the north will not be harnessed. Hydropower plants generate 64 TWh in a normal year, but only minor capacity expansions are possible.

End use of energy totaled 384 TWh in 1994, of which 141 TWh was used in industry and 157 TWh in housing, services, and district heating, and 86 TWh in the transport system. The eight largest production companies generate 90% of the electricity in Sweden and the state and municipalities together control most of the production. The largest companies in the power market are the state-owned Vattenfall AB and Sydkraft AB, which have municipal owners in southern Sweden plus German and French companies.

Denmark. The Danish power industry has two electric cooperatives divided in area by the Great Belt: Elsam in the East and Elkraft in the West. In Denmark, there are 20 power plants with a capacity exceeding 100 MW. Eleven of these plants have more than 300 MW. Coal-fired plants account for 92% of the power production, with the remaining 8% coming from oil, natural gas, biomass, and wind. Most of the coal-fired power generation takes place in large central heat and power plants which are largely supplied with cogenerated heat.

Denmark has made advances in the area of wind technology due to geographic location and strict environmental laws. According to the Danish Ministry of Energy, a major goal of the Danish energy policy is to reduce overall energy consumption by 15% and carbon dioxide emissions by 20% by the year 2005. More than a quarter of the capacity has desulfurization and 32% has low-NOx burners.

Switzerland. Switzerland's generating companies are preparing for deregulation of the electric energy market. The 475 power generating firms are an important segment of Swiss industry, with $7 billion(US) of revenues, accounting for 2% of the Swiss gross national product. Deregulation plans are partially the result of similar moves by neighboring European Union countries.

The electric power network is fully integrated with those of the French, German, Italian, and Austrian neighbors. Swiss power companies hold significant shares in six major French nuclear power plants, from which they import 8,200 GW annually. Exports top 12,000 GW, particularly to Italy and Germany.

Germany. Energy consumption and production differs markedly between the western and eastern German states. In western Germany, production is based principally on coal, lignite, and nuclear power plants. In the east, by contrast, production has been based almost exclusively on lignite, though new plants are expected to be based partly on natural gas and coal in addition to lignite. (Table 8–7)

Table 8–7
Breakdown of German electricity generation sources

Fuel	Percentage
Coal	57
Nuclear	32
Gas	5
Hydro	2
Wind/Solar	1
Other/Misc.	3

In western Germany, current power generating capacity is expected to meet the demand for electricity into the foreseeable future. Local industry projections predict a new cycle of investment and

modernization in power generating plants will occur around the year 2005 to meet the growing demand for electricity driven by industrial innovation and increased automation in telecommunications and information processing.

There is a growing trend toward independent power producers in Germany. Cogeneration facilities and plants using waste, hydropower, and biomass are becoming an increasingly attractive option for producing electricity. Since there are no restrictions on auto production, and IPPs may negotiate individual contracts to sell power to the utilities, the IPPs are introducing an element of competition into the German energy market.

Another trend affecting the market is the development of increasingly strict environmental standards, which in Germany are significantly more stringent than in the rest of Europe.

Energy use in Germany totaled 528 billion kWh in 1994, up 0.2% from 1993. Electric power generation remained constant at 526 billion kWh, of which 87% was generated by public utilities, 11% by private industry, and 1% by the railroad industry. Power generation by public utilities increased by 0.5% in 1994 to 455 billion kWh.

Coal-fired plants account for approximately 56% of the power generated in Germany; nuclear, 33%; natural gas, 5%; hydroelectric, 4%; and renewable energy sources, including solar and wind, account for approximately 1%.

Electricity is supplied principally by nine large electric companies: RWE Energie, Preussenelektra, VEW, Bayernwerk, Badenwerk, EVS, HEW, Bewag, and VEAG. These companies have state-guaranteed regional monopolies and distribute to smaller regional and municipal utilities as well as to end-users. The large utilities also own some of the regional and local power companies, and together produce about 80% of Germany's power. Another 50 companies own and operate power plants that distribute electricity to other utilities. Industrial companies and the federal railway system generate another 15% of the electricity, most of which is fed into the public grid. Another 70 smaller companies retain some generating capacity, as do most large cities.

Netherlands. The Netherlands' national grid, with its 380/220-kV network, is overseen by Samenwerkende Elektriciteits-Produktiebedrijven. This federal organization is also responsible for the coordination and control of electric production. The Netherlands operates four main power generation companies: EPON, EPZ, EZH, and UNA. They sell power to 50 distribution companies. Among these are 12 larger, regional distribution companies, responsible for the operation and maintenance of the 110/150-kV networks. Greater independence has been given to distribution companies to generate power and buy from wider sources. In addition to the centralized power producers, distribution companies and private firms are legally entitled to generate electricity. Decentralized production is substantial and growing.

France. Electricité de France is the national electricity company of France. Although most strongly relying on nuclear power, France has announced that it is not likely to place any more orders for nuclear power before 2000.

France is the leading innovator in implementing the infrastructure for electric vehicles (EV) in the European community, and possibly in the world, as Electricité de France (EDF) stepped into the fray early with pilot tests, manufacturer and governmental partnerships, and utility diversification. EDF has more than 20 years of experience in research and development of battery recharging systems and engines. The utility recently completed a $5.7 million(US) three-year study of various aspects of EV technology. It is backing research to improve performance of lead/acid, nickel/cadmium, and lithium/polymer batteries. EDF has developed a recharge terminal system and is working to perfect rapid recharging. It is also instituting a self-service car program.

In 1992, the Ministers of the Environment and Industry cosigned a framework agreement with the chairmen of EDF, Peugeot Citroen, and Renault to develop the EV. Twenty-two pilot cities in France are experimenting with EVs. To make EVs more attractive, EDF and other partners are implementing a battery rental network to help customers stagger the expenses.

As a utility that generates and distributes electricity, EDF is developing the EV for personal use or as part of a company car fleet, in response to the French public's interest in reducing air pollution in cities, along with the corresponding reduction in noise pollution. EDF is working to implement a self-service car program, intended to help reduce congestion and traffic jams in urban areas by providing electric cars that can be used by several different drivers during the day. Several communities in the United Kingdom are also considering the option. The system is based on the use of small electric cars in reserved parking lots in the city center. Cars are available for members who have subscribed to the system and who possess a payment card which gives them access to the cars. Each car is fitted with an automatic charging system that connects the car and initializes the charging process. This program is being carried out by EDF, Renault Automobile, and the Compagnie Generale Francaise de Transports ed d'Entrepreises.

EDF reports that even if France had one million EVs, each traveling 10,000 miles annually, no additional power plants would be needed. Currently, French EVs average 2,000 kWh annually, so total EV consumption for one million cars would be between 3–4 million kWh, less than 1% of all power now generated in the country.

Belgium, with 10 million inhabitants, has a well-developed and modern electric power generation and distribution system. Sixty percent of its electricity comes from nuclear power, with coal-fired plants accounting for 25% and natural gas contributing 12%.

Around 60% of Belgium's electricity is generated by nuclear power plants, but for political and environmental reasons following the Chernobyl disaster, no further nuclear capacity is planned within the foreseeable future. Coal accounts for 25% of generation, and gas, 12%.

Annual investment in new and refurbished electricity generating capacity is expected to

average more than $1 billion(US) in the next three to five years. (Table 8–8)

Table 8–8
Data on Belgium's electrical power systems

	Figures are in millions of US dollars		
	1994	**1995**	**1996**
Import market	$1,773	$1,945	$1,863
Local production	$2,180	$2,407	$2,163
Exports	$1,493	$1,664	$1,617
Total market	$2,460	$2,689	$2,560

Estimated future inflation rate: 2-3%

1995 import market share: Germany 32%, France 20%, Holland 11%, and US 6.6%

Electrabel, a public limited company and subsidiary of the Tractebel industrial holding group, accounts for 84% of electricity production and 86% of distribution. Small, independent producers/distributors account for the balance. The industry is closely supervised by the Control Committee for Electricity and Gas.

THE FORMER SOVIET UNION

Reliance on nuclear power varies widely throughout the former Soviet Union. Lithuania generates 76% of its electricity in nuclear plants and Russia only 11%. Several countries have plans for nuclear capacity growth but the uncertain economic and political future in these states creates challenges to construction plans. The EIA projects a small net loss in nuclear capacity for the region in the coming decade if outside financing does not support nuclear construction efforts or a small net gain in nuclear capacity if Eastern European countries and international lending institutions provide aid.

Hydroelectric generation is the most popular renewable energy source in Eastern Europe and the former Soviet Union. A variety of wind-generating projects are under way in this region, many with the support of institutions such as the World Bank and the European Bank for

Reconstruction and Development. Other European nations also are assisting the struggling former Soviet Union utilities.

Free markets are taking root in the New Independent States (NIS) with 20,000 major enterprises and 100,000 small businesses in Russia alone that have been transferred into private hands. There is, however, resistance to change and weakness in popular knowledge of how free markets work, which hamper reform. In the next few years, these republics will focus on seven key issues:

(1) developing capital markets,

(2) establishing equity and commodity exchanges,

(3) forming responsible regulatory agencies,

(4) instituting modern financial and accounting standards,

(5) drafting commercial laws,

(6) establishing a fiscally sound tax system, and

(7) completing a comprehensive land reform program.

The NIS power sector covers one-sixth of the world's land surface and has the largest combined proven energy reserves of any region in the world—but it has problems. There is an energy crisis with a decline in energy production, nonpayment for fuels, and skyrocketing energy costs. Many of the power sectors are bankrupt, and inadequate electricity rates do not cover the cost of producing the power.

A variety of factors have contributed to the crisis, including destruction of economic links between the republics, a slump in the production of energy resources, and a lack of adequate investment in the industry. There is not enough funding to pay for the essential components of the energy sector—fuel, maintenance, repairs, and capital investments. Development of the NIS energy sector has the potential to make a significant contribution to meeting the world's energy needs. Efficient development of these resources will require unprecedented cooperation within the international energy industry, and therefore will provide tremendous opportunities.

Problem areas tend to be uniform from republic to republic. The age and status of the thermal power plants is one of the biggest problems. Most of the thermal power plants are between 30–40 years old and nearing the end of their useful lives. The thermal sector was neglected under the Russian regime as a higher emphasis was placed on nuclear plants, with the intention of phasing out the thermal facilities.

Fuel cost is also a problem. Many of the republics do not have indigenous fuel supplies, making them dependent on the other countries. Also, much of the coal is of low quality and difficult to mine. For example, coal in Ukraine rests 2,000 feet below the surface in seams 14 inches thick which lie on a 45 degree angle. Once mined, the coal has a high ash content, high moisture content, and a low heating value.

Spare parts are also a problem. One eight-unit power plant in Georgia has only three units running, as the other five are being used for parts. Safety programs for workers are lacking and environmental protection equipment such as dust collectors and precipitators are noticeably absent.

Maintenance is poor because staff does not have the technology or knowledge to utilize preventative maintenance. Water quality is also poor, as many plants use no chemical treatment of the water going into the boilers.

Instrumentation is out-of-date and slow in response, and bill collection processes often include bartering rather than cash. Still, approximately 30% of the residential customers do not pay their bills, which in many countries are only 0.5¢ per kW.

But the republics are working to overcome these many crippling difficulties, working to modernize their existing energy systems with life extension programs and modifications to the transmission systems, controls, and instrumentation. They would like to add pollution controls.

The utilities are learning many aspects of running a business in a market economy, including ways to raise foreign capital and to learn acceptable bookkeeping methods.

Legal reform has been dramatic in this region, but in the drive to shed old laws, new legislation was often enacted so quickly that laws came in conflict with one another. The lack of a market economy tradition and the experience of applying commercial laws mean steeper learning curves. The Soviet legacy also includes a highly politicized judiciary, where the rule of law gave way to a practice in which party leaders instructed the judges by telephone on how issues would be resolved by the courts—commonly called telephone justice. Increasingly legislation in this region is being reconsidered in an attempt to reform it.

During the Soviet era, the government gave everyone a job and ran all the plants. The struggling nations are now trying to outperform this inefficient legacy. The NIS and the countries of Central and Eastern Europe are making ambitious plans to expand their electric power infrastructure, with an estimated 136 GW of installed capacity to be in place by 2010, according to U.S. Trade and Development Agency statistics.

Russia. The Far East region of Russia is approximately 6.2 million square kilometers with a population of nearly eight million people. It has a large supply of natural energy resources, with more than 34% of the estimated coal reserves of the Russian Federation and 30% of the hydroelectric potential. (Table 8–9) There are also gas and oil fields, geothermal springs, wind, and ocean resources. The largest fuel and energy sources are not distributed evenly, however, and are located mainly in uninhabited areas. Power generating plants and electricity consumers are separated by large distances, so there is an extensive transmission network, with existing transmission lines carrying 220 kV and construction of a 500-kV network under way in the south. Coal constitutes 69% of the fuel used in fossil power plants; fuel oil accounts for 22%; diesel oil, 1.5%; and gas, 7.5%. About 80% of the coal comes from local mines.

Table 8–9
Russia's eastern power grid

Number of regional power systems	4
Installed capacity	7,048 MW
Fossil power plant capacity	5,718 MW
percentage of total capacity	81%
Hydroelectric power plant capacity	1,330 MW
percentage of total capacity	19%
Electric power generation	30.1 million MWh
Fossil power generation	25.1 million MWh
percentage of total generation	83%
Hydroelectric power plant generation	5.0 million MWh
percentage of total generation	17%
Number of power plants	16
Capacity of the largest fossil fuel unit	215 MW
Capacity of the largest hydroelectric unit	225 MW
Length of 220-550 kV transmission lines	7,723 miles
length of 500 kV lines	1,130 miles
length of 220 kV lines	6,593 miles

[Courtesy Vostokenergo]

The Eastern Power Grid (EPG) covers a majority of the territory, serving five million people, including most of the industrially developed parts of the Far East. EPG covers 70% of the installed capacity in the region with 16 plants and a total capacity of 7,048 MW. EPG is planning to expand after merging with Nikolaevsk and Central power systems.

The economy in the Far East is expected to stabilize soon, leading to an increase in electricity demand. Expansions are planned at Bureyskaya Hydroelectric Power Plant, plus a variety of upgrades and modifications to existing power plants. Major demand increases are expected in the south of the region with up to three million MWh of electricity imports projects.

Major projects scheduled by the turn of the century include:

- complete construction of 2,000-MW Burey Hydroelectric Power Plant,

- start construction of Urgal 1 Hydroelectric Power Plant in Khabarovsk Territory,

- start construction of Nishine-Burey Hydroelectric Power Plant in Amursk Territory, and

- complete Vilyuy Hydroelectric Power Plant Unit 3, Yakut Central Fossil Power Plant, Magadan Heat and Power Plant, and Ust-Srednekan Hydroelectric Power Plant.

The decade of 2000 to 2010 is expected to be the turning point in the national economy with positive growth in the industrial and economic markets. New hydroelectric facilities are being contemplated in Khabarovsk and Amursk territories in this era, along with one or two nuclear power plants in Khabarovsk and Primorsk territories.

One of the biggest projects under way is the Urgal Fuel and Energy Complex in the Khabarovsk Territory. When completed, it will include:

- Urgal Hydroelectric Power Plant 1, on the Neman River, 600 MW,

- Urgal Hydroelectric Power Plant 2, in the Bureya River, 290 MW,

- Urgal State Regional Power Plant, first phase 645 MW, full capacity 2,200 MW,

- Urgal Gas Turbine Power Plant, sited on a natural gas field near the Elga railway station, and

- Urgal 1 Coal Mine, output expected to reach about six million tons.

Russia's first independent power producer soon will be a reality, as Magnitogorsk Integrated Iron and Steel Works (MMK) plans to enter the cogeneration business. Magnitogorsk awarded KMR Power Corp. a mandate to develop, construct, own, and operate a 150-MW, natural gas-fired, combined-cycle plant at its facility to help meet the firm's increasing demands for electric power and steam. The term of the agreement is 20 years, after which the facility will be transferred to MMK. A joint venture has been arranged between Stone & Webster and Westinghouse to act as the equipment contractor and to provide turnkey supply.

Foster Wheeler International Corp. also has entered the Russian market, with a recent announcement of a contract for Tonar Corp., a Moscow-based state and joint stock corporation. Foster Wheeler is performing a feasibility study and design for a 480,000-metric-ton-per-year municipal solid waste (MSW) processing complex. The Timokhovo Ecocomplex will include recycling and waste-to-energy sections. The waste-to-energy section will be based on Foster Wheeler's advanced, circulating, fluidized-bed, boiler technology, to convert waste cleanly into electricity.

Ukraine.

Ukraine's total installed capacity is 54,200 MW, with fossil-fueled plants providing 67.6% and nuclear plants providing 25% of that total. There are 104 fossil-fueled plants, ranging from 150 MW to 800 MW, with a combined capacity of 28,700 MW. However, 82% of all operating units already have reached their designed service life limit of 100,000 hours, and 48% already have exceeded maximum allowed service life limits of 170,000 hours. Twenty units have been in operation for 200,000 hours. Constant daily cycling with units going out of service for the night and consequent start-ups for morning load has caused deterioration and maintenance problems. The nuclear plants are baseload stations and are not used to control network frequency. None of the fossil-fueled plants are equipped with NO_x or SO_2 emission control systems.

Hydroelectric plants play an important role in maintaining peaking function. Ukraine has 4,700 MW of hydroelectric capacity, 8.8% of the national capacity. Most of the hydroelectric plants have been in service for 20 to 40 years, so they also have severe maintenance problems.

Poor coal quality has led to capacity loss and decreased reliability, and has affected operator ability to control power output range. Fuel consumption increases as equipment deteriorates, and emission problems worsen. Oil and natural gas are being used at the coal-burning plants to improve combustion problems, to increase cycle efficiency, and to reduce pollution. However, nonpayment by consumers combined with an outdated and unstable tariff rate system are restricting the resources of the Ministry of Energy in import oil and natural gas. All this has resulted in reserve shut-down and long-term lay-up of the most efficient and reliable gas- and oil-fired units, which have a combined capacity exceeding 6,000 MW. Reforms are called for, and the Ukrainian power industry is attempting to provide a foundation for the financial investments needed, with initial restructuring recently completed. These include:

- The National Energy Control Center has been working to create an electricity market. Ukraine is working toward a competitive market where all major electricity generators would function as a system, regardless of the form of ownership. Local governments will have control of local electric tariff rates and work to stimulate power industry development.

- The National Electric Co. has been organized to handle transmission lines of 220 kV and higher.

- Twenty-seven regional state-controlled corporate electric utilities have been established.

- Six state-controlled power generating corporations have been established.

- Former construction division of the Ministry of Energy, manufacturing and fabricating plants, design institutions, and other branches of the ministry have become public corporations in the past two years.

Free market conditions have been established, but the functioning has been hampered by the unstable financial and credit conditions. The National Energy Program through 2010 calls for widespread reconstruction and major technical upgrading of existing power plants and other power sector components with the latest domestic and foreign technologies. Projects are to be financed by the utilities, using funds from increased electricity and heat tariff rates. Some programs are to be funded by the government and foreign investors. The improvements to fossil power plants, electric distribution, and heating networks are estimated to require $9 billion(US).

Armenia is a small, landlocked country with a land area of 29,800 square kilometers and a population of approximately 3.5 million. The country depends heavily on the national network of power and gas distribution for personal, commercial, and industrial purposes. The electric network is one of the most developed branches of industry and is spread throughout the country. Armenia only can produce an average of 12 million kWh of electricity daily toward meeting a demand approaching 30 million kWh daily.

Before 1988, the installed capacity of power plants in Armenia was about 3,500 MW, with 1,750 MW from fossil-fueled power plants, 800 MW from one nuclear plant, and 950 MW from hydroelectric power plants. The Armenian distribution network is a well-developed network of electric transmission and distribution. The extension networks are 35 kV and higher, and there are 35 200-kV substations giving a total capacity of 13,772 MA.

However, Armenia is experiencing a crisis for power due to blockades from Azerbaijan and Turkey, lack of rail transport to the European part of the former Soviet Union, frequent disturbances of rail and gas pipelines through Georgia, and shutdown of the one nuclear plant following a 1988 earthquake. As a result of these factors, current generating capacity is only one-quarter of the 1988 total. The government is scrambling to shore up the electric industry, including:

- equalizing tariff rates to all consumers,

- normalizing and centralizing collections of tariffs for hydroelectric and fossil energy,

- technically upgrading via World Bank financing and USAID,

- reorganizing the energy sector with a goal of making the electrical network and all thermal power stations self-supporting and self-financing, and

- repairing the nuclear plant.

The government of Armenia expects the energy sector to build its own finances for development, but in the meantime is looking to foreign credits and investments.

Before the present crisis, hydroelectric plants generated about 15% of the nation's total electricity. Of the estimated 21.8 billion kWh of hydropower produced, 85% was generated on large- and medium-size rivers and 15% on small rivers. Today, because of the reduction in nuclear, oil, and gas generation, the hydroelectric plants account for more than 70% of the electricity generated in the country. In 1993, to increase the nation's hydropower capacity, the Ministry of Energy conducted a survey of potential sites, identifying 40 priority sites suitable for development of small hydropower stations. Armenia is also working to upgrade existing hydro facilities.

Thermal power plants are another significant source of the energy supply in Armenia. There are three fully-operating plants: Yerevan, 550 MW; Hrazdan, 1,110 MW; and Vanadzor, 96 MW. All have exceeded their projected operating lifespans, operate inefficiently, and need renovation.

Armenia is working to link its grid with Iran at Meghri on the border. The project is expected to be completed by the end of 1996 at a cost of $12 million(US). It includes construction of a 230-kV line with a capacity of 200 MW. A projected electricity grid link between Iran and Turkmenistan, if completed, would allow Armenia also to buy power from Turkmenistan.

Alternative energy resources have potential for easing the crisis. The country has significant solar, wind, and bioenergy potential. On average, 10,000 square meters of Armenian territory receive about 2,500 to 2,700 hours of direct sunlight annually, which converts to potential power of 2,000-2,200 kW per square meter. High-speed wind energy in

mountainous regions could generate another 1,000 MW of electricity annually. About 85% of the country has low-speed wind potential.

Development of the energy sector is a high priority for the government, and is supported by the United States and other foreign nations, along with international organizations in the country, but the government lacks financing for many of the potential projects in the energy sector.

Kazakhstan. The power generation system of Kazakhstan is comprised of fossil fuel and hydroelectric power plants with combined power output of 16,000 MW interconnected with the transmission lines from 110 kV to 1,150 kV. To achieve independence in its power supply and create conditions for national economic stabilization and future growth, the government realizes the need to build up its power generation industry. Production and consumption of electricity in the country decreased 24% from 1990 to 1994, from production of 104.7 million MWh to 79.5 million MWh, and was projected to fall to 75.2 million MWh for 1995. The generation drop is caused by the physical and technological deterioration of the power plants combined with economic difficulties.

The main power generating units are at their 45% life-level, but each year 500 MW of capacity reaches its designed maximum service-life limit, and by 2000 this number will reach 800 MW.

By 2010 electricity consumption could increase to 115–125 million MWh. There is an existing deficit of approximately 12 million MWh, so the country needs to add 38–48 million MWh of additional capacity. This will require new generating units with a total capacity of 4,400 to 5,300 MW by 2010.

The most complex problem exists in West Kazakhstan which is not connected to Kazakhstan Common Power Grid. The Russian Federal supplies 4–5 million MWh per year to this region, but in 1994 alone, due to the price difference between locally produced and imported electricity, the state lost more than $50 million(US). This region's economy has a strong influence on national currency stabilization, so a priority has been placed on stabilizing the power supply in the region, primarily through construction of Aktubinsk and Uralsk power plants plus an additional unit at Atyrausk. Kazakhstan is working to attract foreign capital to assist in operation of existing plants and construction of new ones.

In June 1995, Kazakhstanenergo and a consortium of Siemens, Babcock, and BMB Group signed a turnkey contract for a combined-cycle, 954-MW power plant in Aktubinsk. Construction will be financed with the help of foreign credits, guaranteed with sales of crude oil.

Other projects include Akturbo Corp. and ABB Craftwerke, Germany, installing a 100-MW, gas-turbine generator at Aktubinsk, and Traktebel of Belgium developing plants for combined-cycle units at Ural Power Plant No. 1 which Traktebel will finance 100% in a build-own-transfer arrangement.

Kyrgyzstan.
This republic is rich in hydroelectric resources and coal. It also has oil and gas reserves. Coal deposits are reported to include 620 million tons of industrially-explored coals and an estimate of 1,360 million tons as the total resource. The deposits appear to comprise 64.5% brown or lignite coal and 21.5% high volatile coal and are distributed throughout the country. Coal mining production has fallen from almost four million tons in 1990 to about 1.7 million tons in 1993 and less than one million tons in 1994. Energy production is increasingly shifting from coal to hydroelectric and the demand for residential heating is declining because electricity is more convenient and can be purchased on credit.

Heating plant consumption is declining because the plants are not generating enough revenue to pay their fuel expenses and they are being taken out of service when steam production is not essential.

There are no funds to support pilot or demonstration facilities in the republic, although there are some test facilities set up near Osh. Since all energy sources—coal, gas, oil, electricity, hot water, and steam—are subsidized in different ways, the task of evaluating the economics of an energy form is formidable. The price of heat, hot water, or electricity delivered to the consumer is set by a government agency on the basis of the amount the consumer can afford to pay in the local economy. If the consumer cannot afford to pay for the energy received, the energy provider receives no revenue, but still must provide the energy.

The republic plans gradually to replace its coal generation facilities with new hydroelectric plants, but the financing has not been secured for major construction efforts on these projects. To meet demands, construction of the hydroelectric facilities and associated transmission and distribution lines needs to be accelerated dramatically.

Low efficiency of the power plants is evident from high particulate emissions and high levels of unburned carbon in the fly ash. In some instances carbon content in the ash is near 40%. Power generated is bartered for coal and oil with Kazakhstan. Because of the low plant efficiency, an unnecessarily high amount of fuel is used for producing electricity, rather than for heating and transportation. Inefficient combustion also raises the costs of hot water and steam for district heating.

High carbon in the coal ash limits the ability of pollution control equipment to collect the ash. The high carbon content also makes the ash unsuitable for paving material or other uses; therefore, it must be disposed of in landfills.

Kyrgyzstan is seen as a strong candidate for clean coal technologies. As the economy strengthens, post-combustion control systems will be needed. Utilities are considering pulse-jet baghouses for particulate controls and coal cleaning technologies to reduce the sulfur content of local coals, although some local coals are naturally low in sulfur. Integrated gasification combined-cycle (IGCC) technologies are seen as a promising element in Kyrgyzstan's future. IGCC could provide a source of energy and raw materials to support

other industrial development within the country without substantial deterioration of the environment. Electricity, hot water, steam, gas, chemical feedstocks, and other materials could be derived from coal in a single integrated facility and distributed to existing industrial complexes, new greenfield sites, and to the population to replace use of coal and high-priced electricity.

Slovak Republic.

The Slovak electrical power plants of Bratislava generated 22,861 GWh of electricity in 1995. Of that, approximately 50% is credited to the nuclear power plant in Bohunice, which produced 11,437 GWh. Coal and gas plants produced 6,269 GWh or 27.4%. Hydroelectric power accounted for 22.5% at 5,155 GWh.

Forecasts predict electricity sales to increase by 1,700 GWh in 1996, but after-tax profits for the state utility are expected to drop, as the increase will include a 3,786 GWh increase in electricity imports.

In October 1994, the Slovakian government transformed the state-owned Slovensky Energeticky Podnick (SEP) into a joint stock company, Slovensky Elektrarne a.s. (SE a.s.). SE a.s. is the Slovakian power system which operates nuclear, thermal, and hydroelectric power plants and supplies about 85% of the nation's electric power. Three power distribution companies purchase power from SE a.s. and resell it to customers. Slovakia is in the midst of a total energy policy review, including a study of demand and load management, supply and generation options, impacts on the economy, and environmental policy. SE a.s. is working to complete a new nuclear plant, and is considering closing an older plant.

SE a.s. produces electricity in nuclear, thermal, and hydroelectric facilities, operates 400- and 220-kV transmission networks, and delivers electricity to the distributing companies. It has one 760-MW nuclear power plant, two thermal plants of 198 MW and 9,230 MW of hydroelectric facilities. Another 215 MW of capacity belongs to the distributing company. Total production is 23,400 GWh with a total installed capacity of 6,829 MW.

Annual electricity consumption per capita is 4,390 kWh. Industry consumes 53.5% of the total generation, residential consumption accounts for 43.6%, and transportation uses 2.9%. SE a.s. reports its power sources as: liquid fuel, 17.9%; coal, 36.4%; natural gas, 25.9%; nuclear power, 16.3%; hydroelectric, 1.9%; imports, 0.8%; new sources, 0.5%; and 0.3% from other sources.

SE a.s. reports major objectives of:

- maintaining the balance between generation and consumption,

- substantial reduction of negative impact of power generation on people and the environment,

- keeping electricity generation as economical as possible, and

- providing consumers with perfect services while striving to reduce power consumption.

It has an environmental improvement program which is focusing on reducing emissions. Specifically they are reducing particulate emissions through precipitator enhancement, implementing environmentally acceptable solid waste disposal from coal plants, using reliable radiation control for the nuclear power plant environment, and implementing cleaner production technologies in generation.

Estonia

is a small country on the southern Gulf of Finland coast of the Baltic Sea with a total area of 45,226 square kilometers and a population of 1.56 million. Installed capacity of the state utility, Eesti Energia, is 3,268 MW and the thermal capacity is 4,199 MW.

The energy system produces 99% electrical and 35% thermal energy in the republic, exporting 35% of the electricity to the neighbor states of Latvia and Russia. (Table 8–10) All of the nation's power is produced by thermal power plants. The largest power stations in Estonia are the 1,390-MWe Baltic Power Station and the 1,610-MWe Eesti Power Station. Both stations use the ground powder of oil shale for fuel.

Table 8–10
Latvia, Lithuania, Estonia

Latvia	
Installed capacity	2,021 MW
Hydro	74%
Thermal	26%
Total demand	6.4 TWh
Lithuania	
Installed capacity	5,929 MW
Thermal	44%
Nuclear	44%
Hydro	12%
Total generation	14.7 TWh
Estonia	
Installed capacity	3,268 MW
Thermal	100%

The Estonian government and the Ministry of Environment have been amending environmental legislation since the beginning of independence. A calculated, annual, minimal emission amount has been set for every pollutive substance.

Estonia is working to reduce sulfur emissions 50% by 1997. Its progress will depend on several factors, including the size of the electricity market and the opportunity of raising the sale price of electricity to make bigger investments into building sulfur-cleaning equipment. There is concern regarding the environmental effects of Estonia's use of oil shale to generate electricity.

Electricity generation is mainly through two thermal stations with a total capacity exceeding 3,000 MW. The Estonian plants are interconnected to the other Baltic nations, Belarus, and Northwestern Russia. There is a major need for energy efficient methods and products, and environmental restoration.

Latvia. As one of three Baltic States with Estonia and Lithuania that recently achieved freedom from Soviet domination, Latvia has struggled with its transition to independence. Latvia has had to compete with a new economic system and an electrical separation from the old, unified Soviet system. Demand for electricity has declined substantially over the last three years. Latvia has an installed capacity of 2,021 MW, with 74% of its power coming from hydroelectric sources and the other 26% coming from thermal sources. Electricity demand is 6.4 TWh.

Electricity is an urgent problem in Latvia because it does not have its own significant energy resources to supply its needs. The economy is fully dependent on foreign energy resources, so the energy crisis in Russia has caused a crisis in supply to Latvia. Of the Baltic States, only Latvia has an unfavorable electricity balance, as domestic generation covers only about one-half the total demand.

Lithuania has an installed capacity of 5,929 MW, of which 44% is thermal, 44% nuclear, and 12% hydroelectric.

Electricity production in 1993 was 14.7 TWh. Lithuania exported approximately 20% of the electricity it generated in 1993. Lithuanian officials are interested in increasing energy efficiency through price reforms and demand-side management programs. Many electricity consumers in this nation are not accustomed to receiving or paying an electric bill. Much of the country's electric system was designed to serve the needs of the former Soviet Union. Lithuania, like many other regional nations, is examining alternatives to its older or questionable nuclear facilities. Lithuania is working closely with Latvia and Estonia in a coordinated effort to share electricity resources and transmission and distribution assets.

CENTRAL AND EASTERN EUROPE

Romania. At the close of 1993, installed capacity of the Romanian Power System was 22,365 MW, of which 94% belonged to Renel. Formed in 1990, Renel manages the generation, transmission, and distribution of electricity in Romania. Renel has 8,588 MW of coal-fired capacity and 5,840 MW of hydroelectric power.

Gross electrical energy production in Renel's plants for 1993 was 53,846 GWh, a 2.87% increase from 1992. Electricity demand in Romania was 54.1 TWh in 1992.

As the second largest country in Central and Eastern Europe, Romania has a massive power generating and distribution system that was built to support a centrally planned economy. The transition to a market economy has presented major challenges to Romania and its utilities, including Renel. Despite the country's large generating capacity, the poor conditions of the thermal power plants, combined with fuel shortages and a lack of hard currency to buy fuel, have created problems. In the past, these led to the need for a fuel rationing system.

The future looks brighter, however, as Renel has commissioned a large nuclear plant. Romania is also planning to restore about 3,500 MW of thermal capacity by converting lignite plants to hard coal. Romania is working to make organizational and legal changes to its power sector, with a new electricity law and regulatory systems pending.

The development and rehabilitation program, which projects through the turn of the century, includes proposals to reduce pollution from the generating facilities in ever-lowering levels. Specific plans include restoring boilers, upgrading electrostatic precipitators, changing to low-NO_x burners, upgrading control systems, and converting to higher quality coals.

Bulgaria has an installed capacity of 12,074 MW and an available capacity of 8,700 MW, of which 53% originates at thermal facilities, 31% is from nuclear sources, and 16% is from hydroelectric sites. Electricity demand, as of 1993, was 38.2 TWh.

Bulgaria is working to implement a market-oriented economy, improve industrial sector performance, and tighten environmental protections. However, unlike most nations, power demand in Bulgaria has been dropping. The decrease in demand started in 1990 and total consumption of primary energy has decreased by

40% in comparison with 1989. After several years of decline, the recession seems to have abated. After a decline in gross domestic production and electricity demand of nearly 20%, the country is showing a turnaround and small increase. The country is highly dependent on imported energy, particularly of oil, gas, and coal. The electric system is based on nuclear and lignite/coal units. A major issue is the safety of the large nuclear power plant at Kozluduy. Bulgaria's Natsionalna Elektricheska Kompania is the state power company, handling generation, transmission, and distribution of electricity throughout the nation.

Czech Republic. The Czech Republic is a landlocked country in the heart of Europe with a population of 10.3 million and a territory of 79,000 square kilometers. Its key resources include hard coal and lignite, keolin, uranium, glass sands, and limestone. It is a highly industrialized country. CEZ, a public limited company, is the dominant generator in the republic, accounting for 78% of domestic generation in 1994. Total installed capacity of CEZ is 10,655 MW, of which 7,677 MW is coal-fired; 1,760 MW, nuclear; and 1,218 MW, hydropower. (Table 8–11) Eight regional electric power distribution companies were privatized in 1994. CEZ also sells electricity directly to six large industrial customers. It exported 2.0 TWh of electricity in 1994, mostly to Italy and Switzerland. CEZ owns and operates 10 large coal-fired plants, two nuclear plants, and 14 hydroelectric plants. It is also owner and operator of the Czech Republic's national high voltage power transmission grid which has 4,276 kilometers of 400- and 220-kV lines and a transformer capacity of 14,650 MVA. A downturn in the economy has led to decreasing electricity demand by about 15% between 1990 and 1993. In 1993, the electricity consumption demand reached its lowest point. It began growing again in 1994, with a 2.6% increase and grew again in 1995.

CEZ is working to reduce emissions in a variety of ways, including shifting generation responsibility from coal-fired plants to the nuclear ones, and using higher quality coals and improved emissions

Table 8–11
Centrel statistics

| Country | Beginning of 1995 | |
	Installed capacity (MW)	Peak load (MW)
Czech Republic	13,826	9,631
Hungary	7,317	5,700
Poland	33,171	22,050
Slovak Republic	6,935	3,778

These four nations comprise Central Europe, and their combined state utilities form Centrel.

reduction systems. Total investment costs of the air protection program between 1995 and 2000 for CEZ alone will represent approximately $600 million(US).

Macedonia seceded from Yugoslavia in 1991, but due to opposition of the use of the name Macedonia, the country's independence was not immediately recognized by much of the international community. In 1993, the nation was admitted to the United Nations as The Former Yugoslav Republic of Macedonia, and most of the international community recognized it. The Electric Power Co. of Macedonia is state owned and responsible for production, transmission, and distribution for the entire country. Macedonia has an installed capacity of 1,380 MW, of which 72% is thermal and 28% hydroelectric. Electricity demand in 1993 was 6.4 TWh.

Albania. The electrical power system of Albania was created in 1957. It has 20 electric power plants with an installed capacity of 1,670 MW. (Table 8–12) Some 11 of these plants are hydroelectric and nine are thermal, with 1,446 MW and 224 MW respectively. Productive capacity of the hydroelectric facilities varies from 3.5–4.8 to 7 billion kWh. There are 51 generating units, 29 of them hydrogenerators and 22 turbogenerators.

The most powerful sources of electricity are the three hydropower stations built on the cascade of

Table 8–12
Albanian power system statistics

Plant	# of Units	Output/Unit (MWh)	River Location
Hydropower Plants in the Albanian Power Systems			
Komani	4	150	Drin
Fierza	4	125	Drin
Vau I Dejes	5	50	Drin
Ulza	4	6.3	Mati
Shkopeti	2	12	Mati
Bistrica I	1	77	Bistrica
Bistrica II	1	5	Bistrica
Smokthina	2	4.5	Vijose
Bogova	1	2.3	Osum
Gjanci	1	3	Devolt
Lanabregas	2	2.5	Shkumbin
Total Hydropower Units	27		
Total Hydropower Output (MWh)	1,537.9		

Plant	# of Units	Output/Unit (MWh)	Fuel
Fossil and thermal Power Plants in the Albanian Energy System			
Ballshi	2	24	Gas-liquid fuel
Cerrik	3	8.5	Pulverized coal
Elbasan	3	6	Pulverized coal
Fier	6	159	Gas-liquid fuel
Korce	1	6	Pulverized coal
Maliq	3	7	Pulverized or grated coal
Tirana	2	4.9	Pulverized coal
Vlore	2	3	Grated coal
Kucove	2	5.6	Gas-liquid fuel
Total Fossil Power Units	24		
Total Fossil Power Output (MWh)	224		
Total Power Output-Solid Fuels	35.4		
Total Power Output-Liquid/Gas Fuels	188.6		

[Courtesy Unirex International Inc.]

the Drini River, the hydropower plants of Vau I Dejes, Kiomani and Fieza, with 250, 600, and 500 MW respectively. Their combined power is 80% of the installed power. The electric transmission network is 3,550 km long, with 1,150 km of 35-kV, 1,180 km of 110-kV, 1,100 km of 220-kV, and 120 km of 400-kV. Urban and rural distribution is composed of 31,200 km of 4-kV lines, 6,120 km of 6-kV lines, and 6,450 km of 10 kV lines. There are 185 high voltage substations, with a total installed power of 4,645 MVA.

Chapter 9

Middle East and Africa Electricity Supply

ANN CHAMBERS
ASSOCIATE EDITOR
POWER ENGINEERING INTERNATIONAL AND
POWER ENGINEERING

OVERVIEW

The Middle East and Africa are struggling to develop the electricity infrastructure to bring electricity to their rural areas and to the poorer urban areas. The Middle East seems to be a few paces ahead, at least in terms of installed capacity. Since this region is rich in oil, this resource serves as both a fuel for generation and a means of raising the necessary capital for construction.

(Table 9–1) Africa, on the other hand, has relatively small amounts of natural energy sources and the nations lack the capital to develop the costly infrastructure to expand electrical grids and capacity. (Table 9–2) A few African nations have excess capacity, but most have shortfalls. Even those that currently have excess will need more capacity if they develop their infrastructure to bring electricity to more of the unserved population.

Table 9–1

Middle East nation statistics

Country	Population (millions)	GDP (billion US$)	GDP growth (%)	Inflation rate (%)	Generation capacity	Electricity production (million kWh)
Iran	65	56.5	2.5	60	20.9 GW	70,000
Iraq	20.6	15	n/a	75-100	5 GW	25,700
Israel	5.4	70.1	4.9	10	4.3 GW	25,000
Jordan	4.1	17	6	5	1.1 GW	4,200
Kuwait	1.8	25.3	13.5	3	7.2 GW	11,500
Oman	2.1	11.7	5.1	1.3	1.5 GW	7,000
Qatar	0.5	10.7	3	1	1.6 GW	4,800
Saudi Arabia	n/a	118.5	2.5	5.1	18.4 GW	65,000
Syria	15	10.5	-3.7	20	4 GW	5,700

Table 9–2
African nation statistics

Country	Population (millions)	GDP (billion US$)	GDP growth (%)	Inflation rate (%)	Generation capacity	Electricity production (million kWh)
Algeria	28.5	97	2.9	33	5.8 GW	18,400
Angola	10.1	6.1	-1	20 monthly	620 MW	1,900
Congo	2.5	2.4	-2.2	30	162 MW	360
Egypt	62.8	40.6	5.3	8	14 GW	45,400
Gabon	1.4	3.4	3.4	25	300 MW	1,000
Libya	5.2	32.9	2.7	5-30	4.6 GW	16.1 TWh
Nigeria	101	49	2.3	60	5.1 GW	9,000
South Africa	42.8	61	2.3	9.1	40 GW	168,000

MIDDLE EAST

The nations of the Middle East are working to privatize at least portions of the power industry. While they are moving slower than some other areas, advances are being made. Many of these nations are working to diversify generation sources and to incorporate renewables into their generation mixes. Nuclear power is not a big contender in the Middle East, although there are a few nuclear plants sited there, and construction is under way on two more units.

More traditional fuels such as oil and gas are predominantly in use today. Iraq lags behind because much of its generation and transmission equipment was damaged or destroyed in the Gulf War. Several of these nations have stated commitments to the development of their electricity infrastructure and are backing those commitments with financing and cooperation of the private sector, and by cooperative agreements with neighboring countries. (Tables 9–3, 9–4, 9–5)

Iran hopes to raise its electrical generating capacity from 21 GW at present to 35 GW by 1998. A $1.4 billion(US), 2,090-MW plant in southern Iran is one major project under construction. However, U.S. sanctions may affect further progress on this project. China has agreed to provide four 325-MW generators for a new $700 million(US) plant in Arak. This project is expected to come on-line by 2000.

In mid-1995, Iranian officials stated their intent to build 10 nuclear power plants by 2015. The goal of the program would be the use of nuclear

Table 9–3
Electric power investments by region, 1995-2010

Type	(in billions of US dollars)		
	Middle East	Africa	World
Generation			
Solid fuel	2	27	734
Natural gas	27	16	298
Oil	2	6	29
Nuclear	0	0	129
Hydro/renewables	3	5	235
Subtotal	**34**	**54**	**1,426**
Transmission	4	12	200
Distribution	10	19	480
General	5	7	173
Subtotal	**18**	**38**	**854**
Total	**52**	**91**	**2,279**
Annual Average	3	6	152

Table 9–4
Projected cumulative investment in electric power for the Middle East and Africa, 1995-2010

(In billions of US dollars)				
	Electric Power Investment		Total Private	Electric Power
Region	Total	Official	Private	Investment	% of private $
Middle East	52	8	44	600	6.9
Africa	91	56	35	800	4.3
Total	143	64	79	1,400	n/a

energy to provide about 20% of the country's power needs. In January 1995, Iran took a major step toward attaining nuclear generating capability when Russia signed a $780 million(US) contract to complete the Bushehr nuclear power plant. Construction on this plant began in 1975, but halted after the 1979 Islamic revolution. The plant was 80% complete. The Russian deal calls for the

Table 9–5
Private investment in the Middle East and Africa

Region	Source	In billions of US dollars							
		1987	1988	1989	1990	1991	1992	1993	1994
Middle East and North Africa	Int'l. Private Debt	2.6	4.6	3.2	(2.2)	(0.7)	(0.8)	0.3	3.5
	Int'l. Portfolio Equity	0.0	0.0	0.0	0.0	0.0	0.0	0.0	0.3
	Foreign Direct Invest.	1.2	1.9	2.0	1.6	1.2	1.6	1.7	2.1
	Subtotal International	3.8	6.5	5.2	(0.6)	0.5	0.8	2.0	6.0
Sub-Saharan Africa	Int'l Private Debt	0.6	(0.2)	0.8	(1.0)	(1.2)	(1.4)	(2.6)	1.2
	Int'l Portfolio Equity	0.0	0.0	0.0	0.0	0.0	0.2	0.4	0.8
	Foreign Direct Invest.	1.4	1.1	2.5	0.1	1.9	1.8	1.8	2.2
	Subtotal International	2.0	0.9	3.3	(0.9)	0.7	0.5	(0.4)	4.2

completion of the two 1,300-MW, pressurized, light water units as well as the possible supply of two modern VVER-440 units. Preliminary work on the reactor began in early 1996.

Iran's current installed capacity is 20.9 GW with production of 70 billion kWh. Total energy consumption is 3.49 quadrillion Btus with a per capita consumption of 55.2 million Btus.

Iraq. Approximately 90% of Iraq's national power grid was destroyed during the Gulf War. Existing generating capacity of 9 GW in December 1990 was reduced to only 340 MW by March 1991. Roughly 85% of Iraq's 20 power stations were damaged or destroyed in the Gulf War. In early 1991, transmission and distribution infrastructure was also destroyed, including the 10 substations serving Baghdad and about 30% of the country's 400-kV transmission network. In 1991 the United Nations estimated that while it would cost $12 billion(US) to rebuild the entire national power grid, expenditures of only about $2 billion(US) would be required to restore half of the pre-Gulf War capacity. In early 1992, Iraq claimed that it had restarted 75% of the national grid. However, western estimates place Iraq's generation capacity in 1994 at 5,000 MW, or around 55% of the pre-Gulf War levels. Generation capacity is estimated at 5,000 MW with a total production of 25.7 billion kWh annually. Total energy consumption is 0.9 quadrillion Btu, or 46.7 million Btus per capita.

Israel has about 6.4 GW of installed capacity, with 2.6 GW accounted for by coal-fired plants,

2.2 GW by oil-fired units, and 1.6 GW by gas turbines. Israel's current long-term plan calls for building a fourth coal-fired plant, scheduled to come on-line in 1999 or 2000, at Ashkelon on the Mediterranean coastline. A possible fifth coal-fired station will be built sometime after that.

Besides coal and oil, future sources of electric generating capacity may include gas supplies, particularly from Egypt and/or the Persian Gulf region. Israel also is looking at its own indigenous resources, including oil shale from the Dead Sea region, as well as renewables, particularly solar power. As of late 1995, two Israeli companies were discussing the possible construction of a 100-MW solar power facility and the nation was negotiating a 150-MW shale oil-fired power plant. Nuclear energy is not considered an option for at least 20 years.

One area of potential regional cooperation involves integration of individual, national, power transmission grids into a regional power network. Such a network would, among other benefits, allow power companies to take advantage of differences in peak demand periods, reduce the need for installation and maintenance of reserve generating capacity, and provide outlets for surplus generating capacity. Israel and Jordan have tentatively agreed to link their grid in the near future, and have also discussed several proposed joint power stations, including a 100-MW wind farm and a 150-MW solar plant in the Arava desert.

Israel's installed capacity is around 4.3 GW with an annual production of 25 billion kWh. Total

energy consumption is 0.55 quadrillion Btus with a per capita consumption of 105 million Btus.

Jordan. In July 1995, energy ministers and officials from Turkey, Egypt, Jordan, Syria, and Iraq discussed a $590 million(US) project to link their electric power grids. According to at least one estimate, such a linkage could save Jordan up to $250 million(US) annually in investments and running costs to meet seasonal peak electric power demand. Plans for a $370 million(US) system linking the electricity networks of Jordan, Egypt, Israel, and Palestine also have been discussed.

As with other areas of its economy, Jordan is moving to privatize its electric power sector. In addition, Jordan hopes to diversify its electricity generation options by burning oil shale directly, instead of turning it into oil first. A feasibility study has concluded that this could be an economically viable operation. Jordan has an installed capacity of 1.1 GW with annual generation of 4.2 billion kWh.

Syria. In September 1993, President Asad declared that a secure supply of electricity was the right of every Syrian. Following this declaration, contracts were awarded for the construction of several new, gas-turbine power stations. These plants began coming on-line in late 1995, including a 600-MW station built by Japan's Mitsubishi Heavy Industries. In addition, eight 125-MW gas turbine plants are being built throughout the country. A 630-MW hydroelectric plant is under way. The Saudi Fund for Development has agreed to provide $200 million(US) in funding toward construction of a 1,000-MW steam power plant near Aleppo. Syria's Electricity Minister has announced plans to spend $2 billion(US) on energy investments.

Syria has an installed capacity of 4 GW with annual generation of 5.7 billion kWh, predominantly fueled by oil and gas, with about 25% hydroelectric.

Turkey. Increasing electricity generating capacity is a top priority for Turkish energy officials.

Electric power demand grew at an average 9.1% annual rate between 1980 and 1994, one of the fastest rates in the world. Turkey's Electricity Generating and Transmission Corp. (TEAS) expects national power consumption to more than triple by 2010 to 260 TWh, from 78.3 TWh now. This will require $45–50 billion(US) in new investments in the next decade. Build-own-transfer (BOT) projects are expected to play a major role in the restructuring of the Turkish power industry. The challenge for Turkish authorities is to reassure foreign lenders that the complex financing structures required for these projects will be honored and protected. Investors have balked at Turkish investment risk as a result of political uncertainties and over privatization laws. In November 1995, Turkey's first BOT contract, for a $1.6 billion(US) hydroelectric plant on the Euphrates River, was signed. Turkey's energy ministry plan for 24 lignite-fired units, 27 natural gas-fired units, 21 coal-fired plants, two nuclear power plants, and 113 hydroelectric units. Although estimates are that geothermal power in Turkey could amount to 31.5 GW, little progress has been made on exploiting that potential. Also, plans to build the country's first nuclear plant have run into public opposition.

In January 1994, Turkey reached an agreement with Iraq, Egypt, Jordan, and Syria to build a common electricity grid, expected to be in place in 1998. In November 1995, the European Investment Bank agreed to lend Turkey funding for the project, with calls for construction of a 115-mile transmission line from Aleppo in northern Syria to the Attaturk dam in southeastern Turkey. Turkey has announced plans to spend $715 million(US) on electric power projects in 1996. Much of the government's spending allotment will go to electricity generation, with about one-fourth earmarked for transmission needs and miscellaneous equipment.

Capacity stood at 20,951 MW at the close of 1995, and the government hopes to increase capacity to 21,217 by the end of 1996. (Table 9–6) The government of Turkey issued Decree No. 96/8007 on April 17, 1996, defining a new tariff for excess energy sales and wheeling charges. The new regulations encourage increased self-generation of power or autogeneration, as well as movement of energy to primary end-users such as textile, paper, steel, petrochemical, and ceramics manufacturers.

Table 9–6
Turkey statistics

Population (million)	63.4
Gross Domestic Product	$305.2 billion(US)
GDP Growth Rate	7%
Inflation Rate	94%
Generating Capacity	20.3 GW
Electricity Generation	75,000 million kWh
coal	44%
hydroelectric	37%
oil	14%
natural gas	5%

Turkish industrialists continue to consider autogeneration as a viable power supply option, given expectations of a projected power shortage starting toward the end of next year. Turkey's Ministry of Energy & Natural Resources (MENR) drafted the new regulation to motivate industrial investors to establish their own power generation facilities. The stimulus for self-generation stems from changes in Turkey's excess electricity tariff regulations. Previously, the sale price of electric power was set at 60% of the Turkish Electricity Distribution Co.'s (TEDAS) average price for hydropower plants and 65% for thermal facilities. Now, the price of excess capacity from autoproducers has been boosted to 70% of average after surcharges are deducted.

Changes in wheeling rates are another advantage of the new regulations—the old, fixed-percentage charge has been replaced with a distance-based scale starting at 6% for plants within the same region and ending at 17% for plants 600 km or more from their end-users. The government's goal is to foster badly needed power projects, and it hopes that energy savings of 15–20% will tempt Turkey's large private-sector holdings to singly or jointly establish large cogeneration plants serving several manufacturing facilities.

Autoproducers in Turkey commonly create joint ventures. By working together, companies can increase generation profile requirements while adding flexibility for equipment selection and cycle optimization.

Revised regulations have made the economic viability of either wheeling or selling to the national power generation and transmission company (TEAS) a little more favorable to autoproducers. Also, for Turkey's industrial groups, there still are uncertainties relative to fuel supply. The fuel cost-to-kilowatt ratio could be a later risk in some projects.

To address this problem, the government of Turkey and Turkish firms have plans to invest more than $800 million(US) in various oil and gas projects in nearby Turkmenistan. Further, since 1994, the Algerian State Petroleum agency has been delivering liquefied natural gas (LNG) and liquefied petroleum gas (LPG) to Turkey.

Cogeneration in Turkey is set to continue its slow but steady growth during the next five years; during the second half of 1996, eight projects with 100 MW of installed capacity are moving forward. This type of infrastructure growth remains a driver in the country's quest for low-cost power.

AFRICA

South Africa, which covers less than 4% of the continent of Africa and has just more than 5% of its total population, supplies more than one-half of the total electricity generated on the continent. Key energy-sector goals in Africa include:

- fostering economic development through increased trade and investment,

- removing barriers to investment,

- transition to market economies,

- implementing environmental standards,

- encouraging efficient energy use, and

- diversifying energy sources.

South Africa produces 60% of Africa's electricity, but Central Africa contains 50% of the continent's hydroelectric potential. Growth in electric power demand is being driven by the exploding population, urbanization, and the growing industrial base. The urban power infrastructure is subject to frequent power outages and breakdowns in service.

The total population of Africa exceeds 590 million people, of which around 10% are connected to an electrical source. Throughout much of Africa less than 10% of the population has access to electricity. Grids are established in southern Africa, west Africa, and the Horn of Africa.

There are ongoing efforts to expand the use of renewable energy resources. A U.S. Department of Energy and Botswana Energy Ministry project recently set up a demonstration site in Manayana village, providing electricity for lighting, small appliances, and communication in homes, schools, and clinics. Egypt, Ethiopia, and the Red Sea coastal African nations have great wind-power potential. Africa's solar energy potential is equal to or better than that of the southwestern United States, with great potential for developing manufacturing jobs through this clean energy source. Senegal already has 2,500 homes with rooftop photovoltaic panels providing power for outside communication links and electricity.

Biofuels are being used to substitute crop residues for wood burning to protect remaining forests. Also, programs are under way to encourage growth of crops for energy use.

In 1993, more than 155,000 million kWh were sent out in South Africa, and Eskom, the South African utility, supplied more than 90% at an average price of 9.59¢/kWh. The electricity not supplied by Eskom came from industries and municipalities operating their own power stations, many of which also buy electricity in bulk from Eskom to supplement their self-generation. Eskom exports electricity to all neighbor states. Consumers are supplied via a national transmission grid of 238,964 kilometers of overhead lines and 5,841 kilometers of underground cables.

Coal is the main fuel for electricity generation. In 1993, approximately 94% of Eskom's generation came from its coal-fired stations. The remainder was supplied by Eskom's nuclear, hydro, pumped storage, and gas-turbine facilities. Eskom has a nominal capacity of 9,720 MW. Koeberg, South Africa's first nuclear power station, with a net maximum capacity of 1,840 MW, entered operation in 1984. During the past 20 years, electricity consumption increased at an average growth rate of 4.86%, slowing to around 2.5% in the last five years.

Eskom has eliminated costly voltage dips, which were once an ongoing problem, through a systemwide dip-proofing project. Prior to 1990, Eskom experienced many trips in its large power stations during voltage depressions in the auxiliary supply system. The dips, introduced by faults on the auxiliary system or the station's interconnected high voltage transmission network, interrupted the operation of auxiliary plants, causing units to be tripped.

Due to small amounts of reserve on the Eskom interconnected power system, loss of more than one 600-MW unit could result in severe deviations in system frequency. In 1990, Eskom introduced protection against voltage dips at its large power stations. The auto tripping and reclosing voltage dip-proofing system on the switchgear boards was removed and voltage dip-proofing inverters were installed. Before dip-proofing was introduced, a voltage-dip-related trip of a 600-MW unit occurred every 34 days, costing approximately $30,000(US) to restart the unit and $43,000(US) to replace the generation. The dip-proofing project is thought to have saved the utility approximately $3.42 million(US). The project cost $1.39 million(US).

Eskom operates what is reported to be the largest coal-fired power station in the world—Kendal Power Station, 60 miles east of Johannesburg. Opened in October 1994, the 4,116-MW station took 12 years to build. By the year 2000, Kendal is expected to meet the

electricity needs of more than 2.5 million households.

The Electric Power Research Institute of the United States and Eskom are forming an African Center for Essential Community Services (CECS) to bring more electrification and beneficial electrotechnologies to the people of Africa. Emphasis is particularly on those technologies that help supply clean water and improve health conditions. The CECS is working as a technology transfer mechanism to bring EPRI technology to sub-Saharan Africa. The local government has stated that the center is expected to be a key element in spreading rural electrification.

Renewable Energy for African Development (REFAD) has announced an agreement with the Department of Mineral and Energy Affairs of the government of South Africa to implement the first phase of a program to bring electricity from solar and other renewable resources to 4,000 households. This is expected to assist up to 20,000 people and to aid in building the needed educational and industrial capacity in South Africa. The multimillion-dollar first phase in South Africa will include the establishment of a credit facility to allow consumers to purchase up to 4,000 photovoltaic home power systems.

Benin has two central organizations charged with overseeing the generation and distribution of electricity. One—Societe Beninoise d'Electricite e d'Eau—has a total rated capacity of 28 MW, generating in the largest city—Contonou—burning gas, diesel oil, and fuel oil. The second—Communaute Electrique du Benin—is a binational venture with neighboring Congo purchasing and transmitting electricity from Ghana's Volta River Authority hydroelectric site. Small diesel facilities are scattered throughout the less-populated central and northern regions.

In 1993, Benin had a total electricity consumption of 260 GWh, with maximum loads exceeding 45 MW. The governments of Benin and Congo are considering construction of an Adjarala River hydroelectric plant, to be sited 97 km downstream from Nagbeto on the Mono River in Benin. This proposed 60-MW plant would include a dam, powerhouse, and related transmission lines.

Simple-cycle, gas-fired turbines are a top contender for this market, because they are considered a relatively clean technology. Benin is considering taking some debt equity in power projects, and the country is viewed favorably by both the World Bank and the U.S. Export-Import Bank.

Botswana has announced plans for Mmamabula, a coal-fired power plant. The first phase, consisting of two 600-MW units, is expected to come on-line as soon as 1998, with plans for this station to eventually double to 2,400 MW. Botswana plans to use conventional, pulverized, coal-fired boilers with air-cooled, mechanical, draught condensers. Fuel would be coal from the Mmamabula coal fields. The government is considering some equity financing.

Botswana currently has an installed capacity of 197 MW. Approximately 75% of the total electricity in this country is used by the copper and diamond mining industries.

The country is developing an extended rural-electrification strategy, with ongoing projects being extended to serve the needs of farmers in the Tuli Block on the Limpopo River.

Congo has an electrical generation capacity of around 160 MW. Hydropower is the predominant method of generation. In particular, the 74-MW Bouenza and the 15-MW Djou hydroelectric plants have served as the mainstays of Congo's power generating capacity since 1980. Congo is a net electricity importer. According to recent government estimates, the country purchases approximately 37% of its requirements from Zaire's state-owned SNEL.

In August 1995, the government launched a three-year, $312 million(US) program to raise Congo's generating capacity to 412 MW and alleviate its dependence on imports. With this program, the government hopes to provide electricity to 56% of the country's population, up

from the present 27%. Congo's capacity expansion plan includes renovation of the Djou plant. However, it is the $925 million, 1-GW Sounda Gorge hydroelectric project which could make Congo a significant regional exporter of electricity. Presently, a three-phased construction plan is under way at the Limpopo River site, located 85 miles north of Pointe Noire.

The $50 million(US) first phase will include installation of two axial bulb turbines by late 1997. These turbines will be capable of supplying 10 MW and will be used to generate cash flow for subsequent phases. The second phase will involve construction of a 130-foot-high dam which will boost the plant's generating capacity to 240 MW. A third phase will increase the dam's height to more than 300 feet and its generating capacity to 1 GW. However, feasibility studies for the third phase are still in progress and financing remains an issue.

Congo currently has a capacity of 162 MW with annual production of 360 million kWh. Total energy consumption is 0.02 quadrillion Btu with a per capita consumption of 8.3 million Btus.

Egypt has installed generating capacity of 14,000 MW, with plans to add an additional 3,000 MW by 2000. A 1,200-MW, gas-fired power plant is under construction at Kureimat. A $200 million(US) grant from the U.S. Agency for International Development will provide financing for Kureimat as well as several other projects to modernize the electricity network. Two 60-MW, wind-powered plants are under construction in Zaafarna on the Gulf of Suez. Contracts have been awarded for 650-MW, gas-fired power plants at Sidi Kerir and Ayun Musa, with the facilities scheduled to enter operation in 1999 and 2000, respectively.

The Electricity and Energy Minister has announced that three build-operate-transfer (BOT) projects will be offered to investors. The BOT projects will be used to fund large-scale public infrastructure without affecting the country's debt profile. The private developers will be allowed to recover their construction costs through operation of the plant for a fixed period before handing it over to the state. The first BOT to be considered is a 200-MW, wind-powered plant at Zaafarna. The second will be a 600-MW, pumped, storage plant on the Gabal Galala plateau, above the Suez. The final will be a 650-MW, thermal-power plant at a site yet to be determined.

The 650-MW BOT will probably be gas-fired as Egypt has undertaken an aggressive campaign to convert existing thermal generation from oil to natural gas. Gas currently accounts for 80% of the hydrocarbon-fired electricity generation, and Egypt plans to increase that to 90% in a couple of years. Egypt also is working to connect its grid into a regional grid to include Jordan, Syria, Turkey, and Iraq, and in a separate project, to connect its grid with those of Jordan, Israel, and the Palestinian self-rule areas. Local companies are constructing a connection between Egypt and Libya. North Africa's power grids will be interconnected when the Egypt-Libya and Libya-Tunisia links are completed.

Malawi. All baseload electricity in Malawi comes from hydroelectric plants operated by Eskom, the electrical supply commission. Its gas turbines and diesel units are for standby use only. In 1991, Malawi's hydro capacity was 146 MW; thermal units added another 23 MW. Another 2 MW of diesel are sited in the northern tip of the country, and self-generators are estimated to have 24 MW of capacity from steam plants, diesels, and two small hydro stations.

Malawi is looking to build Kapachire Hydroelectric Power Project, with a planned commissioning date of 1998. The project includes a dam at the head of the Kapachire Falls, a power tunnel bypassing the falls, and a surface power house set in a deep tailrace channel. The powerhouse will accommodate four 32-MW units. The 128-MW project is expected to be financed through a combination of World Bank, other investment banks, and government funding.

Morocco is planning to convert Kenitra and Mohammedia power plants from No. 2 fuel oil to natural gas. Kenitra has four 75-MW units and

Mohammedia has two 150-MW units and three 33-MW units. The plants would use gas from the Maghreb-European pipeline.

Rural Morocco is almost totally without electricity, but the Office National de L'Electricity (ONE) is working to extend service to 2,000 villages. Three 100-MW combustion turbines are being completed, and an expansion of eight 330-MW units is being planned for Jorf Lasfar station. The government has announced plans to spend $1 billion(US) on the power sector in 1996 and has invited the private sector for equity-participation.

Tanzania's electricity is primarily hydroelectric power, and the country is experiencing generation shortfalls in drought or dry weather conditions. Some diesel-powered units are available, but they are expensive to operate and drain the country's foreign exchange reserves. The government is exploring plans to use its indigenous coal to generate electricity. Tanzania has coal reserves estimated between 200 and 300 million tons. The government wants to build a 400-MW thermal station, near the Mchuchuma/Katewaka coal field.

Tanzania is a light electrical consumer with an installed capacity of 482 MW, of which 445 MW is in the interconnected grid system and 37 MW in isolated generating stations. The grid transmits 328 MW of hydroelectric power and 117 MW of diesel power.

Zambia is looking to expand its hydroelectric capacity through Kafue Gorge Lower Hydroelectric Plant. Hydroelectricity is the leading source of power in Zambia. It has seven hydroelectric facilities, totaling more than 1,670 MW, and these have made the Zambia Electricity Supply Corp. an exporter of electrical power. The main stations are: Kafue Gorge Upper, 900 MW; Kariba North, 600 MW; and Victoria Falls, 108 MW.

The proposed Kafue Gorge Lower Hydroelectric Project would be sited in the Kafue Gorge, about 65 kilometers south of Lusaka, the capital of Zambia. The Kafue River drops about 600 meters in a distance of 30 kilometers to join the Zambezi River below the Kariba Dam. The upper 400 meters of this was developed in 1976 to produce the Kafue Gorge Upper site. The proposed project would use the remaining 200 meters of available head.

Zimbabwe is planning to upgrade Hwange Power station, its largest coal-fueled station. It is a minemouth power plant with four 110-MW units and two 220-MW units, with a total nameplate-rated capacity of 980 MW. Power is delivered to the country's transmission system through a 330-kV transmission interconnection. The Zimbabwe Electric Supply Authority (ZESA) has sole responsibility for generation, transmission, and distribution of electricity there.

Chapter 10
Asia and Pacific Electricity Supply

MICHAEL T. BURR
SENIOR EDITOR
INDEPENDENT ENERGY

OVERVIEW

The past several years of economic growth in Asia have resulted in power consumption that is quickly outstripping the supply capabilities of current power systems across much of the region. The result is regular brownouts and inadequate power capacity to support expansion of industrial growth. This impairs the sustainability of economic growth, and can have a significant effect on development.

Power supply levels vary widely in Asia. (See Table 10–1.) South Korea is relatively well off, with an installed capacity of 36,000 MW, providing the Thai people with 2,460 kilowatt hours (kWh) per capita annually. For comparison, conditions are not as good in Indonesia, with 200 kWh per capita, while Pakistan, with 122 million people, has about 13,000 MW of capacity on-line, generating just 30 kWh annually per capita. (See Figure 5–1.)

Table 10–1
Asia power profile

Country	Tariff (cents/kWh)	Load Factor	System Losses (%)
China	2.78	N/A	12.9
Indonesia	5.80	67.4	20.4
Korea	7.61	71.2	10.2
Philippines	7.61	71.2	23.1
Thailand	7.05	69.5	13.6
Bangladesh	6.34	58.5	36.2
India	4.88	55.0	28.6
Nepal	3.70	48.3	29.1
Pakistan	4.99	64.5	22.8
Sri Lanka	5.80	56.0	17.2

[Courtesy World Bank]

The Asian region is expected to require 150,000 MW of new capacity through the year 2000, and 465,000 MW through 2005. (See Table 5–1.) This would more than double the current installed capacity of about 500 GW. Through 2000, this would require installing the equivalent of 123 projects on the scale of the 1,220-MW Paiton II project in Indonesia, or 3.4 such projects a month for the next three years. Through 2000, 381 Paiton

IIs would be necessary, with four of the plants a month through 2005. At the plant's $1.4 million per-megawatt installed cost, such expansion would require investment of $210 billion by 2000, or $5.8 billion a month for the next three years.

Figure 10–1. Estimated power investment requirements, 1995

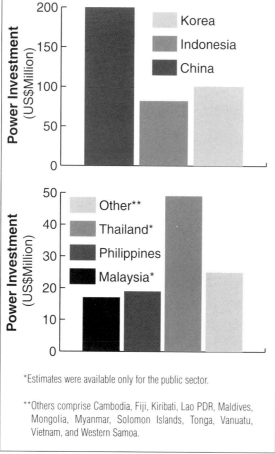

*Estimates were available only for the public sector.

**Others comprise Cambodia, Fiji, Kiribati, Lao PDR, Maldives, Mongolia, Myanmar, Solomon Islands, Tonga, Vanuatu, Vietnam, and Western Samoa.

[Courtesy World Bank]

These financing requirements far exceed governments' resources, and thus are unlikely to be met under existing power industry structures and with current sources of funds. (See Figure 10–1.) To facilitate the flow of funds from the international financial community, Asian nations are adopting policies to attract private investment by international developers and lending institutions. Governments are creating regulatory and economic frameworks to support a commercial, private power industry. However,

international private power financing during 1995 totaled $11 billion, just 6.4% of the estimated $70 billion annual need.

In any case, pouring such enormous foreign investment into the economies of countries already struggling to manage high economic growth rates would spur a sudden increase in demand for all manner of goods, services, and infrastructure. Hyperinflation likely would result, as industrial, commercial, manufacturing, and infrastructure sectors were strained beyond their ability to keep up. Indeed, for those runaway-train economies in danger of overheating, suppressed power supply has been viewed as a necessary coolant. For example, in the People's Republic of China the government has approached capacity expansion plans with caution, fearing that abrupt power system expansion would derail efforts to control inflation. Now, as inflation figures have stabilized and economic growth has slowed to a more manageable pace, the State Planning Commission is beginning to break the logjam of projects waiting for central government approvals.

PROJECT FINANCING

The private power industry's ability to meet countries' expectations relies largely on resolving a number of political, regulatory, and economic questions. Many countries have stated ambitious intentions to reform and privatize their power industries and encourage independent power development. In many cases, however, official policies regarding private power have been vague, seeming to shift along with the political winds. As a result, independent power producers (IPPs) have been financed in only a handful of countries, and many such financings have occurred only after years of negotiation—and at a cost considerably higher than similar projects in developed countries.

As a practical matter, financing costs are higher in countries where higher levels of risk are perceived. Power off-takers in Asia are usually

state-owned utility companies, which for decades have been burdened with unrealistic rate structures and inadequate financing. As a result, such entities are often in poor financial shape, and thus are not strong enough to satisfy the lending criteria of commercial lenders. Consequently, financing costs are higher for commercially financed IPPs, and thus power rates are also higher—often higher than utilities themselves are able to collect from customers. Of course, the subsidized power supplies typically provided by Asian state-owned utilities are often sold below the cost of production, and thus provide an unfair basis for comparison with commercially produced power.

Regulatory structures and policies vary widely from country to country. Nevertheless, clear progress has been made in Asia toward increased private-sector participation across a range of industries traditionally controlled by government entities. As a result, private power has met considerable success in some Asian markets. Countries where private power has become well-established include the Philippines and Malaysia, where numerous IPPs either are operating or are in construction, and privately produced power represents a significant share of total capacity. Today, models for private power are developing quickly elsewhere in Asia, and projects have recently reached financing and begun construction in China, Hong Kong, Indonesia, India, and Pakistan.

The tallest hurdle for most projects involves achieving financeability. Ensuring the creditworthiness of the power purchaser, mitigating exchange rate risks, and forging sound contracts are all central to establishing a financially viable project. Developers are faced with the difficulty of building a contractual framework that will take the place of government ownership. Where these issues have been adequately addressed, a growing number of options exist for financing projects in Asia. Major sources of debt financing include: multilateral and bilateral development agencies, such as the ADB and the International Finance Corp. (IFC) of the World Bank Group; export credit agencies, especially the

Export-Import Bank of the United States (U.S. Exim) and the Japan Export-Import Bank (JEXIM); commercial lenders, including banks, institutional investors, and large trading companies from Europe, Japan, the United States, and Australia; and the U.S. and international capital markets.

Additionally, a number of investment vehicles have been formed to finance infrastructure in Asian markets, including: Global Power Investments, a fund led by GE Capital of Stamford, Connecticut, and George Soros Fund Management of New York; investment consortia sponsored by Hong Kong's Peregrine Ltd., American International Group (AIG), and Goldman Sachs; publicly traded development groups launched by AES Corp. of Arlington, Va., Sithe Energies Inc. of New York, and Hong Kong-based Hopewell Holdings Ltd. AES China Generating Co. Ltd. and Sithe/China Holdings Ltd., subsidiaries formed to develop projects in China, are both publicly traded in U.S. stock markets, and have become involved with several projects in China. Hopewell's venture, Consolidated Electric Power Asia (CEPA), was spun off as a holding company for Hopewell's power assets, and has been very active developing projects in the Philippines, Indonesia, and elsewhere. The company is publicly traded in the Hong Kong stock exchange. Additionally, California Energy Co. Inc. issued senior discount notes totaling nearly $530 million in 1994 to fund its geothermal development activities, primarily in Indonesia and the Philippines. A number of quasi-public financings in the international bond markets have followed for projects in the Philippines.

It is unclear how private power projects will be financed over the long term, as governments run out of credit to guarantee the power sales commitments of noncreditworthy utilities. Multilateral guarantee agencies such as the Asian Development Bank (ADB) and the World Bank, as well as export credit agencies, have begun providing significant credit support for projects, but their guarantee capacity may prove inadequate to meet the rising financing needs of a fast-growing power sector.

As power industries are restructured and privatized in Asia, more utility companies are expected to become creditworthy. Also, as market reforms come to fruition, Asian power industries will be more able to support commercial financing of the type that has served to build the private power industries of such countries as the United States and the United Kingdom. Already, the amount of international commercial financing flowing into Asian power industries is increasing significantly from its level only a few years ago.

Even now, however, the power industry must compete with other infrastructure sectors for a slice of the commercial financing pie. (Figure 10–2) Commercial debt funds are beginning to flow into Asia's power markets from institutional investors and public debt and equity markets, and the contribution of these areas is expected to increase as commercial financing conditions improve and as investors become more familiar with the markets and the risks they present. These sources of financing are indeed vast, with the combined resources of numerous pension funds, insurance companies, and multinational trading companies, as well as the broader public capital markets. Their appetite for power project debt in emerging economies, however, is not as large as the power sector needs it to be.

The conclusion of these facts is inescapable: Eventually, domestic financing resources must

increase to fund project development. Toward this end, multilateral development agencies are funding projects to create capital markets in countries across Asia, and governments are beginning to support policies intended to increase the amount of domestic funds available to finance infrastructure development.

Malaysia provides an example of a country with capital markets that are well-enough developed to support the country's private power development activities. Local capital markets are emerging in other countries as well, including Thailand, India, Indonesia, and the Philippines. The Philippines is relatively advanced in this regard, having financed a geothermal power project in late 1995 with entirely domestic, commercial-debt funds. Uncertainty remains, however, regarding whether these markets will become large enough or mature enough to provide adequate financing for the infrastructure requirements of these fast-growing economies.

REFORM AND PRIVATE PARTICIPATION

Numerous questions remain unanswered regarding regulatory procedures, ownership issues, and financing. The complexity of resolving these questions, while trying to address the power demands of a growing industrial sector, has been a primary cause of the delays and difficulties of bringing additional power supplies on-line in Asia. Private power is a new idea for most governments, and leaders are struggling to develop coherent policies and strategies for creating a private power industry.

On an individual project level, the challenge for developers is to persevere through the painstaking process of forging viable regulatory structures. To assist this effort, project sponsors continue to focus considerable effort on communicating the rationale behind private power, project financing, and firm power sales agreements. At the same time, developers find themselves balancing on the

Figure 10–2. Infrastructure investment in Asia, 1995-2004

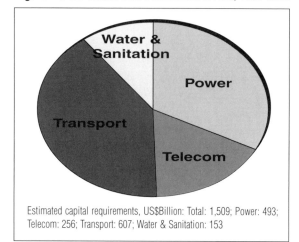

Estimated capital requirements, US$Billion: Total: 1,509; Power: 493; Telecom: 256; Transport: 607; Water & Sanitation: 153

[Courtesy World Bank]

fine line between educating government officials and telling them what to do. Success in this endeavor requires sensitivity, skill, and patience in countries where achievements are measured in decades and centuries, rather than quarters and fiscal years.

To date, most private power activity in Asia has consisted of development of greenfield projects. That is changing, however, as countries begin restructuring their electricity sectors and tapping private capital sources to finance new investment. In some cases, utility services are unbundled, with the constituent groups sold off in pieces—through stock flotations, sales to private investors, or a combination of the two. In other instances, utility assets are privatized, with some individual utility plants, or projects are offered for sale to private companies.

SOLICITATION SYSTEMS

Most private power projects in construction or operation in Asia today were awarded using direct-negotiation methods. Now, however, competitive bidding is beginning to emerge as a preferred method of procuring new private power capacity in Asia. Some countries beginning to use competitive bidding processes to select IPPs include China, India, Indonesia, Korea, Pakistan, the Philippines, Taiwan, and Thailand. Additionally, nations planning to use competitive IPP solicitation processes in the future include Bangladesh, Kazakhstan, and Malaysia.

The need to satisfy the requirements of development banks and export credit agencies are major forces driving Asian countries toward competitive bidding. Additionally, power planners are attracted by the downward pressure competition exerts on prices. In Malaysia, for example, the first independent power procurement process was based on direct negotiation, because the country was facing severe power constraints. In the future, however, the government expects to employ competitive bidding. In fact, the country has already

used competitive bidding for projects in the Sabah region, and prices have dropped as a result.

The success of competitive bidding programs in Asia has been mixed so far, with solicitations in only a few countries resulting in projects that proceed to financial closing. On the other hand, direct-awarded projects have faced controversy and encountered severe delays. Time will tell whether open, competitive bidding systems are the best alternative for meeting power supply needs in Asia.

FUEL USE

A majority of Asia's electric power is generated by coal-fired stations, with considerable hydropower, oil-, and gas-fired resources. Power-sector regulatory reforms are expected to increase the amount of natural gas used in many Asian nations. The U.S. Energy Information Administration (EIA) projects natural gas-fired generation will grow by 5% each year in non-OECD (Organization of Economic Cooperation and Development) countries, providing nearly 20% of generation by 2015. Coal is expected to remain dominant, however, and will likely increase its share of overall generation in Asia by 5% per year, to provide more than one-third of generation by 2015.

Considerable equipment sales have been evident in Asia during the past few years. Turbine equipment totaling almost 90,000 MW of generating capacity was imported into Asian markets since January 1, 1994. (See Tables 10–2, 10–3, and 10–4, and Figures 10–3, 10–4, and 10–5.)

Table 10–2
Asia turbine sales by region

	GT Units	ST Units	Total Units	GT MW	ST MW	Total MW
China	16	30	46	895	15254.75	16149.75
East Asia	151	93	244	15082.35	26379	41461.35
South Asia	41	18	59	1634	1979	3613
SE Asia	111	45	156	8510	10329.4	18839.4
Other	27	34	61	3159	6621	9780
Total Asia	346	220	566	29280.35	60563.15	89843.5

Table 10–3
Turbine equipment sales in Asia

	GT Units	ST Units	Total Units	GT MW	ST MW	Total MW
ABB	32	NA	32	5277	NA	5277
Siemens	18	12	30	1800	3000	4800
GE PS	20	40	60	4841	12836	17677
GE MIE	40	NA	40	1180	NA	1180
GEC Alsthom	77	39	116	3040	10730	13770
Westinghouse	36	17	53	3350	5492	8842
Mitsubishi HI	60	107	167	8448	16267	24715
Toshiba International	NA	NA	0	1078	12122	13200
US Turbine	10	NA	10	42	NA	42
Allison Engine	42	NA	42	199	NA	199
Mitsui Engineering	11	5	16	25.35	116.15	141.5
	346	220	566	29280.35	60563.15	89843.5

Table 10–4
Asia turbine sales by export region

	GT Units	ST Units	Total Units	GT MW	ST MW	Total MW
China						
European Companies	8	14	22	574	7870	8444
US Companies	8	11	19	321	4790	5111
Japanese Companies	0	5	5	0	2594.75	2594.75
East Asia						
European Companies	77	18	95	7305	2420	9725
US Companies	62	29	91	6169	9971	16140
Japanese Companies	36	50	86	4194.35	14558	18752.35
South Asia						
European Companies	18	7	25	822	335	1157
US Companies	23	4	27	812	547	1359
Japanese Companies	0	7	7	0	1097	1097
Southeast Asia						
European Companies	47	16	63	3762	3675	7437
US Companies	44	11	55	1742	2841	4583
Japanese Companies	20	18	38	3006	3813.4	6819.4

A country-by-country analysis of major power supply markets in the Asia/Pacific region follows:

Australia.

Total generating capacity in the Australian electricity industry is just under 36,500 MW, with coal accounting for 72.9% of primary energy consumption, hydropower accounts for

Figure 10–3. Asia turbine equipment sales — market share — gas turbines

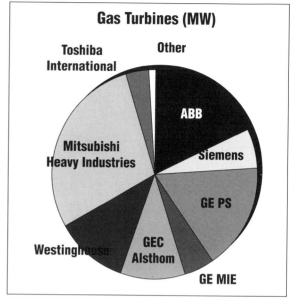

20.3%, and natural gas for 5.6%. Australia has reliable, low cost power. Competition is advanced in electricity markets, and international utilities and independent power producers are encouraged to compete in this market. Privatization and deregulation are now a reality, offering companies investment opportunities. Electricity reforms have been initiated in all Australia's states. There is considerable variation in the generation systems of each Australian state considering total installed capacity, number of units, plant type, size, and age. These variations can be explained by differences in each state's fuel sources and the historical development of electricity supply industries.

Victoria: Victoria has about 18% of Australia's generating capacity, which is sourced from low-grade brown coal, natural gas from the Bass strait, and some hydropower. Victoria's electricity supply industry is implementing the most competitive measures. The integrated system has been split into separate distribution, generation, and transmission systems with distribution and generation being privatized. Generation Victoria is responsible for its own state-owned power generation assets. Victoria Power Exchange manages the central coordination and control of

Figure 10–4. Asia turbine equipment sales — market share — steam turbines

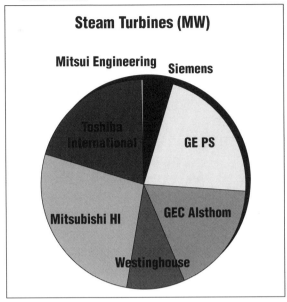

Figure 10–5. Asia turbine equipment sales — market share — total turbines

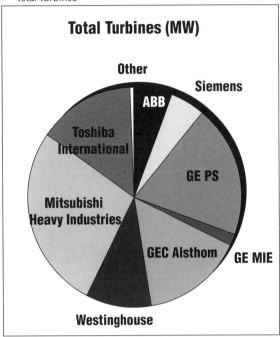

the electricity system, and Powernet Victoria maintains the high voltage transmission grid.

The five new generation businesses are the coal-fired plants at Loy Yang-A, Yallourn-W, and Hazelwood, two gas-fired plants at Newport and Jeeralang, and the hydroelectric stations at Kiewa, Dartmouth, and Eildon/Rubicon/Cairncurran.

Victoria introduced private sector involvement in generation with the sale of 51% of the Loy Yang B Power Station in 1994 to Edison Mission Energy Co. of Irvine, California, for $1.9 billion(US). Tariff reforms were announced with immediate effect to some customers and an open competitive market structure by the year 2000. A second generation company, Yallourn-W, was sold early in March 1996 to M.K. Co. Powergen, and later, Hazelwood, Loy Yang-A, and the hydroelectric plants will be sold.

The 30-year-old, low cost, 1,600-MW Hazelwood Power Station is next on the block and could be sold as early as August 1996, fetching up to $1 billion(US). The plum asset, however, is the Loy Yang-A generator, which may bring up to $3 billion(US), and transmission company, Powernet Victoria, could sell for $1.8 billion(US). Additionally, the state's five distribution companies were sold to U.S. utilities and their consortia.

New South Wales: NSW has about 32% of Australia's generating capacity. Reforms in NSW have focused on the separation of Pacific Power's generation and transmission corporations. The NSW electricity supply is less vertically integrated than Victoria. Electricity transmission and generation were under the control of Pacific Power Corp.—previously the Electricity Commission of NSW. Pacific Power's total generating capacity is 11,512 MW, excluding NSW's entitlement to the Snowy Mountains hydropower.

Currently there is little private-generation capacity in NSW, though Sithe Energies of New York and Broken Hill Proprietary (BHP) of Australia have begun construction of a 160-MW cogeneration plant at Smithfield, and Energy Developments Ltd. is involved in a small-scale generation of 4-MW, landfill, gas-fueled power plant, and a proposed 90-MW, coal-steam, methane power plant at the BHP Coal Mine at Appin.

Queensland: Electricity generation in Queensland was undertaken by the Queensland Electricity Commission (QEC), which is estimated

to have produced 29,800 GWh of electricity from 1993 to 1994. The QEC has been split into two divisions—Austa Electric for generation, and The Queensland Transmission and Supply Corporation (QTSC) to operate generation and transmission and distribution (T&D) businesses of the QEC.

Generation is principally from coal-fired power stations with some hydropower, gas turbines, and oil-fueled generators. QEC operates 14 power stations in all, constituting about 17% of Australia's generating capacity.

The Queensland model for reform was to introduce competition into generation with the $500 million(US) sale of the Gladstone Power Station to a consortium led by Comalco and NRG Energy. Collinsville Power Station also is owned by NRG and Transfield. Private sector involvement has increased with Sithe Energies announcing its intention to build a cogeneration power plant, and Energy Equity's plans for a gas-fired facility at Barcaldine. More recently, Pacific Gas & Electric has purchased the state's pipeline.

The state is currently considering supply options for new generating capacity required from 1998. The following projects will help meet the state's electricity demand through the year 2006. Recommissioning of Collinsville-1 (180 MW) and Callide-A (120 MW), and interconnection with the New South Wales east link (500 MW); 440 MW of peaking capacity, with at least 110 MW at Townsville, and the remainder in Central and Southern Queensland; 600 MW and up to 1,400 MW of baseload capacity in Southern or Central Queensland

South Australia: South Australia constitutes 6.5% of Australia's total generating capacity. The Electricity Trust of South Australia (ETSA) is a vertically integrated, publicly owned utility that generates, transmits, and distributes electricity throughout South Australia. Baseload electricity is produced in steam-cycle plants fired by coal or natural gas. While it produced 8,900 GWh of electricity from 1993 to 1994, South Australia also imported 1,500 GWh from Victoria. Under current demand forecasts, a new plant to provide peaking capacity will be required this year. A special

industry task force has been set up to examine reforms within the state.

Snowy Mountains: With about 10.3% of Australia's capacity, the 3,740-MW Snowy Mountains Scheme (SMS) represents a vital part of Victoria and New South Wales' electricity supply arrangements. An average annual energy production of 5,130 GWh is supplied by seven generating stations, providing a significant proportion of the State Energy Commission of Victoria's (SECV) and Pacific Power's peak demand, particularly in the winter months.

Tasmania: Tasmania's generating capacity is about 6% of Australia's total. The Hydro-Electric Commission of Tasmania (HEC) launched a major commercialization program in March 1992, and was split into six business units. Construction of large hydropower stations has been completed in Tasmania. Issues such as the introduction of gas from Bass Strait and the $350 million(US) Basslink proposal are high on the agenda. The state concluded that annual benefits totaling $95 million(US) would accrue should Basslink be given the go-ahead. The Basslink will allow Tasmania to source baseload power from Victoria via a single, 300-MW, underground cable on the national grid. It will also allow Tasmania to supply the east coast of Australia with peaking capacity.

Western Australia: Currently, Western Australia generates about 7.2% of Australia's capacity. The State Energy Commission of Western Australia (SECWA) has been broken up into two independent specialist units—Western Power and Alintagas. The two only have been corporatized at this stage, but they may be privatized by the end of the decade. The extension of the Collie Power Station is expected to add about 10% to the state's present capacity, and further production of electricity will result from future use of gas-fired power stations and interstate energy trading.

Bangladesh. Most of Bangladesh's existing 2,500 MW of capacity is hydropower, with some natural gas. The state-owned Power Development Board (PDB) was incorporated last year into the Power Cell within the Energy of Ministry, with the

goal of reforming the country's power structure to encourage private investment.

The Bangladesh government opened the power sector to private investment in 1995, and has since signed 11 agreements with developers to build nearly 1,000 MW of new capacity. A number of plant expansion projects are being implemented, including China National Machinery and Equipment Import & Export Corp.'s construction of the second generating unit of the Rauzan power plant in Chittagong.

A number of power sector projects are in development in Bangladesh, including a 300-MW, Meghnaghat combined-cycle project, to be developed under a build-operate-transfer (BOT) structure. A request for qualifications (RFQ) was issued for the project, located 20 kilometers outside the capital city of Dhaka. The Asian Development Bank has selected K&M Engineering and Consulting Corp. to provide technical assistance to the government of Bangladesh in structuring private sector participation for implementing the project. The project is expected to be developed for the Bangladesh Power Development Board (BPDB) on a BOO transfer structure, and will be awarded on a competitive basis.

The ADB is considering a $100 million loan for the Tenth Power Project, sponsored by the Bangladesh Power Development Board, the Dhaka Electricity Supply Authority, and the Rural Electrification Board. The ADB loan would fund transmission, distribution and substation equipment, and engineering design of a 60-MW, gas-fired, combined-cycle power plant to be located in the Mymensingh area. The project could eventually be expanded to provide 180 MW of capacity. The loan would also provide for expansion of distribution networks totaling about 2,900 km, and 50 MVa of substation capacity. The ADB is expected to provide $50 million of the loan, with other sources providing the rest.

Another project being considered by the ADB involves building the 1,500 km Indus Grid transmission system. The project includes the involvement of the United Kingdom's National Grid Co., and would require $730 million in financing. Equity would comprise about 28% of the project's financing, with ADB potentially providing $20 million, the project sponsors providing $104 million, and other investors providing $79 million. The ADB would provide $30 million in debt funds and $50 million of cofinancing, and political risk cover to support a $50 million syndicated commercial loan. The United Kindom's Export Credit Guarantee Agency (ECGD) would provide a political risk guarantee of $248 million, while other sources would provide $97 million in debt.

China. In addition to building new generating capacity, China is expanding its power grids and is refurbishing existing power plants to improve efficiency and availability. Total power generation in China during 1995 reached 1,070 billion kWh, with a total of 10,110 MW of large- and medium-sized power units installed last year. A large portion of China's power is supplied by coal-fired plants, with hydropower and other sources contributing a significant minority of generation.

China has 26 different provinces, each of which has electric power generation systems managed by state-owned utility entities. While the central government has considerable authority for final authorization of projects in China, state-level officials are of growing importance, as individual provinces gain authority over development projects.

What portion of China's enormous power capacity needs might be supplied by private power producers is not clear, but the Chinese government is actively seeking foreign assistance. China opened its power industry to private sector development in June 1992, and encourages build-operate-transfer (BOT) transactions. Overseas developers and investors can expect more success stories in China this year after two and one-half years of frustration and uncertainty. Despite continued debate and disagreement among top Chinese leaders and experts, most officials now agree that China has realized a soft landing after the two-year-long austerity program

starting in 1993. As a result, China has made substantial progress in reforming the power sector.

Most importantly, the newly passed Electricity Law began implementation April 1. It helps clarify ownership and regulatory responsibilities in the power sector. A major change is the clarification that while the state maintains sovereignty control and management of the national grid, all interested parties, including foreign sponsors, will be allowed majority control—and even complete ownership—of power stations in China. More joint ventures with foreign partners have been and will be approved. However, the credit market will not loosen dramatically this year because the nation's priority is still placed on controlling inflation from 14.8% last year to 10% this year. Although China's foreign reserve has reached $73 billion(US), the government's relatively tight monetary policy will continue.

During 1996, the power industry ministry is being restructured to be the China National Electric Power Company (CNEPC), a group company for the sector. Following the restructuring model that China used in its textile and light industry ministries, the power and metal ministries will be the pilot sectors for restructuring China's heavy industrial sectors. This is considered part of China's strategy for restructuring infrastructure management. Preparation work has already begun for major subsidiary companies of the CNEPC, such as the National Grid Construction Co.

The central government of China is ready to totally open up the generation segment, while it improves its control of transmission and distribution management. All new power stations will be built and operated as limited liability companies according to the new Company Law. The State Development Bank will only honor credit to a power plant as an independent legal person. The relationship between power supplier and power network is one of seller and buyer, which must be formed by signing a power purchase agreement. All new power plants will follow this principle. Further, for plant expansion projects, the new, expanded part will follow the principle for new power stations and will be organized as an independent company, while the old part is changed step by step.

Foreign partners in power plant development will be allowed to have majority equity and even whole ownership. The logic behind this new consensus is that since all power generation companies will be limited liability companies, it really does not matter who has the majority control.

The cap on rate of return already has been eliminated. However, most Chinese developers still consider 12–17% to be the range, since most of them think 18% and higher return rates are unrealistic.

The new policy change in importing power equipment is that, beginning this year, there will be no tax holiday for imported equipment, unless it is a large (60 MW) unit. This is different from the trend two years ago when foreign investment was encouraged with tax breaks on imported equipment.

About one-third of Chinese cities have comprehensive, cogeneration heating systems. The Chinese central government has issued a document to regulate against building small-sized power plants without heating. Many local cogeneration projects have been rejected by the central government due to their lack of a feasibility study for district heating. The state wants to control those low-efficiency projects which require excessive fuel and cause heavy pollution.

Together with the city construction department of the Construction Ministry, officials of the State Planning Commission are researching a comprehensive plan for city heating for medium and large Chinese cities. Before the plan is finished and more regulatory framework is composed, the cogeneration market in China will be active but limited.

India's current installed capacity totals about 81,000 MW, most of which is generated by coal-fired power capacity. Though the country's power demand since the late 1980s has grown steadily, capacity additions have failed to keep

pace. Of the installed base, 96% is under public utilities—the central sector is 27% and state sector is 69%. Today 70% of the country's capacity is thermal and 27% hydropower. This reflects India's increasing dependence on coal-based power despite a hydropower potential of about 130 GW. Of today's installed capacity, 66.5% is coal-fired.

Until the late 1970s, India was a power surplus country. Today, the country is experiencing acute shortage of electricity with average shortfall of 10% and peak shortfall of 20%. Regional shortfall is estimated at 27% in the eastern region; 22%, northern region; 18%, western region; 17%, southern region; and 12%, northeastern region.

Major coal-producing states added a number of coal-based projects between 1965 and 1975. These include: Bihar, six; West Bengal, 11; Orissa, four; Madhya Pradesh, 10; and Andhra Pradesh, five. Only eight coal projects—West Bengal with five and Bihar with three—existed before 1965 in these states. With expanding transportation networks, coal-based projects began growing rapidly in regions of power demand, which explains why non-coal-producing states of Maharashtra and Gujarat have maximum, coal-based generating capacity.

Hydropower projects are uniformly distributed by river states with the top 10 hydropower states comprising only 44% of installed hydropower. Maharashtra, Gujarat, Uttar Pradesh, West Bengal, and Madhya Pradesh account for 50% of coal-based power. The major gas-producing states of Maharashtra, Gujarat, and Assam account for 68% of the total gas-based power. The availability of gas in domestic and international markets and the relative costs will determine whether the optimistic addition of gas-based power—6.8 GW in the eighth five-year plan—is achievable. India has 1.8 GW of installed diesel and wind-power plants, and 2 GW of nuclear-based plants. Issues of nuclear waste disposal, funding constraints, and political sensitivity have been a deterrent to nuclear energy addition.

While government investment in the power sector has been inadequate, there also has been a slowdown based on lack of funds and the expectation that IPPs will add the required capacity. In the eighth five-year plan (1992-1997) the government had planned to add 45 GW. Successive revisions reduced the target to 30 GW. The government capacity addition is expected to be 19 GW or 42% of the original target for the eighth plan. With IPPs including fast-track projects facing slow development, the crisis is deepening further.

The eighth plan of the government (1992-1997) allocated $23 billion for the five-year plan or an average annual amount of $4.6 billion. This is planned for the entire power industry, not just for capacity additions. Private sector investment is not a matter of choice, it is a critical need.

Cumulatively the installed base and projects under development present an unrealistic picture of Indian power with a power project sited for every 50 kms of habitable land in India, sometime in the future. However, preliminary analysis at the project level suggests a maximum addition of about 95 GW within the next 10 years. IPPs are expected to account for almost 60% of the total addition. Analysis further suggests that power projects currently under development will undergo an attrition of almost 60% in the future based on demand-based analysis alone.

The call for private participation in the power sector by the government has been overwhelming since mid-1994. In December 1995, the ministry of power recorded more than 225 proposals by developers totaling about 100,000 MW in power generation capacity. Since then the crisis in the power sector has worsened and projects have continued to be slow developing. The government has responded by initiating several measures to accelerate project development, weed out less serious projects, and streamline the project clearance process.

One of the most significant initiatives has been to eliminate the mandated clearance required from Central Electricity Authority (CEA) for projects costing less than Rs. 400 crore ($115 million(US)), thus giving a boost to medium and small power project development. The clearance issued by the CEA is a techno-economic clearance that

examines all parameters of a project. However, many say that the CEA clearance—which is to be applied for after the rigors of detailed feasibility studies, securing a PPA and FSA—is too general in nature, adds little value, and unnecessarily delays projects. According to some former, senior, power-sector officials and industry leaders, India's CEA does not possess the resources to assess the large number of private power projects of increasing structural, technical, and financial complexity. The CEA clearance was initially not required for projects under Rs. 25 crore ($7.2 million(US)). This limit has been increased progressively to Rs. 1 billion ($28.7 million(US)), then Rs. 2 billion ($57.37 million(US)), Rs. 4 billion ($114.7 million(US)), and finally, Rs. 10 billion ($285 million (US)).

State governments have taken advantage of these changes and taken independent initiatives to woo private power developers. Asia Consulting Group's National Project Track is currently tracking almost 1,300 projects under development in the country. These projects include IPPs, captive projects, new government projects, as well as small projects. Collectively these account for 250,000 MW of capacity under development with IPPs accounting for almost 189,000 MW.

Currently the State Electricity Boards (SEB) are the primary purchasers of power. PPAs signed by the SEBs have to be supported by revenues. Given the highly subsidized tariff structure in India, T&D losses, theft, and collection irregularities, the demand forecasts will not be reflected in the revenue streams of the SEBs. Hence, the SEB ability to sign up and honor PPAs is substantially lower than what the demand figures suggest. Even in the event of tariff rationalization and reduction of losses, the situation is unlikely to improve dramatically.

Inefficiency of state electricity boards is a significant problem. The central government has suggested several models of restructuring programs to facilitate reformation of SEBs to make them commercially viable, to regulate and rationalize the tariffs, and improve the T&D network.

Orissa is the first state to opt for restructuring. Orissa's electricity reform bill was passed in November 1995, and subsequently the SEB was broken into three separate entities in charge of generation, T&D, and an independent regulatory body which will set the operating norms and fixed tariff structures. Haryana also is undergoing a similar process by forming three separately managed entities and a regulatory commission which will safeguard the interest of consumers. Bihar, too, has made a policy decision on restructuring its board, and Uttar Pradesh has initiated restructuring studies with external assistance. However, the government is delaying the process of reforms keeping in view the discontent among the employees and its likely effect on elections. At the same time, the SEBs of other states like Rajasthan, Andhra Pradesh, and Punjab are also heading for a change.

Indonesia. Perusahaan Umum Listrik Negara (PLN), the state-owned electric utility, is Indonesia's primary electricity provider. The country has 21,000 MW of installed capacity, of which PLN owns more than 13,000 MW. Most capacity is coal- or oil-fired, with some natural gas, geothermal, and hydropower capacity.

Indonesia's government has begun the process of restructuring PLN in preparation for privatization of subsidiary companies in international stock markets. To strengthen PLN, it has been incorporated and changed from a state-owned entity to a public, limited-liability company. Most shares are owned by the government, but stock is traded in public markets. Two power generation subsidiaries have already been formed in Java, Power Generation Corp. I and II, with privatization to occur in 1996 after the companies' assets are fully appraised.

PLN has canceled plans to build a number of nuclear projects, and is concentrating efforts to bring additional coal- and gas-fired plants, in order to use the country's enormous indigenous resources of those fuels.

Construction has begun on three large, joint-venture IPPs that will sell power to PLN.

These include two private power units at the 5,000-MW Paiton coal-fired complex in eastern Java. Paiton I is being built by a consortium of four partners, including: Irvine, California-based Edison Mission Energy; Mitsui & Co. of Japan; GE Capital of Stamford, Connecticut; and P.T. Batu Hitam Perkasa of Jakarta, Indonesia. ABB Combustion Engineering of Stamford, Connecticut, is providing the plant's pulverized coal boilers, and Schenectady, New York-based General Electric is providing steam turbine generators. A consortium of Duke/Fluor Daniel of Charlotte, North Carolina, and Mitsui and Toyo of Japan will provide EPC services. The plant will burn primarily Indonesian coal, owned by the Indonesian government, under contract arranged by P.T. Batu Hitam Perkasa. The first unit will begin operation in late 1998, and second will come on-line within four months of the first.

The project was financed in 1995, with a limited-recourse package totaling $2.5 billion. The consortium financing Paiton I includes banks from the United States, Japan, Switzerland, and the United Kingdom, as well as export credit agencies from the United States and Japan.

At the same complex, the Paiton II project is being developed by a consortium of Siemens Power Ventures GmbH of Erlangen, Germany, PowerGen PLC of the United Kingdom, and P.T. Bumipertiwi Tatapradipta, an Indonesian Bimantara Group company. The $1.7 billion(US), 1,220-MW project was financed in early 1996 by export credit agencies from the United States and Germany, and consortium of lenders from Switzerland, Germany, Japan, Canada, and the United States.

Third, a construction contract was signed in 1995 for the 1,220-MW Tanjung Jati-B thermal power plant in Semarang, Central Java. The $900 million(US) project is being built by Sumitomo Corp. of Tokyo for Consolidated Electric Power Asia (CEPA), a subsidiary of Hopewell Holdings Ltd. of Hong Kong. Babcock & Wilcox is providing boiler equipment and engineering services.

Japan's electric power is supplied by 10 electric utility companies. In the past fiscal year, power supply by these companies rose 2.2% from a year earlier to 834.82 billion kilowatt-hours. The companies are expected to make significant investments in power generating capacity through the end of the decade to meet increasing power demand. Increased investment in development of diversified sources of power, including the expansion of nuclear power facilities, is expected in Japan.

Japan's 10 utilities are: Tokyo Electric Power, Kansai Electric Power, Chubu Electric Power, Tohoku Electric Power, Kyushu Electric Power, Chugoku Electric Power, Hokkaido Electric Power, Shikoku Electric Power, Hokuriku Electric Power, and Okinawa Electric Power.

Until deregulation in December 1995, Japan's power industry was an oligopoly of these major utilities. Now the power sector is open to power sales from independent power producers. Major Japanese industrial, steel, petrochemical, and oil firms have expressed interest in entering the power supply market. Up to 10% of power supply could eventually be supplied by IPPs.

Early in 1996, major electricity utility Tokyo Electric Power Co., Inc. (TEPCO) issued its first tender to buy electricity from IPPs. The solicitation seeks 1,000 MW of power capacity from fiscal year 1999/2000 to 2001/2002. Power purchase agreements are to be set at 15 years. Awards are expected to be announced in January 1997.

TEPCO recently awarded a $500 million contract to GE Power Systems of Schenectady, New York, to design and build a 1,400-megawatt, advanced combined-cycle power plant at Chiba Power Station No. 2. GE will supply four gas turbines, four steam turbines, and four generators for the project. Additional equipment and services will be supplied by Foster Wheeler of the United States, IHI, Toshiba Corp., and Hitachi, Ltd. of Japan.

South Korea's state-owned utility, Korea Electric Power Co. (KEPCO), is financially sound, in contrast with many state-owned utilities in

developing Asian nations. Korea currently has 36,000 MW of installed generating capacity. About 60% of Korea's power is generated by fossil-fueled plants, while about 29% is nuclear, and 9% is hydroelectric. Virtually all of the country's energy comes from imported fuels. A small amount of hydropower and anthracite coal are the country's only indigenous energy resources.

KEPCO has been the only supplier of power to Korea's national grid, but the government is taking steps to incorporate private power into the system. BOO plants are expected to contribute up to 2,000 MW of new capacity to Korea's power system by 2005, and more than 6,000 MW by 2010. Solicitation processes for the first two liquefied natural gas-fired plants are proceeding, with an announcement of winning bidders expected soon.

Laos

Laos has 260 MW of generating capacity, owned by the state utility, Electricite du Laos (EDL). Most power is supplied by hydropower facilities, with other fossil fuels adding incremental capacity. The country has recently been opened to competition from private companies developing BOT projects.

Laos exports 100 MW of capacity to Thailand, and expects to increase that amount to at least 1,500 MW by the year 2000. Laos has a large untapped hydropower capacity, which it plans to develop to produce power for sale to Thailand. Laos has plans to build dozens more hydropower stations along the Mekong River and tributaries. Plans to build a 210-MW hydropower plant at Theun-Hinboun took a major step forward when the Asian Development Bank approved a $60 million loan for the project's development. Power from the facility is expected to be exported to Thailand beginning in 1998. In a first for Laos, the government will form a joint venture company with private participants to finance, build, and operate the plant. All equipment for the project is to be procured through competitive bidding procedures. Scandinavian firms Statkraft of Norway and Vattenfall and Nordic Power of Sweden have established a joint venture to manage 25% equity interest.

The Electricity Generating Authority of Thailand (EGAT), Electricité de France, and Transfield Corp. of Australia are working on the 600-MW, Nam Thuen 2 project. Also, EGAT has announced plans to build 369 km of transmission facilities linking Laos to Thailand, totaling an estimated $51.9 million(US) in investment. Construction is scheduled to begin in March 1996, with commissioning slated for October 1997.

Additionally, Laos has issued an invitation for bids to build three transmission lines as part of a provincial grid integration project being implemented by Electricite du Laos (EDL). The project is being built with credit support from the World Bank.

Malaysia

Malaysia has three electric utilities. The largest is Tenaga Nasional Berhad (TNB), serving peninsular Malaysia, home to 80% of Malaysia's population. Two smaller utilities serve the island provinces of Sabah and Sarawak—Sabah Electric Board (SEB) and Sarawak Electric Supply Corp. (SESCO). Malaysia's current electric capacity is more than 8,000 MW.

Although Malaysia's electric utilities will continue to serve the electricity needs of the country's 18 million people, the government successfully has opened the generation side of the power industry to competition from independent power producers. In the short term, the transmission and distribution (T&D) of electricity remains a monopoly, but the government is considering options for restructuring T&D as well. Several independent power producers have received licenses to construct power plants, and several hundred megawatts of IPP capacity is now operating.

Malaysia's aggressive pursuit of private power in the early 1990s established the country as a leading Asian model for privatization and restructuring of the electric power industry. In addition to the partial privatization of TNB, Malaysia has brought more independent power capacity on-line than any other Asian nation. This success is due largely to a well-devised regulatory structure in support of IPPs, several domestic

companies with the ability to become private power developers, and capital markets deep enough to finance private power investments.

Malaysia opened its power industry to private investment in 1991, listing TNB on the Kuala Lumpur stock exchange, and soliciting projects from private developers. As a result, several projects were granted licenses to proceed, and at least five have been financed, all using entirely domestic financing. At least five large projects have entered service. These include:

- the first, 150-MW phase of the 1,300-MW, Lumut combined-cycle project built by ABB Power Generation for Sikap Energy Ventures of Kuala Lumpur;

- two projects, totaling 1,212 MW, built under turnkey contract by Siemens KWU of Erlangen, Germany, for YTL Power Generation Sdn. Bhd. of Kuala Lumpur;

- the 687-MW Kuala Langat project, a gas-fired facility owned by Genting Sanyen Malaysia, British Gas PLC of the U.K., and TNB, and built under turnkey contract by ABB; and

- the 440-MW PowerTek project, a peaking unit near Malacca, owned by Cergas Ungal, Arab Malaysian Development and other Malaysian investors.

Additionally, the Port Dickson project, a 440-MW, gas-fired facility has been financed and is under construction at Tanjung Gemok, south of Kuala Lumpur. The project is being developed by a partnership of Malaysian industrial companies, Sime Darby, Malaysian Resources Corp., and Hypergantic, with TNB as a minority shareholder. General Electric Power Systems is building the project and supplying equipment under turnkey contract.

The Ringgit-only financing strategy was possible for these projects because Malaysia's capital markets are well developed in comparison with its neighbors. Additionally, Malaysia has a healthy business climate and a favorable development framework established by the government. Because TNB is considered a stable and financially secure utility, sovereign guarantees are not needed in Malaysia to underpin power purchase obligations. Finally, it is believed the federal government took steps to ensure the availability of financing from the Employees' Provident Fund.

The Paka and Pasir Gudang plants owned by YTL were financed as a single investment, totaling RM2.66 billion (about $1 billion(US)). Financing totaling RM2.67 billion was arranged in two loan packages, both from domestic Malaysian sources. The Employees' Provident Fund, a pension fund serving the nation's salaried employees, contributed a RM1.5 billion fixed-rate loan, and RM1.6 billion came from Bank Bumiputra Malaysia Bhd. (BBMB) in the form of a floating-rate term loan. Power is being sold to TNB under a 21-year, minimum-purchase agreement, and Petronas supplies fuel under a 21-year contract.

The Lumut, PowerTek, and Port Dickson projects are financed under similar structures. The financing for the Lumut project includes: $1.1 billion(US) in debt funds, divided evenly between floating-rate debt, provided by lenders Bank Bumiputra Malaysia Bhd. and Malayan Banking Bhd., and fixed-rate securities, held by the Employees Provident Fund. The remaining $400 million(US) takes the form of subordinated shareholder loans and equity contributed by Sikap Energy Ventures. Sikap is a partnership of ABB Holdings in Malaysia and Malakoff Bhd., a subsidiary of Malaysian Resources Corp.

Finally, PowerTek is financed with a 21-year, limited-recourse debt package from Bank Bumiputra Malaysia Bhd., which expects to syndicate some of the loan to other institutions, and Port Dickson is financed with non-recourse debt from the Employees' Provident Fund.

Several other projects are at advanced stages of development, at least one holding a license to sell power. Notably, the 2,400-MW Bakun hydroelectric project located in Sarawak State on the island of Borneo, recently reached important milestones, including the award of several equipment supply contracts valued at over $5 billion(US). The largest

share of the award went to ABB, which is expected to supply $3 billion(US) in equipment and services. The project is a joint venture of Ekran Bhd., TNB, Employees' Provident Fund, the Sarawak State Electricity Corp., and Malaysia Mining Corp.

Pakistan.

The primary electricity supplier in Pakistan is the Water & Power Development Authority (WAPDA), a government-owned utility company. The country's total installed capacity is about 13,000 MW, about one-half split between hydroelectric and thermal capacity. About 6,000 MW of WAPDA power plants are expected to be privatized in the future. The first of these is the 1,600-MW Kot Addu project in Punjab Province, for which a 26% equity stake was awarded in April 1996 to National Power PLC of the United Kingdom, which bid $215 million(US) in an open, international tender process. National Power will assume management control of the plant, although WAPDA holds a 74% equity stake in the new project company. A 10% share in the project is expected to be floated on Pakistan's stock market. The Kot Addu project will sell power to WAPDA under a 25-year contract.

Kot Addu is the first power station Pakistan has privatized, clearing the way for further power sector divestitures. The 880-MW Jamshoro facility and the Faisalabad Area Electricity Board are expected to be sold next. Following the successful privatization of a share of the Kot Addu power plant, Sind Provincial officials expect to open a 26% share of the 800-MW, oil-fired Jamshoro power plant to competitive tender. Bidding documents are expected to be available in late 1996.

A number of projects have secured financing and are in construction in Pakistan, including the 362-MW, $375 million Lalpir project in Muzaffargarh, Punjab Province, developed by AES Transpower, a Karachi-based subsidiary of the AES Corp. in Arlington, Virginia. The Lalpir project was financed less than six months from the signing of power purchase agreements. Construction of the oil-fired project is nearly half complete, with start-

up scheduled for late 1997. Nichimen Corp. of Japan is the turnkey contractor, with Mitsubishi Heavy Industries supplying equipment.

The Lalpir project represents a milestone in the economic development of Pakistan. Although government policy for establishing private sector, build-own-operate (BOO) power plants had been in effect in Pakistan since 1986, progress was slow until 1994. To attract foreign investors to build power plants, the Government of Pakistan (GOP) issued a new policy with a number of incentives for private power. AES Transpower's Lalpir project is the first IPP developed under this new paradigm.

Since the Lalpir project was financed, a number of other projects have closed financing using a similar structure. An example is AES Transpower's PakGen project, a nearly identical facility at Muzaffargarh, which closed financing in January 1996. More recently, developers of the Uch power project—Midlands Electricity PLC, Tenaska International, GE Capital, Hasan Associates (Pvt) Ltd. of Pakistan, and Hawkins Oil & Gas Inc. of Tulsa, Oklahoma—secured a $690 million(US) international financing package. Another major project that has secured financing is the Rousch 412-MW, combined-cycle project in Punjab Province, sponsored by Rousche Finance, Siemens Power Ventures GmbH, and ESB International. Siemens KWU began building the project under turnkey contract in May 1996.

Financing was secured in early 1995 for the 350-MW, $475 million(US) Khalifa Point project near Karachi, sponsored by the Fauji Foundation and CanAmerican Holdings of the United Arab Emirates. Italy's Ansaldo Group is building the project under turnkey contract, with Babcock & Wilcox of the United States providing boiler equipment.

In June, the U.S. Maritime Administration approved a $402 million(US) long-term loan guarantee to WAK Orient Power and Light Ltd., a project company created to develop, finance, own, and operate a 450-MW, power barge complex in Port Qasim, near Pakistan's southern port city of Karachi. The project will be built and installed by

a consortium consisting of Pittsburgh-based Westinghouse and Raytheon Engineers and Constructors based in Lexington, Massachusetts. Marine Energy Systems Corp., based in Charleston, South Carolina, will build the plant in a U.S. shipyard and transport it complete to Pakistan.

Many major projects are at advanced stages of development in Pakistan, including such projects as the 754-MW Multan project being developed by Enron Development Corp. of Houston, Texas; a 288-MW, barge-mounted project sponsored by Westmont Bhd. of Malaysia; and the 157-MW, Kabirwala gas-fired project sponsored by Fauji Foundation and Sceptre Power Co. of California.

Philippines.
Power generation capacity in the Philippines began falling seriously short in the late 1980s. In 1990, residents and businesses suffered through brownouts every few days. The crisis peaked in 1992 and 1993, with outages lasting from six to 12 hours almost every day. In 1992, Manila spent 258 days without power. These shortages are estimated to have cost the country's economy up to $3 billion per year, with a measurable impact on gross domestic product in 1992 and 1993.

Unable to finance the new power plants needed to end the crisis, the government turned to the private sector. President Aquino issued Executive Order 215, and Congress authorized private involvement in financing, construction, operation, and maintenance of infrastructure projects, by enacting the Republic Act 6957—better known as the BOT Law. The first project implemented under the BOT Law was the 210-MW, diesel-fired, Navotas facility, built under a 12-year BOT agreement by Hopewell Holdings Ltd. of Hong Kong (now Consolidated Electric Power Asia (CEPA)). The facility entered service in 1991.

The Aquino administration continued to pursue private power, approving two additional BOT projects in 1990. Also, many industrial and commercial energy users began installing small, self-generation systems in order to ensure reliable power supplies. By the end of 1992, about 1,000 MW of self-generation capacity was added.

However, these public and private efforts proved too little and too late to avert the power crisis of 1992 and 1993.

Using emergency authority granted by Congress, newly-elected President Ramos promised an end to power shortages. His first executive order, issued June 30, 1992, exempted electric generation equipment from 10% and 20% import tariffs for three years. Subsequently, Congress enacted Republic Act 7636, creating the Department of Energy (DOE) to accelerate the Philippines' power development plans. Other legislative efforts increased the president's authority to negotiate fast-track contracts, authorized the reorganization of NPC, ordered a percentage of national gaming revenues to be provided to NPC, and authorized loan guarantees for BOT contractees.

Six BOT projects were financed using loan guarantees from the government. These include the 700-MW, coal-fired Pagbilao project, built by Hopewell; the 105-MW, diesel-fired, Pinamucan project at Batangas, and the 28-MW, diesel-fired Zambales project at Subic bay, both built by Enron Development Corp. of Houston; the 210-MW, Bauang diesel-fired project at Batangas sponsored by First Private Power Corp. of Manila; and the 58-MW and 40-MW Iligan City diesel-fired projects built on Mindanao by ALSONS of the Philippines in consortium with Tomen of Japan.

The government also established an energy conservation program in late 1993, with the cooperation of large energy users. Combined with some new capacity additions, NPC succeeded in reducing the duration of brownouts by about 50%. Also, the utility refurbished and returned to service a number of existing thermal plants. These efforts, combined with new fast-track projects coming on-line and increased rainfall for hydropower generation, enabled the government to bring the power crisis under control by the middle of 1994. Since then, new IPPs have entered service and the government has begun efforts to effect broader privatization and deregulation.

Numerous private companies have become involved in the country's private power industry. Most IPPs have entered service after 1993,

increasing the Philippines generating capacity by 18% between 1993 and mid-1994, from 6,695 MW to more than 8,000 MW. By June 1995, IPPs represented 27% of the Philippines generating capacity, with 23 projects providing more than 3,400 MW. In the past year, seven IPPs have entered service, adding 2,500 MW of new operating capacity. Most of this capacity is located in the island of Luzon, with about 25% split between Mindanao and Visayas.

The Philippines government expects 13,000 MW of new capacity to be added between 1996 and 2005, with an additional 32,660 MW between 2006 and 2015, and 46,500 from 2015 through 2025. The private sector's share of total generating capacity is expected to reach 60% by 2005. Eventually, this could expand to a larger share, as the government implements plans to privatize government-owned generation assets.

The Ramos administration and NPC are pursuing an ambitious plan to restructure and privatize NPC and to further open the power industry to competition. A DOE-sponsored legislation package, tentatively called the Omnibus Electric Industry Code, promises to significantly extend opportunities for private participation in the Philippines electric utility industry. In principle, NPC intends to divest 100% of its generation assets, totaling more than $5 billion(US) in book value.

Sri Lanka

Sri Lanka currently has about 2,000 MW of installed capacity, most of which—1,400 MW—is operated by the state utility, Ceylon Electricity Board (CEB). The CEB is seeking investments from the private sector in its electricity system, and is expected to invite foreign investors to bid for a $800 million(US), 300-MW, coal-fired power plant, and a $150 million(US), 150-MW diesel plant. Additionally, the government is planning to reissue a solicitation for a 300-MW, coal-fired power plant near Trincomalee, after the expected investors withdrew. The country anticipates that it needs to install new capacity totaling 780 MW, and to invest some $1.8 billion(US) in transmission and distribution systems, by the year 2001.

The Ministry of Irrigation, Power & Energy is the primary government body with authority over the electric power industry. The CEB is the primary utility, operating about 1,400 MW of installed capacity—almost all hydropower. The country is nearing the limit of its hydropower capacity that is viable for development, and thus is directing effort toward thermal capacity. CEB plans to add about 220 MW of hydropower by 2001, and 560 MW of thermal capacity during the same period.

The country has opened the power sector to development by private companies, but regulatory policies and systems remain uncertain and unpredictable. The country supports, in principle, proposals for BOT and BOO projects, but has so far been unable to move many such projects forward.

CEB has a number of small projects in construction and advanced stages of development, including: a $55 million(US), 40-MW, diesel-fired project at Sapugaskanda; a $62 million(US), 51-MW, fuel oil-fired BOT project sponsored by KHD of the United Kingdom; two, 60-MW, barge-mounted, BOT power projects at Negombo and Galle; a 150-MW, naptha-fired, combined-cycle power plant, originally being negotiated with Midlands PLC of the U.K.; a 300-MW, coal-fired project at Puttalam; a 300-MW, heavy fuel-fired, BOT project at Hambantota; and several small hydropower projects totaling 290 MW.

Taiwan's

Taiwan's Ministry of Economic Affairs (MOEA) received 22 project bids last spring, totaling 30 GW, in response to its private power initiative seeking 7.26 GW of new capacity between 1998 and 2002. It selected 11 projects in two rounds of bidding. The first, 11 awarded projects, announced in the first part of 1995, are at various stages of development. A list of winning projects from the second round of bidding follows:

- The 550-MW Hochung Oil-Fired plant is a $670 million(US) project being developed by Full Power International Investment Co., a joint venture of Enserch

International Ltd. of New Jersey and Ambassador Group of New York.

- The Hsin Tao, 600-MW, combined-cycle, LNG-fired project, being developed by the ADI Corporation and Hsin Tao Power Preparatory Office, consists of two or three gas turbines plus one steam turbine.

- The Suao Orimulsion plant is a 600-MW project being developed by the Taiwan Sakura Corp., Sceptre Power Co. & CSW Energy.

- Chang Hung Power is a 1,500-MW, orimulsion-fired project being developed by Taiwan Synthetic Rubber and International Generating Co.

General Electric Power Systems won a $1.8 billion(US) contract in early June to supply equipment for Taiwan's fourth nuclear power plant, but the Taiwan Power-sponsored plant is in limbo following Parliament's vote to cancel it. Taiwan's Cabinet has asked Parliament to reconsider the $4.1 billion(US), 2,700-MW project, which has been under construction in Kungliao since 1994. The Cabinet could veto the Parliamentary ruling, but this veto could itself be overturned by Parliament in a two-thirds majority vote. The Parliament's rejection would also force the country's premier to resign.

Thailand. With real economic growth of 8.2% in the past decade, the Kingdom of Thailand has one of Asia's fastest-growing economies. Installed capacity of 13,000 is inadequate to meet the country's expected future power demands, and the government is trying to bring private power investment into the country to help add at least 4,500 MW by the year 2000, and 11,000 MW of new capacity by 2005. Additionally, Thailand expects to increase power imports from Laos, Malaysia, and Vietnam. Thailand's power demands are expected to triple to more than 30,000 MW during the next 15 years. Installed capacity is comprised of 47% coal- and oil-fired thermal

plants, 32% gas-fired combined-cycle plants, and nearly 20% hydropower.

Private companies are allowed to participate in independent power and industrial cogeneration projects, and the state utility has solicited bids to develop private power generators.

Although initially it moved slowly, the Thai government is working to privatize the Electricity Generating Authority of Thailand. Recently, EGAT finalized privatization of the 774-MW, gas-fired, Khanom generating facilities. Electricity Generating Co. PLC (EGCO), a private power company owned largely by EGAT, signed agreements with EGAT enabling the estimated $700 million(US) sale to proceed. EGCO will sell output from the Khanom complex's 624-MW combined-cycle plant and two, 75-MW power barges to EGAT under long-term power purchase agreements, and EGAT is contracted to provide maintenance for at least six years.

In addition, EGAT is considering a number of IPP proposals and projects that independent power could ultimately contribute 13,100 MW to Thailand's power industry, or nearly one-third of EGAT's total capacity.

EGCO expects to finance the acquisition with equity and debt funds, and has already arranged a $265 million(US) loan syndicated among Industrial Bank of Japan, Sakura Bank, and Thai Farmer Bank. Ownership of the Khanom facilities was expected to transfer to EGCO in late June 1995.

Vietnam has about 4,400 MW of installed capacity, and is expected to add 8,000 MW by 2000, and 12,000 MW by 2005. State-owned Power Companies No. 1, 2, and 3, combined under the auspices of Electricity of Vietnam, provide virtually all of the country's power. More than half of the country's electricity is provided by hydroelectric stations, with the remainder split among coal-, oil-, diesel-, and gas-fired plants.

Private-sector participation is slowly creeping into the market as Vietnam faces a looming capacity shortfall. The Ministry of Energy has invited private firms to submit proposals for BOT projects totaling 1,600 MW. These include the 400-

MW Tuong Dong hydropower project in Hghe An Province; a 400-MW, coal-fired project at Phuoc Thoi in Can Tho Province; the 400-MW Vung Tau gas-fired project near Vung Tau; and a 400-MW, coal-fired project in Kien Plang Province. The Ministry is also expected to open two coal-fired projects and seven hydropower projects, totaling some 6,500 MW of new capacity, to possible development by the private sector.

A number of projects are being developed. For example, BHP Power, Tomen Corp., BP Exploration, Powerfin, and Statoil last year signed a memorandum of understanding with the Vietnamese State Planning Committee and Electricity of Vietnam to develop the 600-MW to 900-MW Phu My III project near Ho Chi Minh City. The project is an integrated power and fertilizer project with fuel to be supplied from large natural gas fields that British Petroleum discovered offshore near Ho Chi Minh City in 1994. Also at Phu My, Mobil Power Corp., Raytheon Engineers & Constructors, and the Vietnamese Ministry of Energy are developing a 400-MW, liquefied natural gas-fired project, known as Phu My II. Mobil Power is also developing Phu My IV, a 400-MW to 600-MW project.

Another project is being developed by Pacific Power International, a subsidiary of Australia's largest electric utility, Pacific Power, based in Sydney. The Pha Lai project near Hanoi consists of two, 300-MW units, burning locally mined anthracite. Construction of the Pha Lai project is expected to begin in early 1997, with completion in 1999.

Fuels Outlook

Chapter 11

Fuel Supply, Availability, and Transportation

TIMOTHY B. DEMOSS
ASSOCIATE EDITOR
POWER ENGINEERING AND
POWER ENGINEERING INTERNATIONAL

OVERVIEW

Despite increasing worldwide concern for the environment and the role energy production plays in the environment's health, economic considerations in developing countries are overwhelming any real or perceived threats from burning fossil fuels, namely coal, oil, and natural gas. Electricity generation in particular is not only an indicator, but a catalyst for economic growth. As such, countries with mature or developing economies seek the lowest-cost means of producing electricity. That lowest-cost means continues to be electricity fueled primarily by coal and natural gas.

Likewise in the transportation sector, no suitable substitute has come forward to displace oil as the most economic fuel. Even electric vehicles ultimately depend heavily on fossil fuels for their power. Another factor which, in the face of environmentalism, drives fossil fuel use, is the

advances in technology that decrease fossil fuels' potential harm to the environment while increasing the efficiency of burning those fuels. Whether this technology creates an environmental windfall or an economic windfall becomes moot when both sides are served by the same advances.

However, new technologies do not address all environmental concerns, and as pressure mounts worldwide to decrease air pollution in particular, the balance will continue to tip in favor of less polluting fuels. As increasing regulations bring economic consequences to energy production, nuclear energy will bear most of the burden because much of the public views nuclear waste as an extreme threat. Renewable energy sources will see increased use, but until the cost of producing electric energy using these sources becomes economically viable, there will be no mass migration toward using them. Coal, despite its relative abundance and low cost, will see no increase in its share of the electric energy pie. The costs associated with cleaning coal pollutants and

ash waste plus the difficulty in dealing with its many forms and qualities in a power plant setting place it at a disadvantage.

The real winner in this scenario appears to be natural gas. The high-efficiency electricity generation possible with natural gas, along with its relatively benign pollutants (CO_2 is a controversial exception in light of the global warming discussion), will make it a favorite over the next two decades in those regions with strict pollution regulations. Natural gas's fuel consumption share for electricity generation is expected to increase by more than 5% over this period.

Despite fears of an "oil shortage" in the 1970s which fanned the flames of doomsaying over the world's fossil fuel reserves, there is no indication that supply will run short over the forecast period. As long as the economics bear out for extracting these resources, fossil fuels appear stable in their perch atop the fuel consumption ladder.

FUEL MIX

In the U.S. Department of Energy's (DOE) Energy Information Administration (EIA) report, *International Energy Outlook* 1996 (IEO96), the agency expects the fuel mix for world electricity generation to change significantly by 2015 (Figures 11–1 and 11–2 and Table 11–1). The natural gas share of total electricity generation is projected to increase worldwide from 16% in 1993 to 21% in 2015, largely due to increased utilization

of natural gas in the Organization for Economic Cooperation and Development (OECD) regions, where its share doubles from 9% of total generation in 1993 to 18% in 2015. The natural gas share declines slightly in non-OECD areas, from 25–24%; however, the heavy reliance of NIS and Middle East nations on natural gas for power generation keeps the overall share of natural gas higher for the non-OECD than for the OECD countries overall.

Coal remains the primary fuel for electricity generation throughout the EIA's IEO96 forecast, with a consistent share of 36%. Non-OECD Asia, which is projected to account for almost one-third of total non-OECD electricity demand in 2015, currently uses coal for about 60% of its total power needs; its reliance on coal is expected to continue over the next two decades. Coal-fired generation in the other Asia subgroup of non-OECD countries, which includes a number of countries in the Pacific Rim region with rapidly growing economies (notably, South Korea, Taiwan, Thailand, the Philippines, and Indonesia), is expected to increase by almost 5% per year over the next 20 years, pushing the coal-fired share of total generation for the other Asia group from 28% in 1993 to 34% in 2015.

For all the fossil fuels (natural gas, coal, and oil), an increasing share in the world's total fuel use for electricity generation is projected—from 62% in 1993 to 66% in 2015. This is a reversal of the trend for the two previous decades, when generation from fossil fuels was losing share—decreasing from 71–62% of total generation—as nuclear power penetrated the market. Nuclear

Figure 11–1. World energy consumption for electricity generation by fuel type—1995

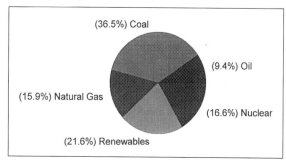

Figure 11–2. World energy consumption for electricity generation by fuel type—2015

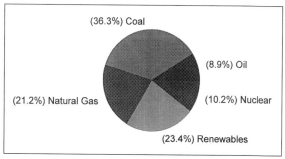

Fuel Supply, Availability, and Transportation

power's generation share is expected to decline slightly—from 22% in 1993 to 21% in 2105—after peaking at more than 24% by the turn of the century. This decline is due in part to the expectation that the number of nuclear reactors retired over the IEO96 forecast horizon will surpass the number of new units being commissioned.

The renewable share of total electricity generation is expected to increase from 21% in 1993 to 23% in 2015. Hydropower, the dominant renewable source of energy for electricity production, is expected to show substantial growth in non-OECD countries. The regions primarily responsible for the continued penetration of hydropower are non-OECD Asia and Central and South America.

Table 11–1
World energy consumption for electricity generation by region and fuel, 1993-2015 (quadrillion Btu)

Region/ Fuel	History		Projections			
	1993	1995	2000	2005	2010	2015
OECD	**74.1**	**77.3**	**84.3**	**91.2**	**97.8**	**103.4**
Oil	5.4	5.7	5.6	5.8	5.9	5.8
Natural Gas	6.8	7.6	9.6	12.4	15.2	19.1
Coal	26.9	27.3	29.3	31.4	33.0	34.2
Nuclear	18.1	19.1	19.6	19.3	18.9	16.7
Renewables	16.8	17.7	20.1	22.4	24.8	27.6
Non-OECD	**58.4**	**61.7**	**72.0**	**82.9**	**95.5**	**109.0**
Oil	7.7	7.5	8.9	10.6	12.0	13.2
Natural Gas	14.3	14.5	17.0	19.3	22.4	26.0
Coal	21.2	23.5	27.3	32.1	37.1	43.0
Nuclear	4.0	3.9	4.8	5.0	5.4	4.9
Renewables	11.2	12.3	13.9	15.9	18.6	22.0
Total World	**132.5**	**139.0**	**156.3**	**174.2**	**193.4**	**212.5**
Oil	13.1	13.1	14.5	16.3	18.0	19.0
Natural Gas	21.2	22.1	26.6	31.8	37.6	45.1
Coal	48.1	50.7	56.6	63.5	70.1	77.2
Nuclear	22.1	23.0	24.4	24.3	24.3	21.6
Renewables	28.1	30.0	34.0	38.3	43.4	49.7

Note: OECD=Organization for Economic Cooperation and Development

COAL

Background

According to the EIA, world coal use is projected to increase by more than 50% between 1993 and 2015, primarily for electricity generation.

Coal demand remains strong despite increasing environmental regulation and competition from other fuels.

Although worldwide coal consumption grew steadily in the 1970s when oil embargoes drove up oil prices, from 1985 to 1993 coal's share of total energy consumption decreased from 28% to 25%. (Figure 11–3) Collapsing oil prices and new, highly competitive technologies for natural gas-fired electricity generation have been major factors in coal's decline relative to these other fuels.

In some regions, coal consumption has decreased in both relative and absolute terms. While increasing in the U.S. and Japan, coal use in other OECD countries has declined by more than 20% over the last decade as a result of competition from other fuels. Eastern Europe and the NIS experienced a 27% decline in coal use between 1989 and 1993. However, economic growth in China and other Asian countries places ever-increasing demands on those countries for electric power and will continue to offset these declines.

Figure 11–3. World energy consumption shares by fuel type

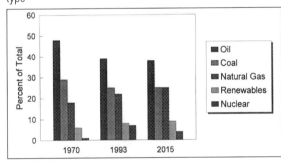

The decline in coal use for OECD countries is partly due to increasing concern about the adverse environmental impacts associated with coal use. Many countries have implemented policies or regulations to limit sulfur dioxide emissions, a significant coal pollutant, requiring electricity producers to switch to lower sulfur fuels or invest in technologies that reduce the amount of sulfur dioxide emitted. Nitrogen oxides, particulate matter, and hazardous air pollutants such as mercury may also be included in many of these regulations. Advances in SO_2, NO_x, and

139

particulate-control technologies for coal-fired electricity production have thus far managed to meet most environmental regulations. Continued advances will help maintain coal's lead role in electric power generation.

Reserves

In 1993, seven regions produced 85% of the world's coal. The United States and the Newly Independent States (NIS), formerly the Soviet Union, produced 23% each; China, 11%; and four other countries—Australia, Germany, India, and South Africa, produced 28% combined. With estimated recoverable reserves at 1,145 billion tons (Figure 11–4), the world's coal should last another 230 years at current production levels.

Figure 11–4. World coal reserves

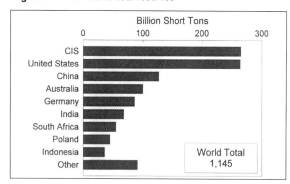

Although 230 years seems like a long time, coal quality, which varies from region to region, will factor greatly in determining the economic feasibility of tapping a reserve. Coal deposits in South Africa, the number three exporter in the world, are high in ash content and require much more preparation to produce a marketable product than do coals from other regions. However, South Africa's easily mined, low-sulfur coal compensates for the higher preparation costs. Much of Germany's coal, on the other hand, is difficult to extract. Consequently, despite the coal's relatively high quality, Germany's coal production requires large government subsidies to ensure its competitiveness with other fuels.

Several countries have only recently entered the coal marketplace, and as these new entries—such as Indonesia, currently ranked ninth in the world—rapidly penetrate the market with high-quality coal, veteran producers such as the United States and South Africa could see their market share begin to shrink. Indonesia's recoverable reserves were estimated at only three billion tons as late as 1989. Today, the country's estimated reserves are 35 billion tons, and their high-quality reserves will be in great demand as the economies of nearby countries balloon in the coming years, requiring low-cost fuel for power generation.

Regional Overview

Worldwide, the consumption of coal relative to other fuels is projected to remain stable, according to the EIA, accounting for 25% of total energy consumption through 2015 (Figure 11–3), and 36% of electric power generation (Figures 11–1 and 11–2).

Asia. As a result of fast-paced economic growth, coal consumption is expected to grow most rapidly in non-OECD Asia. In the EIA's IEO96 forecast, this region's share of total world coal consumption increases from 36% in 1993 to 52% in 2015. The region's coal consumption is expected to rise from 1,777 million tons in 1993 to 3,931 million tons in 2015. China, alone, should increase its coal consumption by 1,725 million tons. India also expects to increase consumption by 320 million tons.

Strong economic growth in China and India (7.7% per year in China and 5.1% per year in India, according to the EIA), and the expectation that much of the increased demand for energy will be met by coal, are the basis for the projected increase in coal consumption. By 2015, coal could meet as much as 66% of the total demand for primary energy in China and 47% in India. The EIA's forecast assumes no significant change in environmental policies in the two countries. It also assumes that the countries will make necessary investments in their mines, transportation, industrial facilities, and power plants.

Japan, the world's largest coal importer, anticipates 26% growth in coal usage. In 1993, Japanese coal imports were 122 million tons, or 29% of total world imports. Although coal imports to Japan are expected to expand to meet increasing electricity demand, its share of total world imports is projected to decline to 21% by 2015.

Europe. The countries of OECD Europe are committed to the stabilization of greenhouse gas concentrations in the atmosphere as established by the Framework Convention on Climate Change. As a result, coal consumption in OECD Europe has declined in recent years in favor of other fuels such as natural gas. The EIA projects increased coal consumption for the region, but does not expect it to reach the levels of the late 1980s.

In Eastern Europe (EE) and the NIS, a market-oriented economy is replacing centrally planned economic systems. The dislocations associated with these changes have contributed substantially to declines in both coal production and consumption. Coal consumption in the EE/NIS region has fallen from 1,441 millions tons in 1988 to about one billion tons in 1993, according to the EIA. Although total energy consumption in the region is expected to rise, coal's projected share declines from 27% in 1993 to 19% in 2015, while the share of natural gas consumption increases from 40% in 1993 to 48% in 2015.

North America. In North America, coal consumption is concentrated in the United States. At 926 million tons, U.S. consumption accounted for 94% of the regional total in 1993. By 2015, the EIA projects U.S. coal consumption will rise to 1,120 million tons. With its substantial supplies of coal reserves, the United States has come to rely heavily on coal for electricity generation and continues to do so in the IEO96 forecast. Coal provided 52% of total U.S. electricity generation in 1993 and the EIA projects a 49% share in 2015. Coal consumption in Canada and Mexico, taken

together, is projected to rise from 59 million tons in 1993 to 109 million tons in 2015.

Africa. In Africa, coal production and consumption are concentrated almost entirely in South Africa. In 1993, South Africa produced 201 million tons of coal, with 71% routed to domestic markets and the remainder to exports. South Africa ranks third in the world in exports, behind Australia and the United States, and is projected to maintain that position over the forecast. For Africa as a whole, the EIA projects coal consumption to increase by 36 million tons between 1993 and 2015, primarily to meet increased demand for electricity.

Natural Gas

Background

As demand for electric generating capacity increases worldwide, natural gas leads the way as the fastest-growing fossil fuel. This strong growth will continue as a result of environmental considerations and advances in gas-fired electricity generation. Super-high-efficiency turbines and the combined-cycle are responsible for much of this growth, particularly in areas with plentiful gas reserves.

Natural gas is the cleanest fossil fuel, and it is an attractive alternative fuel for industrialized OECD countries concerned about reducing greenhouse gas emissions. It is increasingly popular for countries building new electric generating facilities, because natural gas-fired plants often require lower capital costs and shorter construction lead times than solid fuel plants. Technological advances are also lowering operating costs. In addition, natural gas prices are expected to be increasingly competitive with oil prices, and gas reserves are abundant.

The IEO96 forecast predicts worldwide natural gas demand will grow by more than 76% over current levels by 2015. The EIA predicts

consumption will grow to 133 trillion cubic feet in 2015 from 76 trillion cubic feet in 1993. The fastest growth is projected for Europe (both OECD and Eastern Europe), Asia, and Central and South America, with each of these regions making gains in its share of world natural gas demand. OECD Europe is expected to increase its share by three percentage points between 1993 and 2015. Although Asia and Central and South America have not developed their natural gas resources to the same extent as regions with more mature natural gas markets, such as North America, natural gas demand is expected to grow by 6.5% annually in Asia, 4.8% in Eastern Europe, and 4.4% in Central and South America, compared with 1.7% for North America.

The explosive economic growth in many non-OECD countries, particularly in Asia, will require extensive electric power development and natural gas should play a key role in this arena.

Changes in the natural gas industry and technological advances are also facilitating the growth of natural gas demand in the OECD countries. While the U.S. natural gas market is almost completely competitive, many countries of OECD Europe are in various stages of privatization. For most of the non-OECD nations, natural gas utilities remain under state control. However, many non-OECD countries have also begun to explore privatization. As privatization efforts for electric power make headway in these countries, technological developments, particularly increasing the efficiency of natural gas-fired electric power plants, favor the penetration of natural gas in the electric utility sector, especially in OECD Europe.

Reserves

As of January 1, 1996, proven world gas reserves (Table 11–2) were estimated at nearly five quadrillion cubic feet, 46 trillion cubic feet less than the estimate for 1995. Over the past two decades, however, estimated reserves have increased by 94%, mostly because of increases in

Table 11–2
World natural gas reserves by country as of January 1, 1996

Country	Reserves (trillion cubic feet)	Percent of World Total
World Total	**4,933.6**	**100.0**
Top 20 Countries	**4,579.7**	**92.8**
NIS	1,977.0	40.1
Iran	741.6	15.0
Qatar	250.0	5.1
United Arab Emirates	205.5	4.2
Saudi Arabia	185.4	3.8
United States	163.8	3.3
Venezuela	139.9	2.8
Algeria	128.0	2.6
Nigeria	109.7	2.2
Iraq	109.5	2.2
Indonesia	68.9	1.4
Mexico	68.4	1.4
Malaysia	68.0	1.4
Canada	67.0	1.4
Netherlands	65.2	1.3
China	59.0	1.2
Kuwait	52.4	1.1
Norway	47.5	1.0
Libya	45.8	0.9
Pakistan	27.0	0.5
Rest of World	**353.9**	**7.2**

domestic reserve estimates in the Middle East, Eastern Europe, and NIS. While OECD reserves have remained fairly stable between 1975 and 1996, estimated non-OECD reserves have more than doubled, from 1,990 trillion cubic feet to 4,442 trillion cubic feet.

More than 70% of the world's gas reserves are located in the former Soviet Union and the Middle East, with remaining reserves distributed fairly evenly throughout the other regions of the world (Figure 11–5), except for the OECD Pacific. Natural gas reserves in the OECD Pacific region amounted to only 24 trillion cubic feet in 1996, about one-seventh the size of those in OECD Europe.

Despite rapid growth in natural gas use, reserves-to-production ratios are high by standards seen in developed gas markets in North America and Europe. On a worldwide basis, known reserves could maintain production at current rates for more than 60 years. In many countries with emerging economies, the reserves-to-production ratio is twice the world average.

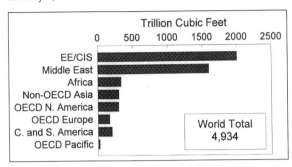

Figure 11–5. World natural gas reserves by region as of January 1, 1996

Infrastructure

Delivery and storage systems are key to making natural gas an economical source of fuel for energy consumption. In the United States, major developments in infrastructure occurred especially in the 1950s and 1960s. In Europe and Japan the energy crises of the 1970s drove rapid development of pipeline and liquid natural gas (LNG) processing facilities. In these established markets, substantial expansion of natural gas handling facilities continues. Although infrastructure development is less advanced in other areas of the world, widespread development is under way, featuring not only major LNG projects but also extended pipeline connections.

In addition, the increasingly competitive global natural gas market has resulted in a need for countries to increase natural gas storage capacity, both to ensure secure supplies of the fuel and to increase market efficiency and, subsequently, market growth. This is particularly evident in countries in North America, OECD Europe, and Eastern Europe, where growing gas imports, deregulation, and competition have increased the demand for flexible mechanisms to transmit gas to customers. The need for more storage is particularly strong in those European countries that are import-dependent and are unable to dramatically increase domestic production.

REGIONAL ACTIVITY

North America

United States. The United States has more than one quadrillion cubic feet of recoverable natural gas, compared with 740 trillion cubic feet in Canada and 250 trillion cubic feet in Mexico, according to the EIA. North America contains roughly 7% of the world's total natural gas reserves but accounts for more than 31% of world production. The United States currently is the second largest producer of natural gas in the world and accounts for roughly 76% of total North American production.

Underground storage capabilities in the United States are approximately eight trillion cubic feet in 375 storage sites, with about 46% of this capacity available to meet demand requirements. On a peak day, the industry can deliver more than 120 billion cubic feet to consumers, and underground storage can supply as much as half of that capacity. Proposed capacity additions through 2000 could increase the U.S. industry's peak-day storage delivery ability by almost 31% from 1993 levels. Despite high levels of domestic production, the United States is still expected to increase imports from 11% of total supply in 1994 to 14% in 2015.

Canada. Natural gas consumption in Canada is expected to grow 1.2% annually between 1993 and 2015. Production should continue to increase as field development intensifies with the aid of technology improvements. Historically, Canada has exported substantial volumes of gas to the United States, increasing from 28% of its domestic production a decade ago to 50% in 1994.

However, existing pipeline capacity cannot handle any significant increases. Several projects are either planned or under way to alleviate this bottleneck. If all the projects announced through the end of 1994 were completed as proposed, pipeline capacity on the U.S.-Canadian border would expand by more than 500 billion cubic feet

per year by 1997. Canada has a current underground storage capacity of 682 billion cubic feet in 11 storage sites, with a peak delivery capability of about eight billion cubic feet per day. Approximately 66 billion cubic feet of new storage capacity is in the planning stage.

Mexico expects 4.5% annual growth in natural gas consumption through 2015, in part because of new environmental standards. Mexico also has the greatest potential in North America for growth in production, with a reserve-to-production ratio greater than 30 years. U.S. and Canadian ratios are 8.5 years and 17.0 years respectively.

Developing these Mexican resources will require foreign and domestic capital investment, and proposed expansion of pipeline capacity between Mexico and the United States should drive this infrastructure development. The EIA reports six proposed pipeline projects: two will increase pipeline capacity at the California-Mexico border, three target the New Mexico-Northwest Texas area, and one connects a pipeline originating in Hidalgo County, Texas, with a PEMEX pipeline near Reynosa, Tamaulipas, Mexico. If all the projects announced were completed as proposed, annual cross-border capacity would increase by more than 600 billion cubic feet. It is unlikely, however, that all the projects actually will be built, because construction of some pipelines may eliminate the need for others.

OECD Europe

Particularly strong growth is expected for natural gas in the electric-utility sector of OECD Europe, and much of the recent pipe-laying activity has focused around plans to expand the international gas grid serving the OECD European markets. Much of this effort involved installing large-diameter international pipeline systems to transport natural gas from the North Sea, North Africa, and Russia. More than 1,600 miles of large gas pipelines (five total) are planned to transport

gas from the Norwegian North Sea to markets in Europe.

France. The main gas suppliers to France are currently Algeria and Russia. Concerns in France about dependence on these two suppliers have led the French public gas utility, Gaz de France, to maintain storage to accommodate disruptions for up to a year from either major supplier. In 1995, Gaz de France signed a 26-year contract with the Norwegian Gas Negotiating Committee to purchase more than 1.4 trillion cubic feet of gas beginning in 2001. A new pipeline at Dunkirk (completion date October 1998) will deliver the gas. Deliveries through the pipeline are expected to peak in 2005 at 70 billion cubic feet. With this contract, Norwegian gas deliveries to France in 2005 should reach almost 530 billion cubic feet, around 35% of the total French gas demand.

Germany. The Norwegian companies Statoil and Norsk Hydro announced at the end of 1994 that they would participate in gas pipeline expansions in Germany, through the newly formed company, Norddeutsche Erdgas-Transversale (Netra). The $720 million, 181-mile Etzel-Salzwedel pipeline project, completed at the end of 1995, will transport between 560 and 630 billion cubic feet of Norwegian gas per year to eastern German markets. In addition, the Etzel-Salzwedel line should connect with an existing 112-mile segment between Salzwedel (at the former East-West German border) and Bernau (north of Berlin). Existing contracts call for Norway to triple its gas supplies to Germany to more than 1,050 billion cubic feet per year by 2005, from 385 billion cubic feet in 1994. By 2005, Norway is expected to supply almost one-third of Germany's natural gas demand.

United Kingdom. The United Kingdom is estimated to have the third-largest reserves of natural gas in OECD Europe, after Norway and the Netherlands. With its large reserves, the

United Kingdom is not expected to import any natural gas in the foreseeable future. In 1994, a consortium of companies led by British Gas agreed to lay a 150-mile pipeline—the Interconnector—between England and continental Europe, with a capacity of 1.9 billion cubic feet per day. Once completed in October 1998, the Interconnector, which is expected to connect into the Belgium gas grid at Zeebrugge, will be the first pipeline link between Britain and the continent. Other pipelines serving the United Kingdom market include a 25-mile subsea pipeline (completion date late 1996) to transport gas from Twynholm, Scotland (Bord Gais Eireann interconnect) to Larne, Northern Ireland (Ballylumford power station).

Pipeline construction is expected to continue in regions interested in feeding the healthy gas markets of OECD Europe. Many European countries are depending on the completion of the proposed 2,500-mile pipeline that will connect Russia with the European markets through Poland and Belarus. Current estimates for its completion are for 2010, although the first gas might begin to flow from already-producing fields in western Siberia at the end of 1996, at a rate of around 483 million cubic feet per day. Construction also continues on pipelines between Africa and Europe. The first phase of the 865-mile Maghreb-Europe pipeline between Algeria and Spain is expected to be complete by the end of 1996. This line would also provide a route for Algerian gas into Portugal, France, and Germany. Spain has plans to expand its pipeline system by more than 20,000 miles by 2004, as well as plans to connect with the gas grids of Portugal and France.

Italy is expected to increase its capacity on the trans-Mediterranean pipeline from Algeria to about 2.5 billion cubic feet per day. The trans-Mediterranean pipeline is being expanded by more than 1,366 miles of new pipe, running from the Algeria-Tunisia border to Minerbio, Italy. Construction also has continued on pipelines connecting Tunisia and Sicily, and within Italy,

there are plans for a 900-mile expansion to the trans-Mediterranean system. In September 1995, Edison SpA, an Italian energy producer, agreed to set up a joint venture with Russia's Gazprom to transport natural gas to Italy. The proposed 620-mile pipeline is expected to begin operation in 1998, and it is slated to be used mainly to supply electricity generators.

OECD European Storage

Increased gas storage capacity is needed in Europe to deal with the increasingly competitive nature of the natural gas market, as well as to ensure supplies in periods of peak demand. The Netherlands utility, Gasunie, announced at the beginning of 1995 that it was losing the ability to provide swing capacity during peak winter demand periods as a result of the growth in gas demand, deregulation, and competition throughout Europe. Other important European exporters, such as Norway, Russia, and Algeria, are not considered flexible enough to accommodate seasonal demand swings. Moreover, these suppliers and numerous LNG suppliers depend upon high-load, inflexible deliveries to make the gas trade economically viable.

In Europe there are plans to expand underground storage by 730 billion cubic feet over the next 10 years. Overall, gas from existing underground storage sites in Europe can, at a maximum, supply about two months of peak winter demand. Currently, European workable underground storage capacity is estimated at 1.5 trillion cubic feet, divided among 76 sites in 12 net importing countries. Most of the sites and storage capacity (61 sites storing 1.2 trillion cubic feet) are located in OECD Europe. Germany, with an expected 300 billion cubic feet of storage capacity expansion between 1995 and 2000, has the most ambitious plans for increased storage capacity in OECD Europe, followed by Italy and Austria, which expect to add 151 and 53 billion cubic feet, respectively, over the same time period.

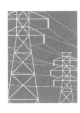

Eastern Europe and NIS

At the end of 1995, Eastern (non-OECD) Europe and the NIS accounted for approximately 41% of the world's natural gas reserves, and exploratory efforts continue to uncover reserves. The vast majority of the reserves (34 of the 41%) are located in the Russian Federation, with the rest mainly in Turkmenistan, 2%; Uzbekistan, 1.3%; and Ukraine, 0.8%.

About 34.5% of the world's total natural gas production in 1994 came from the EE/NIS region—33.0% from the NIS alone. The NIS exported 17.5% of its 1994 production. Key export markets were Austria, Finland, France, Germany, Italy, Turkey, and most of Eastern Europe.

The economic and political transitions occurring in Eastern Europe and the NIS continue to hamper growth in natural gas production and consumption, continuing a decline that began in 1990. The highest consumption drops were seen in Ukraine and the Russian Federation, where consumption fell by 12.4% and 7.1%, respectively.

Turkmenistan experienced the highest production drop, with production falling by 45.5% between 1993 and 1994. Partially offsetting the drastic decline in Turkmenistan production was a 4.9% increase in production in Uzbekistan. Due to increased storage and exports from the NIS, overall production fell less (5.6%) than consumption (7.2%).

The newly relaxed political environment in Eastern Bloc countries is attracting foreign investors, increasing prospects for more development of the countries' natural resources. Substantial natural gas resources over and above already proven reserves appear to exist. However, although foreign capital is funding resource development in several countries, until an investor-friendly petroleum law is passed in the Russian Federation, plans for large expenditures by Western firms are on hold. The legislated willingness of EE/NIS countries to allow foreign investment is key to resource development.

Foreign investment also may play a role in developing Eastern Bloc natural gas transmission and distribution systems. For example, Mitsubishi is investigating building an oil and gas pipeline from Turkmenistan and Kazakhstan through China and Korea to Japan. The project probably will not be feasible in this century. However, a very large resource base is available to serve such a development.

Other key developments include the signing of an agreement in August 1994 between Turkmenistan and Iran to build a pipeline from Turkmenistan through northern Iran to Turkey, and the February 1995 agreement to build the Yamal-Poland-Germany gas pipeline across Poland. The Yamal pipeline will deliver cheap gas to Poland beginning in 1996 and has a large potential for delivery to Western Europe by 2010.

Asia

With its quickly increasing need for electricity, Asia's demand for natural gas is projected to increase by 6.5% annually, reaching 14.5 trillion cubic feet in 2015, according to the EIA. Pipeline construction plans necessary to meet India's growing gas demand have not materialized as hoped. After plans for a proposed pipeline connecting Oman to India fell through at the end of 1995, India's Gas Authority of India Limited (GAIL) began working to develop domestic reserves and to secure import sources that will allow gas demand to double by 2000.

In Southeast Asia, there are some 39 current or probable natural-gas development projects expected to produce an estimated 51 trillion cubic feet of gas. In Indonesia, 14 gas development projects have startup dates between 1996 and 1999. Thailand, Myanmar, and the Philippines also have a number of gas development projects. Current daily gas production in the region is 12.4 billion cubic feet, with an expected increase of 54% by 2002.

China has four offshore, natural-gas projects expected to be operational between 1995 and 1999, with estimated reserves of more than 6.2 trillion cubic feet. In January 1996, Asia's longest

large-diameter subsea pipeline began operating. The 480-mile system links China's Yacheng gas field (South China Sea) and Hong Kong. There are notable efforts to expand the gas transportation system in the Xinjiang Uygur region in remote Northwest China, including a 56-mile pipeline from Lunnan to Korla, a 192-mile pipeline from Shanshan to Urumqu with a capacity of 153 million cubic feet per day, and a 195-mile pipeline from Tazhong 4 field to Lunnan with a capacity of 38 million cubic feet per day.

Myanmar is expected to begin gas production in the Yadana gas field in the Gulf of Martaban by July 1998. The field has estimated reserves of as much as 5.8 trillion cubic feet. A 260-mile pipeline is planned to transport the gas from Yadana to Thailand, and construction is expected to begin by the end of 1995. The Yetagun gas field, discovered in Myanmar's Gulf of Martaban in 1992, should provide Thailand with gas deliveries of about 200 million cubic feet per day by 2000. Plans are to construct a pipeline from Yetagun to Thailand.

Indonesia may be another potential gas supplier for Thailand. In 1996, Pertamina and the Petroleum Authority of Thailand began discussions to consider building a 620-mile pipeline to Thailand. Indonesia also should remain South Korea's largest natural gas supplier, with about 90% of the Korean market. Malaysia and Brunei currently supply the remaining 10%. South Korea has recently added Qatar as a supplier and has also entered negotiations with Australia for gas supplies.

Much of the natural gas pipeline development in the OECD Pacific is projected to occur in Japan and Australia. Japan, which imported almost 65% of the world's LNG in 1994, began construction that year on a 155-mile pipeline running from the west coast city, Niigata, to Sendai City on the Pacific Ocean. This is the first part of a 2,050-mile gas distribution system that by 2005 could transport as much as 82.6 million metric tons of regasified LNG per year. In mid-1995, work began on the 470-mile Australian pipeline, which will link Queensland with Brisbane and Gladstone. The project is expected to begin operation in late 1996.

Central and South America

Development of natural gas resources is expected to be strong in some countries of Central and South America, reports the EIA, in order to meet increasing demand for electricity in a region where natural gas is considered a relatively immature industry. Natural gas and hydropower are the two major energy sources for electricity generation in the region. In 1995, construction of several large pipeline projects was scheduled which, when complete, will transport gas from Argentina to markets in Brazil and Chile. A 750-mile system planned for the Argentina-Chile line is expected to be complete in 1997. A 2,000-mile pipeline system is being developed to deliver gas from Argentina and Bolivia to Brazil, and a 685-mile project is currently under consideration to link Bolivia and Chile.

In 1994, construction began on Colombia's first, large, natural gas pipeline, a 357-mile system running from Ballena, Colombia, into the Barrancabermeja area. For the first 15 years of operation, the gas will be used to supply the domestic market with about 150 million cubic feet per day.

Africa

Algeria, by far, has the most highly developed natural gas resources in Africa. The pipelines linking Algeria with markets in OECD Europe, combined with growing LNG exports, provide the country with a particularly strong commodity. According to the EIA, pipelines are currently under construction to link both Algeria and Tunisia with Italy and Spain, and through them to markets in Belgium, Portugal, and France.

Natural gas resources in North Africa (primarily, Algeria, Egypt, and Libya) are considerably more developed than those in the rest of Africa. There is, however, growing interest in pursuing gas resources outside the north, particularly in terms of fueling electric power. Nigeria, for example, is the site of a $569-million(US) gas utilization project in

Escravos, which is expected to be operational in 1997. A Nigerian LNG project also has been proposed. The country is estimated to have some 120 trillion cubic feet of natural gas reserves, the most of any west African country. Long-term hopes are to expand the Escravos gas project into the West African Pipeline, which would allow gas in eastern Nigeria to reach potential customers in Benin, Togo, and Ghana, as well as other parts of Nigeria's domestic market.

Tanzania is also anxious to develop its natural gas resources. Although Tanzania's reserves are smaller than those of Nigeria, at four trillion cubic feet, the country is seeking financing to construct two small, natural gas-fired electricity plants (one at Songo-Songo and one at Mnazi Bay). Tanzania is interested in increasing the amount of electricity generated by natural gas to counter losses in hydroelectricity—caused by low rainfall and aging facilities—and to replace some of the 90% of its energy consumption currently provided by wood burning.

Middle East

More than 30% of the world's natural gas reserves are located in the Middle East, and about 93% of the Middle Eastern reserves are located in Iran, Iraq, Qatar, Saudi Arabia, and the United Arab Emirates (mostly Abu Dhabi). Electricity demand is increasing rapidly in the Middle East, and much of it is expected to be accommodated by natural gas-fired plants. At present, more than 50% of the region's marketed natural gas production is consumed in electric power generation and for seawater desalination. Most of the thermal power plants in countries that border the Arabian Gulf are fueled by natural gas.

Also there is evidence of increased development of natural gas for export in the Middle East. The region accounted for almost 5% of the world's LNG exports in 1994, all of it exported to Japan. There are plans to develop Qatar's North field gas reserves for export to Japan, with initial plans to produce 195 billion cubic feet per year.

OIL

Background

Oil lags behind other fuels in terms of electricity production. However, it is the major source of energy worldwide and is expected to remain so over the next two decades. (Figure 11–3) Oil use is projected to grow by 2% a year, but oil prices are not expected to rise beyond $25 per barrel before 2015. This leading role as energy provider will be important in determining how each country manages its oil resources.

Since the oil price collapse of 1986, petroleum has reemerged as a premier growth industry in world energy markets. Current oil consumption exceeds 68 million barrels per day and is rising at an annual rate in excess of 1.5 million barrels per day. According to the EIA, the world's daily consumption of oil is expected to reach about 99 million barrels by 2015, as compared with an average of 57 barrels per day in 1973, when the world first experienced an oil price crisis. Despite continued demand growth of nearly 2% per year over the next two decades, oil prices are not expected to rise beyond $25 per barrel. The existence of vast quantities of producible oil reserves, along with actual and potential competition from nonpetroleum fuels, is expected to moderate many tendencies for sustained oil price escalation over the next 20 years.

While natural gas and renewables are making inroads into energy markets in OECD nations, leading to a decline in oil's share in those markets, its share is rising in the developing nations as transportation, industrial, and other uses for oil expand.

Reserves

In the late 1980s, more than 350 billion barrels of crude oil reserves were added worldwide. The additions were made predominantly by OPEC (Organization of Petroleum Exporting Countries) nations (almost 94% of the total). Although OPEC

crude oil production has been increasing steadily since the mid-1980s, crude oil production from non-OPEC suppliers has shown surprising resilience over the past two decades, increasing by more than two-thirds. In fact, the long-term outlook for non-OPEC supply has become increasingly optimistic even in the face of lower world oil prices.

Although forecasters have long been predicting a decline of non-OPEC oil supplies, there is reason to expect that such production will continue to be vigorous well into the next century. Table 11–3 shows estimates of worldwide, proven, crude oil reserves and a forecast range of undiscovered conventional crude oil. Also shown is an estimate of ultimately recoverable resources, which is derived from the sum of cumulative production, undiscovered conventional crude oil (modal value), and identified reserves (assuming current technology and prices). Cumulative production also is included, to give a sense of that portion of ultimately recoverable resources that has already been produced. OPEC producers, led by those in the Persian Gulf region, obviously enjoy an enormous advantage in proven reserves over non-OPEC producers. (Figure 11–6) However, the U.S. Geological Survey estimates that of the more than 450 billion barrels of undiscovered conventional crude oil that would most likely be recoverable, assuming current economic and technological conditions, about two-thirds of that oil would come from non-OPEC producers.

Figure 11–6. World oil production by region

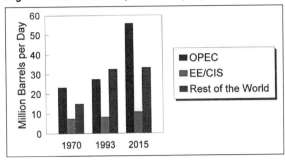

OPEC Production

The IEO96 price projections assume the OPEC countries with large reserves that can be exploited at relatively low cost will have the greatest influence on future oil market conditions. It is assumed that OPEC nations will pursue policies—and that investment capital will be available—to expand production capacity as necessary to meet growing demand.

In the IEO96 reference case, the production call on OPEC producers grows at an annual rate of 3.5%. By 2015, the IEO96 production estimate for OPEC exceeds 55 million barrels per day. This outlook assumes that Iraq will resume exports in 1997 and will gradually build its output to almost three million barrels per day by the year 2000.

Given these production capacity expansion requirements for OPEC, much attention has been focused on the oil development, production, and operating costs of individual producers. The reserves-to-production ratio of Persian Gulf OPEC

Table 11–3
Estimated undiscovered and ultimately recoverable conventional oil resources as of January 1, 1993 (billion barrels)

| Region | Undiscovered Oil | | | Cumulative Production | Identified Reserves | Ultimate Resources |
	Low Estimate	Most Likely	High Estimate			
OPEC	**95.3**	**152.0**	**319.8**	**282.9**	**706.4**	**1,141.3**
Persian Gulf	74.2	116.4	232.0	177.0	583.0	876.4
Other	21.1	35.6	87.8	105.9	123.4	264.9
Non-OPEC	**196.9**	**318.7**	**685.4**	**415.7**	**396.8**	**1,131.2**
OECD	68.4	108.3	223.9	225.4	156.4	490.1
Eurasia	77.5	132.1	330.6	142.3	163.7	438.1
Rest of World	51.0	78.3	130.9	48.0	76.7	203.0
Total World	**292.2**	**470.7**	**1,005.2**	**698.6**	**1,103.2**	**2,272.5**

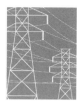

producers currently exceeds 80 years, but the economics of production capacity expansion estimates will play a part in determining production development.

The capital investment required to increase production capacity by one barrel per day in Persian Gulf OPEC nations ranges between $2,515 and $4,866, depending on field size. The total cost of the projected capacity expansion is a relatively small percentage of the gross revenue even in a low-price scenario. For OPEC producers outside the Persian Gulf, the cost to expand production capacity by one barrel per day is considerably greater, ranging from $7,610 (Indonesia) to $10,240 (Venezuela). Nonetheless, even this group of producers in the low-price case can expect margins in excess of 50% on investments to expand production capacity over the long term. Of the non-Persian Gulf OPEC producers, Venezuela has the greatest capacity expansion potential and has already announced plans to expand capacity to nearly four million barrels per day by 2005.

Non-OPEC Production

The growth in non-OPEC oil supply has played a significant role in the erosion of OPEC's market share over the past two decades. Moreover, the non-OPEC oil supply has become increasingly diverse. North America dominated non-OPEC supply in the early 1970s, the North Sea and Mexico evolved as major producers into the 1980s, and much of the new production in the 1990s has come from the developing countries.

In the IEO96 reference case, world petroleum demand rises at an annual average rate of 1.5 million barrels per day through 2015. Although OPEC is expected to benefit most from the projected growth in oil demand, there will be significant competition from a diverse range of non-OPEC suppliers that have shown surprising resilience even in the current low-price environment. While U.S. exploration and development activity has dropped dramatically over the past decade, the country's production and reserve availability have

not fallen proportionately. At the same time, even with lower prices, exploration activity in some of the developing countries has actually expanded. By EIA estimates, non-OPEC supply is expected to remain virtually flat through 2010, ranging between 41.0 and 41.5 million barrels per day. The agency expects a decline of only one million barrels per day coming near 2015, the end of the projection period.

The following regional estimates are from the IEO96 forecast and are based on such parameters as the number of exploration wells, finding rates, reserve-to-production ratios, advances in extraction technology, and the world oil price. By the end of the projection period, the range of non-OPEC supply varies between 38.5 and 47.2 million barrels per day.

North America

Due mainly to the decline in U.S. production, North American output will show steady decline into the early years of the next century. Canada's output should increase modestly over current levels, declining only slightly by the end of the forecast period. Offshore discoveries in the Gulf of Mexico, incremental Alaskan production from Cook Inlet, and technological advances in extraction methods reverse the downward trend in U.S. production for the remainder of the forecast period. By 2015, U.S. production is expected to return to current production levels. Mexico is expected increasingly to make concessions that will encourage foreign investment in its oil sector, resulting in a much-needed infusion of capital and leading to more efficient use of its vast resource base. Production volumes in Mexico are expected to reach 3.5 million barrels per day by 2005 and could increase by another 300,000 barrels per day by 2015.

Western Europe

North Sea production is expected to peak in 1997 at almost 6.4 million barrels per day.

Production from Norway, Western Europe's largest producer, is expected to peak at about 3.3 million barrels per day in 1997 and then gradually decline to about 2.2 million barrels per day by the end of the forecast period, as some of its larger and older fields mature. The United Kingdom sector of the North Sea is expected to produce about 2.8 million barrels per day for the remainder of this decade, followed by a decline of about one million barrels per day by the end of the forecast period. However, recent discoveries, especially in the United Kingdom sector, indicate the possible availability of significant untapped potential.

Asia

Far Eastern producers are beginning to explore and develop what appears to be a promising potential for oil production, which could reap benefits well into the next century. Assuming no barriers for foreign investment, India is expected to increase its current output steadily to about 900,000 barrels per day by 2015, and deep-water fields offshore from the Philippines could produce about 250,000 barrels per day by the turn of the century. There appears to be enough long-term production potential in Vietnam for output to reach 500,000 barrels per day by the end of the forecast period. Australia will have a near-term increase that peaks at more than 650,000 barrels per day by 1997, but production declines are expected to be rather severe beyond the year 2000 unless current offshore exploration pays some dividends. Malaysia's production activity comes mostly from mature fields that are in decline. Preliminary seismic exploration and test wells indicate some production potential for Bangladesh and Mongolia, but it is unlikely that output would be realized until the turn of the century.

Central and South America

In Central and South America, Colombia—which continues to encourage significant multinational investment—is expected to at least double its current output by 2000. By the turn of the century, both Brazil and Colombia are expected to join the relatively short list of producers whose output exceeds one million barrels per day. Brazil has vast, untapped production potential; and given no government impediments to foreign investment, it could approach two million barrels per day of output by the end of the forecast period. Argentina is expected to raise current production levels by up to 150,000 barrels per day by the end of this decade. Former OPEC member Ecuador is expected to increase its production capacity to allow an additional 200,000 barrels per day in output.

Non-OPEC Africa

A few non-OPEC producers in Africa are expected to show modest increases out to the end of the decade. Angola, Congo, and Tunisia, combined, will account for about 200,000 barrels per day of additional output by the year 2000. The absence of significant discoveries, coupled with normal declines from mature fields, has Egypt's production falling by almost 150,000 barrels per day by the end of the decade. Two new African producers, Chad and the Sudan, are expected to bring a combined 500,000 barrels per day of output on-line by the turn of the century. The Ivory Coast, Equatorial Guinea, Somalia, and South Africa have some production potential, but they are unlikely to begin production before 2000.

Non-OPEC Persian Gulf

Two non-OPEC Persian Gulf producers are expected to show production increases at least to the end of this decade. In Oman, enhanced recovery techniques are expected to increase current output by almost 150,000 barrels per day. And assuming that the recent civil strife in Yemen remains dormant, current oil production could

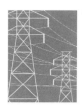

increase by more than 200,000 barrels per day early in the next century. Syria is expected to hold output at its current level for the remainder of this decade, with production declining thereafter.

NUCLEAR

For information on nuclear fuels, please refer to Chapter 14 on nuclear technology.

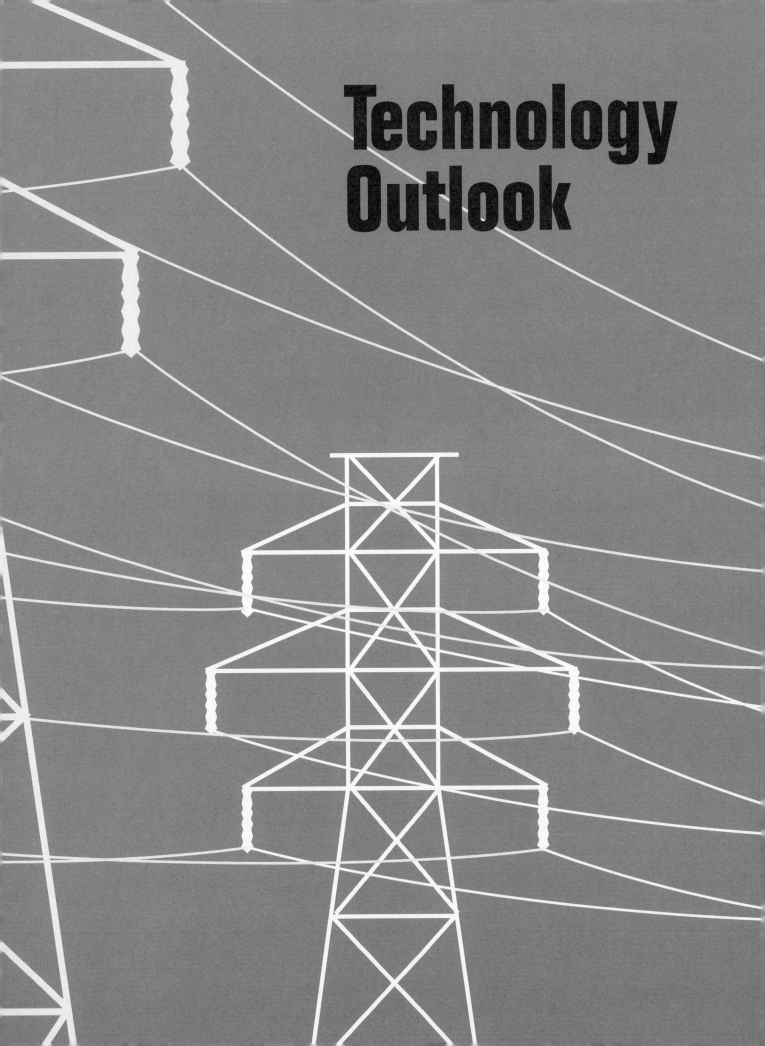

Technology Outlook

Chapter 12
Conventional Boilers

TIMOTHY B. DEMOSS
ASSOCIATE EDITOR
POWER ENGINEERING AND
POWER ENGINEERING INTERNATIONAL

OVERVIEW

Much attention has been given lately to advanced coal burning technologies in light of an increased public awareness of coal burning's environmental impact. This has resulted in increasing regulations on coal-fired power generation worldwide. Many of the technologies spawned as a result of research in clean-coal power generation diverge considerably from the conventional, pulverized-coal (PC), combustion boiler approach. Fluidized-bed combustion and integrated gasification combined-cycle are two of the more popular designs. However, there are two concepts currently being tested to ready pulverized-coal combustion for the 21st century, the low-emission boiler system (LEBS) and the high performance power system (HIPPS). Both technologies are part of the U.S. Department of Energy's (DOE) Combustion 2000 program. Progress to date in the Combustion 2000 program shows there is substantial room for improvement

of the PC design and it can be an option for the next century.

LEBS

The ultimate goal of the LEBS program is an advanced, pulverized-coal combustion system with integrated emission controls and a net thermal efficiency of 42%. Industry teams headed by three major U.S. boiler manufacturers are developing conceptual designs.

The target is an advanced, clean, PC combustion system for baseload electricity generation in the 21st century, with a cost of electricity lower than PC systems currently achieve. It's intended to appeal to utilities who are skeptical about more radical, new, coal-combustion technologies such as pressurized fluidized-bed combustion (PFBC) or integrated coal gasification combined-cycles (IGCC).

Integrated Design

The three main legs of the LEBS design are low-NO_x emissions, flue-gas desulfurization, and advanced, supercritical boiler designs. To date, each of these systems has been designed on its own path. LEBS program director Larry Ruth, who is officially the director of the coal utilization division of the DOE's Pittsburgh Energy Technology Center, believes that an integrated design can yield dramatically better performance in a PC system.

Basic performance goals for all the LEBS teams are:

- SO_2 emission of 0.1 lb/MBtu,

- NO_x emission of 0.1 lb/MBtu,

- particulate emission of 0.01 lb/MBtu,

- efficiency of 42%, and

- cost of electricity less than a current, New Source Performance Standards coal-fired plant.

Use of well-known PC technology should lead to wider acceptance than more advanced technologies have received so far. LEBS designs are expected to be ready for ordering by the year 2000 to meet baseload demand by 2005. No demonstration plants will be needed, according to Ruth.

The total program is expected to cost approximately $85 million(US). Phase I, begun in 1992 and recently completed, saw the technical and economic evaluation of candidate technologies, small-scale testing, and preliminary design of a 350-MW commercial plant. In Phase II, currently underway, new technology will be designed and tested. In Phases III and IV, LEBS teams will develop specific, complete designs.

Three industry teams are currently working on LEBS designs under cost-sharing contracts with DOE:

1. Riley Stoker Corp. heads a team with Sargent & Lundy, Tecogen, and the University of Utah;

2. ABB CE heads a team including Raytheon Engineers and Constructors; and

3. Babcock & Wilcox (B&W) heads a team with Physical Sciences, Inc., and Raytheon.

Slagging, Supercritical Boiler

The Riley Stoker team is developing a new boiler design that features slag-tap firing and a new, regenerable SO_2 system. The design will eliminate solid waste streams. The slagging boiler will have a supercritical, once-through design that features main steam conditions of 4,500 psig at 1,100 F and two, 1,100 F reheat stages. Advanced low-NO_x combustion will be integrated into the design.

Supercritical boilers have gone out of favor in the United States since 1970, according to a Riley Stoker spokesman, but they have continued to be built in Europe. Riley designed the boiler based on a design used successfully by its parent firm, Deutsche Babcock, for boilers in Europe. Materials were the main problem with first-generation supercritical designs in the United States. The advanced steam conditions of the new design will require some advanced, 9–12% chromium steels.

The Riley team's concept also features desulfurization in a moving bed absorber using dry, regenerable copper oxide as the sorbent. The system will yield sulfuric acid or elemental sulfur with no waste products. There will be additional NO_x removal via ammonia injection in the boiler and selective catalytic reduction by the copper oxide. The overall system is shown in Figure 12–1. The Riley Stoker LEBS design offers the lowest-cost option for electricity generators at approximately 5¢/kWh. The capital cost of a 400-MW unit burning Illinois No. 6 coal will be $1,140/kW in 1993 U.S. dollars.

Conventional PC systems cost $1,400/kW in 1992 and $940/kW in 1970. The LEBS cost also compares well to PFBC and IGCC systems. The 30-year leveled cost of electricity from the Riley LEBS boiler even can beat that of a natural gas-fired combined-cycle when coal costs start at $1.50(US)/MBtu and escalate at 1.5% per year, and gas costs start at $2.77(US)/MBtu and escalate at 5% per year.

The ABB-led team has a design based on a supercritical boiler at 4,500 psig, 1,100 F, and double reheat. An ABB spokesman noted that this design is not a leap in technology or a risk, because boilers with these conditions are being built in Japan and Denmark.

ABB's design will achieve NO_x control through the low-NO_x burners in ABB CE's advanced tangential firing system, through use of the SNO_x system and through a catalytic filter. SO_2 reduction will be achieved in the SNO_x system's advanced, wet limestone scrubber, with particulate removal taking place in the catalytic filter. The overall system is shown in Figure 12–2.

The B&W team's boiler is a double reheat, supercritical unit at 4,500 psig and 1,100 F. SO_2 control will be handled by B&W's dry limestone process. NO_x control will be handled by advanced low-NO_x burners that can do the job without using selective catalytic reduction (SCR). One of the major challenges for the B&W team is NO_x control without SCR. Particulate control will be done in a pulse-jet baghouse. The B&W system is shown in Figure 12–3.

LEBS' Future

Repowering with LEBS will initially be the primary use for the technology. LEBS does not require new sites and is a comfortable alternative for utilities burdened with aging power plants. As advanced, high-pressure steam cycles are proved reliable and as experience with the Kalina cycle (using an ammonia/water mixture instead of water only as a heat transfer medium) gains it more acceptance, LEBS efficiencies could increase as high as 50% when integrated with these technologies, making it an even more attractive option.

Some industry experts feel the LEBS concept has a limited future because the program's efficiency target, 42%, is too low to counter increasing pressure for CO_2 reduction. However, combined with the advanced steam technologies

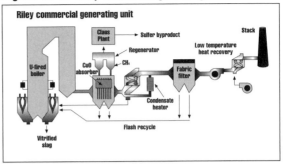

Figure 12–1. Riley commercial generating unit

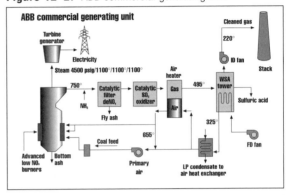

Figure 12–2. ABB commercial generating unit

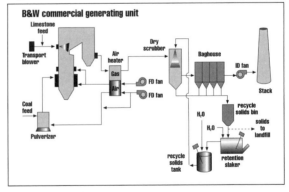

Figure 12–3. B&W commercial generating unit

mentioned earlier and with the current emphasis on combined-cycle technologies, with which LEBS could be integrated, the LEBS approach could emerge as an important concept for future coal-fired power generation.

HIPPS

LEBS is DOE's near-term PC improvement program. A longer term program is the high

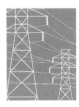

performance power system (HIPPS), which aims at using more exotic technology to get PC technology thermal efficiency up to 47%. The system is shown in Figure 12–4. HIPPS processes are based on an indirect coal-fired combined-cycle and the technology includes a high-temperature advanced furnace (HITAF). HITAF integrates combustion, heat transfer, and emission control in a single unit. In the HIPPS combined-cycle, a commercially available gas turbine is driven with clean air heated indirectly in the coal-fired HITAF. Supplementary firing with clean fuel (such as natural gas) is used to boost the air temperature to achieve optimum gas-turbine inlet temperatures; the gas firing can be phased out as advances are made with the HITAF design. Energy in the turbine exhaust is used to generate steam in the heat recovery steam generator (HRSG). HITAF energy also can be used for superheating and reheating, and the gas turbine exhaust returns to the HITAF for use as coal combustion air.

The HIPPS program has experienced repeated budget cuts, but the system described faces another problem that will delay its commercialization until at least 2004. (The 2004 date was given by the DOE in late 1993; slow progress on HIPPS thus far indicates a later date is more likely.) This advanced design has a HITAF exit temperature of 1,800 F which will require high-temperature advanced materials such as coated superalloys and ceramics, capable of withstanding 2,000 F temperatures. To move up the date for HIPPS demonstration and commercialization, the development teams must

reduce the HITAF exit temperature to one that state-of-the-art materials will handle. Lowering the HITAF exit temperature to 1,500 F should make this possible.

The state-of-the-art HIPPS plant (Figure 12–5) has a target efficiency of 45% and must match the emissions control of PC plants with scrubbers, doing so while using coal for no less than 50% of its total fuel input on a thermal basis.

Several options have been considered for the state-of-the-art HIPPS plant, including reducing the HITAF exit temperature, reducing gas-turbine inlet temperature, and providing gas turbine intercooling. With the HITAF exit temperature lowered to 1,500 F, natural gas is required to raise the gas-turbine inlet temperature to 2,300 F. An air heater preheats ambient air for combustion instead of recycling vitiated air from the turbine exhaust. Table 12–1 compares the results for

Table 12–1
Comparison of advanced and state-of-the-art HIPPS

	Advanced HIPPS[1]	State-of-the-Art HIPPS
Feed coal sulfur: wt %, dry	Illinois No. 6 3.65	Illinois No. 6 3.65
Steam conditions	894 K/9409 kPa (1150 F/1365 psia)	811 K/811 K/10100 kPa (1000 F/1000 F/1465 psia)
Furnace air outlet temperature, K	1255 (1800 F)	1088 (1500 F)
Gas turbine inlet temperature, K	1533 (2300 F)	1533 (2300 F)
Stack gas temperature, K	352 (175 F)	353 (177 F)
Combustion air source	Turbine exhaust	Preheated ambient air
Results Power summary		
Gas turbine, MW	142.3	298.5
Steam turbine, MW	113.5	278.9
Auxiliary, MW	-5.8	-18.9
Net power, MW	**250.0**	**558.6[2]**
System efficiency: %, HHV	47.7	45.3
Natural gas usage, % of thermal input	34.5	44.2

1 Results from previous analysis (Klara and Ward, 1992)
2 Plant size increased to compare with plant costs for a 600-MW PC plant

Figure 12–4. HIPPS indirect coal-fired combined cycle

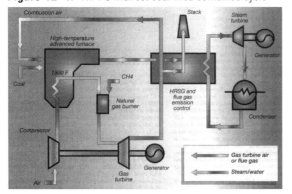

estimated performance of the advanced and state-of-the-art HIPPS.

With a significant portion of the system fired by natural gas, the modified HIPPS plant's SO_2 emissions are less than one-half that of a PC plant equipped with conventional scrubbers, and CO_2 emissions are more than 35% less than a conventional PC plant. The state-of-the-art HIPPS plant is also favored over the conventional PC plant with regard to capital requirement (Table 12–2) and leveled cost of electricity (Figure 12–6). By making these simple modifications to the advanced design and settling for performance that doesn't quite meet the original Combustion 2000 goals, the HIPPS plant stands a better chance in the short term of being competitive compared to other advanced coal-burning designs. (Figure 12–7) Although

Table 12–2

Capital cost for a state-of-the-art HIPPS plant

Plant system	Cost ($1000)	$/kW
HITAF material	74,120	
HITAF erection (with bypass)	37,060	
Steam turbine-generator	33,850	
Gas turbine-generators (2)	72,450	
Heat recovery steam generators (2)	12,480	
Heat recovery steam generator erection	4,620	
Coal handling system	13,255	
Coal train unloading system	8,680	
Wet flue gas desulfurization	53,225	
Electrostatic precipitator	9,445	
Mechanical draft cooling tower	9,500	
Balance of mechanical equipment	22,500	
Electrical equipment	31,479	
Instrumentation and control	7,135	
Civil works	36,410	
Mechanical installation	31,070	
Electrical/instruments and controls installation	15,985	
Indirect construction costs and general expenses	85,230	
Total direct and indirect construction costs	**558,494**	**1000**
Engineering and construction management services (7%)	39,095	
Project contingency (15%)	89,640	
Process contingency (20% of HITAF material)	14,825	
Total project cost (December 92 dollars)	**702,044**	**1257**
Total cash expended (mixed year dollars)	665,603	
Allowance for funds used during construction	109,572	
Total plant investment	**775,175**	**1388**
Organization, startup, inventory, land	28,807	
Total capital requirement (January 93 in-service)	**803,982**	**1439**

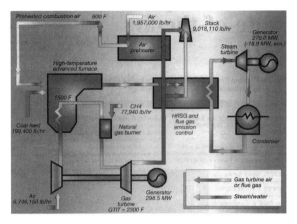

Figure 12–5. State-of-the-art HIPPS configuration

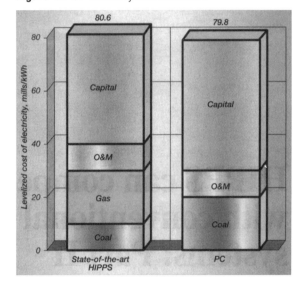

Figure 12–6. Electricity cost breakdown

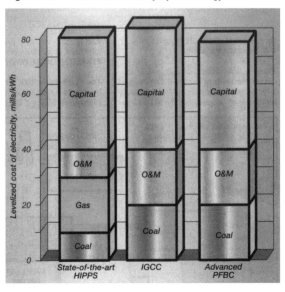

Figure 12–7. Cost of electricity by technology

commercialization for state-of-the-art HIPPS by 2000 seems unlikely, combining the system's emissions performance with its leveled cost of electricity and conventional design could make it a competitive commercial technology within the next decade.

Chapter 13
Fluidized-Bed Combustion

TIMOTHY B. DEMOSS
ASSOCIATE EDITOR
POWER ENGINEERING AND
POWER ENGINEERING INTERNATIONAL

OVERVIEW

With an abundance and wide variety of coal reserves worldwide, it only makes economic sense to find new and better ways to utilize this vast resource for electricity generation. One hundred years ago, the soot from coal-fired boilers filled the air as steam turbines made it possible to centralize the generation of electricity for the first time. Today, we understand the consequences of unmitigated pollution, and many countries have regulations requiring power generation facilities to take extreme measures to curtail the negative effects of burning fossil fuels, coal in particular, to electrify our societies.

Worldwide, coal accounts for 36% of electricity generation, and forecasts for the next two decades predict little or no change in this number. In coal-rich countries like the United States, where coal's share of electricity generation is at a steady 56%, minimizing stack emissions from coal-fired plants is a high priority.

Research efforts like the U.S. Department of Energy's Clean Coal Technology (CCT) Program have confronted the clean-burning coal challenge with great success. As a result of these efforts, advanced coal-burning technologies are in place worldwide, generating power with low emissions and high efficiency. One of the most successful technologies to date has been fluidized-bed combustion (FBC). Fluidized-bed reactors have long been used in noncombustion reactions. However, it was not until the 1950s that experiments began focusing on using a fluidized bed to combust coal. Much of the work in this area was done in England during the 1960s, with the technology making its way to the United States that same decade. Pilot-plant research in FBC boilers led eventually to a scaled-up 30-MW demonstration plant in 1975 at Rivesville, West Virginia. This plant was 15 times larger than any other operating FBC facility. Research continues in the areas of both conventional, bubbling, fluidized beds, characterized by larger particles and low air velocity,

and circulating fluidized beds, characterized by finer particles and higher air velocities. Circulating fluidized beds require recirculation of the particles to maintain the fuel level in the bed.

ATMOSPHERIC FLUIDIZED-BED COMBUSTION

The early demonstration plants using FBC operated their boilers at atmospheric pressure. Atmospheric fluidized-bed combustion (AFBC) is now considered a mature technology and makes up the bulk of FBC plants in operation. There are hundreds of these plants located throughout the world in a variety of sizes, with some units generating hundreds of megawatts. However, efficiency values (percent high heating value [HHV]) for AFBC are around 36%, not much better than a conventional boiler plant. For some plant operators, the advantages afforded by AFBC, such as increased fuel flexibility, were not enough to swing the balance in AFBC's favor.

Studies in the 1980s indicated that pressurizing the AFBC concept could improve the heat rate for a coal-fired plant by more than 10%. Although early indications were that capital costs were not low enough to offset the development risk, cooperation among industry and government worldwide has made significant strides in reducing the cost for pressurized fluidized-bed combustion (PFBC), and today the technology is poised to become a commercial success.

PRESSURIZED FLUIDIZED-BED COMBUSTION

PFBC boilers offer higher efficiency (up to 39% in first-generation systems) and lower costs (about $300(US)/kW less) than a conventional pulver-

ized-coal boiler with flue-gas desulfurization. A pressurized fluidized-bed boiler operates at about 12 to 16 atm., burning coal in a large pressure vessel. Sulfur released during combustion reacts with a sorbent in the boiler, such as limestone or dolomite, reducing SO_2 emissions. PFBC cleans as much as 95% of the sulfur from the coal during combustion. NO_x levels are also reduced because the boiler combusts the coal at lower temperatures (860 C is typical) than a conventional boiler while maintaining high efficiency. Ammonia injection can reduce the NO_x levels even further. NO_x levels of 0.05 lb/MBtu have been reported using this technique. Figure 13–1 compares SO_2 and NO_x emissions for PFBC compared to AFBC, integrated gasification combined-cycle, and pulverized coal with flue-gas desulfurization and selective catalytic reduction. Reducing these pollutants in the boiler eliminates the need for back-end pollution control such as flue-gas desulfurization, and the low operating temperatures help to avoid furnace slagging and fouling.

From this point forward in the PFBC process, the PFBC plant operates much like any other combined-cycle system, with the exception of some further gas cleanup. The PFBC combined-cycle can generate electricity with efficiencies of more than 40% (HHV). Heater tubes in the fluidized bed provide steam to the steam turbine while the bed's combustion gases drive a gas turbine. The steam turbine provides 70–80% of the total electricity generated. Before expanding through the gas turbine, combustion gases pass through a series of cyclones to remove about 98% of the ash in the

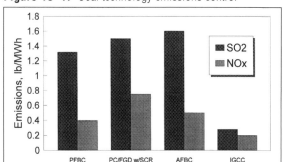

Figure 13–1. Coal technology emissions control

Table 13–1
Repowering a typical power plant with advanced, coal-based systems

	Typical candidate	CAFBC	1st gen. PFBC	IGCC	EFCC	2nd gen. PFBC
Steam turbine, MW (gross)	100	105	105	105	105	105
Gas turbine, MW (gross)	N/A	N/A	24	210	48	75
Gross power, MW	100	105	129	315	153	180
Capacity addition, MW (gross)	N/A	5	29	215	53	80
Efficiency (HHV)	30.2%	33.4%	37.3%	42.1%	36.6%	41.8%
Sulfur dioxide, lb/MMBtu	3	0.4	0.2	0.02	0.1	0.2
Nitrogen oxides, lb/MMBtu	0.8	0.2	0.3	0.08	0.25	0.3
Carbon dioxide reduction lb/MWhr	N/A	229	454	676	418	663
Sulfur dioxide reduction lb/MWhr	N/A	29.8	32.1	33.7	33.0	32.3
Nitrogen oxide reduction lb/MWhr	N/A	7.00	6.29	8.39	6.71	6.59
Repowered total plant cost, $ millions	N/A	112-133	155-181	268-394	176-222	160-214
Repowered total plant cost, $/kW	N/A	1070-1270	1100-1400	850-1250	1150-1450	890-1190

gas. The latest designs use hot-gas filters to remove more particulate and other contaminants, and to protect the turbine from erosion and corrosion damage. Finally, turbine exhaust gas passes through an economizer and an electrostatic precipitator before exiting the plant through the stack. The gas turbine's compressor provides the air to fluidize the coal bed.

According to the United States' Electric Power Research Institute (EPRI), bubbling PFBC technology is near commercial status today, with at least five units operating at 80 MWe and larger units, up to 350 MWe, being manufactured. Scaling up to larger sizes depends mainly on building a larger combustor and gas turbine, and fine tuning the overall system. By EPRI estimates, the levelized cost of electricity for large-scale, coal-fired PFBC units starting up in 2000 should be as much as 15% less than subcritical, pulverized coal-fired units with flue-gas desulfurization, and 5–10% less than these units' advanced, supercritical siblings.

REPOWERING

One place to look for this technology to make a significant impact is in repowering. With so many of the world's conventional coal-fired boilers reaching retirement age, using PFBC to breathe new life into these units can be an economically viable alternative to dismantling them, compared to other advanced, coal-based systems. (Table 13–1)

Plants no larger than the PFBC demonstration plants could conceivably repower today, although the U.S. Department of Energy (DOE) predicts full commercialization is still a couple of years away. The first full-scale PFBC demonstration plant in the U.S. was a repowering project. The 70-MWe Tidd Plant in Brilliant, Ohio, went on-line in 1990 and has provided valuable experience for PFBC repowering research. The demonstration project for the plant, originally commissioned in the 1940s, reused much of the plant's existing infrastructure.

FUTURE IMPROVEMENTS

PFBC demonstrations thus far have been with bubbling bed combustors. One of the next steps for improving these first-generation designs is to apply circulating fluidized-bed (CFB) technology to the basic system. No CFB PFBC demonstrations have been built to date, but the technology does offer some improvements over the bubbling bed design.

EPRI describes these improvements this way:

Compared to bubbling PFBCs, circulating PFBCs operate with a

considerably higher fluidizing velocity, which results in a smaller boiler cross section and a reduced number of fuel-feed points. The diameter of the pressure vessel is also smaller compared to bubbling PFBC, although vessel height increases somewhat. Because circulating PFBCs do not require a deep bed, sorbent particles can be smaller than those fed to bubbling PFBCs. The use of smaller particles results in a more efficient conversion of calcium carbonate to calcium sulfate, hence reducing sorbent consumption for equal levels of sulfur reduction. As there are no in-bed tubes, NO_x emissions can be reduced through staged combustion. Emissions can be reduced further by injecting ammonia into the boiler. Load following is simplified by eliminating the need to adjust bed level and transfer hot bed material to and from storage.

ECONOMICS

EPRI conducted a series of engineering studies comparing PFBC to other fossil-fueled technologies, including a pulverized-coal plant with flue-gas desulfurization and selective catalytic reduction, gasification combined-cycle, and natural gas combined-cycle. Figure 13–2 shows the total capital requirement for these technologies and bubbling and circulating bed PFBC. The only fossil fuel-fired technology with a lower capital requirement than PFBC, which requires $1,200 to $1,300/kW(US), is a natural gas-fired combined-cycle plant, at about $600/kW(US).

Figure 13–2. Total capital requirement

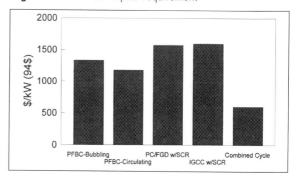

EPRI also looked at the cost of electricity (COE) for each of these technologies. (Figure 13–3) While operations and maintenance costs are similar for all of the coal-fired technologies, reduced fuel costs (as a result of improved efficiency) and lower capital costs made PFBC the low levelized COE winner.

Figure 13–3. Levelized cost of electricity

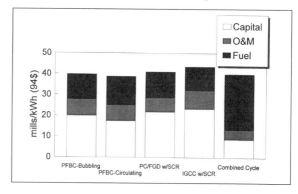

An important aspect of the COE numbers is that fuel is the major component of electricity cost for the natural gas-fired combined-cycle. The price for natural gas is expected to increase 1.5–2% per year. If this does happen, when the difference in the 30-year levelized cost of gas and coal reaches $2.00(US)/MBtu, PFBC will gain the advantage over gas combined-cycle.

HOT GAS CLEANUP

One remaining hurdle for commercial deployment PFBC is the development of a reliable

hot gas cleanup (HGCU) system. HGCU is necessary in PFBC plants, especially the advanced PFBC plants discussed later in this chapter, because the system's cyclones are not capable of cleaning 100% of the ash from the combustion gas before it encounters the gas turbine. The presence of ash in the gas requires ruggedized gas turbines, limiting the performance of the combined-cycle. Furthermore, ash that does make it past the cyclones requires electrostatic precipitators (ESP) at the stack to meet particulate emissions standards. Capturing particulates early in the cycle would eliminate the need for secondary cyclones and stack gas ESPs, in addition to permitting a wider selection of gas turbines.

The basic design for HGCU is a ceramic barrier filter system. A filter pressure vessel houses hundreds of ceramic filter elements, called candles, which collect ash on their surface while allowing the gas to pass through. In the Westinghouse design (Figure 13–4) used at the previously mentioned Tidd facility in the United States, ceramic filter element arrays were formed by attaching individual candle elements (Item 1) to a common plenum and discharge pipe (Item 2). Periodic backpulses of compressed gas from a single-pulse nozzle source clean the fly ash collected on the surface of the filter elements, and the ash is discharged from the filter vessel's hopper. When arranged vertically from a support structure, individual plenum assemblies form a filter cluster (Item 3).

Figure 13–4. Westinghouse candle filter system

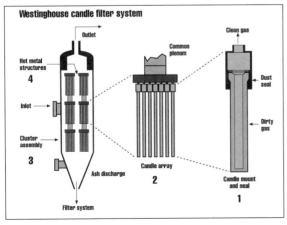

The filter cluster represents the basic module needed for constructing a large filter system. The individual clusters are supported from a common, high-alloy tubesheet and expansion assembly (Item 4) that spans the pressure vessel and divides it into "clean-gas" and "dirty-gas" sides. The cluster approach also permits efficient maintenance and replacement of individual filter elements.

ASH BRIDGING

The Westinghouse system is structurally adequate, but experience at the Tidd plant, and at other demonstration plants with similar systems, revealed that more research is needed in the design of hot gas cleanup systems. Early tests at the Tidd plant revealed a problem with ash "bridging" between candles. Besides making ash removal and filter cleaning difficult, ash bridges broke several of the candles by producing bending moment stresses at the candle bases. Testing of the Westinghouse system at Ahlstrom Pyropower in Finland and of a similar HGCU system at the Wakamatsu Coal Utilization Research Center in Japan indicated that severe thermal gradients also can break candles.

Several facility and filter modifications addressed these process problems, but the long-term durability of ceramic candles at extreme temperatures remains a major hurdle for HGCU system engineers. One design approach taken by LLB Lurgi Lentjes Babcock (LLB) attempts to sidestep these problems, caused in part by inadequate candle materials.

In LLB's filter concept, instead of suspending candles in a tubesheet, which produces unfavorable tension in the ceramic material, designers arranged the candles upside down with the open end held in a seat arranged on a horizontal header. In addition to the compressive stress given by the weight of the candle itself, a weight on top of the candle is responsible for keeping the candle seated when operators

444

Figure 13–5. LLB candle filter

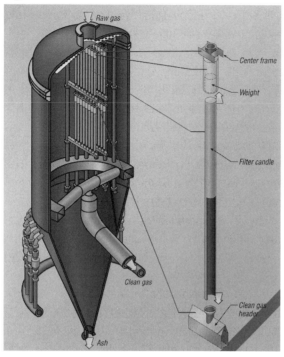

backpulse the system. (Figure 13–5) A special candle configuration ensures that the candle does not experience excessive horizontal forces and bending moments. The inverted candle arrangement was successful in eliminating candle damage once engineers isolated vibration from the fluidized bed's operation.

Although HGCU system testing has provided solutions to many of the problems facing PFBC engineers, more experience is needed with different fuel types before HGCU is ready for commercialization. Solving these problems is essential for PFBC to enter successfully its next advanced phase.

ADVANCED PFBC

With first-generation PFBC ready for commercial deployment, a new technology with its roots in PFBC is poised to emerge as a clean coal technology leader. Second-generation or advanced PFBC (APFBC) will soon be demonstrated under the U.S. DOE's Clean Coal Technology program, with private interests conducting research and development as well. APFBC can be described loosely as a combination of first-generation PFBC and integrated gasification combined-cycle (IGCC).

In an IGCC system, applying heat and pressure to coal synthesizes a fuel gas, which in turn is used to fuel a gas turbine. Steam for the bottoming cycle is generated using exhaust heat from the gas turbine and from heat rejected by water used to cool the syngas.

The marriage of PFBC and IGCC is made possible by converting a portion of the coal's Btu energy into syngas. This partial gasification takes place in a carbonizer at a temperature below the coal's slagging temperature, producing syngas and char. Limestone, fed into the carbonizer along with the coal, plays a vital role as sulfur remover in the APFBC process. Just like first-generation PFBC, the limestone sorbent captures sulfur as CaS, later converted to calcium sulfate in the fluidized-bed by feeding excess air to the combustor. By using staged combustion, the fluidized-bed combustor lowers NO_x emissions as well.

Cyclones and particulate control devices (PCD) remove light char and calcium sulfide from the syngas before it is introduced into a topping combustor for the gas turbine, the key to increased efficiency possible with APFBC. All char and particulate matter is combusted in the fluidized bed, with calcium sulfate and ash as the only waste products. The hot flue gas from the fluidized-bed combustor also passes through the gas cleanup system on its way to the topping combustor, where it acts as the oxidant for burning syngas from the carbonizer.

EFFICIENCY ADVANTAGE

Like first-generation PFBC and IGCC, APFBC is a combined-cycle. Figure 13–6 shows the APFBC system. A fluidized-bed heat exchanger and an HRSG provide the steam for the bottoming cycle. Using this design changes the ratio of steam-gen-

Figure 13–6. Second-generation PFBC

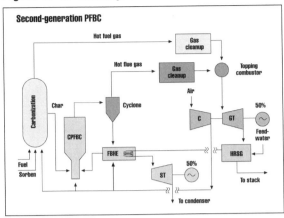

Figure 13–7. Efficiency comparison

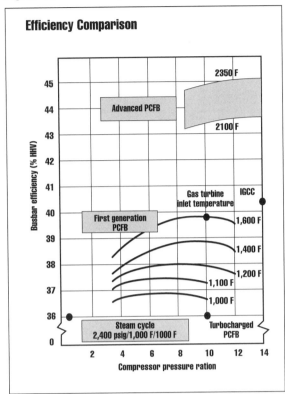

erated power to gas-generated power from 4:1 to 1:1 compared to first-generation PFBC. By taking advantage of this shift from Rankine to Brayton cycle, engineers predict that commercial-scale APFBC combined-cycles will enjoy a considerable efficiency boost to as high as 46% or more. Advances in gas turbine technology could increase the efficiency level to more than 50%. Such efficiency increases will result in coal consumption that is 25% lower per unit than a pulverized coal or atmospheric FBC plant. A comparison of APFBC efficiency to other advanced coal technologies is shown in Figure 13–7. Table 13–2 shows a performance and economic comparison of commercial advanced-PFBC and conventional coal-combustion technology.

Much of the increase in efficiency is due to the increased gas-turbine inlet temperature, more than 1260 C, made possible by burning the syngas in the topping combustor. At these temperatures, molten coal ash would damage the turbine, so the hot gas cleanup becomes essential in the APFBC design. Even if the HGCU system were able to successfully clean particulate matter from the gas, the syngas would still contain fuel-bound nitrogen which would convert to NO$_x$ if burned in a standard combustor. The combustor also must be able to withstand the 870 C combustor inlet temperature. Most gas-turbine combustors are designed for 370 C. Research also continues in this area.

Table 13–2
Commercial plant comparison

Power summary	Advanced PFBC	Conventional PC w/scrubber
Net capacity, MWe	538.2	500.9
Net plant efficiency, %(HHV)	46.2	35.9
Topping combustor temp, °F	2,425	—
Gross power, MWe		
Gas turbine	278.2	—
Steam turbine	282.2	540.4
Main steam flow, lb/hr	1.62×10^6	3.97×10^6
Economics ($1987)		
Total plant cost, $/kW	875.8	1,192.6
Total plant investment, $/kW	947.8	1,307.7
Total capital requirement, $/kW	1,002.1	1,375.3
Levelized busbar cost, mills/kWh (65% capacity factor)	72.9	93.2
Cost of energy advantage, %	21.8	—

OPERATIONAL FLEXIBILITY

An additional advantage of APFBC which might appeal to power generators is that the technology offers widespread applications from

new-construction, greenfield sites to repowering. The independent combined-cycle nature of APFBC, its ability to process energy in several process paths, makes this possible. There are several possible operating configurations:

- with the carbonizer out of service, the PFBC can be independently fired with coal;

- with the PFBC out of service, the char from the carbonizer can be stored for later use, and the topping combustor and HRSG can be fired with a supplementary fuel gas such as natural gas or propane;

- with both the carbonizer and the PFBC out of service, the topping combustor and HRSG can be fired with another fuel gas;

- with the topping combustor out of service, the PFBC and the HRSG can be used in a steam cycle similar to a first-generation PFBC; and

- the HRSG can be fired on its own if the rest of the plant is unavailable.

Utilities could use this same flexibility to construct a greenfield plant in phases as shown in Figure 13–8.

Figure 13–8. Phased construction of a second-generation PFBC plant

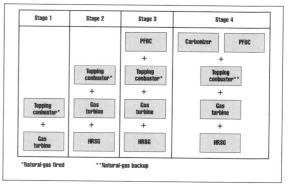

TOWARD COMMERCIALIZATION

Research and development programs conducted at various companies are producing valuable experience and data to further the overall development of advanced-PFBC systems. What is lacking so far are demonstration plants similar to the first-generation PFBC demonstrations mentioned earlier. Table 13–3 lists planned and possible future PFBC plants worldwide.

Foster Wheeler Development Corporation has conducted tests on individual components of the APFBC system in preparation for a demonstration

Table 13–3
Planned/possible future PFBC

Project	Type	Location	Capacity	Status
Midwest power	Circulating	Iowa, U.S.	80 MWe	Due for commissioning in 1998
Mountaineer	Bubbling	W.Virginia, U.S.	350 MWe	Due for commissioning in 2002
Four Rivers Energy Modernization	Advanced	Kentucky, U.S.	70 MWe + process steam	Due for commissioning in 1998
Trebovice	Bubbling	Czech Republic	60 MWth + district heating and process steam	Contract awarded
Teruel	Bubbling	Spain	350 MWe	Feasibility study
Wakefield	Bubbling	UK	80 MWe	Under study
Linkou	Bubbling	Taiwan	350 MWe	Feasibility study
Kyushu Electric-Karita Station	Bubbling	Japan	350 MWe	Due for commissioning in 1998
Chugoku Electric	Bubbling	Japan	250 MWe	Planned
Hokkaido Electric	Bubbling	Japan	85 MWe	Due for commissioning in 1995/6
Hokkaido Electric	Bubbling	Japan	350 MWe	Under study
Chubu Electric	Circulating	Japan	300-400 MWe	Feasibility study
Okinawa Electric	Bubbling	Japan	150-250 MWe	Under study
Southern Co. Sites	Bubbling	U.S.	80,160,350 MWe	Under study

[Courtesy EPRI]

plant at Southern Company Services Power Systems Development Facility in Wilsonville, Alabama.

Experience from the Wilsonville plant will provide much-needed data, but the commercialization of APFBC may lie in the success of a U.S. DOE CCT project, the Four Rivers Energy Modernization Project (FREMP). Air Products and Chemicals, Inc., principal contractor for the project, is using the advanced-PFBC technology to repower their chemicals manufacturing facility in Calvert City, Kentucky.

Foster Wheeler will design, fabricate, and erect the APFBC power island with LLB supplying the flue-gas PCD, fuel paste feed, and ash disposal system. Westinghouse will supply the carbonizer flue-gas PCD. The 95-MWe FREMP plant will provide data on the system components and the integrated system just like the Wilsonville pilot plant, only at a commercial scale. Conservative estimates place APFBC commercialization around 2005. FREMP should provide a needed stepping stone to achieve commercialization by this date. Despite the success enjoyed with the research programs to date, advanced-PFBC must still clear some formidable hurdles before it is ready for full commercialization. Issues that require resolution are:

- reliable coal/char transfer,

- high-temperature, high-pressure gas filters with commercially acceptable operating lives,

- a topping combustor which achieves the required turbine inlet temperature while restricting NO_x emissions to less than 0.1 lb/MMBtu,

- ash discharge material that is sufficiently low in sulfides, suitable for utilization applications, and can be disposed of readily,

- a gas turbine inlet gas that is sufficiently low in alkali vapor so as not to cause blade-corrosion problems, and

- for the full advanced-PFBC system, a fuel gas control valve that can operate at a high-temperature reducing atmosphere.

Another problem, according to EPRI's John Wheeldon, is that none of the specialized components for APFBC have undergone long-term testing. It is this unknown that could determine the success of the APFBC projects. Wheeldon said accelerating advances in the hot gas filters is essential for commercialization to occur very soon.

Chapter 14
Nuclear Outlook

DR. JOHN ZINK
MANAGING EDITOR
POWER ENGINEERING

OVERVIEW

The nuclear energy industry worldwide had a good year last year, and there is every reason to believe the favorable trend will continue. Operating nuclear power plants throughout the world generally performed well. Plants in the United States set new records for reliability, economy, and personnel safety, surpassing the targets established by industry groups. The next generation of nuclear technology, with enhanced safety and operability features, has finally begun to move from design to construction and operation, although construction of new plants has essentially halted in North America and Western Europe. The nuclear fuel business has reached a better balance between supply and demand, indicating that, perhaps, the fuel suppliers' downsizing may be coming to an end. The nuclear services business, which continues to be the backbone of most nuclear suppliers as existing plants grow older, shows signs of even more significant business opportunities in the future. And there was even a little progress, worldwide, in handling nuclear waste.

NUCLEAR PLANT OPERATIONS

The Nuclear Energy Institute, the U.S. trade organization for nuclear power operators and suppliers, said, "1995 was a take-charge year" for the nuclear energy industry. The U.S. nuclear plants' capability factor (the percent of the ideal maximum production a plant is actually capable of producing during a given year) is currently higher than that of any other country's nuclear fleet, and the average cost per kWh for nuclear generation decreased by 12%. During the twelve-month period ending June 30, 1995, the last for which full

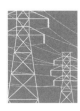

data are available, the unit capability factor of U.S. nuclear plants reached a median of 84.5%, far above the 68% experienced less than 10 years previously. The impact of forced outages was also the lowest in history, with the unplanned capability loss factor declining to 4.2% in 1995. Capacity factors for the 109 nuclear plants in the U.S. fleet averaged 78.2%. Worldwide, reports from various national organizations show that nuclear power plant operators continued to improve their performance, with experience similar to that in the United States.

Industry observers expect this trend of improving operating performance to continue for the next several years, although the rate of improvement will necessarily slow as performance gets better and the room for improvement gets smaller. Figure 14–1 shows the trend of U.S nuclear plant capacity factors over the past 20 years. This unrelenting upward trend in plant performance since 1985 is the result of a focused effort in the U.S. and throughout the world. The industry is focusing on day-to-day activities in operating plants, and concentrating on more efficient work techniques and effective training of personnel. As part of this effort, two organizations, the World Association of Nuclear Operators (WANO) and the U.S. Institute of Nuclear Power Operations (INPO) share experiences and "best practices" as identified by each organization, with

a mutual goal to optimize nuclear plant safety and performance. In addition, the Electric Power Research Institute (EPRI), the research consortium composed of most of the electric utilities in the United States, operates the Nuclear Maintenance Applications Center in Charlotte, North Carolina, to serve as an international forum for developing and demonstrating techniques for successful plant maintenance.

In the United States, a major factor affecting productivity in operating nuclear plants is regulation. Prescriptive regulation requires periodic testing of equipment, status checks, etc., that may not be necessary on the prescribed frequency. The industry is looking for ways to move from such prescriptive regulation toward performance-based regulation, where measurable performance goals are established and the individual plants are allowed some leeway in how to reach those goals. There already has been some success in this arena, and there is every reason to believe that further progress will be made and that capability factors will continue at a high level for the foreseeable future. This program can make a difference in the length of maintenance outages, for example. European nuclear plants, which already operate under less prescriptive regulation, have shorter maintenance outages in spite of the fact that they, typically, have one-half the staffing of U.S. plants.

Refueling outages constitute the largest portion of the nuclear unit's expected down time. Typically, a nuclear power plant must shut down every 12 to 24 months to replace a large portion (one-quarter to one-half) of the fuel rods that make up the core of the nuclear reactor. As recently as 10 years ago, these refueling outages were expected to last 60 to 90 days—time when the expensive power plant asset was not productive for the owning utility. In fact, refueling was commonly scheduled to be an annual maintenance until fuel vendors were able to design longer-lasting cores at the request of plant owners, who preferred to be shut down for the long, expensive refueling process less frequently.

Figure 14–1. U.S. nuclear power plant capacity factors, 1974-1994

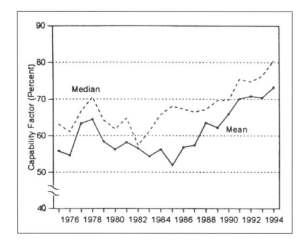

Now, however, through improved scheduling and work control, the average refueling outage takes 48 days, and several U.S. nuclear plants have reduced their refueling outage duration to as little as 20–30 days. For example, workers at TVA's Browns Ferry Unit 2 completed the spring 1996 outage in only 32 days, and a similar outage at the South Texas Project was completed in only 23 days. These reduced shutdown times in the United States are now matching the best performances in the world, and contributing to the improved economics of those plants.

Figure 14–2 shows that with the productivity improvements that have been made, the average annual operating and maintenance costs per megawatt of nuclear generation in the United States have leveled off since 1989 and actually began to decline slightly in 1993. This occurred in spite of the fact that the U.S. nuclear fleet is aging and, hence, plants require more major repairs and replacements than they did in their earlier years.

Looking forward, the recent impressive performance that has resulted from years of concerted effort by the nuclear industry worldwide can be expected to continue. This improvement will have continuing favorable impact on the economics of nuclear generation as companies focus on reducing their variable operating costs in an increasingly competitive environment.

Figure 14–2. Average annual operating and maintenance costs per megawatt-electric of U.S. nuclear capacity, 1982-1993

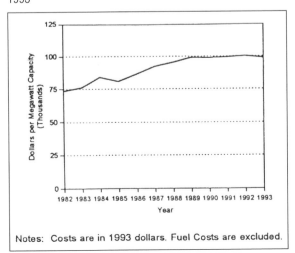

Notes: Costs are in 1993 dollars. Fuel Costs are excluded.

WORLD NUCLEAR CAPACITY

As of January 1, 1996, there were 431 nuclear power plants in operation in 31 countries throughout the world, representing more than 342,000 megawatts (MWe) of net electric generation capacity, according to the annual survey published by the American Nuclear Society. An additional 64 units are in various construction stages and account for an expected addition of 52,000 megawatts. It is interesting to note, as one indicator of the maturity of the nuclear power industry, that 66 units have been retired or otherwise permanently shut down for various reasons. Table 14–1 summarizes the

Table 14–1
Nuclear power units by country

Country	No. of Units in operation
Armenia	1
Argentina	2
Belgium	7
Brazil	1
Bulgaria	6
Canada	21
China	3
Cuba	0
Czech Republic	4
Finland	4
France	56
Germany	20
Hungary	4
India	10
Japan	51
Kazakhstan	1
Korea	11
Lithuania	2
Mexico	2
Netherlands	2
Pakistan	1
Philippines	0
Romania	0
Russia	29
Slovakia	4
Slovenia	1
South Africa	2
Spain	9
Sweden	12
Switzerland	5
Taiwan	6
Ukraine	16
United Kingdom	35
United States	109
Totals	**437**

[Courtesy International Atomic Energy Agency]

status of nuclear power in various countries throughout the world as compiled by the International Atomic Energy Agency. These numbers differ slightly from the American Nuclear Society numbers because of different criteria that determine whether a plant is operational.

In the United States and in Western Europe (with the possible exception of France) the growth of nuclear power has slowed to a crawl, at most. The growth in nuclear capacity is very much commensurate with the general growth of energy needs throughout the world. That is, the emerging nations of the Far East and of Eastern Europe make up the bulk of the current construction of new nuclear capacity. For example, there are eight nuclear units under construction in India, four in China, four in Japan, and one each in the Philippines and Pakistan, for a total of 18 units. There are 23 units under construction in various parts of the former Soviet Union. The U.S. Energy Information Agency (EIA) projects that worldwide nuclear generating capacity in 2005 will be between 364 and 366 GWe (1 gigawatt-electric (GWe) equals 1,000 MWe), and by the year 2015, the worldwide installed nuclear capacity will be between 313.9 and 409.7 GWe compared to the current total of 342.5 GWe. This 20-year trend is illustrated in Figure 14–3.

The decline in capacity in the Low Case assumes that few new nuclear baseload electricity

generating plants will be commissioned in Western Europe and the United States over the next 20 years. For these regions, the focus will be on extending the operation of existing plants. For the countries of the former Soviet Union and Eastern Europe, some growth in nuclear power is projected. However, adding safety features and upgrades to western standards currently are the major issues. Asia may be the only region of the world with significant growth in nuclear capacity between now and 2015. Countries like China, South Korea, Taiwan, Indonesia, and Thailand are experiencing a tremendous increase in energy consumption, and nuclear power will fill part of this demand.

Breakdowns for each of the specific regions of the EIA study, updated to include operating plants as of the end of 1995, are included.

United States. With one newly-completed unit and only three nuclear units officially under construction, future plant shutdowns, not construction, produce the greatest uncertainty in the long-range projections of nuclear capacity in the United States. The EIA projects that the United States is likely to have nuclear capacity between 61.4 GWe and 76.0 GWe by 2015, down from the 100.3 GWe expected in 2005. It is assumed that none of the three units under construction, but categorized as indefinitely delayed, will be completed, and that plants that reach the end of their useful life will not be replaced by other nuclear units.

Figure 14–3. 1994 world nuclear capacity and projected capacity, 1995-2015

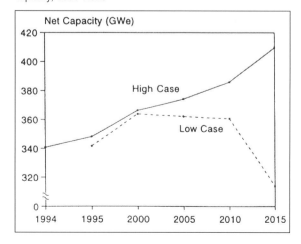

Canada. The outlook in Canada is much the same as that in the U.S. There are no nuclear units under construction, and the primary concern is maintaining the reliable and economical operation of the 22 existing units. One unit has been shut down in the past year, but not decommissioned. Nuclear capacity is expected to decline slowly over the next ten years, and probably beyond.

Western Europe. The ten countries of Western Europe have a total nuclear capacity of 121.9 GWe from 151 nuclear units, with nuclear

plants accounting for more than 40% of total electric generation. Recent economic slowdowns throughout the region have reduced the current use of electricity, but growth is expected to pick up again, soon. When new power plants are planned, however, nuclear power probably will not play a large role except, perhaps, in France. The EIA projects that net nuclear capacity in this region in 2005 will be 121.7 GWe, and by 2015 it will be in a range from 141.4 GWe to 109.8 GWe.

Eastern Europe. At the end of 1995, the ten Eastern European countries had 62 operating nuclear units with a net capacity of 44.6 GWe. Over the next 10 years EIA expects their capacity to grow to somewhere between 47 GWe and 51 GWe. And at the end of the next 20 years, EIA expects this capacity to be in a range from 36.2 GWe to 62.1 GWe. Most of the future gains in nuclear capacity will come from Russia, Romania, and the Ukraine. An important factor is whether or not adequate financing will be available to provide these countries the capital they need to expand their electricity generation.

Far East. This region, composed of China, Japan, Korea, Taiwan, and the Philippines, had 69 operating nuclear reactors with a net capacity of 54.8 GWe at the end of 1995. That capacity is expected to increase to 70–75 GWe in the next 10 years and to continue to increase to a low of 82.2 GWe or a high of 96.2 GWe by the year 2015. This is the only region of the world in which EIA expects there to be a steady and unambiguous trend in the upward direction. The Far East is a region of rapid economic growth, calling for rapid growth in electric generation to support the developing economies there. For example, electricity consumption has more than doubled in China over the past 10 years. Most of the Far East countries have no indigenous energy resources and, having suffered severe dislocations from the oil shocks of the 1970s, they have turned to nuclear fuel to decrease their dependence on imported fuels.

Other. The EIA includes Argentina, Brazil, Cuba, India, Mexico, Pakistan, and South Africa in this category. There are 18 operable units in these seven countries, with a capacity of 6.5 GWe. These countries are expected to see substantial growth in their nuclear capacity so that, by 2005, they will have between 9.3 GWe and 12.1 GWe of nuclear capacity, and by 2015, their nuclear capacity is estimated to be in the 12.3 GWe to 18.7 GWe range. Table 14–2 summarizes the EIA projections for all regions of the world, while Figure 14–3 graphically illustrates the worldwide trend.

Table 14–2
Projected nuclear capacities

Region	Projected 2005		Projected 2015	
	Low	High	Low	High
United States	100.3	100.3	61.4	95.0
Canada	14.1	14.1	12.0	15.3
Western Europe	121.7	121.7	109.8	141.4
Eastern Europe	47.0	51.2	36.2	62.1
Far East	69.9	74.9	82.2	96.2
Other	9.3	12.1	12.3	18.7

ADVANCED REACTOR TECHNOLOGIES

Over the past 30 years of designing and operating nuclear power plants, manufacturers and utilities have learned a great deal about how to make plants more reliable and more economical. They are now incorporating that knowledge into the next generation of nuclear plants.

Over the same 30-year period, regulations have required continual redesign, backfit of new hardware not contemplated in the original design, and more-complex operating procedures. Since the mid-1980s, manufacturers, utilities, and regulators have engaged in a major effort to reverse this trend of increasing complexity while, at the same time, improving safety and reducing personnel radiation exposure. In April 1989, the U.S. Nuclear Regulatory Commission (NRC) made the first major step in this direction when it issued

new regulations that made the regulatory process more predictable and less costly for future plants. These regulations emphasize standardized plant designs and provide for early and final resolution of site, design, and construction issues. This gave manufacturers the confidence to invest substantial sums in engineering and testing new designs that would be marketable because of their better economy and enhanced safety. Those investments are now beginning to bear fruit.

In 1995, the NRC issued proposed rules for certification of the ABB System 80+ and the GE Advanced Boiling Water Reactor. The smaller, "passive" Westinghouse AP-600 successfully completed all safety testing, and GE's next generation Simplified Boiling Water Reactor received NRC approval for its testing program. Details of these advanced reactor developments, based on company product information, are given.

THE GENERAL ELECTRIC ADVANCED BOILING WATER REACTOR (ABWR)

The ABWR is the farthest along of the evolutionary advanced designs. The first ABWR has been constructed in Japan and was put on-line at low power on January 29, 1996. The plant will undergo exhaustive testing at low power, then at progressively higher levels up to its full electrical output of 1,346 MWe, and is expected to be in commercial operation by the end of 1996. In May 1996, GE announced that Taiwan Power Co. had also ordered two ABWRs.

The goal of the evolutionary design of the ABWR was to achieve enhanced safety and reliability, enhanced operability and maintainability, improved economy, and reduced occupational radiation exposure and radioactive waste.

Enhanced Safety and Reliability

- **Simplified Primary System Piping.** The adoption of ten reactor internal pumps around the periphery of the vessel bottom head eliminates the troublesome external reactor cooling loops used on earlier BWRs. Also, with no openings in the reactor vessel below the fuel region, this design ensures that the core and fuel always are covered and cooled by water during all design basis accidents.

- **Diversity of Control Rod Drive Mechanisms.** An electric drive system has been added to the existing hydraulic system to give finer control of power variations, and also to provide diversity and redundancy for reactor shutdown, thus increasing the safety margin.

- **Optimized Emergency Core Cooling System (ECCS).** The ABWR has enhanced safety by separating the ECCS into three physically and electrically independent divisions thus always maintaining a redundant backup system.

- **Wet, Pressure-Suppression Containment.** The wet, pressure-suppression containment requires a 30% smaller volume to contain the discharge from a vessel blowdown.

- **Passive Severe Accident Mitigation.** Passive accident mitigation features have been added and, as a result, the calculated core damage frequency is reduced from 2×10^{-6} to 1.7×10^{-7}, improvement by a factor of 10. No operator action is required for up to 72 hours after a design basis accident.

Enhanced Operability and Maintainability

- **State of the Art Instrumentation and Control System.** Optical multiplexing of

signal transmission significantly reduces cable volume. A fault-tolerant triplicate control system allows single channel malfunction while data are still being retrieved by other channels.

- **Advanced Man-Machine Interface.** The control room features a one-man, sit-down operation with touch-screen control and large mimic plant system displays. Plant operation is automated from startup through full-power operation. Artificial intelligence assists in plant status diagnosis.

- **Greater Maintainability.** Inside the reactor building, equipment at all levels is accessible by stairs and platforms which encircle the vessel and equipment.

Improved Economy

- **Reduced Construction Cost.** The building volume and materials required are much reduced, including shorter wire and cable runs, less piping, and reduced HVAC ductwork.

- **Reduced Operating Cost.** The design reduces the inspection frequency of key components.

Reduced Occupational Radiation Exposure and Radioactive Waste

- **Reduction of Radiation Sources.** The expected occupational exposure will decrease from the current level of 350 person-rem/yr to less than 100 person-rem/yr because of a number of design changes.

- **Reduction in Radioactive Waste.** The amount of low-level waste generated will decrease from the current level of 800 drums to an expected 100 drums per year

as a result of design changes for the ABWR.

THE GENERAL ELECTRIC SIMPLIFIED BOILING WATER REACTOR (SBWR)

The next step beyond the evolutionary ABWR is the more revolutionary design, the SBWR. This is a smaller unit, 600 MWe, that aims at even greater reliability through simplified design, natural circulation rather than forced (pumped) circulation, and passive safety systems. The passive safety design will eliminate emergency diesel generators and their associated valves, auxiliaries, and power distribution equipment. It is anticipated that there will be further reductions in both radioactive waste and in-plant radiation exposure. The SBWR is still in the design stage and no orders have been placed at this early stage of the process of developing a commercial product. It is not likely that any commercial plants of the SBWR design will be in operation in the next 10 years.

THE WESTINGHOUSE AP-600

Westinghouse has chosen to go directly to the smaller, simplified plant design for its next generation of nuclear units, without first going through the iteration of an advanced version of their current product offering. The AP-600 is a 600 MWe plant that embodies safety systems that rely on a combination of proven technologies and natural forces. The design was developed as part of a cooperative effort with EPRI and the U.S. Department of Energy's Advanced Light Water Reactor (ALWR) Program.

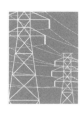

All AP-600 safety testing was completed in 1995, and the NRC has written a Draft Safety Evaluation Report as a result of the tests. A Final Safety Evaluation Report is expected during the first half of 1997, with final design approval coming near the end of 1997. More than likely, the first AP-600 plant will be built in Asia.

Westinghouse called upon its many reactor-years of PWR experience to focus the AP-600 design changes on simplification, economy, and enhanced safety. Compared to a 600-MWe power plant built the conventional way, the AP-600 has only one-half as many valves, two-thirds as many pumps, and one-fifth as many HVAC units to be operated, tested, and maintained. Its compact layout also means there is 70% less cable, 80% less piping, and a 45% smaller seismic-qualified building. All of this translates into fewer challenges to safe and simple operation and maintenance.

The design philosophy of the ALWR program, as embodied in the AP-600, was as follows:

- Simplify plant systems, equipment, operations, inspections, maintenance, and quality assurance requirements. The AP-600 safety systems are predominately passive, depending on the natural forces of gravity, circulation, convection, evaporation, and condensation instead of mechanical components.

- Use known components that offer high reliability. The reactor vessel, internals, and fuel are of essentially conventional design. Steam generators, turbine-generators, and other major components incorporate the best design experience to date.

- Provide a high degree of licensing certainty so no demonstration plant is required. Detailed testing has verified the functionality of the natural safety systems, safety system components, and containment.

- Shorten construction time by maximizing factory-fabricated modules. This also enhances the quality control of the fabrication process.

- Utilize the benefits of standardization, pre-engineered components and assemblies, and early detailed design to make costs lower and predictable.

Current projections are that the AP-600 "overnight" construction costs are about $1,370 per kW. Westinghouse expects the AP-600 will be competitive with gas at about $3 per million Btu and they feel it is competitive with coal, now. Organizations from more than 23 countries have provided some support or services for the ALWR program, and this involvement could provide a favorable opening for the AP-600 into all of these 23 markets.

THE ABB-CE SYSTEM 80+

The ABB-CE System 80+ is the standard design for the Korean nuclear power program, and is an evolution of the standard System 80 design used at the Palo Verde plant in the United States. The System 80+ can be built quickly and economically because of its standardized design, and it qualifies for licensing under the U.S. NRC's new one-step process. As part of that process, in 1995 the NRC issued its proposed rules for certification of System 80+.

The System 80+ is the most conventional of the three advanced nuclear plant designs, consistent with incorporating the design characteristics required under the DOE ALWR program. This evolutionary design includes:

- dual containment, with a reactor cavity that is able to cool molten core material and prevent it from entering the containment atmosphere,

- improved steam generator design that increases cooling capacity and, hence, provides more time for the operator to respond to an upset in the plant condition,

- increased redundancy, with four trains of safety systems utilizing two different power sources,

- separation of safety and non-safety functions to simplify maintenance and to reduce the challenges to the safety systems,

- simplified operator interface that unburdens the operator from the task of sorting through redundant information, and

- modular structures that can be shop-fabricated, saving construction time and improving quality control.

The company anticipates that, because of the evolutionary design of the System 80+, no demonstration unit will be required before these plants can be offered commercially.

Manufacturers Continue Design Improvements

Thus, in spite of there being no new U.S. orders on the horizon, the U.S. reactor manufacturers are moving forward with new and improved designs that could take advantage of the new licensing regime in the United States. And they are selling these new, improved plants in Asia—by far the most active market in the world for electric generation equipment. If U.S. utilities, generating companies, or independent power producers order new nuclear units within the next 10 years, these new, simplified designs will be the ones they will order.

NUCLEAR FUEL

World uranium production must increase significantly from current levels to meet future reactor requirements, according to the International Atomic Energy Agency (IAEA). The market for enrichment services, an essential refining step in producing nuclear fuel from uranium, has firmed during 1995. Also the market for the fabrication of the nuclear fuel elements appears to be in reasonable balance in early 1996. But these hopeful-sounding indicators come on the heels of a painful few years for all companies involved in the nuclear fuel business.

Uranium Supply and Demand

Uranium demand is unique in the world of energy fuels. It depends upon the number of nuclear power plants in operation in the world more than it does on the overall demand for electricity. Nuclear plants are expensive to build but, once built, generate large quantities of electricity at relatively low fuel cost. Therefore, to generate electricity as economically as possible, and to maximize the use of their large investment in a nuclear power plant, utilities "base load" these plants. Other plants that burn coal, oil, or gas may be shut down if the demand for electricity is low, but nuclear plants will seldom run at anything but maximum output. So, while the demand for coal and gas to fuel power plants is sensitive to the demand for electricity, the demand for nuclear fuel is sensitive only to the number of nuclear power plants and their reliability.

The slowdown in the construction of nuclear power plants throughout the western world over the past 10 years has had a devastating effect on the demand for uranium. The only uranium production in the United States at this time is from the unconventional production means of in-situ leaching processes and uranium recovery as a byproduct of phosphate production. All of the conventional open pit and underground uranium mines in the United States have been shut down. In the 1970s, many uranium miners entered into contracts for long-term uranium sales to supply the nuclear plants then in the construction pipeline. Since then, utilities have canceled plans for many of these plants in the United States, and

the demand throughout the rest of the world also has experienced a lull. As mentioned earlier, nuclear generation will probably experience real growth only in Asia and in a few other countries scattered throughout the world.

One would expect the price of uranium to fall as demand decreased and left a surplus of production capacity. That is exactly what happened throughout the 1970s and 1980s. The picture began to change in the 1990s, as more producers shut down their mines and factories, and supply and demand came more into balance. In addition, early 1996 saw the market affected by the bankruptcy of one of the largest uranium brokers in the world, leaving some demand uncovered. Figure 14–4 shows the average annual price of uranium, as published by the Uranium Exchange Co., quoted in dollars per pound of its typical chemical form, U_3O_8, from 1990 to early 1996. The most-common index of uranium price was at just under $16 per pound in March 1996. While the trend on this graph might look like encouraging news for uranium producers—and it is, compared to how the market has been—it is good to keep in mind that uranium was selling for $43 per pound in 1978. Nuclear Assurance Corporation estimates

that the full production costs of "all but a handful" of western producers exceed the current spot price of uranium, although current operating expenses are covered.

As uranium prices were plunging during the 1980s, uranium buyers reacted in a rational manner: they stopped making long-term commitments, lest they get locked into purchasing at above-market prices. This caused drawdown of user inventories instead of new purchases, and many suppliers were forced out of business. Consequently, since 1990, world production of uranium has been below reactor requirements. Annual inventory drawdowns during 1993 and 1994 supplied about 45% of the world's uranium requirements, according to the IAEA. The market now is in a position where significant portions of future fuel needs for existing power plants are uncommitted and, according to Edlow International, uranium producers will need to add capacity in the next three years or so. Reactor operators' realization of this fact has helped lead to the firming of uranium prices.

Figure 14–5 shows the United States and worldwide uncommitted uranium demand through 2005 as compiled by the Uranium Exchange Co. The increasing nuclear capacity in Asia adds growth of about 1% a year to the demand. Even with the slow growth of nuclear power in most of the Western world, existing plants' improved performance (i.e., operation at higher capacity factors) leads to increased fuel demand. The combination of these two market

Figure 14–4. Average annual Ux U_3O_8 spot price

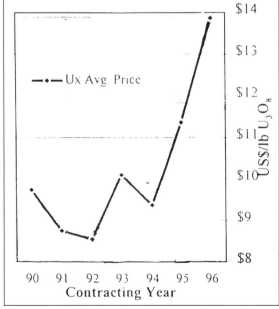

[Courtesy The Uranium Exchange Company]

Figure 14–5. Utility uncommitted uranium demand

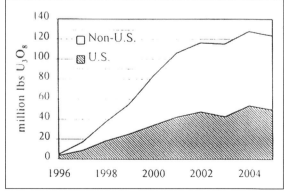

[Courtesy The Uranium Exchange Company]

factors leads to further pressure on the uranium market, and the uncommitted uranium demand becomes significant. Even more important to the market is the balance between this uncommitted demand and the producers' uncommitted supplies. It is possible that, in the near term, before production can expand to meet the uncommitted demand, supplies will not be adequate to meet the demand. This will lead to further upward pressure on prices and, in the absence of other factors, the current price trend will probably continue in the near term.

A wild card in the uranium supply situation is the introduction of low enrichment uranium (LEU) used in power plants, that is produced from dilution of high enrichment uranium (HEU) that comes from the destruction of nuclear weapons. This material is now entering the market, and Tenex, in Eastern Europe, plans to ship up to 360 tonnes of LEU from this source in 1996. Furthermore, it appears that this amount could increase by 50% in 1997 as a result of the meetings of the Gore-Chernomyrdin Commission on the disposition of surplus nuclear weapons. While these amounts are relatively small compared to the uncommitted demand in future years, they would take some of the immediate pressure off the supply side of the market. The IAEA estimates that from 2000 to 2010, diluted weapons material may meet about 10% of the annual world requirements for uranium. Reprocessed reactor fuel may meet another 5%. This means that world uranium production must increase by about 70% from current levels. Several suppliers, RTZ and ERA, for example, have taken steps that could increase their production by up to 50%. Others may do so, also, if prices continue firm, but producers still remember their past bad experiences. Also, changed political conditions have made it possible for South African uranium to enter the world market now. And, finally, there is serious talk about using plutonium from old weapons as reactor fuel. It will probably be at least 10 years before this has much impact on uranium demand, but it all helps cloud the supply-side picture.

Thus in 1996, uranium supply and demand came into better balance than they have been for the past five years or more. As a result, prices have firmed a bit. Although there is significant uncommitted future demand, supply options to fill that demand are increasing, also, and it is possible that some order may soon return to the uranium market. The pressure of the uncommitted demand is expected to keep prices firm over the next five to 10 years.

Conversion

Conversion is a relatively simple chemical process by which the uranium powder, called yellowcake, is made into a gaseous material, uranium hexafluoride (UF_6), in preparation for the enrichment process. Conversion plants, like most chemical operations, can be operated quite flexibly by shutting down process lines, operating for more or fewer hours a year, etc. Thus, with the exception of one casualty to a combination of market and environmental forces, conversion suppliers have been able to cope with the slowdown in the need for their services without the devastating effects the slowdown had on uranium miners.

Conversion capacity appears to be available when it will be needed to meet the demand, so it will probably not have much effect on the overall nuclear fuel prices for the next five to 10 years.

Enrichment

Enrichment is the process by which the useful species of uranium is increased about five-fold from its level in natural uranium. In the early days of the enrichment business, the governments of the United States, USSR, England, France, and Germany controlled this process because of its strategic importance to the production and control of nuclear weapons. The United States had a monopoly on enrichment for power reactors in the West during the 1960s and 1970s. Now,

however, a number of companies are involved, and four organizations control about 80% of the enrichment business in the world, with the U.S. portion being about 40%. The U.S. Enrichment Company, a quasi-governmental company made up of the enrichment assets of the U.S. Department of Energy, is expected to be spun off into a wholly private company, although the timing is somewhat questionable, as this action became embroiled in the congressional budget battles of 1996. South Africa also expects to enter the enrichment business by 2001, and HEU from the former weapons material will displace some more enrichment requirements.

The enrichment business experienced dislocations similar to the uranium business when the spate of reactor delays and cancellations occurred in the early 1980s. Companies operating under long-term enrichment contracts had to accept more fuel and more enrichment services than they needed until they could adjust their commitments, creating excess inventories of enriched uranium. Now, however, most of these excess inventories have been liquidated and supply and demand have achieved better balance. This is reflected in the price for enrichment services, which has increased from $78.42 per separative work unit (SWU) in 1993, to $85.63 in 1994, and up to $98.00 by first quarter of 1996. Worldwide capacity will continue to outstrip demand by more than 25% over the next 20 years, however, so the pressure on enrichment prices should not intensify.

Fuel Design and Fabrication Services

Fuel design and fabrication play a defining role in the market for uranium, conversion, and enrichment. Fuel designers must account for the past several years' operating history of a power plant, must predict future performance of the plant, and must observe the nuclear operation and safety parameters associated with the fuel. Then the designer must consider economic tradeoffs in determining the amounts of uranium and enrichment used for a particular fuel load. Most fabrication suppliers are positioning themselves for the coming era of competition in power generation, and are seeking ways to establish long-term "partnering" relationships with their customers, structured with incentives tied to plant performance. They know that their long-term success depends upon making the utility successful in keeping costs low and reliability high.

The industry trend toward higher capacity factors for operating plants, and a desire for longer times between refueling shutdowns and shorter time to do the refueling, all present particular challenges to the fuel designer. While higher capacity factors increase the demand for fuel fabrication, the more-efficient use of fuel (higher "burnup") tends to reduce that demand. Fabricators are able to adjust rapidly to the varying demand by activating or deactivating existing fabrication lines as required, but the feedstock for fabrication, enriched uranium, is determined at an early date because of the front-end processing involved. In general, the fabrication market is in reasonable supply/demand balance, although all the major fabricators have the capacity to produce more.

The U.S. and Western Europe markets are flat, as would be expected from the lack of growth in nuclear generation there, and opportunities elsewhere are limited because fabrication is usually a localized business, with European fabrication plants serving European customers, and Asian fabrication plants serving Asian customers, etc. In general, it can be expected that the fabrication business will closely track the installed nuclear capacity in a region. The price of fabrication services is highly dependent upon the full range of services rendered, the size of the fuel reload, the type of reactor, and a myriad of specific contract provisions, so it is not possible to quote a market price for this part of the fuel cycle.

In spite of the flat market for fabrication, the service and design portion of the business may trend upward independently. John Bohart, president of Framatome Technologies, has

observed that fuel design and services hold the prime opportunity for innovation in the nuclear fuel cycle. Heavy competition and customer demands for better-performing fuel, along with the economic pressures of deregulation affecting utilities, will tend to speed fuel design innovations to the market.

Waste Disposal

No discussion of nuclear fuel is complete without some mention of nuclear waste disposal—specifically, the disposition of spent nuclear fuel or the byproducts from reprocessing spent nuclear fuel. Worldwide, some countries are successfully disposing of nuclear waste while others, such as the United States, are stymied by public debate that continues without reaching a public consensus. There can be no doubt, however, that the amount of spent fuel or reprocessed waste will continue to increase as nuclear plant operations continue throughout the world.

Figure 14–6 shows low-case and high-case projections of the accumulation of spent fuel in the United States as estimated by the EIA. Worldwide projections would follow the same pattern, but would show a steeper increase as nuclear generation continues to grow in Asia and Eastern Europe. If the used fuel is not

Figure 14–6. Projections of cumulative U.S. spent fuel discharges, 1995-2040

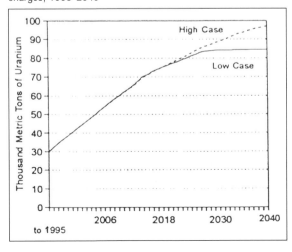

reprocessed, with the reusable uranium recycled, then the entire volume of spent fuel must be considered high-level nuclear waste. Reprocessing and recycling would decrease the absolute volume of waste to less than 5% of the original, but the growth trend would be the same.

Currently, reprocessing plants are operating in France, England, and Japan, while countries with smaller nuclear programs, typically, rely on long-term storage of the spent fuel. In March 1996 a U.S. Senate committee passed legislation to facilitate the long-term disposal of spent fuel, but the legislative process appears to have bogged down in election-year politics before any final action could be taken. Nevertheless, the U.S. nuclear industry considered this vote a hopeful sign, given the level of inaction up to that time.

NUCLEAR SERVICES

In the absence of orders for new plants, reactor manufacturers have sustained themselves and maintained their technical expertise by providing operation and maintenance services for operating units. As utilities strive for higher productivity, it is likely that they will outsource more of the activities they have usually performed for themselves. Also, as existing plants get older they will require more major maintenance and more major equipment replacements. Thus, the market for servicing nuclear plants should be an increasing market until the world's installed nuclear capacity begins to decline. Current projections are for a significant decline beginning in 2010 for the EIA's Low Case, or for no decline at all in the foreseeable future for their High Case. More than likely the actual experience will lie somewhere in-between these two extremes, meaning that the services sector will probably grow, albeit slowly, for the next 10 to 15 years.

The nature of the nuclear services rendered varies greatly. All manufacturers are providing updated controls systems for their older plants and are providing specialized NDT (non-destructive

testing) and repair services for aging reactor components. Several are providing new safety systems, fire protection systems, and other plant modifications to bring plants in Eastern Europe up to western safety standards. All equipment suppliers are trying to provide products and services that will enhance the productivity of power plant personnel, reduce the length of refueling and maintenance outages, and generally reduce the operating costs of nuclear plants. Although most plant operators feel more comfortable contracting with the original equipment suppliers for help with major components, the market is becoming more competitive, with manufacturers regularly bidding to work on each others' equipment and many independent companies also furnishing specialized services. Manufacturers are counting on success in the services business to sustain themselves until they can begin significant production of their next generation of power plants.

Chapter 15
Gas-Turbine and Combined-Cycle Technology

TERESA HANSEN
ASSOCIATE EDITOR
ELECTRIC LIGHT & POWER AND
POWER ENGINEERING

OVERVIEW

Gas turbines have taken a dominant role in new power generation capacity development. Despite some recent reliability problems, they promise to continue their leading role into the 21st century.

The basic reason for this dominance is high efficiency. The rapid pace of gas-turbine technology improvement in the 1990s drove combined-cycle thermal efficiency to nearly 60% with natural gas as the fuel. It will probably go even higher after the year 2000.

Gas-fired combined-cycle generation is also a bargain. Gas-turbine and combined-cycle plants have a much lower up-front capital cost than coal, nuclear, or renewable electricity generation plants. The cost of new combined-cycle generating capacity has dropped from around $600 per kW five years ago to about $350 per kW today.

In addition, with today's low natural gas prices, gas turbine and combined cycles are the least-cost generation technologies for power producers with access to gas. New gas-fired combined-cycle plants can produce electricity at a cost of less than three cents a kilowatt hour in the United States. And, since natural gas prices are predicted to increase at an average annual rate of only 1.5% well into the next century, gas-fired combined cycles will probably remain the low cost producers.

Clean fuel and increased efficiency give gas turbines and combined cycles another advantage over other generation technologies—lower emissions. (Figure 15–1) Electricity generators currently produce 36% of the nation's carbon emissions. Coal accounts for just over one-half of the total electricity generated in the United States but produces 87% of electricity-related carbon emissions. In contrast, gas-fired generators account for 15% of generation and produce only 9% of electricity-related carbon emissions.

Figure 15–1. CO₂ emissions and efficiency of various types of power plants

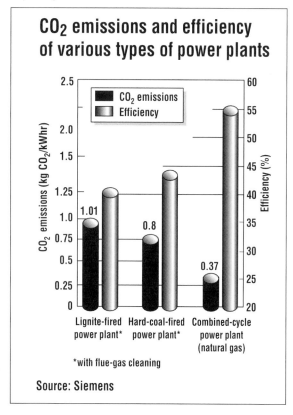

CO$_2$ emissions and efficiency of various types of power plants

Source: Siemens

All of these advantages are making gas-turbine and combined-cycle technology the power generation technology of the future. The U.S. Department of Energy (DOE) says that by 1998, 3,500-3,700 generating units in the United States will be more than 30 years old. Many power producers are expected to replace these older, high-cost power plants with new gas-fired combined-cycle capacity.

HISTORY

Although the major principles associated with gas-turbine technology were demonstrated during the ancient Greek, Roman, and Egyptian eras, gas turbines were not developed as a cost-effective means of generating electricity until the mid-1900s. During World War II, the U.S.

government and its allies began funding aircraft engine development programs, and in early 1943 Westinghouse tested the first wholly American designed and manufactured jet engine. This early aircraft-engine technology set the stage for development of the gas turbines used by today's electricity producers.

After the war, utilities became interested in the new engine technology and began installing a few gas turbines. These units had firing temperatures around 1,300 F (700 C) and pressure ratios of about 6.5. In July 1949, the first U.S., commercial, power-generation gas turbine was installed at Oklahoma Gas and Electric Company's Belle Isle Station. It was a General Electric (GE) MS3000 heavy-duty gas turbine rated at 3,500 kW.

After the big Northeast Blackout of 1965, utilities began to install gas turbines to supply peaking capacity. Improved technology, such as air cooling and more durable materials, allowed firing temperatures of more than 1,550 F (850 C) (Figure 15–2) and efficiency near 25%, making gas turbines well suited for the needed peaking capacity.

The Fuel Use Act of 1978 required the phasing out of natural gas as a fuel, causing the gas turbine market to become sluggish. Some producers even abandoned the U.S. market. Nevertheless, materials technology continued to develop, and when the market returned in the late 1980s, manufacturers were ready with more compressor refinements, higher-temperature resistant materials, and better cooling methods. Firing temperatures climbed toward the current state-of-the-art 2,300 F.

Today, simple cycle units rated at up to 150 MW with efficiencies around 35%, and combined-cycle units rated at over 200 MW with efficiencies around 55%, are up and running. (Figure 15–3) The uncertainty in today's electricity industry, both for utilities and nonutility generators, puts a premium on generation technologies that can be built with short lead time, at reasonable cost, and in affordable increments. Both simple-cycle and combined-cycle configured gas turbines fit these requirements well.

In 1988, orders for gas turbines and combined cycles worldwide totaled only 3,900 MW. By contrast, in 1994 and 1995, 26,000 MW and 24,000 MW, respectively, were ordered worldwide. These figures illustrate just how far and how fast gas-turbine technology for electricity generation has come.

Advancing Technology

Domestic Manufacturers

After advancing at rapid speed, the pace of new gas-turbine technology appears to have slowed. The industry reached a peak in 1994 when eight

Figure 15–2. Terminal efficiency of gas turbines and combined-cycle plants

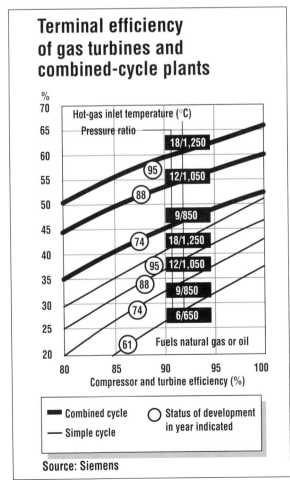

Figure 15–3. Comparison of efficiency and power output of various power producers

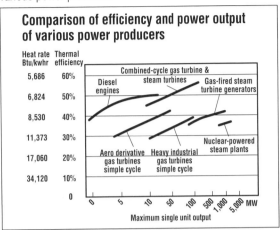

new machines were announced by various manufacturers. There were a few more significant advancements announced in 1995, but the pace is slowing. The current state-of-the-art for gas turbines, "F" technology, got its name because F is part of the product number designation used by both General Electric (GE) and Westinghouse (but not by other major gas-turbine manufacturers such as ABB and Siemens). This technology utilizes a design with first-stage turbine blade inlet gas temperatures of roughly 2,300-2,350 F, a maximum unit size of 150-170 MW (in the 60-Hz configuration), and a combined-cycle efficiency in the 56-58% range. (Figure 15–4)

GE, which currently holds the largest share of the gas-turbine market worldwide (Figure 15–5), has a wide range of 50-Hz and 60-Hz F machines in a variety of unit sizes. The manufacturer reports commitments for more than 100 of its F machines

Figure 15–4. Gas-turbine product positioning diagram

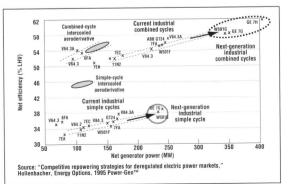

187

worldwide. GE's first F machine went into service in the early 1990s, and in 1995, the smallest of the GE F gas turbines, the 6FA, a 70-MW (60-Hz) F machine, was announced.

Figure 15-5. Worldwide market share 1990-95 — gas turbine/combined cycle

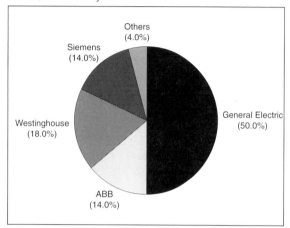

[Courtesy General Electric]

The next step for GE will be "G" and "H" machines. The basic G technology will feature an inlet temperature of 2,600 F and a unit size of 240 MW at 60 Hz and 282 MW at 50 Hz. The 60-Hz machine is being developed in parallel with the 50-Hz machine which will be introduced to the foreign market.

The H machine is a combined-cycle version of the G technology. It will feature steam-cooled turbine blades in the first two turbine stages, 2,600 F inlet temperature, 23 to 1 pressure ratio, and a combined-cycle efficiency of 60% (2,400 pounds per square inch (psi), reheat steam cycle). The simple-cycle G option will have air-cooled turbine blades and compression ratio will be 30 to 1. Projected nitrogen oxide (NO_x) emissions for the G/H machines are 25 parts per million (ppm) dry. The machines are designed to eventually reach nine to 10 ppm dry, but GE has yet to announce the availability of that level.

GE says the steam-cooled blades are the key to this design. It claims that this is the technology that will carry its gas turbines into the next century. Its goal is to have a 50-Hz H machine

ready for shipment in 1998 and have it in operation by 2000.

Westinghouse's newest available machine is the 501F. The manufacturer reports that 24 of these units will be in service by the end of 1996. The first one began commercial operation in 1992. Four of these units were installed at Florida Power & Light Company's Fort Lauderdale station in 1993. The four units have an average reliability of more than 99%. Originally rated at 153 MW, the Westinghouse 501F is now rated at 168 MW.

The next step for Westinghouse will be the 2,600F, 230-MW (60-Hz) 501G machine which will have a steam-cooled transition piece. Turbine blades will be air cooled. The G design will have a compression ratio of 19.2 to 1. Westinghouse says that two machines are being manufactured for initial operation in 1997.

Westinghouse is also working on an even more advanced machine, based on the 501G. It will be one step above the G machine, with a burner outlet temperature of close to 2,700 F and a pressure ratio planned for 25:1. NO_x emissions will be single digit. This machine will have closed-cycle cooling to cool not only the blades, but the vanes and some other components as well. To accommodate the higher temperature, the advanced machine will have different barrier coatings than the 501G. This latest machine is being designed as a single-shaft system with a large hydrogen-cooled generator. It will generate about 435 MW—300 MW from the gas turbine and 135 MW from the steam turbine.

Westinghouse believes the real future for gas-turbine technology lies in ceramic materials which don't have to be cooled. The company expects the military's use of small ceramic blades in aero engines to reach power generation gas turbines some time in the near future.

Both GE and Westinghouse are developing the advanced 60-Hz machines as part of the DOE's Advanced Turbine System (ATS) program. The ATS program was established to help ensure that the United States remains the world leader in supplying gas turbines.

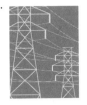

The program is designed to aid in the development of an advanced, ultra-high efficiency, environmentally superior turbine system that will be less expensive than today's system. DOE also feels that high-efficiency turbine systems will reduce U.S. fuel consumption, helping meet the national goal of becoming more energy efficient. DOE has been providing some funding to GE and Westinghouse for ATS development, however, the total funds that DOE committed at the beginning of the program (1993), are not expected to be available to complete the development.

Both GE and Westinghouse say they will continue with advanced technology development. However, both also say the lack of funding may slow the development of the 60-Hz domestic machines.

Overseas Manufacturers

Neither GE or Westinghouse can afford to slow down too much on advanced technology development. The other two major, world, gas-turbine technology suppliers, Siemens and ABB, continue to make advances in gas-turbine technology in hopes of capturing more of the future market.

Siemens has developed a 2,300 F class machine, called the V84.3 for 60-Hz applications and V94.3 in the 50-Hz option. Its latest version is called the V84.3A and is rated at 163-170 MW with an inlet temperature of 2,390 F. Combined-cycle efficiency is rated at 58%. The V84.3A features a new circumferential combustor with 24 burners, a departure from the two large combustion chambers which have been a significant feature of previous Siemens gas-turbine design. The new design is the result of a collaboration between Siemens and Pratt & Whitney, the jet engine manufacturer. NO$_x$ emissions from the new Siemens machine are said to be less than 25 ppm.

The first .3A Siemens machine will be operated under a partnership development agreement between the manufacturer and Kansas City Power & Light Company (KCPL). KCPL will take over operation of the unit once all operational testing has been completed. Two other units have been ordered by utilities in Germany and Portugal.

Siemens is not announcing any new gas-turbine technology beyond the .3A. Its philosophy is to have a new design on its test stand before it makes an announcement. However, Siemens says it is working on new technology with Pratt & Whitney, noting that the need for even larger unit sizes is still an open issue.

ABB introduced its latest gas-turbine design, the GT24 (60 Hz), in 1993. It is a 166-MW, 2,255 F inlet temperature machine. ABB uses what it calls sequential combustion to allow a lower inlet temperature than its major competitors use to achieve high efficiency. The first GT24 started operating in September 1995.

The official efficiency rating for a combined-cycle plant based on the GT24 is 58%. It is based on the 50-Hz/241-MW version, the GT26. However, ABB recently announced the sale of a 2,000-MW, combined-cycle plant using the GT26 and said the plant will achieve an overall fuel efficiency of "nearly" 60%.

ABB says it is working toward the same basic goals as the other manufacturers, but it does not plan to push the limit on temperature. The GT24 design is capable of moving up the temperature curve, but ABB has not disclosed when the next major step will be. The manufacturer's philosophy is to stay at the lowest possible temperature to achieve the optimum efficiency.

RELIABILITY

The only cloud on the gas turbine horizon is reliability. The rapid pace of technical advancement has led to the inevitable, debugging-type problems associated with all new technology.

A rash of problems in 1995 has caused some to question the industry's rapid development pace. Some think it has been too rapid. Some insurers

are reportedly reluctant to back modern gas turbines. Some buyers are looking back at older, proven technology, foregoing the advantages of higher efficiency and large unit size offered by the newer machines. All four large gas-turbine and combined-cycle unit primary manufacturers have experienced some sort of problem with their products.

GE's F machines experienced a series of problems in 1995, including a variety of isolated problems that could be expected with any new technology. However, 21 of 36 total incidents involved a design problem with the machine's rotor flexibility. GE has resolved the rotor problem and there were no catastrophic failures. The root cause of the problem has been determined and all installed units are being corrected. The company has designed a new rotor that is thicker and the flexibility has been eliminated. All new designs will incorporate the fix.

The problem with the GE F machines was not related at all to the high firing temperature or advanced materials, or to any of its advanced technology features. GE is moving ahead aggressively with its next generation G and H machines.

GE is not the only manufacturer that has had problems. There have been others, leading to some speculation that gas-turbine technology has gone too far, too fast. A Siemens V84.2 (not the most advanced Siemens machine) threw a last stage blade at a combined-cycle facility. The incident caused damage to the gas turbine, the generator, the air intake system, the heat-recovery steam generator, the air filter core, and the exhaust diffuser. The machine was down four months.

One of Westinghouse's early 501F machines threw a last-row turbine blade shortly after startup, but has generally operated well. An ABB GT11N2 (an ABB simple-cycle machine) suffered a fourth-stage blade failure in 1995. It was not a catastrophic failure and was an isolated event. However, ABB has redesigned those particular blades and will replace them in operating machines.

Results of a comprehensive, gas-turbine reliability study released in 1995 covered gas-turbine operations from 1989 through 1994. Even though the study did not include the latest F machines, it did include 115 modern units operating for 415 unit years. The general conclusion was that the majority of these gas turbines have performed well. The overall mean availability factor was 93.51% and the median was 95.36%. Units larger than 75 MW, generally the more modern units, had higher average availability than the smaller units. Units in heat-recovery (cogeneration) applications had higher availabilities than simple-cycle or combined-cycle electricity-only producers. Cogeneration applications did slightly better than utility or industrial self-generation applications.

Table 15–1
Gas-turbine availability

Summary data for 100 units		Units 50 to 75 MW (14 units)	
High	99.22	High	96.09
Low	70.43	Low	85.66
Median	95.36	Median	91.99
Mean	93.51	Mean	91.88
Std Dev	5.38	Std Dev	3.09

Frequency distribution		Units over 75 MW (86 units)	
Availability factor	# of units	High	99.22
70-75	1	Low	70.43
75-80	1	Median	95.76
80-85	7	Mean	93.77
85-90	11	Std Dev	5.62
90-95	26		
95+	54		

Heat recovery application (35 units)		Heat recovery application (35 units)	
High	98.45	High	98.45
Low	86.28	Low	86.28
Median	95.33	Median	95.33
Mean	94.97	Mean	94.97
Std Dev	2.05	Std Dev	2.05

Combined-cycle application (26 units)		Combined-cycle application (26 units)	
High	97.81	High	97.81
Low	70.43	Low	70.43
Median	92.50	Median	92.50
Mean	90.61	Mean	90.61
Std Dev	7.00	Std Dev	7.00

Simple-cycle application (39 units)		Simple-cycle application (39 units)	
High	99.22	High	99.22
Low	77.77	Low	77.77
Median	96.22	Median	96.22
Mean	94.13	Mean	94.13
Std Dev	5.46	Std	5.46

The report results show that the gas turbine/generators included in the study have generally experienced a high availability factor, with a median value of almost 95.4%. (Table 15–1)

Recent problems with gas turbines do not appear to challenge this overall conclusion. They do not appear to be directly related to higher firing temperatures or larger unit sizes. Despite the unease caused by the rapid advancement of gas-turbine technology, it appears that gas-turbine technology will continue at a fairly rapid pace.

Maintenance

Most experts believe that correctly operated and maintained gas turbines have the same life expectancy as other forms of baseload generation. However, most also feel that to ensure reliability and longevity, certain components will require inspection and replacement at scheduled intervals. Owners and operators of the machines most likely will have to adopt maintenance routines that are as stringent as the jet engine maintenance programs performed by airline companies. Tight quality control on the advanced machines will be a necessity.

The new advanced gas turbines and combined-cycle units, operating at such extremely high temperature and high pressure, are pushing the parts and materials closer and closer to their operating limits. Sophisticated cooling equipment is required in these latest models, and malfunctions in this cooling equipment can cause catastrophic damage.

In addition, since materials are being pushed to the limit, defective materials or components that are installed have an even greater chance of failure. Failure of one component can very easily cause other components or equipment to fail.

The combustion technology responsible for reducing emissions to as low as nine ppm NO_x in some of the models also requires a great deal of sophisticated equipment. Extremely accurate and dependable control equipment is necessary to ensure that fuel is mixed correctly. Malfunctions in this equipment can cause improper fuel mix or fuel injection at the wrong time resulting in hardware failures downstream.

Advances made in the aircraft industry will play a key role in improved reliability. The use of advanced design and analytical methods such as Failure Mode and Effect Analysis (FMEA) has contributed to the aircraft engine reliability improvement. FMEA looks at possible failures of engines before they occur and attempts to identify the areas or components that will be affected by failures. FMEA is being developed for use on advanced gas turbines.

Since gas turbines and combined cycles have not been used extensively in baseload applications, owners of baseload machines have limited operating experience. With little operating history, failure analysis and maintenance scheduling can be extremely difficult. To make these tasks easier, Electric Power Research Institute (EPRI) began a long-term program to study performance, operation, and maintenance track records of advanced gas turbines.

One of EPRI's main focus areas is on-line monitoring of hot blade temperatures. EPRI is using this information to help determine remaining life of blades, vanes, and nozzles. The organization has also written the *Operating Practices Guidebook,* aimed at helping gas-turbine plant managers and project planners. The book is based on a survey of utilities and independent power producers, as well as in-depth interviews at six gas-turbine sites. It provides owners and operators of gas turbines, combined cycles, and cogeneration units with information on current industry practices. It is a tool that gives readers a look at what other owners have been doing and what has been successful.

Future Design

Continuing gas-turbine technology ultimately may become the responsibility of materials

developers. Advanced materials will allow higher firing temperatures than the turbines currently under development. However, increasing combined-cycle efficiency does not necessarily have to happen in the gas-turbine industry alone. Combined-cycle designers also may be able to increase efficiency from the cycle components and the cycle concept itself.

The basic design—gas turbine, steam turbine, heat recovery steam generator (HRSG)—is the foundation for almost every combined-cycle design. (Figure 15–6) The efficient combination of the Rankine and Brayton cycles is easy and relatively inexpensive to construct. Maintaining cost-effectiveness while finding innovative ways to increase cycle efficiency and keep emissions low is the challenge plant designers are facing.

Of the basic three combined-cycle components, gas turbines have received most of the attention. Advances in cooling techniques and heat resistant materials have been at the center of the latest efficiency increases. However, progress is being made in steam-turbine and HRSG efficiencies as well. Innovative engineering has created a number of technologies and ideas which will

Figure 15–6. Functional diagram of a combined-cycle block

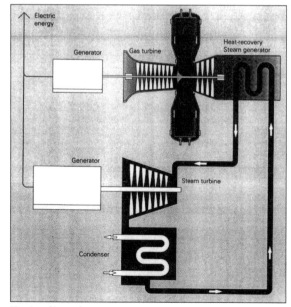

[Courtesy Siemens]

continue to allow combined-cycle design to evolve.

For example, gas-turbine inlet air cooling is no longer limited to conventional means such as evaporative cooling, which is less effective in humid conditions, and refrigeration, which fails to reduce auxiliary power consumption. The latest technique involves applying thermal-energy storage technology similar to that used in some district cooling applications. By cooling inlet air with ice made during off-peak hours, power plants can boost capacity and efficiency during on-peak hours.

The move to raise Rankine-cycle efficiencies also is being explored. Besides the latest gas-turbine developments, the introduction of relatively straightforward system improvements, such as the use of supercritical steam cycles, will help make it possible to achieve combined-cycle efficiency of 60%.

Compared to a "base" combined-cycle design, which has a dual-pressure subcritical steam cycle (1,100 psi, 1,000 F), a triple-pressure subcritical cycle can have an overall efficiency gain of 0.6% and a triple-pressure subcritical cycle with reheat can have a 1.2% gain. A supercritical cycle (3,600 psi, 1,000 F) compared to a base design will have a 1.9% gain with dual pressure, a 2.3% gain with single pressure and reheat, and a 2.4% gain with triple pressure at 1,050 F.

In a single-shaft design, the cycle can have an even higher efficiency and capacity, and the machine is more reliable and easier to maintain. Siemens is building a single-shaft, combined-cycle plant in Portugal that combines several efficiency-boosting options. The plant will feature the company's V94.3A gas turbine with a triple-pressure, reheat steam cycle, fuel preheating, and a hydrogen-cooled generator. Siemens is guaranteeing 55.4% efficiency for the plant, scheduled to begin operation in 1998, with the potential for 56% efficiency. Although this is not the 60% efficiency that is being predicted by some, it sets the groundwork for proving the viability and reliability of the technologies that can make 60% possible.

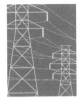

Kalina Combined Cycle

GE is looking toward efficiency of even greater than 60%. The company is involved with the development and commercialization of the Kalina combined cycle. ABB holds the license for direct-fired Kalina plants.

The Kalina cycle, invented by Alexander Kalina, offers a way to increase combined-cycle efficiency by changing the working fluid of the bottoming cycle. This change improves efficiency by increasing the thermodynamic availability, or exergy, of energy transferred from the topping cycle to the bottoming cycle.

In a conventional combined-cycle system, gas-turbine exhaust provides the energy to produce steam for expansion in the steam turbine and subsequent condensation. In a Kalina combined cycle, gas-turbine exhaust energy vaporizes an ammonia-water working fluid mixture, which then expands through a vapor turbine. The key features of the Kalina cycle are its ability to exchange energy from topping to bottoming cycle and to reject heat from

bottoming cycle to heat sink in a non-isothermal manner. This reduces the exergy loss caused by gas/steam temperature differences, which is an area of inefficiency in combined-cycle machines. In addition to exergy loss by gas/steam temperature differences, the traditional combined cycle also suffers exergy loss as a result of HRSG exhaust gas temperatures compared to stack temperatures.

The Kalina combined cycle reduces exergy loss and increases bottoming-cycle output by mixing two working fluids (ammonia and water) and varying their composition, tailoring the fluid properties at each point in the cycle to achieve non-isothermal evaporation. This results in higher efficiencies than a single-pressure Rankine cycle. By adding reheat and a regenerative evaporator (Figure 15–7), the advanced Kalina cycle achieves significantly higher efficiency than the best triple-pressure Rankine bottoming cycle.

The mixed working fluid does have a downside in terms of fluid condensation. Because the mixture (approximately 80% ammonia) requires a 22 F temperature for condensation, a distillation

Figure 15–7. Advanced Kalina combined-cycle

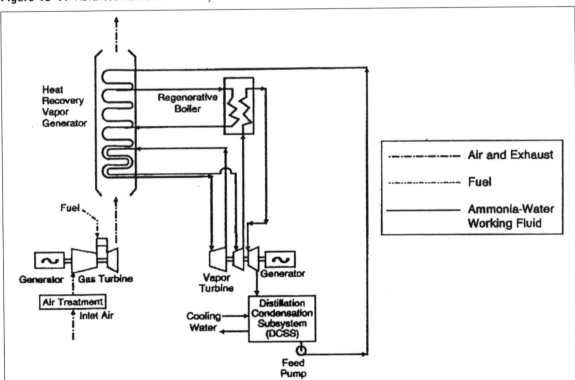

condensation subsystem is necessary to regenerate the working fluid. This system requires three stages to return the fluid to a liquid composition which can be returned to a heat recovery vapor generator for heating.

Using the Kalina cycle, GE has recorded efficiency gains up to 2.5% with its F combined cycle. The same machine produced an additional 25 MW of net power.

GE has performed an economic evaluation of the Kalina cycle versus the conventional Rankine cycle, assessing life-cycle cost in terms of capital, fuel, operations, and maintenance costs. Based on improved efficiency and assuming a 10% discount rate, a 20-year life, an 18% fixed charge rate, and a 4% fuel cost escalation, the Kalina cycle provides an equivalent total combined-cycle capital cost savings of $30 to $100 per kW. This savings does not consider additional power output alongside efficiency increases, which could further enhance the value.

GE is currently trying to resolve some material issues and drive down system costs for the Kalina combined cycle, but the company is ready to build a commercial-scale plant to demonstrate the technology. The manufacturer feels the system would be especially beneficial for high fuel-cost generating plants.

By the turn of the century, it is conceivable that many of the technologies now being tested and developed will be available commercially. As engineers continue to combine these technologies, 60% combined-cycle efficiency may become commonplace.

OUTLOOK

DOE's Energy Information Administration predicts steady growth in natural gas consumption after 2000 due to both increased utilization of existing gas-fired power plants and to the addition of new combined-cycle facilities. Conventional steam coal-fired plants' share of generation is expected to decrease not just in the United States,

Figure 15–8. Development of orders placed worldwide for fossil-fired power plants

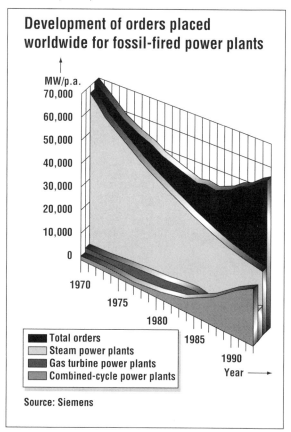

Figure 15–9. Contracts awarded worldwide for fossil-fueled power plants per annum

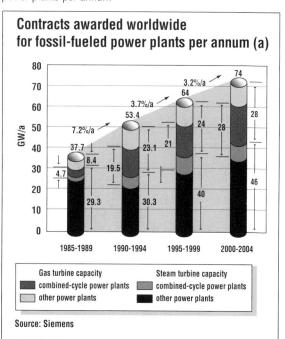

Figure 15-10. Technology forecast — 1995-2000 orders

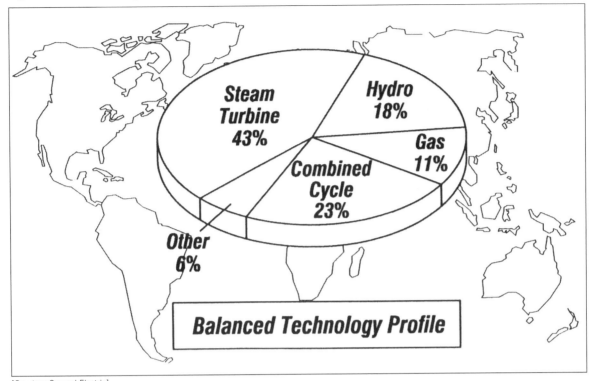

[Courtesy General Electric]

but worldwide, while gas turbines and combined cycles are expected to increase. (Figures 15–8 and 15–9) Early in the 21st century, 34% of electricity, worldwide, will be generated by gas turbines and combined-cycle facilities. (Figure 15–10) While capacity growth in the United States will remain somewhat limited, gas-turbine and combined-cycle manufacturers see potential in foreign markets. (Table 15–2)

Table 15–2

Predicted orders for electric capacity worldwide, 1995-2004

	Total	Gas Turbine	Combined Cycle
North America	70 GW	7.7 GW	16.1 GW
Latin America	55 GW	6.1 GW	12.7 GW
Asia (including China)	300 GW	33 GW	69 GW
Europe & East Africa	250 GW	27.5 GW	57.5 GW
Other	206 GW	22.7 GW	47.4 GW

Chapter 16
Gasification

TERESA HANSEN
ASSOCIATE EDITOR
ELECTRIC LIGHT & POWER AND
POWER ENGINEERING

OVERVIEW

Fossil fuels are the chief source of electricity, currently providing almost 90% of the United States' energy. Of these fossil fuels, coal is the nation's largest resource and the source of 56% of its electricity—38 of the 50 states have coal reserves. Coal has been the U.S. fuel of choice for electricity generation for decades because of its availability and low cost. A dozen states obtain more than 85% of their electricity from coal. Worldwide, coal-fired power stations generate almost 40% of the electricity, more than twice that generated by any other fuel.

Coal-burning utilities account for an estimated two-thirds of the nation's sulfur dioxide (SO_2) emissions. In the year 2000, all utility power plants over 25 MW must reduce SO_2 emissions to 1.2 pounds per million Btu of fuel consumed. Many utilities are looking for a technology that will reduce emissions and still allow them to burn coal and avoid costly fuel switching.

Coal gasification technology fills that bill and is beginning to stand out as the coal-based technology that can meet the requirements for clean, efficient power generation. By the early 21st century, predictions are that with gasification technology, coal-fired power plants will emit 99% less sulfur dioxide (SO_2) and flyash and 90% less nitrogen oxide (NO_x) than today's commercial plants. These future plants also are expected to reduce carbon dioxide (CO_2) by 35–40%, reduce solid wastes by 40–50%, and produce electricity at a cost savings of 10–20%.

Gasification technology combined with advancing gas-turbine technology will play a major role in integrated gasification plants' achieving lower electricity costs than pulverized coal plants equipped with scrubbers.

Gasification of coal as well as residual oils is already occurring. Biomass applications using wood waste or sugar cane bagasse also holds promise. As environmental pressures increase, gasification will likely be the technology that

allows coal to maintain its leading position as a generation fuel.

Major commercial-size gasification projects based on coal, petroleum residuals, biomass, and waste are being planned, designed, and built in the United States and around the world.

HISTORY

The West has known for several centuries that energy-rich vapors can be drawn from liquid and solid hydrocarbons. In 1670, the Reverend John Clayton of Yorkshire recorded his success in distilling flammable vapors from coal. Recorded instances of gas manufacturing for commercial purposes were reported in England by the end of the 1700s. In 1820, the chemist John Dalton provided a credible scientific explanation for the synthesis of flammable gases.

Organic solids and liquids emit flammable vapors when heated in an oxygen-poor environment. Absent oxygen, these substances will not burn, and these vapors can be collected and used elsewhere as fuel. The flammable vapors comprising gas made from coal are principally hydrogen (H_2), carbon monoxide (CO), and methane (CH_4). All of these gases are capable of adding oxygen to their structures and in so doing will emit energy in the form of heat and light. Carbon monoxide in manufactured gas, though flammable, is toxic. In the early days of the industry, gas was notorious as a means of suicide and frequently caused accidental asphyxiation.

Throughout the 19th century, gas produced from coal illuminated streets and homes in most towns east of the Mississippi River. Gas was produced in one or more "gas works" in each urban area. Usually, the same company that manufactured the gas operated the pipelines and distribution system. Throughout the history of manufactured gas, a surprising assortment of organic substances has served as feedstock. In addition to coal, gas works used crude oil, refined oil, wood, pine tar, rubbish, and almost any other organic substance that was cheap and abundant.

When manufactured gas began to capture city lighting markets during the first half of the 19th century (Table 16–1), coal was by far the dominant feedstock, and the distillation technology was primitive. Around 1870, an abundance of refined petroleum products triggered construction of gas works that used a mixture of coal and oil.

Table 16–1
Introduction of town gas in major U.S. cities

East and Southeast	
Baltimore	1816
New York	1823
Boston	1829
New Orleans	1832
Louisville	1832
Pittsburgh	1836
Philadelphia	1836
Providence	1848
New Haven	1848
Buffalo	1848
Rochester	1848
Washington, D.C.	1848
Norfolk	1849
Memphis	1852
Atlanta	1854
Scranton	1857
Pacific Coast	
San Francisco	1854
Portland	1860
Oakland	1867
Los Angeles	1867
Seattle	1873
Tacoma	1885
Spokane	1887
Midwest	
Cincinnati	1840
St. Louis	1846
Detroit	1849
Cleveland	1849
Chicago	1850
Columbus	1850
Indianapolis	1852
Milwaukee	1853
Toledo	1854
St. Paul	1857
Kansas City	1867
Omaha	1868
Minneapolis	1871

Coal gas, oil gas, and various techniques for synthesizing water gas were all still in use during the late 1800s. In selecting a feedstock and technology, a gas company considered the regional availability and comparative costs of coal and oil, the market demand for "enriched vapors," and the threat of competing enterprises.

In the last decade of the 19th century, the "coke" industry supplied much of America's synthetic gas. Flammable vapors were emitted as a result of the coking process, which transformed wood or coal into almost pure carbon for use in steel manufacturing. By 1930, about 90% of all U.S. coke was produced in ovens that jointly manufactured gas, and coke-ovens accounted for 37% of the synthetic gas sold nationwide. After World War II, natural gas became widely available and almost completely captured the manufactured gas business in North America. However, coal gas remains an important fuel for markets, such as Japan, that lack their own resources and must import fuels that are easily transported by sea.

During the energy crises of the 1970s, many U.S. companies began to experiment with more advanced coal-gasification technologies. Curtailments and the seemingly bleak outlook for domestic gas supplies prompted an interest in commercial production of a superior grade of coal gas that could be used interchangeably with natural gas. However, by the time corporate and government interests reached agreement on financing arrangements, the gas shortages were over. Coal gas was once more overshadowed by natural gas.

Growth in the demand for electricity, along with the nation's strict environmental protection measures, have again resurrected an interest in the development of advanced gasification technologies. While growth is expected in the use of renewables and natural gas to generate electricity, it is predicted that coal will continue to provide about one-half of all electricity through the year 2010. (Figure 16–1)

INTEGRATED-GASIFICATION COMBINED-CYCLE TECHNOLOGY

Because coal provides an indigenous, stable supply of relatively inexpensive energy, more than

Figure 16-1. U.S. electricity generation by coal

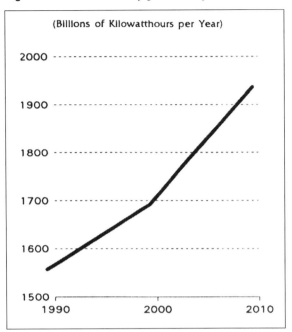

55% of new electric capacity added in the United States between 2000 and 2010 is expected to be coal-based. Integrated-gasification combined-cycle (IGCC) technology is expected to play a major role in supplying this new capacity.

IGCC integrates two commercially proven technologies to produce electricity, taking a totally different approach than conventional combustion technologies. In the gasification process, feedstock (coal, petroleum residual, etc.) reacts under controlled conditions to produce a fuel gas (syngas) which, when cleaned, is comparable to natural gas. The coal or other feedstock is ground into a slurry and is then pumped into a gasification vessel where oxygen is added to form the hot, raw gas through partial combustion. Most of the non-carbon material in the feedstock melts and flows out the bottom of the vessel forming slag, a black, glassy, non-leaching, sandlike material.

The syngas is then cooled in a heat exchanger to generate high pressure steam. The hot gas is further cleaned by an advanced cleanup process to remove particulate, sulfur, and other hazardous air pollutants before being burned in the gas turbine to generate electricity. The gas-turbine

exhaust heat is recovered and used to power a conventional steam turbine that generates additional electricity (Figure 16–2).

The IGCC systems that are currently available commercially have demonstrated exceptional environmental performance. Unparalleled success has been shown in SO_2 removal, NO_x reduction, and particulate removal. SO_2 and NO_x emissions are less than one-tenth of that allowed by federal regulations.

Solid waste problems that occur with conventional coal-fired plants are also avoided with IGCC. The "pre-combustion" technology used in coal gasification removes potential pollutants and converts them to marketable products before the fuel is burned. Sulfur, removed from the fuel gas and recovered in pure elemental form, is a commodity traded on world markets.

Conventional coal-fired power plants use "post-combustion" technologies, such as scrubbers, to clean the air after combustion has occurred, resulting in large amounts of solid wastes, most notably sludge and gypsum. Although some of the ash and gypsum may be sold, about 75% of the waste is disposed of in landfills. The high temperature of the IGCC process converts ash and other solid matter in the coal into inert, non-leachable, granular slag. The slag is nonhazardous and can be used as an aggregate for road and building materials.

Besides being environmentally superior to conventional coal-fired plants, IGCC plants are also more efficient. The plants' efficiency levels are better than 40%, while the base-line efficiency of a conventional coal-fired plant is around 34%. From 1950 until today, conventional power plants have only increased efficiency slowly from around 25% to the current level. IGCC offers a step up in efficiency improvement.

Advancing IGCC Technology

More advanced IGCC systems target efficiency levels of up to 45% and lower capital costs by the year 2000. The U.S. Department of Energy (DOE) predicts that improvements in hot-gas desulfurization and hot-gas particulate removal will be responsible for lowering capital costs from today's $1,400–$1,600 per kW to only $1,200 per kW by 2000. Lower capital costs and increased efficiencies will result in lower electricity costs.

Efficiency improvements currently under development by the major combined-cycle manufacturers are expected to increase IGCC efficiency even earlier in the next century. DOE says that net system efficiencies will reach 52% by the next decade's end, and the capital costs will be lowered to $1,050 per kW. (Figure 16–3)

According to DOE, by the year 2010, the cost of electricity from an advanced coal-fired plant with emissions controls will be 49 mils per kWh, while that from a natural-gas combined-cycle will be 37 mils. DOE predicts the cost of electricity from an IGCC plant will also be 37 mils per kWh. (Figure 16–4) However, the cost of producing electricity from natural gas is expected to increase at a steady rate, as the price of natural gas climbs. By 2010, DOE predicts fuel costs for a coal-fired IGCC plant will be less than one-half of the fuel costs for

Figure 16–2. IGCC system components

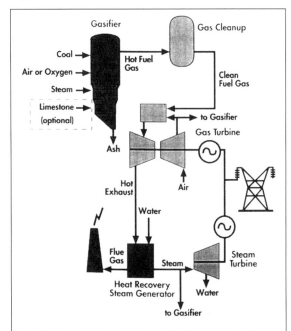

Figure 16–3. Increasing efficiency and decreasing costs in IGCC development

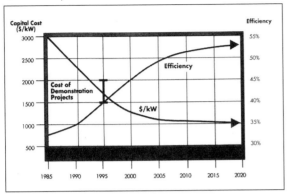

Figure 16–4. Comparison of achievements by 2010

Year 2010	IGCC	Natural Gas Combined Cycle	Advanced Coal Plant
Efficiency	52%	60%	38%-42%
Emissions SO₂ + NOx in #/MMBtu	0.12	0.06	0.6
Capital*	$1,050	$500	$1,400
Fuel Cost* $/MMBtu	$1.80	$3.82	$1.80
Cost of Electricity* (mils/kWh)	37	37	49

1,000 mil = 1 dollar
MMBtu = million Btu
* Costs given in 1990 dollars

natural-gas combined-cycle—$1.80 per million Btu, as compared with $3.82 per million Btu for natural gas. (Figure 16–4)

Advancing technologies have the potential to make coal-fired power plants almost as clean as plants that burn natural gas. It is predicted that SO_2 and NO_x emissions in 2010 from an advanced coal-fired plant with installed anti-pollution scrubbers will be 0.6 pounds per million Btu of coal, but from an IGCC plant they will be only 0.12. (Figure 16–4) At least 99% of the coal's sulfur will be removed from the coal by converting it into a gaseous form in an advanced gasifier before combustion. Predictions are that carbon dioxide (CO_2) production will be further reduced when fuel cell technology is incorporated into the IGCC.

IGCC DEMONSTRATION PROJECTS

Coal now accounts for 56% of the electricity generated in the United States. There are currently six major, U.S., commercial, IGCC demonstration projects in various stages of construction and operation that will account for 1,200 MW of the total coal-based generation. (Figure 16–5) These projects are part of DOE's Clean Coal Technology program and are designed to demonstrate a full range of variations of the IGCC process: different gasifiers, different sizes, different coals, different

cleanup systems, and different applications (grassroots and repowering).

Wabash River Repowering Project

In a joint venture to upgrade an existing plant with advanced technology, Destec Energy, Inc., and PSI Energy, Inc., have repowered one of six units at PSI Energy's Wabash River Generating Station in West Terre Haute, Indiana. The demonstration unit generates 262 MW of electricity using an IGCC system.

The project is demonstrating Destec's two-stage coal gasifier, which produces a medium-Btu syngas from high-sulfur coal. The syngas is piped into a General Electric MS 7001FA high temperature, gas-turbine generator which produces approximately 192 MW of electricity. Steam is supplied to an existing steam-turbine generator in PSI's plant to produce an additional 109 MW (plant auxiliaries consume approximately 33 MW). The technology is expected to boost the heat rate of the repowered unit by about 20% to around 8880 Btu/kWh.

Construction of the Wabash River Repowering Project began in September 1993 and was completed two years later (Fall 1995). The $438 million project, funded 50% by DOE, is the largest single-train IGCC plant in operation in the United States.

The first three years of operation will serve as a demonstration period. During this time, plant performance data will be collected and an evaluation of the new technology for future

Figure 16–5. Demonstration and research facilities

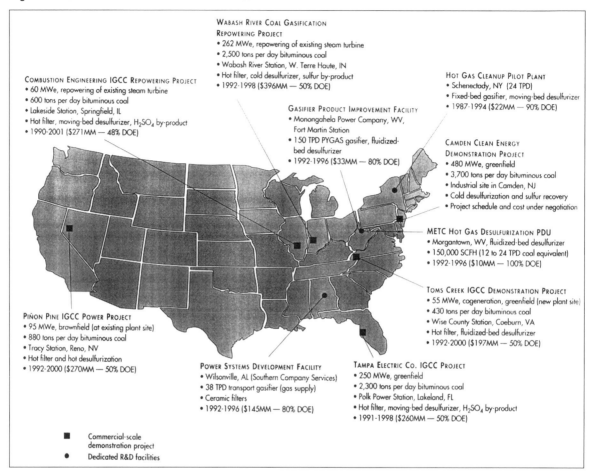

COMBUSTION ENGINEERING IGCC REPOWERING PROJECT
• 60 MWe, repowering of existing steam turbine
• 600 tons per day bituminous coal
• Lakeside Station, Springfield, IL
• Hot filter, moving-bed desulfurizer, H_2SO_4 by-product
• 1990-2001 ($271MM — 48% DOE)

WABASH RIVER COAL GASIFICATION REPOWERING PROJECT
• 262 MWe, repowering of existing steam turbine
• 2,500 tons per day bituminous coal
• Wabash River Station, W. Terre Haute, IN
• Hot filter, cold desulfurizer, sulfur by-product
• 1992-1998 ($396MM — 50% DOE)

GASIFIER PRODUCT IMPROVEMENT FACILITY
• Monongahela Power Company, WV, Fort Martin Station
• 150 TPD PYGAS gasifier, fluidized-bed desulfurizer
• 1992-1996 ($33MM — 80% DOE)

HOT GAS CLEANUP PILOT PLANT
• Schenectady, NY (24 TPD)
• Fixed-bed gasifier, moving-bed desulfurizer
• 1987-1994 ($22MM — 90% DOE)

CAMDEN CLEAN ENERGY DEMONSTRATION PROJECT
• 480 MWe, greenfield
• 3,700 tons per day bituminous coal
• Industrial site in Camden, NJ
• Cold desulfurization and sulfur recovery
• Project schedule and cost under negotiation

METC HOT GAS DESULFURIZATION PDU
• Morgantown, WV, fluidized-bed desulfurizer
• 150,000 SCFH (12 to 24 TPD coal equivalent)
• 1992-1996 ($10MM — 100% DOE)

TOMS CREEK IGCC DEMONSTRATION PROJECT
• 55 MWe, cogeneration, greenfield (new plant site)
• 430 tons per day bituminous coal
• Wise County Station, Coeburn, VA
• Hot filter, fluidized-bed desulfurizer
• 1992-2000 ($197MM — 50% DOE)

PIÑON PINE IGCC POWER PROJECT
• 95 MWe, brownfield (at existing plant site)
• 880 tons per day bituminous coal
• Tracy Station, Reno, NV
• Hot filter and hot desulfurization
• 1992-2000 ($270MM — 50% DOE)

POWER SYSTEMS DEVELOPMENT FACILITY
• Wilsonville, AL (Southern Company Services)
• 38 TPD transport gasifier (gas supply)
• Ceramic filters
• 1992-1996 ($145MM — 80% DOE)

TAMPA ELECTRIC CO. IGCC PROJECT
• 250 MWe, greenfield
• 2,300 tons per day bituminous coal
• Polk Power Station, Lakeland, FL
• Hot filter, moving-bed desulfurizer, H_2SO_4 by-product
• 1991-1998 ($260MM — 50% DOE)

■ Commercial-scale demonstration project
● Dedicated R&D facilities

replication both in the United States and overseas markets will be conducted.

Tampa Electric IGCC Project

As part of a major expansion, the Tampa Electric Company in Florida is building a 250-MW IGCC facility as a grassroots plant. The project will demonstrate Texaco's oxygen-blown, entrained-flow, pressurized-coal gasifier coupled to a General Electric combined-cycle system. The project also will incorporate an innovative hot-gas cleaning system to boost efficiencies even further. The plant will process 2,300 tons of high-sulfur coal per day, using a moving-bed desulfurizer, integrated air separation, and parallel hot- and cold-gas cleanup.

Construction started in 1994 and is currently nearing completion. The facility will undergo four years of operational testing.

Pinion Pine IGCC Project

Sierra Pacific Power Company is hosting an IGCC demonstration at its Tracy Station near Reno, Nevada. The 99-MW unit is using the KRW air-blown, pressurized fluidized-bed gasifier, which produces low-Btu syngas, with hot-gas cleanup. General Electric's gas turbine will be used.

After evaluating several options, including pulverized-coal and natural-gas, single- and combined-cycle systems, the Nevada utility chose the IGCC technology to meet anticipated load growth. The Public Service Commission of Nevada

cited the technology's advantages of "flexibility, diversity, and reliability."

Low-sulfur western coal will be used in the plant, although high-sulfur eastern coals also will be tested.

Construction began in February 1995 and is scheduled to be completed in early 1997, which is also when the unit is set to begin operation. Sierra Pacific and DOE will split the cost of the project.

Toms Creek IGCC Demonstration Project

Tamco Power Partners has developed a 55-MW cogeneration project in Coeburn, Virginia, on a 50/50 private/government cost-sharing basis. The idea behind the project is to reduce the cost and complexity of IGCC plants still further by using air instead of oxygen in the gasifier. The project will demonstrate the Tampella U-Gas, air-blown, fluidized-bed gasifier with in-bed desulfurization, ceramic filters, and external fluidized-bed desulfurization for hot-gas cleanup. Toms Creek Mine will supply the bituminous coal.

Camden Clean Energy Demonstration Project

Duke Energy, in cooperation with General Electric and Air Products and Chemicals, Inc., has proposed that it provide 480 MW of IGCC-generated electricity to Public Service Electric and Gas Company of New Jersey. The project will demonstrate the use of the British Gas/Lurgi fixed-bed, slagging gasifier in an IGCC system. The plant, to be located in Camden, New Jersey, will produce medium-Btu coal-gas from high-sulfur eastern bituminous coal. Negotiations for the proposed project are currently underway.

Combustion Engineering IGCC Repowering Project

Lakeside Station in Springfield, Illinois, is the site of a repowering project designed to demonstrate Combustion Engineering's air-blown, two-stage, entrained-flow gasifier and hot-gas cleanup. The 60-MW plant will process 600 tons of bituminous coal per day.

These six projects are by no means the only IGCC projects under way. Other commercial projects are operating or being constructed in Europe and Asia (Figure 16–6), with many more in various stages of planning and design throughout the world. Four large-scale research and development facilities have also been set up to focus on research supporting commercial market entry of IGCC systems. (Figure 16–5) These facilities explore and demonstrate system integration of hot-gas desulfurization, component scale-up of particulate control devices, and gasifier product improvement.

GASIFICATION IN THE REFINING INDUSTRY

While viewed primarily as a clean, efficient, coal-based, power generation technology, gasification also is becoming increasingly recognized as a cost-effective option in the refining and chemical industry. It cleanly and efficiently converts low-value or negative-value refinery steams to higher value power, steam, and synthesis gas for on-site use or for export.

Gasification is providing a solution to many of the problems associated with petroleum refining in industry. The prevalence of heavy, sour, metals-laden crudes, the highly competitive nature of the refining industry, and environmental regulations are all making gasification an attractive option for refiners. When these petroleum-based gas fuels are fired in gas turbines and combined cycles, minimal amounts of SO_2, NO_x, particulates, volatile organic compounds, and CO_2 are produced.

The reasons for including a gasifier in a refinery are often derived from a combination of crude oil quality and increased restrictions on

Figure 16–6. Gasification technology — illustrative worldwide experience

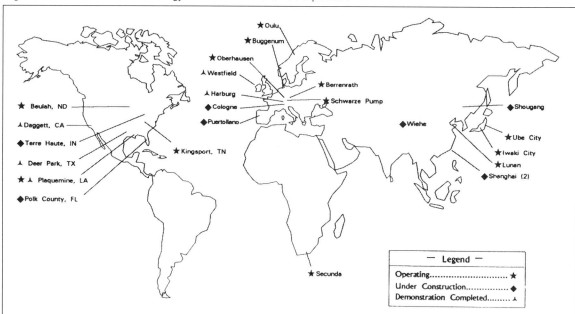

Country	Location	Size (tpd)	Feedstock	Product	Technology	Status
South Africa	Secunda	88,000	Coal	Fuels/Chemicals	Lurgi	Operating
USA	Beulah ND	13,200	Lignite	Gas/Chemicals	Lurgi	Operating
USA	Plaquemine LA	2,400	Coal	Electricity	Destec	Operating
Netherlands	Buggenum	2,200	Coal	Electricity	Shell	Operating
Japan	Ube City	1,500	Coal/Coke	Ammonia	Texaco	Operating
China		1,080	Coal	Ammonia	Lurgi	Operating
USA	Kingsport TN	1,000	Coal	Chemicals	Texaco	Operating
Finland	Oulu	960	Peat	Ammonia	HTW	Operating
Germany	Oberhausen	800	Coal	Chemicals	Texaco	Operating
Germany	Berrenrath	730	Coal	Methanol	HTW	Operating
Germany	Schwarze Pump	720	Coal	Methanol	GSP	Operating
China	Lunan	400	Coal	Ammonia	Texaco	Operating
Japan	Iwaki City	200	Coal	Electricity	Govt. of Japan	Operating
Germany	Cologne	2,880	Coal	Gas/Electricity	HTW	Construction
Spain	Puertollano	2,600	Coal/Coke	Electricity	Prenflo	Construction
USA	Terre Haute IN	2,500	Coal	Electricity	Destec	Construction
USA	Polk County FL	2,300	Coal	Electricity	Texaco	Construction
China	Shougang	1,500	Coal	Town Gas	Texaco	Construction
China	Wiehe	1,360	Coal	Ammonia	Texaco	Construction
China	Shanghai	1,100	Coal	Gas/Methanol	Texaco	Construction
China	Shanghai	800	Coal	Town Gas	U-Gas	Construction
USA	Plaquemine LA	1,600	Coal/Lignite	Electricity	Dow/Destec	Demo Comp.
USA	Daggett CA	1,100	Coal	Electricity	Texaco	Demo Comp.
UK	Westfield	450	Coal	Electcitity	Brit. Gas/Lurgi	Demo Comp.
USA	Plaquemine LA	400	Coal/Lignite	Electricity	Dow/Destec	Demo Comp.
USA	DeerPark TX	250	Coal/Coke	Electricity	Shell	Demo Comp.
Germany	Harburg	200	Coal/Lignite	Syngas	Shell	Demo Comp.

Source: Prepared by the Coal Gasification Committee of the Council on Alternate Fuels based on information provided by the McIlvaine Company and other sources. The illustration and table represent gasification facilities using solid feedstocks (coal, lignite, and petroleum coke) in operation, under construction, or that have completed demonstration of the technology. The list is not intended to be exhaustive, especially with regard to facilities that are in various stages of planning.

levels of SO_2 from the combustion of heavy fuels. Another compelling reason is the ability to use the syngas to generate electricity, thus reducing both costs and emissions. Excess electricity is often sold on the grid, thus providing additional revenue. IGCC plants operating on heavy oil are somewhat less complex than coal-based IGCCs and cost a little less—$1,200–$1,500/kW for heavy oil as compared to $1,400–$1,600/kW for coal.

Several refinery-oriented IGCCs are currently under construction. (Table 16-2) Texaco Inc.'s refinery at El Dorado, Kansas, will use a General Electric Model 6000B, 40-MW system for in-house power generation from petroleum coke and waste oil, plus some supplemental natural gas. It is scheduled for operation sometime in 1996.

Table 16–2
Refinery gasification projects

Company	Location	Feed	Products
API	Italy	Visbr. res.	250 mw + steam
ISAB	Italy	Asphalt	500 mw + steam + hydrogen
Sarlux	Italy	Visbr. res.	550 mw + steam + hydrogen
AGIP	Italy	Visbr. res.	251 mw + hydrogen
Texaco	El Dorado, Kan.	Coke, wastes	35 mw + steam
Shell Nederland	Pernis, Netherlands	Visbr. res.	113 mw + steam + hydrogen

Shell's refinery at Pernis, Netherlands, will use two GE 6000B machines with steam turbine generators to supply refinery needs and export some power to the grid. It is scheduled for startup in early 1997. Some large plants are in the advanced design stage in Italy. The Sarlux refinery in Sardinia and the ISAB refinery in Sicily have joined separately with independent power producers to sell power to the grid using heavy oil feedstock. These plants are 550 MW and 500 MW, respectively.

Gasification technology has the unique ability to generate electricity, chemicals, or both, depending upon the choice of equipment. The ability to produce different products makes the overall economics of an IGCC project attractive to many refiners. The primary components of the fuel gas can be separated from the syngas mixture and sold as pure components, or they can be reacted with other compounds to make a wide range of more complex chemicals. (Figure 16–7)

The ability to produce chemicals from syngas has been proven well, with a number of plants now in operation. An example is the Eastman Chemical Co. facility in Kingsport, Tennessee, which converts coal-derived syngas to methanol and carbon monoxide. These are reacted with

Figure 16–7. Integrated-energy gasification facility

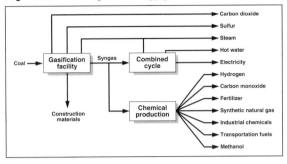

other chemicals to produce cellulose acetate. A plant in Germany produces oxo-chemicals from syngas, and operating plants in India, Japan, and China produce ammonia.

Gasification technologies for refinery applications are offered by Destec Energy, Inc., Noill-LGA Gastechnik GmbH (Germany), Shell Synthetic Fuels, Inc., and Texaco. Heavy oil gasification has been licensed by Shell and Texaco for 40 years, making it a proven method for converting petroleum-based feedstocks to a clean fuel gas.

FORECAST

The continued low cost of coal and the increasing demand for electric power in the United States and abroad have created a tremendous commercial opportunity for advanced power generation technologies, including IGCC.

DOE estimates that capacity additions to the U.S. electric power market will grow at an average rate of 1% per year. In addition, it predicts a considerable market in the repowering of older plants. IGCC systems are expected to make enormous inroads into three key market areas in the next few decades. (Figure 16–8) IGCC technology is predicted to be used widely for new power plants and for the repowering or conversion of others. IGCC plant investments will track the capacity additions and will total over $400 billion by the middle of the next century, according to DOE predictions. Estimates predict

that the IGCC market share will increase to as much as 30% of electricity generation by that time, resulting in 450,000 MW of capacity.

All indications are that the market for coal-based power generation outside the United States will be significantly larger than the U.S. market, and also will represent a more immediate need. Coal represents 70% of the world's proven resources, and there is an urgent need for clean, high-efficiency technologies that will allow developing countries to continue to use it. Essentially all countries with significant coal reserves have expressed a strong interest in using IGCC systems to produce needed electricity.

When efficiency, cost-of-electricity, and environmental benefits are compared, IGCC technology scores very high. Many believe that IGCC will be the power generation technology of choice for the 21st century.

Figure 16–8. IGCC market goals

Market Area	Market Share for Period		
	1995 to 2010	2010 to 2030	2030 to 2050
Coal Plant Additions or Steam Plant Replacements	1%	20%	30%
Repowering of Steam Plants Built Over 30 Years Ago	0.5%	20%	80%
Natural Gas Combined Cycle Conversions	0%	10%	50%
IGCC Market (in thousand megawatts)	6	155	450

Chapter 17
Renewable Energy

DR. JOANTA GREEN
J.H. GREEN ENTERPRISES

OVERVIEW

Many renewable energy resources are relative newcomers to the electric power market. Electricity generation using wind, geothermal, and solar was greatly increased during the 1970s and 1980s. This was due to technological advancements, the implementation of favorable governmental policies, and reactions to the energy shortages of the 1970s. Its continued use has been encouraged due to the perception of renewable energy as being more environmentally acceptable than energy generated from conventional power supplies, such as nuclear and coal. And as renewable energy resources become available domestically, the issue of relying on imported supplies is reduced.

However, renewable energy (energy from solar, wind, hydroelectric, biomass, and waste) currently provides only a small percentage (about 7%) of the nation's energy supply. In 1994, the majority (approximately 49% of the total) was generated

Table 17–1
U.S. renewable energy consumption by source, 1990-1994 (quadrillion Btu)

Energy Source	1990	1991	1992	1993	1994
Conventional Hydroelectric Power	3.113	3.196	2.871	3.156	3.037
Geothermal	0.327	0.331	0.349	0.362	0.357
Biomass	2.632	2.642	2.788	2.784	2.852
Solar energy	0.067	0.068	0.068	0.069	0.069
Wind energy	0.024	0.027	0.030	0.031	0.036
Total	6.163	6.265	6.106	6.403	6.350

Table 17–2
U.S. energy consumption, 1990 (quadrillion Btu)

Energy Source	Consumption	Percent
Petroleum	33.55	39.8
Natural gas	19.30	22.9
Coal	19.12	22.7
Nuclear	6.16	7.3
Renewable Resources	6.26	7.4
Conventional hydropower	2.97	3.5
Geothermal	0.32	0.4
Biomass	2.90	3.4
Solar	0.04[a]	[b]
Wind	0.02[a]	[b]
Total	84.40	100.0

[a] Excludes unmeasured direct use
[b] Less than 0.05 percent

Table 17–3
U.S. electric generating capacity, 1990-1994 (MW)

Source	1990	1991	1992	1993	1994
Hydroelectric	72,693	73,228	77,029	77,504	78,560
Geothermal	2,720	2,663	2,993	3,065	3,082
Biomass	9,114	9,872	10,276	10,636	11,081
Solar/PV	404	392	362	365	358
Wind	2,267	2,156	1,822	1,814	1,745
Total renewables	87,198	88,266	92,484	93,384	94,826
Non-renewables	692,980	701,743	654,079	667,365	669,617
Total	**780,178**	**790,009**	**746,563**	**760,749**	**764,443**

from hydroelectric power. Biomass and municipal solid waste (MSW) combined contributed about 45% of the total. All other renewable resources, including geothermal, wind and solar, provided about 5% of the total. (Tables 17–1—17–3) These resources, however, account for more than 93% of the total of U.S. energy resources. Of these, geothermal, wind and solar are particularly plentiful but not usually economically feasible to access. (Table 17–4)

Table 17–4
Total U.S. energy resources, accessible resources, and reserves (quadrillion Btu)

Resources	Accessible	Resources	Reserves
Geothermal	1,497,925	22,782	247
Solar (including biomass and MSW)[a]	1,034,940	586,687	352
Wind	1,026,078	5,046	5
Shale oil	159,604	11,704	1
Coal	87,458	38,147	5,266
Petroleum	2,767	1,102	156
Natural Gas	1,705	887	231
Peat	1,415	354	–[b]
Uranium	1,177	731	42
Conventional Electric	986	157	58
Total	**3,814,057**	**667,597**	**6,358**

[a]Solar includes all biomass and the natural resource base for MSW energy. Although biomass is not estimated separately for resources or accessible resources, biomass is estimated to account for 334 quadrillion Btu (95 percent) of total solar reserves.

[b]Less than 0.5 quadrillion Btu.

In 1994, the electric utility sector accounted for nearly 50% of the total renewable energy consumption. The industrial/nonutility sector accounted for 40%, and the remaining 10% in the commercial and residential sector. (Table 17–5)

Table 17–5
Renewable energy consumption by sector and energy source, 1990-1994 (quadrillion Btu)

Sector and Source	1990	1991	1992	1993	1994
Residential and Commercial					
Biomass	0.581	0.613	0.645	0.592	0.582
Solar energy	0.060	0.060	0.060	0.060	0.060
Total	0.641	0.673	0.705	0.652	0.642
Industrial and Nonutility					
Biomass	1.948	1.943	2.042	2.084	2.152
Geothermal	0.146	0.162	0.179	0.204	0.212
Conventional hydroelectric power	0.082	0.083	0.097	0.118	0.136
Solar energy	0.007	0.008	0.008	0.009	0.008
Wind energy	0.024	0.027	0.030	0.031	0.036
Total	2.206	2.223	2.357	2.446	2.543
Transportation					
Biomass	0.082	0.065	0.079	0.088	0.098
Electric utility					
Biomass	0.021	0.021	0.022	0.020	0.020
Geothermal	0.181	0.170	0.169	0.158	0.145
Conventional hydroelectric power	2.929	2.899	2.511	2.766	2.540
Solar and wind energy	*	*	*	*	*
Net renewable energy imports	0.102	0.214	0.234	0.271	0.361
Total	3.234	3.304	2.965	3.217	3.066
Total renewable energy consumption	6.163	6.265	6.106	6.403	6.350

*less than 0.5 trillion Btu

HISTORY OF RENEWABLE ENERGY IN ELECTRICITY GENERATION

The use of renewable energy technologies for electricity generation has increased over the past 20 years. However, hydropower and wood have had much longer histories and have provided significant amounts of electricity since the early days of electrical generation. Conventional hydropower (large-scale—i.e., over 10 MW) has been a major contributor to the electrical industry, and power generated from this source predates utility generation. In 1880, two years before Thomas Edison's Pearl Street Station inaugurated the modern electric utility industry, the Grand Rapids Electric Light and Power Company in

Michigan illuminated 16 lamps with hydroelectric power. Sixteen years later, the installation of hydroelectric generators at Niagara Falls by George Westinghouse transformed the industry. This project allowed for the transmission of power over great distances using alternating current (AC) which usurped the dominance that direct current (DC) power had. DC was the standard which was utilized by Edison. During the following years, hydropower generation increased rapidly.

Federal interest also helped to disseminate this technology during the 1930s and beyond. The Mussel Shoals development located in Alabama, which was begun during World War I, was the first large-scale, federally funded hydroelectric project. Later the Tennessee Valley Authority, the Bureau of Reclamation of the U.S. Department of the Interior, and the U.S. Army Corps of Engineers implemented massive hydroelectric programs. Many of the projects were located in the northwest with the first large-scale project, the Grand Coulee with a capacity of 6,500 MW, built on the Columbia River in the 1930s.

During the 1970s, fossil fuel costs rose dramatically which directed more interest to renewable energy. In 1970, U.S. renewable energy generation capacity totaled about 63,000 MW (approximately 18% of the total). (Table 17–6) Of that, more than 96% came from conventional hydroelectric power. Approximately 1.6% of the generation came from the combustion of wood and wood waste, and the remainder is distributed among the other renewable energy resources. About 95% of the hydroelectric power generated was used exclusively by the electric utility sector. By the 1940s, hydroelectric power supplied the United States with 33% of its electric power. The hydroelectric share of the market has declined since then.

Table 17–6
U.S. electricity generating capacity, 1970, 1980, 1990 (GW)

	1970	1980	1990
Fossil	284.9	472.4	548.1
Nuclear	7.0	51.8	99.6
Conventional hydroelectric	61.5	69.1	72.9
Other renewable	1.4	2.8	12.3
Total	354.9	596.0	733.0

Wood also has been used to generate electricity. Since early in this century, scrap wood and waste have provided the wood, wood products, and pulp and paper industries with process heat and some electrical energy. This has had the added advantage of allowing these industries to dispose of their waste in a cost-effective manner.

The majority of the wood-fired, electric-power generation facilities existed outside of the electrical utility industry. This is due to the fact that this industry must collect and store waste which adds cost, and the fact that wood has a lower-energy density limits some of the benefits.

About 75% of this wood-fired electric power is used in the industrial sector to produce process heat. The main source of industrial and nonutility generation is from black liquor (a pulpwood by-product waste fuel). (Table 17–7)

Table 17–7
U.S. generating capacity using renewable resources, 1990

Source	Electric Utility	Nonutility	Total
Conventional hydroelectric	71,423	1,476	72,899
Geothermal	1,614	961	2,575
MSW	244	1,765	2,009
Biomass	221	5,750	5,971
Solar	3	360	363
Wind	d	1,403	1,403
Total	73,505	11,715	85,220

d Less than 0.5 MW

During the 1970s, fossil fuels costs rose rapidly spurring interest in renewable energy systems. The 1980s, however, saw the biggest growth in technical progress in renewable energy. In general, all the renewable energy systems benefited from government and private investment for research, development, and demonstration as well as for commercial projects. Costs dropped for most of the systems during this time period as well. Cost of generating power from geothermal reached 4.5–6.5¢ per kWh in California, with cost from biomass at 5¢ per kWh as well. Photovoltaic systems made significant progress in cost reduction, but still remained higher than energy generated from conventional power supplies, at about 30¢ per kWh.

The dominance of nonutilities in renewable energy is due to three factors:

(1) Nonutility generation is often a by-product of other industrial activities.

(2) Renewable resources are encouraged in nonutility markets by PURPA which exempts renewable-fueled power plants built by nonutilities from being regulated as electric utilities.

(3) Electric utilities slowed construction of new capacity and instead relied on nonutility facilities to meet their requirements.

BIOMASS

In 1994, biomass provided 2.852 quadrillion Btu of energy (45% of the total of renewable energy consumption). Only hydroelectric systems provided more power from renewable energy sources. Consumption of biomass energy has grown at a yearly rate of 2% since 1990, compared to a growth rate of 0.8% per year for total renewable energy consumption. Biomass energy is generated from three resources: wood, waste, and alcohol fuels.

Wood energy consumption amounted to 2.266 quadrillion Btu (approximately 80% of the total biomass energy consumption). Wood energy is derived from harvested wood and from wood waste streams. The largest source of energy from wood is pulping liquor (black liquor) and it amounts to 60–70% of the total wood and wood-derived energy consumption.

Waste, the second largest source for biomass energy, consists of municipal solid waste (MSW), manufacturing waste, and landfill gas. Of these, MSW accounts for approximately 67% of the total energy derived from waste. Energy from waste sources has grown at the rapid rate of 5.4% since 1990, reaching a total of 0.488 quadrillion Btu in 1994.

Biomass alcohol fuel, also known as ethanol, is formulated almost exclusively from corn and is utilized as an oxygenate in gasoline. The passage of the Clean Air Act of 1990 (CAA90) provided for the increased use of ethanol consumption which has grown by 4.6% per year since 1990 to 0.098 quadrillion Btu in 1994. (Table 17–8)

Electricity generation from biomass increased at a rate of 7% per year between 1990 and 1994, reaching 59,380 GWh in 1994. Most of this growth occurred in the industrial sector, where electrical generation from biomass increased from 43,297 GWh in 1990 to 57,392 GWh in 1994. In contrast, the electrical utility industry's use of biomass has remained flat since 1990 at around 2,000 GWh.

Table 17–8
Biomass energy consumption by energy source, sector, and census region, 1990-1994 (trillion Btu)

Energy Source	1990	1991	1992	1993	1994
Wood Sector	2,155	2,151	2,249	2,228	2,266
Residential	581	613	645	548	537
Commercial	—	—	—	44	45
Industrial	1,562	1,528	1,593	1,625	1,673
Electric Utility	12	10	11	11	11
Census Region					
Northeast	256	224	264	277	278
Midwest	330	290	286	222	223
South	1,064	1,167	1,234	1,405	1,437
West	505	469	466	324	328
Waste	395	426	460	468	488
Census Region					
Northeast	119	134	148	151	157
Midwest	89	99	84	85	88
South	114	109	128	130	134
West	73	87	100	102	107
Alcohol Fuels (ethanol)	82	65	79	88	98
Census Region					
Northeast	*	*	*	*	*
Midwest	55	45	55	61	68
South	17	11	13	15	16
West	10	9	10	11	12
Total Biomass Energy Consumption	**2,632**	**2,642**	**2,788**	**2,784**	**2,852**

— Not available

* Less than 0.5 trillion Btu

GEOTHERMAL

In 1994, geothermal energy consumption in the United States totaled less than 0.4 quadrillion Btu

providing approximately 17,000 GWh of electricity generation. Compare this to 1992 when geothermal to electricity generation amounted to 349 trillion Btu. Other uses during this time period totaled 4,000 GWh. Energy generated from this source increased at a rate of 2.2% per year since 1990. However, consumption in the industrial and nonutility sector has grown by 9.8% per year with a decrease of 5.4% per year in the electric utility sector. Much of the utility sector generation comes from The Geysers facility in California which produced 10 times more power than the second largest utility-owned facility and four times that from the largest nonutility-owned facility. About 90% of the geothermal energy came from California in 1994 and another 10% originated in Nevada. (Table 17–9)

Geothermal has three applications: electricity generation, low-temperature process heat, and heating and cooling applications for buildings. Of the geothermal used to produce electricity, almost 60% is used by the industrial sector.

WIND

Wind energy consumption is smaller than any of the other renewable energy sources measured by the Department of Energy. In 1994, wind energy consumption was less than 0.04 quadrillion Btu and provided less than 3,500 GWh of electrical generation. (Table 17–10) However, consumption has grown much more quickly than the other renewables at a rate of 11% per year. Most of this generation occurred in California where tax credits have stimulated the development of large wind energy farms during the 1980s. The majority of wind energy is generated by nonutility facilities.

SOLAR

In 1994, solar energy consumption totaled 0.069 quadrillion Btu. This consisted of 0.060 Btu quadrillion in the residential/commercial sector and 0.008 quadrillion Btu in the industrial/nonutility sector. (Table 17–11)

In 1994, nonutility power producers had a reported installed capacity of 358 MW with a gross electrical generation of 824 million kWh (equivalent to 0.8 trillion Btu of thermal energy) from solar thermal collectors. Nine operating Solar Electric Generating System (SEGS) plants in southern California, SEGS I through IX, accounted for 98% (354 MW) of the total nonutility,

Table 17–9
Geothermal energy consumption and electricity generation, 1990-1994

Estimate	1990	1991	1992	1993	1994
Geothermal energy consumption (quad Btu)					
Electric utility	0.181	0.170	0.169	0.158	0.145
Nonutility	0.146	0.162	0.179	0.204	0.212
Total	0.327	0.331	0.349	0.362	0.357
Electricity generation (1000 kWh)					
Electric utility					
California	8,429,403	7,900,814	7,917,440	7,422,851	6,745,833
Other states	151,825	186,241	186,369	148,148	194,804
Total	8,581,228	8,087,055	8,103,809	7,570,999	6,940,637
Nonutility					
California	6,027,290	6,583,321	7,361,287	8,003,990	8,294,586
Nevada	844,459	990,782	1,214,404	1,587,686	1,636,592
Other states	44,251	120,897	2,309	157,324	190,822
Total	6,916,000	7,695,000	8,578,000	9,749,000	10,122,000
Total geothermal electricity generation	**15,497,228**	**15,782,055**	**16,681,809**	**17,319,999**	**17,062,637**

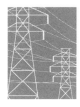

Table 17–10
Wind energy consumption and electricity generation, 1990-1994

Estimate	1990	1991	1992	1993	1994
Wind energy consumption (quad Btu)					
Electric utility	*	*	*	*	*
Nonutility	0.024	0.027	0.030	0.031	0.036
Total	0.024	0.027	0.030	0.031	0.036
Electricity generation (1000 kWh)					
Electric utility					
California	43	0	0	0	0
Other states	355	285	308	243	309
Total	398	285	308	243	309
Nonutility					
California	2,284,000	2,617,000	2,893,000	3,030,000	3,422,000
Other states	11,000	33,000	23,000	22,000	60,000
Total	2,295,000	2,650,000	2,916,000	3,052,000	3,482,000
Total Wind-powered Electricity Generation	**2,295,398**	**2,650,285**	**2,916,308**	**3,052,243**	**3,482,309**

*Less than 0.5 trillion Btu

Table 17–11
Solar energy consumption by sector, 1990-1994 (quadrillion Btu)

Sector	1990	1991	1992	1993	1994
Residential/Commercial	0.060	0.060	0.060	0.060	0.060
Industrial	0.007	0.008	0.008	0.009	0.008
Total	0.067	0.068	0.068	0.069	0.069

solar-generating capacity. Electric utilities, on the other hand, reported 3,472 thousand kWh of net electrical generation from photovoltaic modules in 1994. Of this, 91% was generated in California and 63% of this generated from a single plant. (Table 17–12)

Table 17–12
U.S. utility capacity and new electricity generation from photovoltaic modules, 1994

Utility	Plant	Nameplate Capacity (MW)	1994 Net Generation (MW)
Sacramento Municipal Utility District (CA)	Solar	2.00	2,195
Austin Electric (TX)	Decker Creek	0.30	293
Pacific Gas & Electric (CA)	PVUSA 1	1.00	973
	PVUSA 1	0.50	0
	PVUSA 3	0.50	0
Virginia Electric Power (VA)	North Anna	0.06	11
Total		4.36	3,472

RENEWABLE ENERGY FORECAST

Renewable energy sources (wind, geothermal, and solar) are likely to be promoted because of increasing environmental consideration, but it is unlikely that rapid growth will occur in the period 1997-2001. Electricity generation from these sources during this time period will increase but not to any great extent. Biomass, industrial, and municipal solid waste will also increase their contributions in electricity generation, although their main use will continue to be the production of heat and nonutility, electrical-based generation.

The potential for new, large hydroelectric projects will be limited by the availability of sites in the United States, and although there are plans to expand capacity by renovating existing plants, these are likely to be offset by tightening environmental constraints on the operation of hydroelectric facilities. Hence, output from hydropower is projected to grow at only 1.7% per year.

The single most important factor in the development of a commercial renewable energy market was the passage of the Public Utility Regulatory Policies Act (PURPA) in 1978. Among

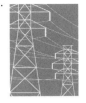

other things, PURPA encouraged the development of small-scale electric power plants, especially those utilizing renewable resources. The renewable energy industry responded to this incentive, and during the period following the passage of PURPA many such power plants were built.

However, new and proposed regulatory reform during the 1990s and especially in 1995 has adversely affected the outlook for renewable energy technologies. Potentially critical regulatory and legislative changes have been proposed in two areas: changes related to PURPA, including the possible repeal of sections of the act, and changes related to the restructuring and deregulation of electricity generation. However, some state and regional programs continue to provide incentives for renewable energy usage, but the federal changes have the potential to adversely affect the entire renewable energy industry.

The Federal Energy Regulatory Commission (FERC) which is responsible for PURPA has had several rulings which will limit the use of above-avoided-cost renewable set-asides, and this may have the effect of severely limiting the commercial viability of the renewable energy industry. PURPA defined a class of independent generators as "qualifying facilities" (QFs) and mandated that utilities purchase power from QFs at the utilities' full avoided cost. This means that utilities were required to pay what they would otherwise have spent to generate power or procure power.

Green pricing has become another option to encourage the development of renewable energy in the deregulated environment. This involves allowing customers to pay a price premium for renewable energy development by direct payments on their monthly utility bills. By using green-pricing programs, utilities state that they can better judge customer support for renewable energy under semi-competitive conditions. There are several green-pricing programs currently in effect but it is still too early to measure the long-term impact that this will have on renewable energy development and usage.

The immediate future of renewable energy systems is dependent on three factors:

(1) Renewable energy depends upon public support. This can be provided through green-pricing programs or through direct, state, and federal government incentives.

(2) Continued improvements in system technology and better economics will increase the likelihood of renewable energy commercialization; but the systems must become more cost competitive for any great gains to be made.

(3) The price of fossil fuels will determine the baseline for deciding whether or not renewable energy is cost competitive.

According to the Energy Information Administration (EIA), U.S. electrical generation is projected to grow moderately through 2010 at an average rate of 1.5% a year. However, the overall conclusion would have to be that energy from renewable resources is not likely to replace fossil fuels as a major contributor of electricity supply over the next 20 years.

The greatest expansion for renewable energy generation is projected to be in the use of MSW. Electricity generation using MSW is expected to expand from 2.0 GW in 1990 to 11.4 GW by 2010 increasing at a rate of 9.1%. This is mainly due to the reduced availability of landfill space and population growth. Geothermal-based electrical generating capacity also is expected to grow rapidly from 2.6 GW in 1990 to 8.5 GW by 2010. This is equivalent to a growth rate of about 7.2% per year. Wind energy is expected to expand at a rate almost nine times the projected overall rate of total U.S. electrical generating capacity. This is an increase from 1.4 GW in 1990 to over 6.3 GW by the year 2010. In spite of that, wind will account for less than 0.7% of the U.S. total at the end of this projected expansion. (Table 17-13) Some expansion in solar-thermal electrical generation will occur especially with Solar Two coming on-

line in 1996. Most of the new expansion in renewable energy generation will come from municipalities and industries as most new investment will occur outside of the utility sector.

Table 17–13

U.S. electric generating capacity and net generation projections for 2010

Technology	1990	2010 Reference	High economic growth	Low economic growth	High world oil price	Low world oil price
Net summer capability (GW)						
Conventional hydropower	72.9	76.9	76.9	76.9	76.9	76.9
Geothermal	2.6	8.5	8.5	8.5	9.7	7.3
MSW	2.0	11.4	13.9	10.9	11.4	11.4
Biomass	6.0	8.1	8.3	7.2	8.1	8.1
Solar	0.4	1.9	1.9	1.9	2.2	1.7
Wind	1.4	6.3	6.3	6.3	7.3	5.3
Total capacity, renewable	85.2	113.1	115.9	111.7	115.5	110.7
Fossil/nuclear/other	647.8	767.0	814.2	722.1	759.4	780.6
Total generating capacity	733.0	880.1	930.1	833.8	874.9	891.3
Percent renewable	11.6	12.9	12.5	13.4	13.2	12.4
Net generation (billion kWh)						
Conventional hydropower	288	306	306	306	306	306
Geothermal	15	62	62	62	72	53
MSW	10	54	70	50	54	54
Biomass	31	59	60	54	59	59
Solar	1	4	4	4	4	3
Wind	2	16	16	16	19	14
Total renewable	348	501	519	492	513	488
Fossil/Nuclear/Other	2,675	3,611	3,816	3,393	3,576	3,679
Total net generation	3,023	4,112	4,335	3,885	4,089	4,167
Percent renewable	11.5	12.2	12.0	12.7	12.5	11.7

Chapter 18
Utility Automation Technology

DON BLOCK
D.E. BLOCK & ASSOCIATES

OVERVIEW

"An era of change" is a phrase which best describes the state of today's electric utility industry. Utilities, just like phone companies, have operated as regulated monopolies. With the recent advent of industry deregulation, utilities are experiencing the same pains as the telephone industry. As utilities downsize, reengineer their companies, and attempt to decide how to compete profitably, not only with their neighboring utility but with new entrepreneurial organizations that are literally startup companies, they must continue to provide reliable service to their customers and a reasonable return to their stockholders. These changes are affecting all facets of a utility's business. The impact on automation within the industry will, over the long term, be very positive; however, during this present transition period, capital expenditures are expected to be reduced.

In the past, the utility industry, although considered very conservative and cautious in adapting new technology to everyday operations, was very open and communicative. Ideas were shared, committees made up of members from several utilities focused on common problems, and companies were proud to tell their counterparts what they were doing. This situation is changing rapidly as utilities are now preparing to do battle for the same customers. Technical conferences such as IEEE/PES are seeing a drop in support. Many of those that do attend these technical meetings are doing so to gain knowledge of what others are doing, with instructions not to divulge information to others.

"Islands of automation," a phrase coined several years ago, still describes the state of automation within the industry. Systems have been designed to do specific jobs. Each manufacturer has used a proprietary protocol, for example, making it difficult for the user to move

to a different supplier. Additionally, the ability to interconnect systems and share data has been minimal. Recently this situation began undergoing change. Standards bodies have been hard at work establishing inter-operability standards in a number of areas. Utility Communication Architecture (UCA), initially defined by the Electric Power Research Institute (EPRI), has established guidelines for utilities, while the AMRA/IEEE SCC 31 Standards Coordinating Committee has been working on communication standards for automatic meter reading (AMR) and other customer-related services. The industry has been striving to achieve a plug and play capability. Considerable progress has been made over the last two to three years in this area. Will it continue with the new competitive environment? It has in other industries because manufacturers felt there was a benefit to them in cooperating on a standard. This has not proven to be the case in the utility industry. If utilities can continue to work together for the good of all, these standards will be established.

The recent passage of the Telecommunications Act of 1996 has added an additional element of confusion to the picture. Utilities are now free to compete with local communication suppliers, including both telephone and cable companies, to provide communication services. Will utilities attempt to compete in this highly competitive market? It is too soon to tell but if they do they will need to hire new management personnel with the vision and understanding of the business. They will have to match the marketing, service, and support which the existing carriers have built into their infrastructure over many years.

The remainder of this chapter will provide insight into the present state of automation in the electric utility and offer perspectives on where the industry will be in 2002. Areas which will be addressed include customer service, generation, distribution, and system operations. A quick passage through time will set the stage for the discussion to follow.

BACKGROUND

Advances in computer and communications technology are driving forces for automation in any industry. This technology has been and continues to be especially true within the electric utility industry. Electric utilities began automating, by remotely monitoring equipment in the field, well over 50 years ago. Some of that early equipment is probably still in operation some place in the world today.

In much the same way as the early computers of the 1950s and 1960s were a precursor to the computational capabilities of today's computers, the early remote monitoring and control systems, rudimentary by today's standards, were a precursor to today's sophisticated automation systems. Specialized hardwired systems were developed for locally monitoring the operation of power plants and for remotely monitoring and controlling switches in transmission substations. The Remote Terminal Units (RTU) of these early monitoring systems were implemented with relay logic, while the master stations consisted primarily of large banks of annunciator panels with red and green lights indicating the state of points being monitored with a flashing light indicating a change in state or an alarm condition.

The era of computers used for real-time monitoring and control applications on a commercial basis began during the 1950s. In the electric utility industry, this early use of computers occurred primarily in generating stations, where individual monitoring and control points could be hardwired directly to the master control system. The memory, speed, and computational capabilities of these early computers limited their use. To take advantage of these early computers at all, required specialized programming of specific applications to be done in either assembly language or in some cases directly in machine language.

The decades of the 1960s and 1970s saw a considerable growth of automation within the

industry as the age of mini-computers such as the Scientific Data Systems (SDS) Sigma 5, the Control Data Corp. (CDC) 1700, the IBM 1800, and the Digital Equipment Corp. (DEC) VAX, designed specifically for process control and real-time applications became available. More extensive use of CRTs to display information in a combination of tabular and limited graphics form eliminated the bothersome and difficult-to-see annunciator panels, and solid state devices replaced much of the relay logic in the RTUs. The additional capabilities of computers also enabled utilities to expand the use of digital systems beyond just SCADA to perform functions such as load frequency control and economic dispatch on a systemwide basis.

The great Northeast blackout caused most utilities to recognize the importance of sophisticated monitoring and control systems. Not only did the requirements for supervisory control and data acquisition (SCADA) systems to gather information on the conditions on the utility network grow, but engineering analysis software, revised to operate from real-time information, was used to predict potential weak spots in the network and the EMS (Energy Management System) was born.

The use of automation continued to grow within the industry with each system purchased specifically designed to meet a set of requirements defined by the purchasing organization. Investment decisions usually were made primarily to automate a set of existing manual tasks. Very little, if any, thought was given to the benefits gained by sharing information between organizations or to perform functions that weren't presently being done manually. As a result, what might otherwise have been a more rapidly growing use of automation was stifled, since each project had to be justified completely on its own merits. This philosophy created islands of automation within a utility which in many cases still are very difficult to bridge without completely replacing installed systems. For example, different architectures, communication capabilities, and database structures established

in the corporate Customer Information System (CIS) from those in the Geographic Information System (GIS) and from those in the Automatic Meter Reading (AMR) system make the sharing of information difficult if not impossible to accomplish.

In the competitive environment of tomorrow's utility companies, these organizations will have to focus on the application of technology to business solutions. This is already under way as processes and organizations are being reengineered to be more responsive to the needs of the customer. Today's stand-alone systems with closed or proprietary architectures are inadequate to support tomorrow's organizational needs. The blending of these systems is not going to happen overnight but functions such as SCADA, trouble call, and work order scheduling will share information with AMR, distribution automation, and distribution asset management, for example. Not only will information be shared, but both computational resources and communication resources will be shared as well.

Many suppliers have given up doing business with utilities due to the frustrations of the long gestation cycle which has been inherent in the utility modus operandi. Companies spent considerable research and development funds developing new products in anticipation of high volumes only to find that the programs never got beyond the pilot phase. This has been especially true in the areas of distribution automation and AMR. Whatever the reasons, it is safe to say that this will not be the case in the future for two primary reasons:

(1) Utilities need to become leaders in the use of new technology if they are to be successful in a competitive environment.

(2) Utilities no longer can afford to fund R&D experimentation which does not have an objective of implementation behind it.

Automation has had a major impact on utility operations and will have an even greater impact in the future.

COMMUNICATIONS

No discussion of automation in the utility industry would be complete without a discussion of communication systems. In many ways, the growth in automation that has taken place over the last five years and the future growth of automation over the next five years are a result of technological improvements made in the communications industry. Five years ago, the economic use of satellite systems, broadband fiberoptics, or cellular communication systems was just a gleam on the horizon. Today, these technologies have matured to the point where utilities are not only considering their future use, but a number of utilities have made decisions to invest in the technology while others have established subsidiary companies focused on selling additional bandwidth on a utility-owned broadband network. Efficiencies in the use of 900 MHz radio frequencies have improved also to the point that utilities using these frequencies as part of a backbone infrastructure are also looking at potential additional revenue by the sale of excess channel bandwidth.

Electric utilities own and operate the largest, highest-capacity private communication systems in the country. At most utilities, these systems were not the result of planning, but were the result of the installation of independent networks used to support individual functional requirements within the utility. Examples of this might include voice and/or data trunk radio systems for service dispatch, 900 MHz MAS radio, or a single-channel fiberoptic channel for distribution automation. Typically, at large utilities a microwave backbone is used for communication between utility district offices and for long-distance, high-speed communication.

The upgrading of these communication systems to form an infrastructure capable of supporting the integrated application requirements of tomorrow will be a challenge. An additional variable has recently entered the picture which is causing utilities to reevaluate their overall business direction.

The Telecommunications Act of 1996, recently signed by President Clinton, has given utilities the ability to openly compete in the information systems business with telecommunication services providers. Some utilities, including Entergy and Central & South West, have already made decisions to become service providers. Several municipals, by looking at the overall needs of the municipality to communicate with its residents, are also looking at expanding into the telecommunications field by providing their customers a "total services" package taking advantage of the bandwidth of a combination of fiberoptics and cable. A number of municipals are presently piloting these technologies.

Utilities are in a prime position to compete in this market. They own both the land and the poles needed to hang fiber and/or cable. In addition, they already have installed numerous radio towers within their service territory which can be used for radio antennas. Most important of all they have customer access with a larger number of customers in a given area than any service provider, be it long distance telephone, cable, or satellite. The driving force behind many of these systems is the utilities' desire to provide additional services to their customers. Many of these services include, in one way or another, the reading of the customer's meter. It is interesting to note that AMR, after laying almost dormant for so long is now the perceived "cash cow" on which most new service and communication plans are based.

CUSTOMER SERVICE
Automatic Meter Reading

Nowhere has the dynamics of change been more heavily felt and its impact on automation been greater than in the customer service area. Most utilities have recognized the future need for AMR in one form or another for many years but the cost to implement this has been a limiting factor in

their plans. Many have been piloting AMR technology, or pieces of AMR technology; however, most of these have focused in one of two areas:

(1) large industrial users where the economics justify dedicated systems, and

(2) on short-term reduction in the high cost to read residential meters which typically constitutes about 5% of the meter population.

Rather than establishing a long-term direction and strategy with high cost to read the first step, the solution selected has been one which only provides a short-term expediency. This approach has changed considerably over the last three years driven by the major changes taking place in the industry itself.

These changes could very well only be the tip of the iceberg. Deregulation and the anticipated move to "Open Transmission Access" have forced utilities to analyze their business in a completely different light. No longer can returns be guaranteed based on invested capital. The important driving force for the investor-owned utility in the competitive environment of today is to find ways to reduce costs, improve service, or face the threat of losing its customer base. This has led to major reengineering undertakings in many utilities as well as an exploding number of mergers and acquisitions as companies sense that economies of scale and reductions in overall fixed costs can be achieved by consolidating many elements of the business.

With the threat of "retail wheeling," utilities are now looking at a variety of ways to keep their present customer base in the same way any other competitive business does—provide more value for the dollar. At the same time, the pressures of maintaining or reducing the overall cost/kilowatt of delivered energy is having a major impact on their decision making. These conflicting pressures represent a drastic change for an industry which for many years has been able to grow and prosper in a regulated environment.

Electricity is a commodity—it is impossible to distinguish one kilowatt from another. As a result,

utilities must find ways to differentiate themselves from their competition by providing additional services to their customers.

Although "open access" was anticipated to impact the wholesale portion of the utility business, it is having a major impact throughout the industry. As regulated monopolies, utilities were able to keep the cost of energy low to their large, residential customer base by artificially increasing the cost to industrial customers. Instead of lower rates based on volume usage industrial customers have been paying higher rates for many years. Now, industrial customers are in a very attractive negotiating position for the first time. If they buy elsewhere or become power producers, the utility is left with costly excess generation. As a result, they have been able to negotiate contracts at reduced rates and also obtain commitments from the supplying utility to provide a variety of additional services. These include: time-of-use pricing, interruptible rates, direct computer access to energy use information, guarantees of power quality, technical help in better managing their energy usage to improve their power quality, and lower consumption.

Reductions in staff, both from layoffs and early retirement programs, have forced utilities to more reliance on automation and the outsourcing of many services previously considered sacred only a few years ago. In an attempt to distinguish itself from its competition, each utility has, in its own way, attempted to become more attuned to the needs and desires of its customers. The answer is the use of automation to establish better communication and more services for the customer. How it will be implemented and when is still a big question at a number of utilities. Major questions include: Do I outsource my meter reading services or do I build a communications infrastructure which will support AMR and can be used by others? Many utilities are exploring the possibility of using the communication system which is needed to support AMR to provide additional customer-oriented services such as outage monitoring, customized billing, time-of-use rates, real-time pricing, and even security

monitoring. Not only do these additional services provide benefits to the utility customer but, since the customer in many instances is willing to pay for them, it also provides an additional source of revenue to the utility.

Even after almost 10 years, AMR is still in its infancy but it has been receiving considerable attention over the last two to three years with interest growing almost exponentially. A good example of this increased interest is the attendance at the AMRA Symposium. Attendance has increased over 21% in each of the last two years, even though utilities have reduced their budgets for trade shows and conferences as part of their cost reduction programs. In addition, AMR-related activities at other conferences such as the DA/DSM (DistribuTECH) have also increased considerably over what was presented at prior conferences.

The number of utilities that have been installing fixed network AMR systems, either as a pilot or as part of an extended implementation plan, continues to rise rapidly. Available information indicates a variety of communication media have been and continue to be selected, although implementations beyond the pilot phase presently are favoring wireless communication of one form or another.

Table 18–1 shows information on the communication media employed on electric utility, fixed network, AMR systems obtained from an AMRA multi-utility survey on overall AMR systems.

Table 18–1
Installed electric AMR systems

Communication	Installations	Pilots	Total	% of Total
Powerline	11	15	26	38.8
Telephone - Inbound	8	12	20	29.8
Radio	5	7	12	17.9
Telephone Outbound	2	2	4	6
Fiber	0	3	3	4.5
Cellular	0	2	2	3
TOTALS	**26**	**41**	**67**	

Table 18–2 shows information from the results of the 1996 UA Research report "Automatic Meter Reading Market Data Report" on what types of

communication systems are being presently considered for future AMR projects.

Table 18–2
Methods of communication for planned AMR projects

Method of Communication	Number of Projects
Fiber Optics (FibO)	1
Leased Telephone Line (LLn)	4
LLn, Power Line Carrier (PwrLC)	1
PwrLC	7
PwrLC, Cellular (CL)	1
Radio	17
Radio, Cable or Coax	3
Radio, LLn	7
Radio, LLn, PwrLC	1
Radio, Microwave (Mcwv)	1
Radio, PwrLC	2
Satellite (Sat)	1
Undecided	60
Total	**106**

Comparing Tables 18–1 and 18–2 shows the changing dynamics within the industry as future AMR projects become more of a driving force for a backbone communication system to support additional customer services with the combination of radio and fiber increasing from 17.9% to 29% of those utilities that have decided on a communications media.

Some utilities already have become communications and services providers either by joint venture, Ameritech Utility Services (a joint venture between WEPCO and Ameritech), partnering arrangements with communication companies (PG&E and TCI, PSE&G and AT&T), by becoming a total services provider themselves through an unregulated subsidiary (C&SW), or by selling additional bandwidth on their own infrastructure (PEPCO and Entergy).

Other utilities have looked at AMR from a completely different perspective and rather than invest in their own systems, are outsourcing their meter reading to third-party providers that have guaranteed to manage the system and provide timely meter readings along with added services (KCP&L and CellNet, Union Electric and CellNet, Duquesne and Itron among others). The outsourcing of many services such as meter reading was considered sacred only a few years ago.

Additional Services

Utilities have been spending considerable time and money in determining what their customers really want. This is a complete change for an industry that until a few short years ago was internally focused with little regard for the desires of its customers. All of the following services are presently being considered as part of a shopping list of services and options by a number of utilities.

Real-Time Outage Monitoring and Reporting.

A customer's perception of what the utility knows about the state of its power system differs greatly from the truth. Customers think, for example, that a utility knows when the power is out. Many people are surprised to hear this isn't the case. Now utilities are looking at supplying outage monitoring capability as an added value. This capability is a fallout of many of the AMR systems on the market today. When power is lost at a location, the location reports that an outage occurred. In addition, several companies make outage monitoring devices which the customer plugs into an electric outlet and a telephone. When an outage occurs it phones the information to the utility. This information then can be transferred directly into a trouble call system to identify the extent of the outage. With this capability in place, additional services can be provided. A number of utility-sponsored surveys have indicated that customers would pay for a service that lets them know when a power outage alarm was received. People with summer cottages, merchants who lost power at the shop or store at night, among others would find such a service worthwhile. Individual devices could be flagged for this service and when an alarm was received from those locations an automatic call would be placed to another location.

Customized Billing.

Many advantages accrue as a result of a fixed network AMR system and one of these, customized billing, will be an attraction to many customers. For commercial establishments with more than one location, customized billing could mean a consolidated bill with information from each store taken on the same day and at relatively the same time. This could be provided for all the McDonald's in a city or all the schools, etc. An added benefit to the residential customer would be to establish a billing date that was most convenient for the customer. In addition, some utilities have discussed the possibility of providing for a fee a monthly histogram with usage for each day of the month.

Security Monitoring.

There has been considerable interest in competing with the present security service provider or supplying the provider with the communication system for a fee. This business, like the telecommunications business, is highly competitive and it is too soon to tell if the utilities could make it a profitable business. They do have an advantage in having access to every customer in their service territory. Monthly bills could provide the marketing vehicle, and with some AMR systems, supplying the service could be a low cost item. The NRECA funded development of such a system for the rural electric market and several utilities are now piloting the service.

Demand Side Management and Home Automation.

This appears to be a big potential winner for the utility, at least as far as interest is concerned. Several utilities are piloting different technologies in this area, but all of the companies presently in the broadband telecommunications area are actively showing this capability at trade shows and conferences. Central & South West has a pilot project in Laredo, Texas using fiber and coax; Entergy also has been piloting the same technology. Key to the system is an intelligent controller which obtains real-time pricing information from the utility and, based on the cost of energy, the user programs turning on or off certain appliances, and setting back the thermostat. Presently several competing powerline technologies are trying for the in-home communi-

cation system and with utilities lined up on each side it doesn't appear there will be a winner.

GENERATION

The dynamics of change in the industry as a result of deregulation and competition is also having a major impact on the generation side of the utility business. To become competitive, utilities must become more focused on their customers' needs and desires. They must begin marketing of a shopping list of added-cost services similar to approaches taken in other deregulated industries. To provide focus on the business issues involved, utilities must restructure their organizations while at the same time decrease their capital expenditures. A number of forward-thinking utilities are already in the process of restructuring into business units in anticipation of independent generation companies (GenCos) and distribution companies (DistCos).

Open transmission access has already led to the establishment of a number of independent power producers (IPP). These IPPs, capable of supplying low cost power to targeted customers, will force the established utility generation organization rapidly to become competitive. Third party marketing organizations also are beginning to emerge as the effects of deregulation become more widely felt. These power marketers are engaged in wholesale electric power transactions. The marketing organizations are many times associated with electric utilities, IPPs, financial institutions, and fuel marketers. Power marketing by itself is forecast to be a big business with estimated sales between $2.6 and $7 trillion by 2010. Financial markets, reacting to this emerging market have already created electricity futures and options.

All of these changes are putting a great deal of pressure on the GenCo to bring down the per kilowatt cost of power. Compliance with the Clean Air Act Amendments of 1990 has been a major drain on capital investments for a number of

years. The next major effect of the amendments will be the Title IV SO_2 rule which will begin to affect utilities in 2000. With reductions in staff, aging power plants, and continued environmental pressures, utilities are caught in a Catch 22. To remain, or in some cases become, competitive, they will be forced to increase and upgrade the automation in existing power plants. This will hold true for both nuclear and non-nuclear plants alike. The short-term outlook is not as bright, however, as the pressures for reduced capital expenditures continue to increase.

Figure 18–1 provides information obtained from the latest CSR Electric Utility Generating Plant Control and Monitoring Systems Market Data Report. The report indicates a total of 368 projects valued at approximately $643,290,000 are planned for procurement over the next 30 months. Of this total, there were 26 nuclear projects at a value of $160,300,000. The table shows comparative planned expenditures from similar reports since 1986.

Figure 18–1. Dollars for nuclear and other projects

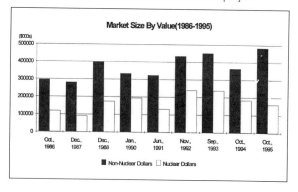

The graph shows a consistent level of expenditures since 1992 except for 1994. This reduced level of expenditures was the result of the Phase I CEM installations made by utilities in 1993. Most generating plants have completed these requirements and budgets for non-nuclear plants have moved to the levels where they were before the new regulations. The dollar value of budgeted nuclear projects has steadily decreased since 1992, and will continue to decrease.

Figure 18–2, which shows the average budget of planned nuclear and non-nuclear projects since 1986, indicates an increasing or flat trend in the per project cost of nuclear projects with less projects being undertaken. It also shows the average cost for non-nuclear projects has remained fairly constant over the total period.

Figure 18–2. Average cost of nuclear and non-nuclear projects

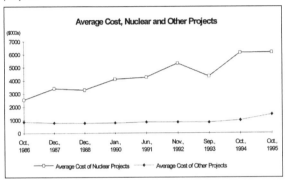

DISTRIBUTION OPERATIONS

Distribution operations within the utility is responsible for ensuring the reliable operation of the distribution system. With the changing dynamics within the utility industry as a result of deregulation and open access, there are questions about where the responsibilities of distribution end. Will load control and demand side management continue to be the responsibility of marketing or will they now fall under the distribution department? For the purposes of this report, they have been included in the section on distribution functions for the following reason: This author believes that the long-term benefit of these functions will be in better managing the distribution system on a feeder-by-feeder basis rather than reducing system peaks. This same philosophy also ties into functions such as capacitor control. Rather than managing system vars they will be used more and more on a feeder-by-feeder basis for both voltage and var control.

This section will address issues associated with automation within the distribution system. There is considerable overlap between functions in a number of areas. For example, as AMR expands (a customer service function), functions such as outage monitoring (typically a distribution function) will in many cases be implemented within the AMR system. In many cases utility organizations will continue to evolve as the impact of deregulation takes effect, and the dividing line for these functions may change from one operating department to another.

Distribution Automation

Distribution automation is the monitoring and/or control of that portion of the distribution system outside the fence of the distribution substation. *Is the control of devices on the customer side of the secondary transformer or devices on the customer side of the meter considered distribution automation? For example, is load control a part of distribution automation?* There has been some discussion on this area for several years. In the context used here, since load control is presently not being used to better manage the load on a feeder, it is not a distribution automation function. However, in the future, when and if distribution operations begins managing the loading on individual feeders by controlling sheddable load, then this same load control function could be considered a distribution automation function.

For purposes of clarity, this discussion will use the definition of distribution automation used by UA Research, "the real-time automation of feeders including reclosers, capacitors, regulators, or switches located in the distribution circuits." This definition of distribution automation starts with the distribution feeder circuit outside the substation fence and ends with the secondary side of the distribution transformer. A typical distribution automation system includes computer hardware and software, communications systems, and remote terminal units (RTUs) or switches

located either in overhead or underground distribution lines.

Distribution automation (DA) has been a future blossoming area of automation for the electric utility industry for almost 10 years, but is one of those functions which never could be cost-justified on a stand-alone basis except in very limited applications. With the changing dynamics of the competitive industry causing the need for increased service reliability while operating equipment closer to its limits, utilities will begin to rely more heavily on and recognize the benefits of distribution automation. Examples of these benefits include reduced service interruption frequency and duration, reduced customer cost-of-outage, and overall improved service quality. For the utility, this translates to increased kilowatt-hour sales, reduced operating and maintenance costs, and deferred or eliminated capital expenditures. Manpower reductions as a result of restructuring have already caused service availability problems at several utilities. To protect its customer base, pressures from the utility marketing department will cause the development of new approaches to cost justification of automation requirements such as DA.

Over the past decade, distribution automation systems have gone through several advancements, including system integration and operating platforms. Currently nearly 21% of installed systems are running on a mini-computer, with 40% on a PC platform, 36% on a UNIX-based workstation, and 3% on a mainframe. There is a continuing move toward PC-based and UNIX systems. The 1995 CSR Report showed 50% of systems running on a mini-computer, 34% on a PC platform, and 16% on a UNIX-based workstation.

For all the benefits of distribution automation to be realized, electric utilities must have other types of automation which can be linked to the DA system. These include SCADA, load management, and automated mapping/facilities management (AM/FM). Less than 25% of the DA systems installed and operating today have a full hardware and software interface to SCADA. Most utilities

indicate this will be a definite requirement for any future procurements.

Figure 18–3 provides information from the latest UA Research Electric Utility Distribution Automation Market Data Report. The report indicates a total of 195 systems projects valued at over $82M are planned for procurement over the next 30 months and show comparative information on planned expenditures obtained from reports since 1986. Figure 18–4 provides information on the total budgeted amounts obtained from each of these earlier reports. The large reduction in budget for the next 30 months is due to several major projects turned into contracts during 1995.

Figure 18–3. Projects in reports since 1986

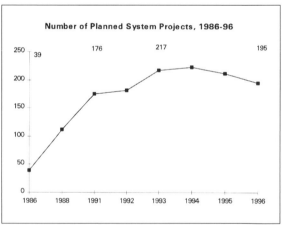

Figure 18–4. Dollar totals of budgets for 1986-1996

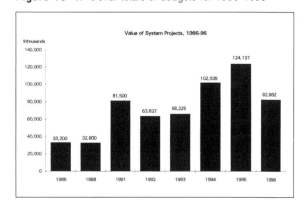

Load Control

Load Control is defined as the ability to remotely control customer loads from a central location. Load control in this context does not include demand-side management systems that provide utilities the ability to set back thermostats and the customer the ability to program his energy usage based on energy cost typically linked to real-time pricing.

For many years, load control has been used as a way of reducing the peak power requirements of the utility during times of energy stress. These systems became popular because the cost of the system was considerably less than the cost of adding the required generation or purchasing the needed short-term energy on the open market. Typically one-way radio systems have been used to turn off or cycle customer appliances such as water heaters, pool pumps, strip heaters, and air conditioners. In addition, load control has been used very effectively to control irrigation systems and heavy loads in large industrial complexes. Table 18–3 shows the type of controls being used by utilities that are presently planning to purchase load control systems over the next 30 months. The information was taken from UA Research's 1996 Electric Utility Load Management Market Data Report. It is interesting to note that the combination of residential air conditioners and hot water heaters make up 24% of the total, a decrease from 31% in the prior report, while the combination of irrigation and industrial loads

make up a total of 21% of the projects, an increase from 10% in the prior report.

Some utilities have found that the one-way system provided marginal reliability with no way to validate the performance of the system without a physical inspection of each site. They began installing two-way communication systems capable of validating operation, detecting tamper, and ensuring controllers have not been bypassed. Although the additional cost for the two-way system does not appear to justify itself, the communication infrastructure has provided the utilities that have taken that step, with a capability to provide other functions such as AMR and capacitor control. In other cases, where broadband fiber has been installed for providing other services, load control has been added to the existing two-way communication system.

The future of load control in today's competitive environment is unknown. With the entry of low cost IPPs, utilities must reevaluate the economic benefit of their load control system. Similarly, generation business units will be in business to sell power and Discos will negotiate with IPPs or through third-party marketers to purchase the power they need. Several utilities have in fact not only decided not to expand further, but also they seriously are considering eliminating their installed systems altogether.

Results of the latest UA Research Electric Utility Load Management Market Data Report substantiate this information. The number of both system projects and add-on switch projects has dropped by about 21% from 1994 until 1996 while the budgets have dropped by over 43%. It is expected that this trend will continue as capital budgets are tightened and utilities continue to search for a new direction in the competitive market.

The future will be determined by the growth of automation within distribution operations. In many cases it may require a more sophisticated load control switch than that in use today. With reduced resources available due to downsizing, increased use of automation will be needed to maintain and improve the reliability of the distribution system. A number of programs are presently in place

Table 18–3
Breakdown by type of units controlled

Type of Unit Controlled	Number of Projects
Air Conditioners (AC)	12
AC, Electric Heaters (EH)	4
AC, Water Heaters (WH)	30
AC, WH, EH	10
AC, Pool Motors (PM)	8
AC, WH, PM	7
EH, WH	9
Industrial Loads	2
Irrigation Pumps	10
WH	17
Miscellaneous Combinations	16
Total	**125**

increasing the automation at the substation level. Within the next few years, substation automation will be a reality and with expanded substation automation and the need to operate the distribution system closer to its limits, utilities will look to load control as a low cost way of deferring capital on system upgrades. When that occurs, funding for load control will again increase.

GIS Systems

Early versions of Geographic Information Systems (GIS) were primarily AM/FM (automated mapping/facilities management) systems initiated within the engineering department to provide mapping and drafting capabilities. Early extensions to these systems added the ability to track distribution facilities. These early systems were limited due to the high cost of computer equipment with large storage capacity, and the cost of the required data entry. Existing handmade drawings had to be scanned into the system and verified. Many of these drawings had been changed a number of times and were, as a result, poor quality and hard to read, but a start had been made. There is a considerable difference between an AM/FM system and a GIS system. An AM/FM system is designed to manage facilities. Most started out as computer-aided drafting systems and provide the ability for mapping the electrical system. GIS systems, on the other hand, include the spatial relationships needed to model the environment in which the utility operates.

Although GIS systems have gone through a period of disfavor with many utilities, the pressures of the changing business dynamics within the industry have recently created an environment where GIS can become a real capability to support the organization's future. The restructuring and reengineering of the organization around core business functions and the need to improve accessibility to information throughout the utility have been brought about by the deregulation of the utility industry. This deregulation has been occurring during a time when new tools for database management and presentation graphics, high-performance client server hardware configurations, and communication technologies have become available. GIS systems of today, if they include a facilities database, can provide utilities the ability to analyze data and not only present information on what the system is today, but also go back in time and provide information on what the electrical system was a year ago.

Rather than continuing to be a separate island of automation, the functions of the GIS system in the future, if it includes access to real-time information and contains a facilities database, will become closely coupled and an integral part of the utility IS (Information System). It will be capable of doing both spatial analysis and network analysis. If and when AMR is expanded to cover major portions of a utility's service territory, the GIS could be used for outage mapping, provide trouble call information, and, in conjunction with SCADA and DA, improve the operating reliability of the system all on an automated basis.

Many of these elements presently are being integrated at a number of forward-thinking utilities. Union Electric, for example, has integrated their GIS and distribution SCADA systems providing distribution dispatchers the ability to see the present status of the system on an actual geographic map. Union Electric presently is installing an AMR system, provided by CellNet Data Systems, throughout the St. Louis metropolitan area. A logical next step would be that as their AMR system becomes integrated into their operation, power outage information from every automated customer location could be fed into the system completely automating the trouble call system in that portion of their service territory.

The integration of diverse systems into a single cohesive entity capable of supporting a number of functional activities is not a task to be taken lightly. In many cases, utilities will find the need to upgrade or completely change out existing systems. Over the long term, however, this advanced use of automation will enable

utilities to remain competitive while providing their customers the service and reliability they expect.

Service Dispatch and Work Order Scheduling

Automating the sectionalizers, switches, and reclosers on the distribution feeder and identifying trouble spots early when there is an outage go a long way toward maintaining system reliability. Without a responsive service capability which can respond to trouble when it is determined, the potential improvements will be lost. Most utilities over the years have established efficient and responsive service capabilities. Usually operations communicates with the service vehicles in the field via a backbone voice radio system. Many of the newer systems are 800Mhz trunk radio with the capability of expanding to both voice and data.

Prescheduled work orders can be downloaded to the service center and provided to the maintenance crews at the beginning of the day. How to reroute crews during the day as a result of emergency situations and provide them with adequate information to efficiently accomplish their work assignment has been a stumbling block to efficient operation. Information from an automated trouble call system can isolate the problem and, linked to a service dispatch system, determine which crew should be dispatched. How to get the crew the information they need rapidly is the problem.

The answer to this problem is more automation in the service vehicle and an efficient data communication system to transmit maps, drawings, and instructions to the vehicle for use by the crew. Several utilities have been implementing this capability using their existing trunk radio system. Other utilities are looking at the capabilities of the communication system being installed for AMR. Whatever the choice, the need is there and in the future service vehicles will have on-board equipment to print out maps

and whatever other information is needed to more efficiently complete the job.

SYSTEM OPERATIONS

In the regulated utility of yesterday, system operations was the place where the decisions were made that affected the profitability of a utility. Decisions on the purchase and sale of power, the scheduling of generation, the forecasting of load based on a weather model, were all made in system operations. In addition, this organization has been responsible for the reliable operation of the utility's transmission system. Since so much of the utility's financial well-being was in the hands of this group, they were provided with whatever tools they needed to help them make decisions.

The bulk power system was the first area of the utility to become automated. Improvements in computer technology, new advanced application software and higher speed reliable communications, coupled with growth in the electrical system itself continued to drive more and more sophistication in this area of automation. By the late 1960s and early 1970s, large redundant computer systems consisting of either mainframes or large minicomputers provided the capability to not only monitor and control what was happening at the transmission substations, but analysis software also provided the system operator the ability to see the weak spots on the system, and make recommendations to remedy them.

The problem utilities faced, however, was that each of these systems was a closed architecture and used proprietary software which made expansion difficult and costly. System projects were anticipated to be almost a decade in length from the beginning of the planning phase until final operation. This time frame meant that by the time the equipment was installed, it was already obsolete and the system supplier was building a completely new generation of equipment. In most cases, to upgrade to a new system meant starting

over again. System operations was literally always in the mode of looking for the next generation.

Industry standards began to be established in this area, as the need for utility "A" to have its EMS talk to the EMS of utility "B". Although these early communication protocol standards led the way, they had a long way to go. There was a separate standard for the western area of the country from that of the eastern. Many years and a lot of hard work have now led to a standard that is being accepted for control center to control center communication. Computers could now be networked together and share data. Open architecture became the buzzword of the industry.

SCADA/EMS technology has made vast improvements over the past few decades. These systems have moved from mainframes and "dumb" RTUs, to minicomputers and microprocessor-based RTUs, to distributed controls with the flexibility to exist under a network of workstations and microprocessor-based computing. One of the latest advancements deals with client-server technology. The client-server approach allows programs to be broken into components. This architecture enables wide-area-network distribution of system networks, as well as peer-linking of multiple systems.

CSR's 1994 study of the Electric Utility SCADA/EMS Market indicated that of SCADA/EMS systems currently installed, the majority, or 53%, were on a minicomputer-based platform, such as Digital Equipment's VAX line of computers. Mainframes accounted for only 4%, with workstations (UNIX-based) at 21%, and PCs accounting for 22% of all SCADA/EMS platforms presently installed.

When comparing these percentages with those for planned systems from the 1996 UA Research SCADA/EMS Market Report, there seems to be increasing usage of PC-based operating platforms. Figure 18–5 shows that 58% of planned systems will use a PC-based operating platform, while only 19% will utilize a mini-based platform. There is also increasing interest for workstation-based platforms at 22% of planned SCADA/EMS systems.

One conclusion which can be drawn from these results is that utilities are expanding their SCADA capability to provide more automation in the distribution area.

The same UA Research report shows the number of projects and total budget for planned systems over the next 30-month period. See Figures 18–6 and 18–7. The sudden drop in projects and budget dollars for 1995 is caused by several factors. The budget is impacted greatly by the fact that several large projects reached the

Figure 18–5. Operating platforms for planned systems

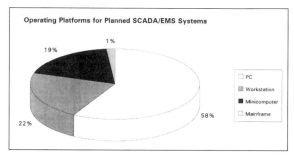

Figure 18–6. Projects in reports since 1985

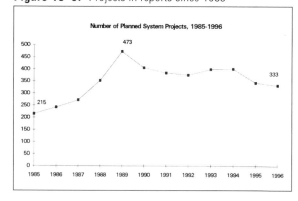

Figure 18–7. Dollar totals of budgets for 1985 through 1995

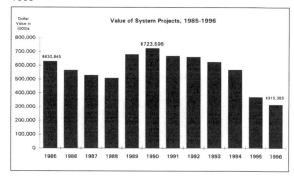

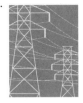

contract stage in 1995. The reduction in the number of projects is indicative of the wait-and-see attitude that has developed as utilities go through reengineering. This trend will continue over the next two to three years as utilities focus their attention to the more competitive portions of their business, namely customer service and generation.

With more reliance on automation as a result of reduced staffing levels, these numbers should recover over the longer three to five year period.

TRENDS FOR THE FUTURE

The changes from a regulated industry to a competitive one will be slow in transition. Although many utilities today are jumping quickly to take a leadership role in this new environment, the conservative decision-making process of the past will not change overnight. Open access will become a reality making it possible for utility customers to buy their electricity from any energy provider, be it their present source of supply, a neighboring utility, or a nonutility energy supplier. Energy consolidators will begin to proliferate throughout the market, negotiating "special rates" which will be attractive to a number of residential customers. The vertical utility will be a thing of the past. Utilities will restructure into generation, transmission, and distribution companies (many utilities are already preparing themselves for this change).

Many issues are yet to be resolved including, most importantly, "who is responsible for stranded assets." A number of alternative approaches are being discussed. So far the issue has not been resolved but at some point it will be. When it is, the fog will lift and a clear picture will begin to take shape. A consensus appears to be emerging, however, which provides insight into the impact on expenditures for automation within the industry.

- Power generation will become a very competitive market. Generation suppliers will be pressured to keep costs to a minimum while maintaining power quality within acceptable limits if they are to sell their product on the open market. This presents ideal conditions for increases in automation and the possible development of new, more sophisticated measurement and control techniques.

- The nation's tightly interconnected transmission grid must stay intact and, as a result, the transmission portion of a utility's business will remain regulated, and possibly operated by an independent third party. In California, for example, the present open access discussions are leaning heavily toward an independent third party, the Independent System Operator (ISO), having responsibility for operating the transmission system, buying power from the power providers, and selling it to the distribution companies and other potential customers. This environment is not one that fosters major expenditures in expanding existing automation equipment over the short term. By 2002 however, expenditures will return to the early 1990s' levels of $600 million to $650 million.

- The future regulation of the distribution segment of the utility's business is still an unknown. Whether it is regulated or not, because of its visibility, the pressure will be on to maintain and improve reliability and power quality and reduce costs. The distribution system at most utilities is the least automated portion of the power system. Advances in the use of integrated distribution management which includes SCADA systems, distribution automation, and the use of GIS systems will take place as utilities increase expenditures to upgrade their capabilities.

- Much attention already has been given to the customer service area as utilities prepare for deregulation. This is one area

that will be heavily impacted by the use of automation within the industry as utilities fight to differentiate themselves from their competition. Increased expenditures in automatic meter reading, customer side of the meter services, and communication systems can be expected over the next five years.

The issue of open access and retail wheeling is being addressed actively in legislative committees across the country in one way or another. Many states are taking a wait-and-see attitude hoping it will go away. Others are looking to California to take the leadership role and be the trendsetter as they have been in the past. Some states are working on their own initiatives and taking the position that what is right for California is definitely not right for them.

The issues rapidly are being brought to a head in California where retail wheeling will be a fact on January 1, 1998. What will the impact be on automation? Listening to some of the meetings of the Direct Access Working Group (DAWG) of the Open Access Committee in California, the impression is that automation will receive a very positive boost. Issues being addressed include methods of providing real-time pricing, the ability to read meters for aggregators on an hourly basis, and the need to provide utilities the ability to offer customers value-added services on the customer side of the meter. In this environment a two-way AMR system, or at least a system which can read meters on a demand basis, will be a requirement. The future for residential AMR will be bright but it is not the only customer service area with potential for the future.

Specialized customer services for the small- to medium-size commercial customer will become important to utilities. The large commercial and industrial customers are presently in a position to obtain special attention and competitive, if not bargain, rates from their utility supplier in order to keep them from changing their source, or provide their own generation capacity. Specialized automation equipment for this class of customer is becoming commonplace. On-line communication

systems will keep the customer and the utility in almost continuous contact with the equipment needed to provide this tailored service easily cost-justified. The small residential customer, based on experiences in other deregulated industries, will not change its supplier in large numbers. It is the commercial customer that will suddenly get the attention of the utility, and depending upon how this customer class responds, will go a long way in determining how successful the utility is.

Most manufacturers of AMR and customer services equipment for areas such as home automation, appliance control, programmable setback thermostats, security services, etc., have, to date, focused on the residential marketplace because of the volumes of equipment involved. There is presently no equipment that has been focused to help the utility satisfy the needs of the small commercial customer.

In the distribution system, the automated substation will come closer to reality. Several companies are today in the process of developing and testing a variety of distributed substation automation equipment. Intelligent substations will enable utilities to manage their distribution system on a feeder-by-feeder basis. Load control and demand side management, after several years of depressed sales, again will become an attraction to the distribution company, not to shave peak power usage, but to manage the distribution system. Strategies will be established to improve equipment reliability and, at the same time, operate the feeders closer to margins, deferring major capital improvement costs.

Although all of these changes will be the result of increased use of automation, major shifts are taking place as utilities contract for services rather than spending capital assets. This shift to services in the area of AMR and distribution automation will be appreciable if the trend continues. Major investor-owned utilities such as Kansas City Power & Light, Duquesne and Union Electric have contracted for AMR services over a 15-20 year period impacting utility capital expenditures for AMR by well over $100,000,000. Two of the largest utilities in the country, Southern California Edison

and Pacific Gas & Electric presently are talking about doing the same thing.

The decisions that utilities make regarding communication systems will have a major impact on both their future structure and their viability as a company on a long-term basis. Will they jump on the information super highway? Will they become service providers themselves or take advantage of their bargaining position to gain access to low-cost or no-cost communications from an existing service provider? Utilities are in an excellent bargaining position to do just that.

The National Information Infrastructure (NII) is a national broadband (high capacity) communication network which will connect homes, businesses, schools, libraries, research laboratories, and hospitals. The vision for the future is a network of networks transmitting voice, data, video, and high-speed computing. Congress and the administration support the competitive development of the NII. In fact, energy management was recognized as a specific NII application.

NII is today a solution in search of a problem. Video-on-demand has not turned out to be the killer application originally anticipated. Service providers are attracting utilities to use NII for AMR applications. In addition, PCS is looking at subdividing spectrum to support AMR, while cable consortiums are planning to provide energy management services. Utilities have a unique opportunity to participate in NII and gain considerable competitive advantage from it. The most obvious is to become a service provider and gain an additional source of revenue. Just as important, however, is the ability to gain access to a low-cost network reducing what otherwise would have resulted in internal construction and operating costs for the communications network required for internal use.

Automation in the utility industry is a billion-dollar business. In the changing dynamics as a result of deregulation, definite shifts will take place that will shift where the automation dollars are spent; however, if utilities are to be successful in a competitive environment, they will be spent. How fast the effects of open access and retail wheeling will be felt at the consumer level is difficult to project. Will we reach the point where we are bothered by telephone calls from power providers, using automated dialing systems, looking for us to switch service like the communication industry? It would be interesting to hear what services they would provide.

Areas of major growth will include communications, AMR and customer-related services, distribution management including integrated SCADA, distribution automation, GIS/AM/FM, trouble call, and generation. Areas which will see reductions in expenditures will include transmission-related areas such as EMS and SCADA, demand-side management programs, and peak-reducing applications such as load control. These areas will recover, once it is determined who has responsibility for what. Will there be an independent system operator for the transmission grid as California is proposing? Will the government let the environmental pressures that led to some demand-side management programs be sacrificed? We are confident they will not.

Decisions must be made that affect the industry as a whole before the fog lifts and the future becomes visible. The next one to two years will be critical ones in that regard. Deregulation will lead to many new automation opportunities for suppliers, and the dynamics of working in a competitive environment will be an exciting change for most utility personnel. Cost-saving ideas using automation will no longer be shrugged off as being of no interest because it all went in the rate base anyway. Exciting times are ahead.

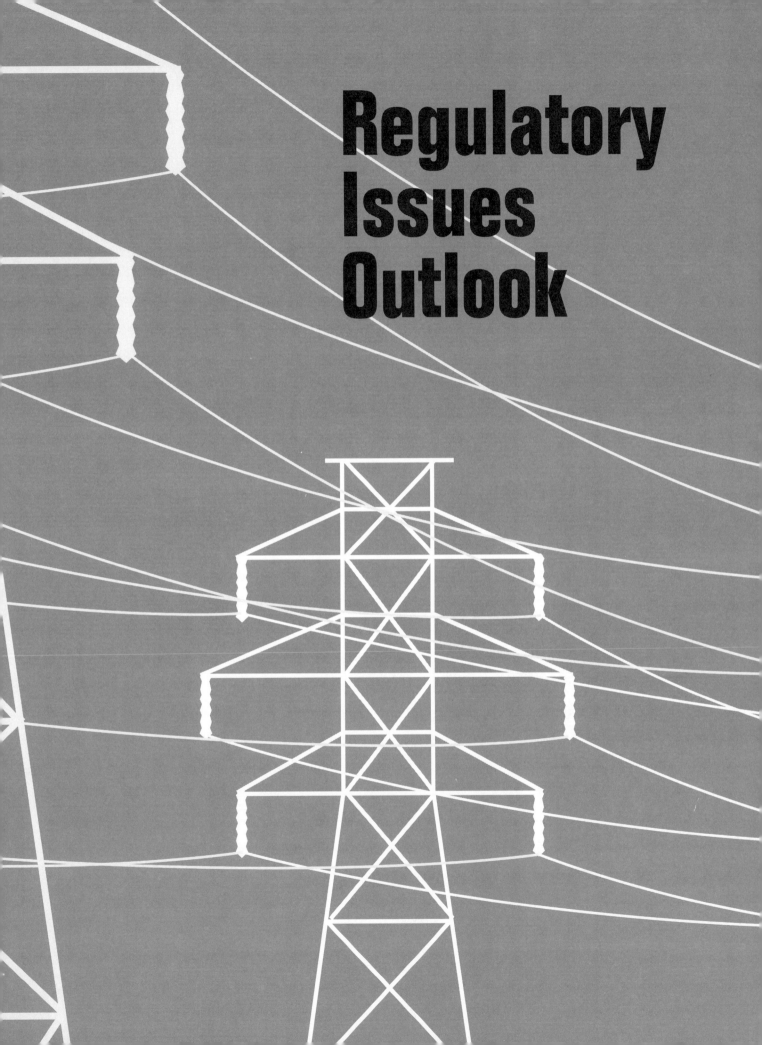

Regulatory Issues Outlook

Chapter 19
Deregulation

DENISE WARKENTIN
NEWS EDITOR, *ELECTRIC LIGHT & POWER*
EDITOR, *ENERGY MARKETING*

OVERVIEW

Deregulation has pervaded the ranks of many different industries in the United States. From telecommunications to airlines and trucking, deregulation has touched industries that in times past seemed untouchable to the likes of deregulation and competition. With this, enter the electric utility industry.

Deregulation of the electric utility industry, which is the last major industry to undergo deregulation, is occurring for much the same basic, underlying reasons that many other industries have deregulated—changes in the economy and the resultant need for competitive pricing.

As has been said on many different occasions in the deregulation proceedings that have been going on in the power industry, "price is king." Just several years ago, it would have been virtually impossible and even unthinkable to have

projected that the "price is king" adage would have been applied and made a common piece of verbiage among key power industry stakeholders.

But, nonetheless, deregulation in the electric utility industry is happening, and industry leaders and stakeholders are grappling with how to interpret and respond to the changes that deregulation is forcing them to contend with. After a general understanding of why change in general has descended upon the electric utility industry, industry leaders and stakeholders must begin the arduous task of positioning their organizations to respond to the changes. Response is, by the way, the only way to react to these changes. Deregulation is happening. It is ill-advised for any electric utility or stakeholder in the power industry to sit back and wait.

As Jerry Demel, assistant general manager of external affairs for Tri-State Generation and Transmission Co. in Denver, Colorado, said at the National Rural Electric Cooperative Association's 1996 annual meeting, "Don't be a member of the

flat-earth society. Accept that deregulation is going to happen."

The changes that are going on in the electric utility industry are the product of evolution. That is, deregulation and competition just have not been dropped on the electric power industry like a hot potato. Rather, deregulation and competition have come as a result of a wide mix of events that have occurred over the history of the industry itself. Table 19–1 lists some of the major changes. These changes are discussed in detail below.

Table 19–1
Changes in industry grounded in historical events

- Energy prices increase.
- Electricity prices increase.
- Oil-dependent units realize new economic realities.
- Passage of PURPA in 1978 creates qualified facilities.
- Nuclear projects grapple with increased costs.
- Economy turns from manufacturing to service-oriented.
- Utilities experience surplus capacity, higher fuel, and capital costs.
- Other industries enter the competitive marketplace.

The electric utility industry was an unregulated non-monopolistic industry from 1879 to the 1900s. Regulation, and thus guaranteed service territories (monopoly conditions) in the power sector began in the mid-1930s, and until the talk of deregulation in the industry over the last five years or so, was expected to remain so.

The apparent true benefits of monopolistic, vertically-integrated electric utilities were at their height during the 1950s and 1960s when technology and manufacturing advancements spurred the production of larger and more efficient turbines, boilers, and other equipment used to produce electricity. Accompanying these technological advancements were lower capital, operating, and maintenance costs. Both large and small customers would reap the benefits of these economy-of-scale developments—mainly, and most importantly, through what was believed to be low and consistent electricity prices.

However, this condition was not to last. The rapid rise in energy prices in the 1970s exposed units too dependent on oil and/or excessive fuel consumption to new economic realities and also resulted in an increase in the price of electricity.

Passage of the Public Utility Regulatory Policies Act of 1978 (PURPA) created a new class of preferred power producers, called qualified facilities, leading many in the industry to begin questioning whether monopolistic, vertically-integrated electric utilities were in fact best suited to provide electricity to consumers.

ECONOMY CHANGES

During the late 1970s and into the 1980s, the nation's economy was being transformed from a growing manufacturing one to a mature and increasingly soft/high-tech manufacturing and service-oriented economy. What did this mean for electric utilities? For the first time in decades, electric utilities would have to face a dramatic decline in consumption.

With reduced consumption by ultimate customers on their hands, electric utilities were hit with yet one more cruel blow—surplus capacity. Following right in step with surplus capacity were higher fuel and capital costs. Consumers were, in many cases, being required to pay as much as three times higher electricity rates than in other parts of the country.

It was getting clearer and clearer that the benefit of a monopolistic, vertically-integrated electric utility industry existed only during the time when they were operated by competent, skilled, and resourceful management and personnel. Many utilities, especially those with nuclear plant-based programs, also found themselves facing the wrath of disgruntled, captive customers as rate shocks began reverberating throughout the industry. Electric utilities and their management were under increasingly heavy scrutiny by consumers and also by policy makers.

As if this weren't enough change, around this same time, AT&T was undergoing deregulation. AT&T was simply following the lead of the transportation, airlines, trucking, and gas industries in deregulating.

Finally, Soviet Union and socialistic/communistic economic models collapsed. The forces of free and open markets claimed victory. The United States and the global economy were thus changed forever.

The premise behind the changes is rather simplistic. Multiple, competing producers can provide a variety of needs to both large and small electricity consumers. If the producers operate under uniform, equal regulations and access to resources and infrastructure, the marketplace will automatically take care of itself in regard to pricing, quality, and availability.

As can be seen from the foregoing background into the events that have led up to deregulation and change in the electric power industry, there obviously is much pressure building for regulatory change to bring about a free and open market in the electricity marketplace. Some may agree, others may disagree, that this condition is desirable, but the simple fact of the matter is that deregulation and competition is a reality. Whether that reality is one that companies choose to accept or reject, the electric utility industry will never be the same again.

mega-NOPR (notice of proposed rulemaking), was adopted by the federal agency on April 24, 1996. The order opens wholesale power sales to competition. Public utilities that own, control, or operate transmission lines are required to file nondiscriminatory open access tariffs that offer others the same transmission service that they provide to themselves. This will:

- bring lower-cost power to electric customers,

- ensure continued reliability of the electric power industry, and

- provide for open and fair electric transmission services by public utilities.

FERC, as part of Order 888, issued a single pro forma tariff, which describes the minimum terms and conditions of service to bring about nondiscriminatory open access transmission service. Under this provision, all public utilities that own, control or operate interstate transmission facilities are required to offer service to others. The pro forma tariff also stipulates that utilities also must use the tariffs for their own wholesale energy sales and purchases.

REGULATORY ACTION SPURS UTILITY RESTRUCTURING

The fact that restructuring is happening in the electric power industry is reinforced by the Federal Energy Regulatory Commission (FERC) and its commitment to ensuring that deregulation of the industry is in everyone's best interest. FERC is a federal agency charged with regulating some 166 public utilities in the United States.

FERC Order 888: The Open Access Rule

FERC Order 888, the result of many months of debate over a FERC, electric utility restructuring

Stranded Cost Recovery

To the delight (and relief) of many public utilities, FERC Order 888 grants full recovery of stranded costs. FERC defines stranded costs as those costs that were prudently incurred to serve power customers and that could go unrecovered if these customers use open access to move to another supplier.

As far as eligibility is concerned, FERC states in its rule that recoverable stranded costs are those that are associated with wholesale requirements contracts signed before July 11, 1994. After this date, the rule states that recovery must be provided for in contracts. Stranded costs will be recoverable from a utility's departing customers. This provision has caused, and is still causing, much debate in the industry.

Utilities Face $135 Billion in Stranded Costs

The whole issue of stranded cost recovery has been a mammoth concern among public utilities. There have been many estimates made on the total amount of stranded costs utilities are likely to face as a result. For purposes of this discussion, an estimate made by Moody's Investors Service will be used. Moody's projects that over the course of the next 10 years, stranded costs are expected to cost the nation's 114 largest, investor-owned electric utilities $135 billion. Utilities in the northeast and the west, according to Moody's, are expected to incur the largest losses.

> **FERC defines stranded costs as those costs that were prudently incurred to serve power customers and that could go unrecovered if these customers use open access to move to another supplier.**

Using conservative assumptions of $20 to $45 per kilowatt as the average price of electricity capacity over the next 10 years, Moody's estimated that the losses on stranded costs from 1996 through the year 2005 would amount to more than 80% of the U.S. investor-owned electric utility industry's total equity—about one-quarter of the industry's total assets. Utilities in the northeast and west would account for more than 40% of total projected losses.

In the northeast, 16 utilities face a potential total loss of $29.5 billion over the next 10 years. In the west, 17 utilities have stranded cost exposure estimated at $28.9 billion. In contrast, a study conducted by Moody's found that the eight investor-owned utilities in the midwestern states of Iowa, Minnesota, North Dakota, and South Dakota would have less than $1 billion in stranded costs. Stranded cost exposures for utilities in other regions fall in between.

According to Moody's, New Orleans Public Service Co., with estimated stranded costs of over $787 million (or about four-and-one-half times its equity), is expected to be among the hardest-hit utilities. Seven other utilities in various regions have stranded cost exposures of more then three times their current equity. These utilities are listed in Table 19–2.

Table 19–2
Utilities with high stranded cost exposure

- Central Maine Power Co.
- Cleveland Electric Illuminating Co.
- Long Island Lighting Co.
- Mississippi Power and Light Co.
- Public Service Company of New Hampshire
- Texas New Mexico Power Co.
- Toledo Edison Co.

Stranded costs are defined earlier, but exactly how do utilities become at-risk for exposure to stranded costs?

Under traditional public utility regulation, historical costs could be collected through approved rates for a bundled service. With the protection of a monopoly franchise, average electricity prices provide the possibility of cost recovery for assets that might not be recoverable in a competitive market.

However, in a competitive market, consumers are free to choose from alternative producers. Large energy users under wholesale wheeling are already choosing. However, smaller users of energy, such as at the residential level, haven't gotten to do so. With retail wheeling, however, this may become a reality. Retail wheeling will be discussed later in this chapter.

Given this freedom of choice, consumers probably will choose the lowest-cost producer. Producers with low-cost assets will not subsidize willingly those with high-cost assets. Therefore, in a market-driven economy, the value of assets will be determined by the present value of the stream of revenues from the goods and services they produce and not by their embedded (or historical) costs.

Should the market price fall for a good or service, the stream of net revenues declines. The effect of this is that certain assets are left "stranded" relative to the market. The success of

the movement toward a deregulated environment depends wholly upon the ability of regulators to structure the transition and assign responsibility for stranded costs. Otherwise, utilities that have considerable financial exposure vigorously will resist regulatory initiatives to establish competition as the primary method of economic control.

FERC Order 889

At the same time that FERC issued its open access rule (FERC Order 888) it also issued a second rule, known as FERC Order 889. This rule is the Open Access Same-time Information System or OASIS rule. OASIS is designed to ensure that transmission owners and their affiliates do not have an unfair competitive advantage in using transmission to sell power.

The OASIS rule requires utilities to:

- obtain information about their transmission system for their own wholesale power transactions in the same way that their competitors do through an OASIS on the Internet, and

- separate their wholesale power marketing and transmission operating functions.

Yet another item FERC took action on the day the two orders were adopted was the issuance of a new NOPR on the Capacity Reservation Open Access Transmission Tariffs or CRT. Under the CRT NOPR, each utility would replace the Open Access Rule pro forma tariff with a capacity reservation tariff by December 31, 1997.

The proposal stipulates that utilities and all other power market participants would reserve firm rights to transfer power between designated receipt and delivery points. FERC stated that its proposed reservation-based service seems to be more compatible with the open access requirement that market participants know how much transmission is available for electric power purchases and sales. FERC also stated that the proposal also may be more accommodating to competitive changes going on within the industry.

RETAIL WHEELING

Retail wheeling, as stated earlier, has the potential to significantly impact the nation's electric utilities and the way they operate. Before getting into the specifics of industry happenings in this area, some background on retail wheeling will be offered.

What is retail wheeling? There are many definitions of this industry buzzword, but the following one is useful: the moving of power between a new seller (one in which a customer chooses) and the customer. Table 19–3 gives a simple summation of what retail wheeling involves.

Table 19–3
What is retail wheeling?

- Moving power between a new seller and the consumer.
- Goal is lower cost.
- A matter of flow of dollars not electricity.
- Energy Policy Act of 1992 bans federally-mandated retail wheeling.

Retail wheeling currently is not permitted on a wide-scale basis. Several states, however, are already putting retail wheeling in the so-called testing labs (before their residential and smaller-user customers) to see how it works. Also, these pilot programs, which are very limited in nature, give utilities a taste of how they would handle the tremendous impacts of retail wheeling if the practice becomes available to its customers on a wide-scale basis.

The Energy Policy Act of 1992 (EPAct) expressly prohibits federally-mandated retail wheeling. Congress left the issue for states to decide on their own whether they wanted to instigate retail wheeling or not. EPAct was pivotal to the whole idea of retail wheeling, and, in fact, its passage marked the beginnings of state attention to retail wheeling.

It is important to note that there is a difference between retail wheeling and wholesale wheeling, which FERC does have some control over. Wholesale wheeling refers to the transmission of power from a seller of the power to a buyer of

the power over the transmission lines of one or more other entities, including utilities and government facilities. The "wheeling" in wholesale wheeling comes from the fact that wheeling occurs when the buyer of the power resells the wheeled power to retail customers. Wholesale wheeling has been in existence for several years, is being used today, and is expected to continue into the future.

Drivers Behind the Retail Wheeling Push

What is driving the push for retail wheeling? According to the National Regulatory Research Institute, several factors are driving the heightened interest in retail wheeling. They are:

- large price differentials between utilities,

- high electricity prices relative to the costs of new generation facilities,

- a recent emphasis on economic development and new jobs that has led some industry stakeholders (including state legislatures, public utility commissions, and industrial groups) to push for more competitive electricity prices,

- a feeling among industrial customers that utility-funded demand-side management (DSM) programs have caused electricity prices to increase; they also argue that most of the benefits from DSM programs have mostly benefited nonindustrial customers, and

- the general belief that more competition in the electric power industry would have positive repercussions.

When Will Retail Wheeling Happen?

The answer to this question is not easy. However, The Arrington Group, a Winter Park,

Florida-based utility consulting firm, has issued some interesting findings as part of an overall report on electric utility industry restructuring, *Electric Utility Industry Survey Report, 1996: The Response of the Electric Utility Industry to Marketplace Change.*

The Arrington Group found that utilities in general feel that retail wheeling is not far from becoming a reality; however, none of the respondents to its survey believe that the practice will be a reality within the next year. The Arrington Group stated that there are some marked differences across industry sectors regarding the arrival of retail wheeling. Cooperatives seem to believe that retail wheeling will not arrive for a long time. Their view of this shift is the furthest out of any sector polled by The Arrington Group.

At the other end of the spectrum, federal, state, and district utilities apparently expect retail wheeling to be a reality earlier than any other group. The view from the investor-owned utility community follows closely behind the expectation of the federal, state, and district utilities.

The Arrington Group stated that the overwhelming opinion of the industry is that retail wheeling will be a reality within five years. For organizations with a typical age of 50–75 years, five years is an incredibly short time. For organizations typically populated by employees with 20 years of service or more in the same place, five years is even a shorter period of time.

The Arrington Group found that while there is consensus within the industry on the inevitability of retail wheeling, there appears to be a general overall lack of understanding of what to do to prepare for it or the will to act on it immediately. The firm found that a tremendous amount of money and energy is being used in the industry in an attempt to prepare for the changes that are occurring. However, The Arrington Group stated that responses to other questions in the survey indicate that there is a significant shortage of results and strategic positioning to deal with the competitive marketplace.

MERGERS AND ACQUISITIONS

Besides retail wheeling, another activity has the potential of significantly impacting the nation's electric utilities—mergers and acquisitions. In fact, mergers and acquisitions already have impacted heavily such industry sectors as investor-owned electric utilities and rural electric co-ops. Table 19–4 lists investor-owned electric utility mergers between 1990 and 1996. Table 19–5 lists electric co-op mergers and acquisitions from 1991 to 1996.

Central to the drivers of mergers and acquisitions is the economy; and, according to economists, they are a logical response to economic conditions. Table 19–6 lists the specific drivers of the merger frenzy. Perhaps the most notable is intensified competition and favorable financial markets.

Table 19–4
Investor-owned electric utility domestic mergers and acquisitions, 1990-1996

Status and year announced	Acquiring utility or merger partner	Acquired utility or merger partner	Merged name, if one and if known
Pending—1996	New England Electric System	Nantucket Electric Co.	
Pending—1996	Kansas City Power & Light	UtiliCorp United	
Pending—1995	Delmarva Power & Light Co.	Conowingo	Delmarva Power & Light Co.
Pending—1995	Cleveland Electric Illuminating Co.	Toledo Edison Co.	Centerior Energy
Pending—1995	WPL Holdings Inc.	IES Industries Inc. and Interstate Power Co.	Interstate Energy Corp.
Pending—1995	Puget Sound Power & Light Co.	Washington Energy Co.	
Pending—1995	Baltimore Gas and Electric Co.	Potomac Electric Power Co.	Constellation Energy Corp.
Pending—1995	Public Service Company of Colorado	Southwestern Public Service Co.	New Century Energies
Pending—1995	Union Electric Co.	CIPSCO Inc.	Ameren Corp.
Complete—1995	Midwest Resources	Iowa-Illinois Gas and Electric Co.	MidAmerican Energy Co.
Proceedings terminated by parties—1995	Central & South West Corp.	El Paso Electric Co.	
Rejected by target utility—1995	PECO Energy	PP&L Resources	Primergy Corp.
Pending—1995	Northern States Power Co.	Wisconsin Energy Corp.	Cinergy Corp.
Complete—1994	PSI Resources Inc.	Cincinnati Gas & Electric Co.	Altus Corp.
Pending—1994	Sierra Pacific Resources	Washington Water Power Co.	
Complete—1993	Entergy Corp.	Gulf States Utilities Co.	IES Industries
Complete—1993	Iowa Electric Light & Power	Iowa Southern	
Complete—1993	Texas Utilities Co.	Southwestern Electric Service Co.	
Complete—1992	Northeast Utilities	Public Service Company of New Hampshire	
Complete—1992	UNTIL Corp.	Fitchburg Gas and Electric	
Complete—1992	Kansas Power & Light Co.	Kansas Gas & Electric Co.	
Complete—1991	UtiliCorp United	Centel Corp.	IES Industries
Complete—1991	IE Industries Inc.	Iowa Southern Utilities Co.	Midwest Resources Inc.
Complete—1990	Midwest Energy Co.	Iowa Resources Inc.	
Complete—1990	Eastern Utilities Associates	Newport Electric Corp.	

Table 19–5
Electric co-op mergers and consolidations, 1991-1996

Merged/consolidated co-ops	Status and year approved
Morrow Electric Co-op/Delaware Electric Co-op	Member elections scheduled—June 1996
Sioux Valley Empire Electric Co-op/Southwestern Minnesota Co-op Electric	Approved—1995
Riceland Electric Co-op/First Electric Co-op Corp.	Approved—1995
East Central Electric Association/North Pine Electric Co-op	Approved—1995
Fayette-Union Rural Electric Membership Corp./Wayne County Rural Electric Membership Corp.	Approved—1995
Sioux Electric Co-op Association/O'Brien County Rural Electric Co-op	Approved—1993
Belmont Electric Co-op/South Central Power Co.	Approved—1993
Waushara Electric Co-op/Adams-Marquette Electric Co-op	Approved—1992
Hardin County Rural Electric Co-op/Midland Power Co-op	Approved—1992
Smokey Valley Electric Co-op Association/DS&O Rural Electric Co-op Association	Approved—1991
Mountrail Electric Co-op/Williams Electric Co-op	Approved—1991

Table 19–6
Mergers and acquisitions: what's fueling them?

The "Fuel"	Explanation
Favorable financial markets	Interest rates are as low as they have been in the past 20 years, and the stock market is at an all-time high. Considered together, they present a perfect climate for mergers. Companies are able to either borrow at low rates to finance their deals or pay for acquisitions with stock.
Modest economic growth	Economies are expanding—in the United States as well as in Europe and Japan—although at a slow pace. In looking to boost profits, companies don't count on growing sales. Mergers present the most obvious way for them to cut costs and increase their bottom line.
Intensified competition	The natural tendency in corporate America is to grow in size in order to survive tough competition. According to Edward Riley, chief investment officer at the Private Bank, "In certain markets, bigger may be better." This certainly has proved true for such companies as IBM, which bought Lotus Development Corp. in 1995.
Globalization	Pressures to merge to take advantage of economies that can be borne out through mergers and consolidations, are bringing with them pressures to break down traditional boundaries. International mergers are now becoming all the norm with many U.S. utilities.

According to The Arrington Group, in the utility industry as a whole, 15% of respondents surveyed on whether or not their organization had been involved in a merger or acquisition, reported having been merged. Fifteen percent reported having acquired another utility; however, no utility reported having been acquired.

Most of the merger and acquisition activity has taken place within investor-owned electric utilities. The Arrington Group report stated that only one cooperative reported involvement in a merger, and only one utility in the federal, state, and district category reported having acquired another utility. Within the investor-owned utility category, 22% reported having merged, and 22% reported having acquired another utility.

On a company basis, 15 investor-owned utilities reported having merged, and 17 reported having acquired another utility. Six investor-owned utilities appeared on both the merged and acquired list. Of the 72 responding investor-owned utilities, 21% reported having merged and 24% reported having acquired another utility.

acquisition activity provides utilities with the ability to average their fixed costs. For some utilities, this is a well thought out strategy to build competitive advantage by dominance in a particular market. For others, it is an effort to remain in business by gathering strength from the potential partner. The Arrington Group maintains that this trend will continue and accelerate in the future.

In addition, the consulting group forecasts that the merger and acquisition trend will continue to be dominated by investor-owned utilities, but that the trend can be expected to spread to municipal utilities and cooperatives as the need arises to compete with invading retail energy marketers.

The Arrington Group stated that a number of industry leaders project that this trend of consolidation will result in fewer than 50 independent investor-owned electric utilities operating within the United States by 2005. This means that fewer than one in four existing companies will remain independent. This belief, according to the consulting firm, was supported by the write-in comments related to pending or projected mergers within the reporting organizations.

OUTLOOK

In analyzing the findings of its survey, The Arrington Group stated that the move to consolidate operations through merger and

Projections Right on Target

Some projections made by Arthur Anderson regarding merger, acquisition, and consolidation activity within the electric utility industry have

been right on target. In 1995, Arthur Andersen, a global accounting firm that provides business advisory and consulting services to the utility industry, indicated that there would be an increasing number of consolidations and mergers, continuing stock volatility, and deregulation. They were right.

In backing up their predictions, Lawrence D. Gilson, a partner in the utilities practice at Arthur Andersen's Los Angeles office, said, "Following the groundbreaking announcement by California regulators of their intention to open the state's electricity market to competition, the bottom dropped out of the Dow Jones utility index."

Gilson went on to say, "Electric companies are scrambling to reposition themselves for a new era of business."

Gilson and another Arthur Andersen colleague, Timothy P. Gardner, of the firm's Washington, D.C. office, predict the following for the future:

- **Industry restructuring.** An increase in the number of takeovers, mergers, and acquisitions is already evident. There were no bankruptcies in the U.S. electric industry prior to 1987, but there have been 10 since then.

- **Increased investment risk.** Arthur Andersen stated that Moody's Investors Service predicts bond ratings of U.S. utilities will come under growing pressure in the next five years. The Dow Jones utilities dropped 31% since its high in 1993. California-based utilities' stock dropped 22% after the public utilities commission in California announced its plans to deregulate.

- **Increased productivity.** Headcount at United Kingdom utilities declined 57% since 1990 industry deregulation/restructuring.

- **Diversification.** United Kingdom electric and water utilities have spent $2.5 billion on diversification since 1989 and have already written off $1.6 billion.

- **Price reductions.** Norwegian commercial and industrial rates, due to deregulation of their utility industry, have dropped 50% in the past four years.

Deregulation Planted Firmly in Utility Industry

It is obvious to most—and no less certain to those who choose not to find it so obvious—that deregulation is occurring in the electric utility industry. Its acceleration has been forecast to occur as early as 1996. From state-initiated retail wheeling activity to the process of unbundling generation, transmission, and distribution, deregulation has firmly planted itself in the utility industry.

In a deregulated electric utility industry environment nothing is more important for utilities than their competitive position. As shown in the Competitive Position Map depicted in Figure 19–1, positioning for strength in the new

Figure 19–1. Competitive position map

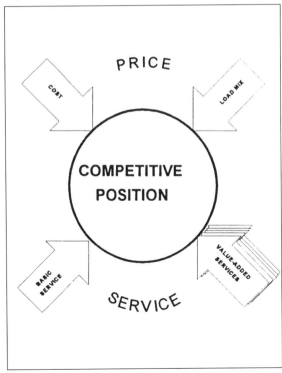

[Courtesy NRECA]

243

market helps ensure that utilities cannot only gain a foothold in the new business era but also retain it. Utilities must be prepared to offer both the best service and best price to all of their customers (commercial, industrial, and residential). On the price side of the competitive position map is cost and load mix, and on the service side of the map is basic service to customers, as well as value-added service.

It has been postulated by some industry analysts and observers that electric utilities must have to work harder than ever before to retain their current customer base. It will, in fact, be very important for electric utilities to take into account their customers' wants, needs, desires, and preferences when making decisions within their companies that will directly affect customers.

A Cambridge Energy Research Associates and Opinion Dynamics Corporation (CERA/ODC) report, *U.S. Public Opinion and the Electric Power Industry: Challenges of Competition,* found that overall the American public is ready to reap the benefits of competition in the electric utility industry. However, the report found that the American public also has some reservations about the potential consequences.

Some of the findings of this report include the following:

- Public support for deregulation is broad but shallow. A solid majority (57%) believe that deregulation would help them either a little or a lot, but are quick to back away if they perceive adverse consequences.

- If competition means higher prices for the average consumer, public support quickly erodes.

- There is little public support for programs that offer price breaks or other special advantages only to business customers. There is a strong undercurrent that any savings from competition must be shared widely among all customer groups.

- People view the question of competition mostly in terms of price. The brand loyalty of the electric power industry's customers is very weak. The report found that three out of every four Americans say they would switch to a new power supplier if they were offered a 5 or 10% discount in the price they pay for electricity, even though they are generally satisfied with their current utility.

The CERA/ODC report found that the public's support for more open power markets dwindles in the face of potentially adverse economic conditions. Most Americans (76%) say they favor the idea of regulators allowing businesses to find cheaper sources of electricity while only 19% oppose it. However, CERA/ODC pointed out that if they knew that as a result of businesses finding cheaper electricity, residential customers might be left paying higher prices, then only 33% would support the idea, and 62% would oppose it.

Although a majority of respondents favored the idea of allowing businesses to build small power plants to generate their own electricity, popular support for other potential consequences of deregulation and competition is tepid. Only 41% would support allowing businesses to buy out-of-state power and require the local utility to deliver it for a flat fee. Only 42% support allowing utilities to guarantee businesses long-term electricity rates lower than those provided to residential customers. Finally, only 44% support allowing utilities to provide (for a fee) services to business customers that they do not offer to residential customers.

According to CERA/ODC, these responses suggest that the ingredients are in place for a public backlash against deregulation and competition if those changes are perceived to give unfair advantage to the business community at the expense of economic damage or disadvantage to ordinary citizens. On the other hand, however, support levels favoring business over residential customers in the 40+ percent range were surprisingly high.

It stands to reason then that customers will play a decided role in the future of deregulation in the electric utility industry. Utilities will do well to heed what their customers are telling them. All signals are pointing to an increased need for utilities to take note.

The future—and success—of deregulation may just hinge on it.

Chapter 20
Privatization

DENISE WARKENTIN
NEWS EDITOR, *ELECTRIC LIGHT & POWER*
EDITOR, *ENERGY MARKETING*

Most changes that are occurring in the electric utility industry are the direct result of evolution. Privatization is no exception. The privatization of public utilities is tightly woven with the powerful force of deregulation that has been brought about by a variety of events in the electric power industry. Taken together with the substantial increase in international independent power projects, it is clear that more competition in the areas of both private power funding and competition for end-users—both of which are intricately tied to privatization—has only just begun.

OVERVIEW

Just a short five years ago, the recent move away from government ownership to investor control of public utilities was, for all practical purposes, unthinkable. This was due in no small part to two presumptions about electric power:

(1) that government control was essential to achieve key planning objectives as they related to the assets of public utilities, and

(2) that electricity was a "natural" monopoly and as such should be under close government control.

However, these presumptions no longer hold true. Although the details of why these presumptions no longer exist will vary by country, there are three related directions that the electric utility industry is moving:

(1) from government to private ownership,

(2) from utilities that are monopolistic in nature to ones that are competitive in nature, and

(3) from jurisdictionally separate entities to global players.

What's more, the changes listed above are spurring corresponding ways in which the

industry is being financed. These new financing trends include:

- private sources (rather than official),

- capital competition (rather than budget allocation), and

- global capital markets (rather than country or regional sources).

Privatization activity currently being undertaken by many nations—including developed as well as developing and post-communist—are in direct contradiction to the historically-held perceptions cited earlier. Privatization activity, not unlike many regime-altering activities, such as liberalization, can take on different meanings for different countries. For instance, some countries are choosing only to privatize certain functions of their electricity markets, such as the power production sector, while others are choosing to privatize the overall market.

To illustrate the sheer magnitude of effects that privatization is having on the U.S. electric power industry, consider that in 1995 alone, the electric utility industry as a whole spent $12.9 billion in asset privatization. Electric power leads all other industries in its actions as they pertain to the privatization of assets. This trend likely will continue as evidenced by the fact that at least another $20 billion of power asset privatization is expected in 1996.

WHAT IS PRIVATIZATION?

Privatization is the transfer of responsibility for various electric power functions to private organizations or to quasi-governmental entities that act like private organizations. Privatization also can take shape from some combination of the aforementioned. Privatization is most generally thought of as the sale of assets; however, incremental private capital is also considered to be a form of privatization.

The magnitude of electric power asset divestitures for 24 nations is shown in Table 20–1.

Table 20–1
Privatizations, 1988-1995

Country	Total ($millions)
United Kingdom	13,515.7
Germany - East	6,607.1
Argentina	4,652.9
Australia	4,276.0
Malaysia	1,474.3
Germany - West	1,350.0
Spain	1,300.0
Hungary	1,248.3
Brazil	1,195.7
China	987.0
Peru	912.6
Canada	654.0
Austria	400.0
Chile	216.6
Bolivia	212.5
Thailand	200.0
Czechoslovakia	173.0
Turkey	114.0
Trinidad/Tobago	112.0
Philippines	98.3
Belize	14.2
Honduras	11.4
Grenada	5.6
Poland	1.7

The dollar amount that a variety of countries have put into asset privatization (as shown in Table 20–1) lends much credence to the fact that much of what the domestic utility market is learning about privatization (including funding and funding strategies) emanates from these foreign countries. There are great lessons to be learned, and the domestic electric power market seems poised and ready to learn.

Table 20–2 shows the significance that international markets have for U.S. investor-owned electric utilities.

Although U.S. utilities have been on what some term a merger and acquisition "frenzy" within the United States (there were 10 either instigated, still under review, or approved mergers and acquisitions in 1995), there is considerable interest in the international market. The reasons behind this interest will be detailed later in this chapter. One company that has been a highly visible player in the international arena has been The Southern Company through its subsidiary, Southern Electric International (SEI). One of SEI's projects is pictured in Figure 20–1.

Table 20–2

Investor-owned electric utility international acquisitions and partnerships—1995

Utility or Consortium	Utility Acquired or Partnered With	Amount of Acquisition Transaction
Entergy Corp.	CitiPower Ltd. (Australia)	$1.2 billion
Texas Utilities Co.	Eastern Energy (Australia)	$1.55 billion
PacifiCorp	Powercor (Australia)	$1.6 billion
Generandes, an Entergy Power Group-led consortium	Has ownership and operation of 60% of Edegel (Peru)	$424.5 million
The Southern Company	South Western Electricity (England)	$1.7 billion
UtiliCorp United	Leading a partnership to purchase United Energy (Australia)	$1.15 billion

In short, this interest by IOUs in the international electricity market is so pervasive because of the extensive number of governments in foreign lands that are privatizing their power sectors. This not only opens up major opportunities for U.S. utilities but also has a great many benefits for the various governments who are loosening their control on electricity.

INDEPENDENT POWER PRODUCERS AND PRIVATIZATION

While independent power producers (IPPs) may not have long-term holdings in assets overseas, they surely do play a major role in the privatization of public utilities.

IPPs hold so-called equity investments in foreign power projects, with some of the assets transferred back to government ownership when the IPP's long-term franchise expires. However, there are some cases in which the assets do stay private.

According to the Reason Foundation, a national public-policy research organization based in Los Angeles, California, IPP investments in foreign assets can be termed "spontaneous" privatization whereby an IPP effects new private capacity into a country which can remain under its existing state-owned power firms.

To illustrate, the top five IPPs based on their project ownership are shown in Table 20–3.

Table 20–3

Independent power producer equity in international projects

IPP	1995 Equity
National Power	4,465 MW
Consolidated Electric Power of Asia	4,391 MW
PowerGen	3,955 MW
Mission Energy	3,463 MW
Enron Development	2,638 MW

Figure 20–1. Southern Electric International's Hidroelectrica Alicura, a 1,000-megawatt hydro plant located at the foothills of the Andes

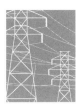

WHY PRIVATIZE AND WHY NOW?

The attractiveness of privatization is most adequately summed up in the following simple equation:

Higher Operating Efficiencies =
Less Risky Private Developments

The above equation is one of the greatest motivating factors currently driving privatization. Why? Because privatization generally improves the economic viability of the utilities and power plants. This is due to the fact that private utilities are less apt to subsidize rates or to allow power theft and other operating inefficiencies. Investors as well as governments that are privatizing or are thinking about privatizing are under the correct assumption that higher operating efficiencies will make private developments less risky.

Why privatize now? As stated earlier, the history behind privatization is rather short; however, there are some specific (brief) historical events that have caused the evolution of privatization.

The United Kingdom (Britain) has served as an excellent example to other nations wishing to privatize their electricity industries. Britain, over the last five years, has privatized the majority of its electricity business assets. This country has served as a model to such countries as Argentina and Australia, for example, that now share many of the same features with Britain's nearly completely privatized assets.

As Britain, as well as other countries have witnessed, the move toward democracy is stimulating privatization and competition. The political stability that is being brought about through the democratic political mood serves to encourage capital investments. All this is positive and actually promotes and supports privatization efforts.

Democracy also has the tendency to bring about new financial regulations, which allow easier access to capital markets. As will be shown (in investment opportunities), these lessened restrictions spell new possibilities for private investment in infrastructure projects.

Britain truly has been an incredible testing laboratory for privatization. It has proven that democracy and the resultant changes that have borne out through the governmental switch to democracy, have increased efficiency in its electric power market. Perhaps most importantly, lower consumer prices have emerged.

Specifically, privatization has four basic areas of concern. These areas and some detail about each appear in Table 20–4.

Table 20–4
Privatization objectives

Area of Concern	Detail
Government Debt	Privatization generally has become an effective tool for governments to raise cash and pay accumulated national debts. Developing countries, in particular, face mounting pressure from the International Monetary Fund as well as development banks to reduce their indebtedness.
Productivity and Economic Growth	Many nations are privatizing to reform their electric power market and to enhance and grow economic productivity. Refer to Table 20–5 for reasons why state-owned power entities are suffering from lagging electric power performance.
External Capital Market	Developing countries often have inadequate internal capital markets to finance large public power projects. Because international government lending is laden with a great deal of red tape, the primary source of financing has become the external market. Of late, international lenders have praised the so-called "spontaneous" privatization of electric power (often effected by independent power producers). These lenders are now pushing for private ownership, and they have great financial and political backing.
Energy Deregulation	As stated in this chapter, privatization is inextricably linked to deregulation. Governments, under this new energy market regime, are no longer the central energy planners. Private investors have stepped in. However, government-enforced monopoly status will not be given to private investors. This makes revenue flows more sensitive to the quality and cost effectiveness of service provided. On the other hand, deregulation allows the privatized entity to enter new markets and to be more responsive to changes in its operating environment. Nations are advised to reform their market processes prior to privatization; otherwise, the desired efficiency improvements will be unattainable. Too, external investors will be apt to steer clear of those nations who have not first put the appropriate markets into place.

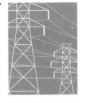

As pointed out in Table 20–4, one of the major areas of concern lies with removing constraints on productivity and economic growth. Table 20–5 outlines the major reasons government-owned power entities generally have been lagging in performance.

Table 20–5
Sources of inefficiency in government-operated power entities

- Weak monitoring of management practices.
- Disincentives to serve consumers.
- An enabler of political favors.

The failings of government-run utility enterprises, then, many believe, can be remedied with the instigation of privatization. Many of the government failures, as listed above, can (and are) being addressed and remedied through privatization. At the same time, electricity (consumer) prices are being lowered and the quality of service is getting a much-needed boost.

INVESTMENT OPPORTUNITIES

Privatization obviously opens up many new opportunities for investors. Depending upon how the privatization is structured, investors may be able to make:

- direct foreign investments,

- portfolio equity investments, and

- private loans.

In privatization efforts, the money to fund electricity generation can come from a wide variety of sources in both the public and private sectors. Particular desires and needs along with overall underlying business and economic conditions will dictate which source of funding will be tapped. All of these factors will vary from country to country.

In privatization efforts, the money to fund electricity generation can come from a wide variety of sources in both the public and the private sectors.

Foreign capital usually comes from two different sources: government and/or international private investment. In addition, it is common for domestic financing to be a part of electricity industry development.

There are four basic methods that can be utilized to finance electric power development. Often used in combination, they include government financing, equity (private) investment, full recourse debt, and project finance. The choice of methods depends in whole upon whether the capital is being raised by a government agency or by a private entity. As stated above, whatever financing sources and methods are used will depend upon a country's economics as well as risk factors such as political stability.

Over the last 10 years, sources of capital that are used for electric power in developing countries have changed dramatically. Overall, capital investment has tripled in the last four years. Private capital market sources have increased dramatically.

In government financing, the creditworthiness of the particular government will determine its ability to raise capital. It must be noted that even in cases where the project is being developed by a private sector entity, the host government's participation is usually critical to the overall financing package. Both developers and financial institutions will continue to view the government as the ultimate guarantor.

Overall, capital investment has tripled in the last four years. Private capital market sources have increased dramatically.

In private financing, private investors need to be able to provide a mixture of equity and debt. Equity investment means that the investor is willing to accept ultimate financial responsibility. Debt financing is accomplished by using either full recourse debt or project finance.

An important part in most private financing is equity investment. Equity investments are generally made by local investors, foreign direct investors, and portfolio equity investors and managers. Should there be a default on the investment, equity investors sometimes will have a higher call on project assets than official development assistance.

Financially strong utilities can take advantage of full recourse debt, which is generally the fastest and most flexible way to raise capital for an investment in a government-owned entity. The requirements for international borrowers are stringent. The borrower must possess an excellent credit history and have promising economic prospects. In addition, the borrower must seek financing in a host country that possesses adequate currency reserves.

If the country is financially weak or currently lacks reserves, the risk is much higher.

Full recourse financing is most often utilized by a strong entity that builds, owns, and operates the power plant or system. In this type of financing, the lender will supply the funds as a general obligation of the borrower, which may be the utility and/or the host government. The lender will look closely at the overall operating revenues and assets of the borrower to help ensure repayment.

If the country is financially weak or currently lacks reserves, the risk is much higher. The reason is that specific revenues are not attachable to secure payment and funds may not be available for payment. In some cases, at this point, the only security is the good faith and credit of the host utility or government. In most instances, this is insufficient to secure financing for developing and transitional economies.

Project finance maximizes the developer's return on equity while minimizing risk. Project finance often is a built-in feature of privatization in many countries—both in developing and in transitional countries. It involves setting up an independent entity to serve as the builder, owner, and/or operator of the power facility. The underlying intent of project finance is to create this entity as solely independent from the host government. That is, the host government, in optimal project finance conditions, could not interfere. A portion of the revenue the project earns is put to the task of repaying the debt.

In a purely project finance deal, the host country will not bear any risks associated with the power project. Lenders will look solely at the assets and earnings of the borrowing entity for repayment of the loan.

As a general rule, project finance is the most preferred form of financing foreign projects. Through spreading risks to parties who are willing, as well as able, to assume them, public and private lending institutions view the projects as less risky to themselves as well as to the utilities and to the host governments. This is in direct opposition to funding under debt financing, where the host country assumes the entire risk.

Investment Criteria

Investors typically have a checklist of items that they use in determining which private power sector investments they will consider funding in developing countries. These items, along with a description, is provided.

- A market for the power must exist. Utilities going into a host country will obviously need a customer base. If there are no customers and there are no projections to point toward the availability of a customer base, then there is no need for the power. This rarely is the case.

- Organizational fundamentals should assure profitability and safety of the investment. The maturity structure of financing must be matched to the cash flows of the particular development. The longer the terms of the financing, the greater the amount of risk. It is important

that interest rate fluctuations be taken into consideration. It is advisable that some portion of the debt be funded at fixed interest rates so that repayment risk remains at an acceptable level.

- Host government support or corporate finance must be available. Guarantors, in order to be viewed as credible, must be capable of being ultimately financially responsible. In developing countries, the government has traditionally been the guarantor. However, with privatization, this may no longer be the norm. Most all other aspects of the electric utility industry are changing, and surely project financing is another such area that is likely to change in the coming months and years. It will be a difficult habit, however, for investors to break. The reason is tradition and because recent surveys have shown that investors still consider the host government ultimately responsible for the debt.

- Political risks must be lessened and government support must be established for private investment and possible privatization. A political climate that is open in nature to the ideas of private investment and privatization greatly minimizes investment risks, such as those connected to changes in sovereign government. This type of change could potentially result in a complete repudiation of existing contracts and obligations. Government regulation, then, of the utility must be clearly delineated so that the utility is free from interference by the host government. This condition, ultimately, will allow market forces to determine appropriate power policies in pricing and revenue collection.

- Currency convertibility, repatriation of profits, and the mitigation of currency valuation risk must be feasible. There must exist the reasonable expectation that an unrestricted conversion of local currency, which is the basis of revenue stream, will be allowed at a market exchange rate, and that sufficient foreign reserves will be available to repay loans and repatriate profits into the specified foreign currency over the term of the loans. This could involve employing a combination of host government guarantees, hedging strategies, and political risk insurance, and/or shifting the problem to the host country by denominating debt repayment in dollars.

Electric utilities, in order to ensure that they will receive the needed financial backing from investors, must be both willing and able to meet the above-listed requirements of investors. The better these requirements can be fulfilled and maintained, the greater the likelihood of success with private investors.

OUTLOOK AND FORECAST

An estimated investment of around $2.3 trillion is needed to finance global, electric-power-sector expansion between now and 2010. This is an average investment of about $152 billion per year. According to the International Energy Agency, about 68% of this total, or $1.5 trillion, will be needed in developing and transitional countries.

It is estimated that over one-third of the world's population does not yet have electricity. And, as stated above, the population in developing countries continues to rise at a rapid pace. As such, a significant amount of electric power development is expected over the entire world in the next 15 years.

Developing countries in East Asia and the Pacific Rim (China, specifically), South Asia, and Latin America are undergoing rapid economic growth. This is being reflected in their electric power usage. In these countries, as well as in other developing countries, electric power is a prerequisite to desired economic growth.

What's more, the transitional countries of Central and Eastern Europe and the Newly Independent States of the former Soviet Union are working to upgrade their current electric power infrastructures to bring them to world standards. So, too, are the developed countries of Western Europe, North America, and the East Asia-Pacific Rim region expected to expand as well as upgrade their current electricity infrastructure.

Developing countries have higher growth rates for population, industrial production, and power consumption than developed countries. While large amounts of capital will need to be raised to meet the power needs of these countries, the investments that will be made will serve to stimulate economies throughout the world and will create a huge market for goods and services that are related to electric power development.

Because of the fact that coal continues to be the most popular energy source worldwide, one-third of all investments will go to coal-fired plants. This will include investments in clean coal technologies in many countries. Investments in gas-fired capacity, in addition, are expected to be large in most parts of the world through 2010. What's more, the International Energy Agency projects that China and Latin America will add considerably to their hydroelectric capacity.

An estimated investment of around $2.3 trillion is needed to finance global, electric-power-sector expansion between now and the year 2010.

The IEA, however, indicates that its projects of capital requirements are figured from relatively uncertain, long-term, energy supply and demand forecasts. For example, worldwide growth in electric power that averages just 0.4% per year higher through 2010 could add $600 billion of investments. This represents a 26% increase.

However, consider this fact. Clean coal technologies, provided that they penetrate the market at a greater than anticipated rate, would greatly increase the efficiency of power supply and reduce environmental impacts. Yet, this occurrence could add in the neighborhood of $135 billion worth of capital requirements—approximately 6% more. The development and deployment of lower-cost clean coal technologies would allow many of these benefits to be effected with much fewer capital requirements.

With Change Comes More Change

As evidenced in the electric power industry, it seems that with change, more change is always on the horizon. As the worldwide electric power industry, then, undergoes the foregoing changes, capital markets are undergoing their own form of transformation. But, it is important to keep in mind that all the changes are interrelated. The world of electricity is changing the world over and it follows that changes in all aspects relating to electricity, including generation, naturally will follow.

The present, as well as the future, will witness a record number of developing and transitional countries seeking investment capital. One of the changes that is following this trend is that the electric utility industry is looking more and more to the international markets and is becoming highly competitive as countries begin to look more seriously at the free markets to meet their power supply demands.

As a direct result, electric power capital in many cases will be provided by private sources as opposed to the traditional government and multilateral sources of the past.

A new and large burden is being placed on the world's capital markets as a result of the amount of power generation financing in developing countries. A recent U.S. Department of Energy Report to Congress projected a $28 billion gap in financing of power generation in developing countries which could only be filled through private finance.

Most financing of electric power in developing and transitional countries largely has been focused on individual projects, countries or regions, and

industry segments. Perhaps this is because the whole idea of privatization is actually quite new. The whole idea is whether an entire electric power industry can be financed to meet each country's expectations and needs. This is important because the traditional sources of capital and external capital will not be adequate enough to meet the needs of the countries needing the most investment. Then there is the question of global need (addressed in the preceding paragraph).

TRENDS IN FINANCING

The following lists some trends in financing that are emerging and are expected to emerge or continue over the forecast period (through 2010 for purposes of this analysis).

- Official development assistance and multilateral lending will no longer solely be sufficient to meet the needs of developing countries.

- More capital is going into power development worldwide than ever before while there are fewer public sector borrowers. Private capital accounted for 30% of total foreign investment in power developments in 1990; by 1994, this had increased to 75%. This trend is expected to continue, and the level of private market funding has increased substantially since 1992. Private capital, rather than government assistance, is now the key seed money for many power sector developments.

- Bank financing is becoming, and will become, less important while foreign direct investment and portfolio equity investments become more important sources in financing the industry. Insurance companies continue to be the most popular capital lending providers. However, other investors have become more

important since 1993. A short-term downturn in equity investments brought on by the Mexican peso crisis of 1994-95 is expected to be mitigated as investors scrutinize currency risk more carefully and consider each country's circumstances individually. The long-term trend is on increased use of portfolio equity investments.

- A blending of techniques and sources is reflecting the needs of the power industry and a willingness to share risks. Among the techniques that have emerged are international project finance and private investment funds. Developing countries now have more funding sources and methods available to them than they did just a few short years ago. Because power projects in today's times require a mixture of these sources and methods, U.S. electric utilities are able to develop projects with more economic risk. This will especially hold true as the industry evolves from project financing of power generating plants to full recourse financing of the entire industry.

- Financing techniques will evolve as the industry continues to undergo changes. These future changes in financing may include greater reliance on domestic capital markets, the use of new financing techniques, and expansion of the base of potential investors.

It clearly is within the interest of the United States, as well as many other countries, to promote and support growth in the worldwide investment in electric power. The United States, in particular, has a significant stake in international electric power development. The reason is worldwide economic development (underpinned by electric power) helps to promote a stable global economy.

The addition of free markets will serve to help improve efficiency, lower costs, and to expand opportunities. In addition, U.S. companies,

because they are at the forefront of international power development, can provide many of the needed (and in-demand) products and services utilized by the industry. Further, U.S. electric utilities can—and already are—playing key roles in the financial markets.

Chapter 21
Energy Marketing and Wheeling

DENISE WARKENTIN
NEWS EDITOR, *ELECTRIC LIGHT & POWER*
EDITOR, *ENERGY MARKETING*

Energy consumers now have a ring all their own. Answering specifically and exclusively to this ring are the multitude of companies that have formed energy marketing divisions or stand-alone entities. Through answering their customers' wants, needs, and desires for clean, efficient, and cost-effective energy sources, energy marketing enterprises are the wave of the present and of the future.

OVERVIEW

The practice of marketing itself is not alien to the electric power industry. Marketing departments exist at most electric utility companies and have since an upsurge in the emphasis on advertising, packaging, and selling electricity to consumers enveloped the industry more than a decade ago.

This upsurge in customer service emphasis was due in large part to a heightened awareness of customer dissatisfaction with their power service. There was a general feeling among many electricity consumers that they were at the mercy of their electricity provider. Should there be an outage, curtailment, or other interruption in power service, many consumers thought that their local electricity supplier simply didn't act quickly enough. Too, consumers over the last several years have become more and more concerned about the environment.

Discovering ways to help conserve energy and to preserve the integrity of the environment once wasn't an area where electric utilities got involved with their customers. Utilities did what they had to do to meet federal Environmental Protection Agency rules, but did very little (if anything) to converse with their customers over what customers themselves could be doing to help the environment.

MARKETING TAKES ON NEW MEANING

However, with the electric power business undergoing deregulation, marketing has taken on a new role, as this chapter will demonstrate. Utilities no longer can assume that they have a toehold on their customers. Wholesale customers already are shopping for the best electricity deal in town. Residential customers soon will be able to make their own "grocery" list of important items they will expect from a power supplier and then make their choices. Utilities are well aware of this fact.

Utilities can no longer assume that they have a toehold on their customers.

Some utilities already have begun offering so–called "value-added services"—including services that cover environmental solutions—for their customers. The offerance of value-added services means that electric utilities are taking very seriously their role in bringing choices coupled with the best value and quality of service to their customers.

An example of such a utility is UtiliCorp United with its EnergyOne brand. EnergyOne is the first nationally-branded line of products and services for both electric and gas utility customers. UtiliCorp, based in Kansas City, Missouri, launched an extensive advertising and marketing campaign to debut EnergyOne in May 1995.

EnergyOne is the first nationally-branded line of products and services for both electric and gas utility customers.

Total energy solutions is the main focus of EnergyOne, which is aptly termed an energy service company or ESCO. EnergyOne offers such

Table 21–1
Portfolio services of EnergyOne

Commercial	Industrial	Residential
Term transportation. Explanation: Small-volume customers are guaranteed savings versus regulated sales rates.	Small power services. Explanation: On-site turnkey generation options.	Appliance financing. Explanation: Low-interest loans for high-efficiency equipment.
Balancing. Explanation: Fee-based service for providing gas volume balancing on local distribution companies' system.	Gas management services. Explanation: Focuses on unregulated gas services such as transport and capacity release.	Appliance repair services. Explanation: Full range of appliance products.
Capacity management. Explanation: Securing gas pipeline capacity on a term arrangement for a fee.	Fuel supply services. Explanation: Contract for supply and distribution of primary and secondary fuels.	Customer power applications. Explanation: Packaged power quality solutions to meet homeowner needs.
Capacity choice. Explanation: Nominated term gas capacity for customers moving third party supply.	Special utility services. Explanation: Extends traditional utility service to customer facilities.	Lighting services. Explanation: New options to meet both security and decorative needs.
Total resource energy evaluation. Explanation: Consists of an audit of customers' facilities and recommendations on energy efficiency improvements that qualify for cash rebates.	Productivity and efficiency services. Explanation: Turnkey tailored technology packages.	Heat pump guarantee. Explanation: Money-back offer if dissatisfied with electric heat pump financed and inspected by EnergyOne.
	Energy profiler services. Explanation: Analyzes the customer's comprehensive energy services.	
	Environmental services. Explanation: Energy technology solutions to environmental challenges.	
	Power quality and reliability services. Explanation: Built on "good, better, and best" offerings and guarantees to include enhanced supply and customer facility options.	

[Courtesy Fitch Investors Service, L.P.]

services as total resource energy evaluation for commercial customers, productivity and efficiency services for industrial customers, and customer power applications for residential customers. Detail on the portfolio of services EnergyOne offers its customers is shown in Table 21–1.

Several utilities are forming and will form ESCOs, however, due to the cost, staffing, and expertise required for such an enterprise, many utilities are instead setting up internal "companies" that address total energy solutions. It must be noted that EnergyOne, however, is highly unique in that it is the only national energy solution provider to date. EnergyOne has contracted with several major companies (Wal-Mart, Appleby's Restaurants, Wendy's, McDonald's, etc.) to be the sole supplier of choice.

All utilities should be commended for their quick-to-act response to the emerging focus and trend of improving customer satisfaction and loyalty through the offerance of services that provide energy solutions.

Other utilities that have formed ESCOs or are doing energy solutions in-house currently are limited in scope to their service territories. However, the fact that some utilities are marketing total energy solutions only in their service territory is highly relevant. All utilities should be commended for their quick-to-act response to the emerging focus and trend of improving customer satisfaction and loyalty through the offerance of services that provide energy solutions.

Management Involvement in Marketing

According to Moody's Investors Service, there has been an increasing level of participation in the marketing effort on the part of executive-level management over the last several years. Many utilities are devising marketing plans that make

senior executives responsible for developing personal relationships with key decision makers at important companies or at companies where the utility is concerned that they may lose a customer.

Incentive compensation, according to Moody's, has increasingly been tied to meeting customer satisfaction objectives. Some companies are even expanding the number of bonus-eligible employees by implementing incentive programs at all levels. Moody's noted that these efforts are hampered by the pervasive downsizing and reorganization that is going on within the industry. Successfully refocusing employees is difficult during a time of great stress and turmoil surrounding the loss of jobs and the fear of the loss of jobs.

Moody's flatly stated that utilities that do not establish a more customer-oriented environment will be at a competitive disadvantage. So, there is no real option. Utilities must become more responsive and more sympathetic to their customers if they want to retain their customers. This responsiveness to large energy users is already occurring, as described earlier. Utilities, by beginning now to cater to their residential customers (with or without the employment of retail wheeling pilot programs), can be one step ahead of the game.

POWER MARKETING COMES OF AGE

This emphasis on marketing electricity to consumers (wholesale, commercial, and industrial) has given rise to the term "power marketing." Unmatched in its irony, power marketing truly is an activity whose occurrence is contrary to what most would have expected in the electric power industry.

In juxtaposition to the past, the delivery of electricity is no longer considered a service. Rather, power has become popularly known as a product. As such, power must be—in order to get

the maximum amount of exposure and thus sales—marketed to its target audience much like any other product.

As a product, electricity (much like oil or natural gas or any other product such as bran or wheat, for example) is a commodity and can now be bought and sold on the open market. The New York Mercantile Exchange, in an unprecedented and as yet still a little foreign to most, launched two electricity futures contracts on March 29, 1996. Those two contracts—the Palo Verde electricity futures contract and the California-Oregon Border electricity futures contract—have a profound effect not only on the electric utility industry but also on other industries as well, particularly the natural gas industry.

> **Unmatched in its irony, power marketing truly is an activity whose occurrence is contrary to what most would have expected in the electric power industry.**

This viewing of electricity as a product is a trend not foreign to the natural gas industry, which has been deregulated for several years. What the natural gas industry has taught the electric power industry, which presently is undergoing deregulation, is that deregulation has the net effect of lowering energy prices. The true power of competition and deregulation has been aptly exemplified in the deregulation of the gas industry.

This makes the deregulation of the electric utility industry even more exciting. Industry stakeholders—as well as some players outside the electric power industry such as natural gas firms—are on the edge of their seats waiting to view first-hand the effects of energy competition. The reason for this is that not only will deregulation in the electric power industry make electric utilities compete against one another, but also it will permit natural gas companies to step up to the plate to woo customers.

> **One of the energy industry's most interesting (and surpris-**
> **ing) cross-industry mergers is that of a merger announced in mid-1996 by Texas Utilities.**

Currently, it is the case that the customers electric utility companies have are also the same customers that natural gas companies have. Competition between the two will run rampant. While it is true that inter-fuel competition is nothing new, deregulation and competition in the power industry will have the effect of increasing it. It already has. Too, it is now the case that cross-industry deals are being struck so that natural gas firms can get more involved in the electricity business and vice versa. The few cases of cross-industry mergers and acquisitions that are currently going on could well become trendsetting.

One of the energy industry's most interesting (and surprising) cross-industry mergers is that of a merger announced in mid-1996 by Texas Utilities. The utility announced that it will acquire Enserch Corp., an integrated natural gas company, for a reported $1.7 billion.

ENERGY MARKETING: AN OVERALL SOLUTION PROVIDER

As stated earlier, utilities are well aware of the fact that their customers have choices. This is particularly true today for wholesale customers. The issue of choice also has come into play recently for selected groups of residential customers as well in certain parts of the United States through retail wheeling pilot programs.

Retail wheeling is the transmission of power to an individual customer from a generator of electricity other than the host or original utility. These pilot programs are giving some residential customers—and their host utilities and "chosen" utilities—a dose of competitive reality. These pilot programs truly are serving as useful barometers of what retail competition will be like.

Retail wheeling is the transmission of power to an individual customer from a generator of electricity other than the host or original utility.

The only, and some believe the best, way for utilities to become the provider of choice for their current customers as well as some new ones is to offer energy choices. What better way to accomplish this than through energy marketing. This means that electric power companies must offer choices, in order to be competitive in today's emerging national energy marketplace. This is the reason the term "energy" in energy marketing has become such a hot topic and one that is likely to dominate the business of providing energy to consumers for years to come.

The rest of this chapter is devoted to presenting some context about why the electricity industry is

---

Common Terms and Their Definitions

Affiliated Power Marketer: An affiliate of an established energy industry company that seeks and achieves power marketer status with the Federal Energy Regulatory Commission.

Aggregators: Marketing companies that pool energy from various sources into packages for resale to end-users.

Commodities Futures Contract: A contract to buy or sell a specific amount of a commodity at a specified future date.

Comparability: The condition that exists when all parties in an energy trading scenario have equal access to the marketplace and can see and take advantage of each other's offers to buy and sell energy.

Competitive Bidding: A process that energy companies utilize in many states to select suppliers of new capacity and energy.

Derivatives: Risk-management financial tools whose values depend upon those of their underlying assets. Examples of derivative instruments include: futures contracts, options, and swaps.

Electricity Futures Contract: Offered by the New York Mercantile Exchange beginning in March 1996, an electricity futures contract gives utilities a market to price electricity up to 18 months into the future.

Energy: Output of generating plants in kilowatt-hours. Energy price does not include the cost of delivery. Energy refers only to the commodity (energy) and not the ability to provide it on demand.

Energy Marketer: Encompasses the marketing of the broad range of energy supply in the United States. Energy marketing refers to the rationalization and evaluation of all energy generation sources by an energy provider to determine the best overall fit in satisfying customer needs. The "energy" in energy marketing not only includes electric power, but also natural gas, cogeneration, self-generation, and a host of other energy alternatives available in the market today.

End-User: The ultimate consumer of energy.

Futures: Contracts whereby an agreement is made to deliver a quantity of goods, generally commodities, at a specified price at a certain time in the future.

Independent Power Marketer: Power marketers that are not classified as affiliated power marketers. Independent power marketers generally are not affiliated with utilities, but rather are independent entities.

Options: A financial instrument (derivative) that gives the buyer the right to purchase or sell a security at a predetermined price.

Power Broker: Brokers who arrange bulk power transactions. Unlike power marketers, however, brokers do not take title to the power but rather act as an intermediary between a willing seller and a willing buyer.

Power Marketer: Like brokers, marketers arrange bulk power transactions. The difference is that power marketers take title to the power and assume the risk of "owning" the power for a time. Marketers, once "owning" the power for a while, resell it on the open market.

undergoing change and also will address the development of an electricity commodity market, present critical factors for developing and growing a successful marketing company or division, and look at the risks energy marketers face. Also contained in the following pages is a listing of all of the power and energy marketers (Table 21–5), the top 10 energy marketers in the first quarter of 1996, and finally, some observations and projections on what lies ahead for energy marketing in the next several years.

A LOOK AT WHAT IS SHAPING THE CHANGES

An open, transparent wholesale market for electricity is rapidly occurring. With the passage of the Energy Policy Act of 1992 (EPAct) and the Federal Energy Regulatory Commission's (FERC) April 24, 1996 adoption of FERC Order 888, open access in the wholesale markets should be brought to fruition by at least 1998.

Camera, Lights, Action: EPAct Sets Stage

EPAct literally set the stage for competition in the electric power industry. The thrust of the act was to promote economic development and energy conservation. However, its major goal was that of encouraging competition. EPAct began what has become a tidal wave of changes in both national policies and state regulations that have defined the role of utilities in the generation, transmission, and sale of electricity.

EPAct literally set the stage for competition in the electric power industry.

Of major importance is the fact that EPAct significantly freed the generation market through creating a new class of power producer, called exempt wholesale generators (EWGs). EWGs may be owned by an electric utility, a utility holding company, or by a developer that is not necessarily connected to a utility.

Wholesale Wheeling: New Opportunities

Another important aspect of EPAct, and one that has received much attention, is that the act mandates utilities allow outside wholesale electricity generators to access their power lines. This transmission of power for a third party is termed "wheeling." In particular, wholesale wheeling occurs when the buyer of the power resells the wheeled power to retail customers.

Wholesale wheeling has been in existence for several years; however, EPAct opened up a plethora of new opportunities. These opportunities not only permit utilities to wheel power among themselves, but also open the door for nontraditional players to enter the wheeling game.

RETAIL WHEELING ON STATE AGENDAS

A practice that has not been existence—or even predicted by many in the industry—is retail wheeling. Retail wheeling is the transmission of power to an individual customer for a generator of electricity other than a utility. FERC is strictly prohibited from ordering retail wheeling. This practice has been left to the individual, state public-utility commissions to handle.

Several states have begun retail wheeling pilot programs. Still yet, other states have adopted or proposed legislation that would permit retail wheeling. New Hampshire currently is leading the way in getting retail wheeling off and running. This state has passed a law that requires full implementation of retail wheeling for all customer classes by January 1, 1998.

While not mandating retail wheeling as yet, the state of California has been a trendsetter with a

statewide deregulation plan it has proposed. Also coming out of California is a national deregulation plan. California's plan to have direct access or retail wheeling privileges has been hampered by the state's legislature, which is still considering the plan. California's public utility commission has proposed that all customers be actively participating in direct access by the 2003.

Some other states, besides New Hampshire and California, that are actively pursuing retail wheeling initiatives include Michigan, Massachusetts, Rhode Island, and Wisconsin.

The Apex of Change: FERC Order 888

Although the foregoing discussion looks at forces shaping great change in the electric power industry, at the apex of change is FERC Order 888.

Adopted by FERC April 24, 1996, FERC Order 888 has all the power of making nonexistent the wholesale transactions consummated by the traditional electric utility industry. To be sure, that tradition, is gone—or will be in short order.

Order 888 opens wholesale power sales to competition. It requires public utilities owning, controlling, or operating transmission lines to file nondiscriminatory open access tariffs that offer others the same transmission service they provide themselves. What does FERC Order 888 hope to accomplish? In a word, competition; competition is the name of the game.

> **Adopted by FERC April 24, 1996, FERC Order 888 has all the power of making nonexistent the wholesale transactions consummated by the traditional electric utility industry.**

Specifically, the order has the following goals:

- bring lower cost power to electric consumers,

- ensure continued reliability of the electric utility industry, and

- provide for open and fair electric transmission services.

COMMODITY MARKET DEVELOPMENT

As presented earlier, electricity is a product. And, as a product, electricity is a commodity and now can be bought and sold on the open market. A bilateral physical market is fast developing and expanding into many regions in the United States.

The bilateral physical market is being accentuated with over-the-counter derivative instruments, which permit market participants to hedge price risk. The New York Mercantile Exchange launched two electricity futures contracts on March 29, 1996. Those two contracts—the Palo Verde electricity futures contract and the California-Oregon Border electricity futures contract—will be expanded to cover at least one eastern delivery point in the near future.

> **Electricity as a commodity will be marked by above-average market price volatility in relation to other exchange-traded commodities.**

All of the forces presenting changes in the electric power industry (including the development of a commodity market for electricity) will have the net effect of economically separating electricity generation from transmission and distribution. Generation will emerge from being a monopoly to being a commodity that will be exposed to risks and price volatility which is encountered by any other single commodity producer. These risks are presented later in this chapter.

According to a May 27, 1996 Fitch Investors Service special report, "Credit Perspective on Power Marketers," electricity as a commodity will be marked by above-average market price

volatility in relation to other exchange-traded commodities. Electricity price volatility, according to Fitch, will be greater than that of natural gas. This price volatility is attributed to weather-related swings in demand, unexpected outages of generating units, and transmission bottlenecks. Fitch also cited the inability to harness significant quantities of electricity as a contributor to the volatility of electricity.

The changing nature of electricity market prices will, no doubt, be a radical departure for purchasers and producers that have grown used to mandated pricing schedules and cost-of-service tariffs.

Fitch projects that cash and physical volume is likely to continue to increase with the expansion of open access transmission beyond the western market region. Further, Fitch projects that financial transactions (exchange-traded and over-the-counter derivatives) will increase at an ever faster pace, along with increased participation by financial institutions and market makers. These aforementioned developments likely will lead to an increase in counterparty risk. As volume increases and contract duration gets longer, credit risk will rise.

According to Fitch, market makers and financial intermediaries will bring with them high credit standards. Power marketers, said Fitch, will need to develop and maintain strong credit to ensure that they qualify as counterparties. In addition, utilities will be developing new skills and disciplines for handling counterparty risk. This may occur due to a default by a poorly capitalized power marketer, or even in recognition of declining and uneven credit quality in the electric utility industry itself.

CREDIT QUALITY SUCCESS FACTORS

In Fitch's special report, the firm indicates that the credit quality of electric power and even gas marketers revolves around the magnitude of

market risk. This is measured by the unhedged exposure in the marketer's portfolio and the level of counterparty credit risk relative to the marketer's capital or other financial resources. Table 21–2 lists some of the most critical credit-related factors that marketers should keep in mind in order to be and remain successful.

Table 21–2
Critical success factors for power marketers

1. Product development and marketing skills.
2. Physical capabilities to schedule, dispatch, and deliver electricity.
3. Well-developed risk management process and effective internal controls.
4. Sufficient capital and credit quality to be accepted as a counterparty on favorable terms.
5. Sufficient size and scale to absorb administrative and risk management costs and operate profitably.

Corporate Structure Dictates Risk Involved

According to Fitch, the corporate structure of a power marketer will make all the difference in how the entity will be able to absorb risks and offset losses. Also important is the amount of capital that is available to the entity.

The following lists the forms a marketer (whether power, energy, or gas) may take:

- a stand-alone company that has independent capital,

- a division of a large company, whereby the marketer enters into contracts and commitments that are binding on the corporation with full recourse to the parent company's capital,

- a nonrecourse subsidiary of a large energy corporation, gas company, or electric utility, with a limited amount of capital invested by the parent company (according to Fitch this is the most common form of marketing organization), or

- a subsidiary of a large energy corporation, gas company, or electric utility whose contractual obligations benefit from a guarantee or strong support agreement

from the corporate parent (currently, this form is rare, says Fitch).

When Fitch goes through the process of analyzing the credit of all businesses, including power and energy marketing, the three key elements it considers are (1) the overall performance and effectiveness of the business, (2) market share, and (3) profitability.

Fitch also considers the rationale of the business objectives and their fit with the company's resources. If the marketer is a subsidiary of a larger parent company and is thus dependent on the parent's financial support, then the marketer's business plan should mesh with that of the overall objectives and resources of its parent corporation.

Fitch projects that near the end of the decade, some companies will develop into retail marketers that specialize in aggregating commercial or residential consumer demands.

According to Fitch, some marketers own and control generating resources or fuel reserves. This business strategy is often that of independent power producers, gas or coal producers, or utility-affiliated marketers. Another class of marketers has as their goal that of physically controlling resources owned by others. This type of marketer earns a spread by enhancing the owners' return on the resources.

Still yet another class of marketers will focus on being a provider of risk management services. These types of services stabilize costs or returns for distributors and generators, and also serve to help customers hedge risk.

Fitch projects that near the end of the decade, some companies will develop into retail marketers that specialize in aggregating commercial or residential consumer demands.

Fitch's analysis of a power or energy marketer's credit quality also takes into consideration the marketer's reputation with customers and counterparties as well as its record of contract performance. Too, the marketer's effectiveness at product innovation and marketing is an equally important consideration when looking at credit quality as is a variety of financial measures (such as the level and stability of operating margins and cash flow).

Bigger Not Always Better

Contrary to popular belief, just because a power or energy marketer is large in size doesn't necessarily mean that it will be more profitable.

Fitch says that larger marketers well may be able to absorb costs associated with new product development, marketing, and sophisticated risk management tools; however, just the sheer fact of greater volume does not necessarily make the enterprise a better moneymaking venture than a smaller enterprise. Consolidation, according to Fitch, is already under way, when small and poorly capitalized marketers are acquired, merge into joint ventures, or in some cases, disappear altogether.

CONTROLLING AND LIMITING RISK

Policies and procedures for bringing risk under control and in managing it properly is extremely important for marketers to investigate and implement. The variety of risks energy marketers face is contained in Table 21–3.

Fitch defines risk management as a process and one that entails the ability to identify, measure, and limit exposures on a portfolio basis. Effective risk management systems should incorporate all physical transactions and commitments as well as derivative contracts.

Risk management: A process that entails the ability to identify, measure, and limit

Table 21–3
Energy marketer risks

The objective of the risk management process is to identify, measure, and mitigate the risks implicit in the marketer's business. Key risks of energy marketing include:

Price Risk: Price risk refers to a company's exposure to changes in the spot or forward price of a commodity. Market-price risk may be mitigated by hedging with physical or financial products, such as swaps, options, or futures. Sometimes the hedging transaction introduces new risks, such as basis risk or credit risk. Another form of market-price risk is the possibility that the relationship of the forward price of a commodity may vary over time relative to spot prices. The forward-price curve may change radically as a result of changes in supply or demand for the commodity.

Basis Risk: Basis risk is the risk that the price differential between a commodity at two locations or between two products will vary from the expected relationship. For example, a marketer may have a contract to deliver energy at Mid-Columbia that he has offset by a contract to purchase a like amount of energy at California Oregon Border. The hedge is not perfect because of the locational basis difference. The price differential between these two points may be hedged using an over-the-counter basis swap or by control of firm transportation capacity at a fixed price. Another form of basis risk occurs when one product is used to hedge another related, but not identical, commodity. For example, a firm may use a natural gas contract to hedge a position in electricity, perhaps because of the availability of longer term contracts in the gas market. While there is some correlation between the prices of natural gas and electricity, the relationship

between the two products is volatile, and this hedge would entail a product basis risk.

Credit Risk: Credit risk means that a counterparty to a transaction will default on its contractual obligation if the contract is unfavorable to the counterparty. If this occurs, then a risk exposure that appeared to be hedged was not actually hedged, and the firm is exposed to the underlying risk. Credit risk is typically greater in over-the-counter (OTC) or bilateral contracts; in exchange-traded instruments, the commodity exchange enforces interim market-to-market and margin requirements and undertakes settlement risk, eliminating a large part of the credit risk. Many techniques can be used to limit credit risk in OTC and bilateral contracts, including: requiring collateral upon changes in the value of a counterparty's position, monitoring limits on the total exposure to individual or related counterparties, and using contract documents that terminate future obligations to deliver or perform in the event of default by the counterparty.

Physical (or Delivery) Risk: Physical risk is the risk that the physical commodity will not be delivered when needed. It is typical in the gas and electricity markets for firm contracts for the commodity and for transportation to be priced at a premium relative to interruptible contracts. This reflects the needs of producers and distributors to minimize delivery risk.

[Reprinted with permission by Fitch Investors Service, L.P.]

---

exposures on a portfolio basis.

According to Fitch, clear and written objectives and policies are essential. These must have buy-in from senior management and the board of directors. In addition, effective management information systems are required to provide risk management reporting, update portfolio positions, and value individual positions and net portfolio exposures at least daily.

Fitch cautions that the evolutionary state of the electric power market in no way diminishes the critical need for portfolio modeling, stress testing (such as an outage of major power plants in a region or extreme weather conditions), and sensitivity analysis.

Beginning with the communication of clear objectives on the firm's intended risk exposure, the risk management process should be marked by frequent and informative reporting of open positions and risk exposures to management and the board. Table 21–4 lists some red flags that signal that there's trouble ahead in a marketer's risk management process.

Table 21–4
Red flags

1. Lack of board-approved risk guidelines and policies.
2. Portfolio exposures are not frequently marked to market.
3. Valuation models and prices cannot be independently confirmed.
4. No integrated measurement or management of physical and financial exposures.
5. No regular reporting of risk exposures and positions to senior management and the board.

[Reprinted with permission by Fitch Investors Service, L.P.]

ENERGY MARKETERS AT THE HEAD OF THE PACK

Table 21–5 provides an exhaustive listing of the current power and energy marketers that have received FERC approval. Of course, it becomes necessary to point out that there are a number of filings by companies currently awaiting approval by FERC. This listing was the latest available by production date of this book.

According to Fitch Investors Service, upwards of 200 marketers have been licensed by FERC to trade in electricity and energy at market-based prices. Table 21–6 lists some requirements FERC places on marketers.

Table 21–5

The power energy marketers: who they are

ACME Power Marketing, Inc.	AES Power, Inc.	AIG Trading Corporation
Alliance Strategies, Inc.	American National Power, Inc.	American Power Exchange Corp.
American Power Exchange, Inc.	AMOCO Power Marketing Corp.	ANP Energy Direct Company
Aquila Power Corporation*	Ashton Energy Corporation	Associated Power Services, Inc.
Audit Pro, Inc.	Bonneville Fuels Management Corp.	Boyd, Rosene & Associates, Inc.
Btu Power, Inc.	C.C. Pace Energy Services	Calpine Power Marketing
Catex Vitol Electric, Inc.	Cenerprise, Inc.*	Chicago Energy Exchange
Citizens Lehman, L.P.	Citizens Lehman Power, L.P.	CLP Hartford Sales, L.L.C.
CMEX Energy, Inc.	CNB/Olympic Gas Services	CNG Energy Services Corp.
CNG Power Services	Coastal Electric Services Co.	CoEnergy Trading Co.
Cogentrix Energy, Inc.	ConAgra Energy Services Co., Inc.	CONOCO Power Marketing, Inc.
Coral Power, L.L.C.	CRSS Power Marketing	Dartmouth Power Associates, L.P.
DC Tie	Delhi Energy Services, Inc.	Destec Energy Services Co.
Direct Access Management, L.P.	Direct Electric, Inc.	Duke Energy Marketing Corp.*
Duke/Louis Dreyfus Energy Services	Duke/Louis Dreyfus, L.L.C.*	E Prime*
Eastern Power Distribution, Inc.	Eastex Power Marketing, Inc.	Eclipse Energy, Inc.
EDC Power Marketing, Inc.	Electrade Corp.	Electric Clearinghouse, Inc.
Energy Alliance Partnership	Energy Marketing Services, Inc.	EnergyOnline, Inc.
Energy Resource Management Corp.	Energy Resource Marketing, Inc.	Energy Services, Inc.
Energy Transfer Group, L.L.C.	Energy West Power Co.	Enerserve, L.C.
Engelhard Power Marketing, Inc.	Enova Energy Management, Inc.*	Enpower, Inc.
Enron Power Marketing, Inc.	Entergy Power Marketing Corp.*	Equitable Power Services Company
Euroamerican Energy Services	Eurobrokers	Excel Energy Services, Inc.
Federal Energy Sales, Inc.	Gateway Energy Marketing	GatewayEnergy, Inc.
GED Gas Services, L.L.C.	Global Petroleum Corp.	Greenwich Energy Partners, L.P.
Gulfstream Energy, LLC	Hadson Electric, Inc.	Heartland Energy Services, Inc.*
Heath Petra Resources, Inc.	Hinson Power Co.	Howard Energy Company, Inc.
Howell Power Systems, Inc.	ICPM, Inc.	IEP Power Marketing, L.L.C.
IGI Resources, Inc.	IGM, Inc.	Illinova Power Marketing, Inc.*
Imprimis Corporation	Industrial Energy Applications*	Industrial Gas and Electric Services
InterCoast Energy Company	International Energy Co.	J Power
J. Anthony & Associates, Ltd.	J. Aron/Goldman Sachs	J.D. Loock & Associates
JEB Corporation	Jefferson Electric Marketing, Inc.	J.L. Walker & Associates
K Power Company, Inc.	Kaztex Energy Services, Inc.	KCS Energy Management Service, Inc.
KCS Energy Marketing, Inc.	Kimball Power, Inc.	KinEr-G Power Marketing, Inc.
KN Marketing, Inc.	Koch Power Services, Inc.	Kohler Company
LG&E Power Marketing, Inc.*	Louis Dreyfus Electric Power, Inc.	Market Responsive Energy, Inc.*
Mesquite Energy Services, Inc.	MG Electric Power, Inc.	Mid-American Resources, Inc.*
MidCon Power Services Corp.	Morgan Stanley Capital Group	MP Energy, Inc.
MPEX*	Multi-Energies USA, Inc.	NAP Trading and Marketing, Inc.
National Electric Associates, L.P.	National Fuel Resources, Inc.	National Power Exchange Corp.
National Power Management Co.	NFR Power, Inc.	NorAm Energy Services, Inc.
Nordic Electric, L.L.C.	Norstar Energy, L.P.	North American Energy Corp.
North American Power Brokers, Inc.	Northwest Power Marketing Co.	Ocean Energy Services, Inc.
Oxbow Power Marketing, Inc.	PacifiCorp Power Marketing, Inc.*	PanEnergy Power Service, Inc.
Paragon Gas Marketing	PennUnion Energy Services, L.L.C.	Peak Energy, Inc.
Petroleum Source & Systems Group, Inc.	Philbro, Inc.	Power Clearinghouse
Power Exchange Corporation	Powerex	PowerMark, L.L.C.
PowerNet Corp.	Power Smart, Inc.	Powertec International, L.L.P.
Prairie Winds Energy, Inc.	Premier Enterprises, Inc.	Progas Power, Inc.
Proven Alternatives, Inc.	QST Energy Trading, Inc.	Questar Energy Trading Co.
Rainbow Energy Marketing Corporation	Rig Gas, Inc.	R.J. Dahnke & Associates
Ruffin Energy Services, Inc.	SCANA Energy Marketing, Inc.*	Seagull Power Services, Inc.
Sonat Power Marketing, Inc.	Southeastern Energy Resources, Inc.	Southern Energy Marketing, Inc.
Stalwart Power Co.	Stand Energy Corporation	SuperSystems, Inc.
Superior Electric Power Corp.	Tenaska Power Services Co.	Tenneco Energy Marketing Co.
Tennessee Power Company	Texaco, Inc.	Texas-Ohio Power Marketing, Inc.
Texican Energy Ventures, Inc.	TexPar Energy, Inc.	Torco Energy Marketing, Inc.
TransAlta Corporation	TransCanada Northridge Power, Ltd.	Transco Power Trading Co.
Universal Power Services, L.L.C.	U.S. Power & Light, Inc.	Utility Management & Consulting
Utility Trade Corp.	Utility-2000 Energy Corp.	Valero Power Services Company
Vanpower, Inc.	Vantus Energy Corp.*	Vastar Power Marketing, Inc.

Table 21–5 (continued)

Vesta Energy Alternatives Co.	VTEC Energy, Inc.	WestCoast Power Marketing, Inc.
Westar Electric Marketing, Inc.	Western Gas Resource Power Marketing	Wheeled Electric Power Co.
Wholesale Power Services, Inc.*	Wickford Energy Marketing, L.C.	Wickland Power Services
Wicor Energy Services, Inc.	Williams Energy Services Company	WPS Energy Services, Inc.
WPS Power Development, Inc.	Yankee Energy Marketing Company	

Owned by an electric and/or gas utility or holding company.

Table 21–6
FERC marketer requirements

Under FERC-mandated rules and regulations, all power and energy marketers must report the following:

- changes in ownership of generation or transmission facilities,
- changes in affiliation with entities that own generation or transmission or affiliation with franchised utilities,
- changes in the arrangements involving an independent power marketer or any affiliate and the entities that buy from or sell power to the marketer, and
- transmission tariff information, which provides for comparable transmission services.

According to Fitch, the top 10 electric power marketers in terms of volume for the first quarter of 1996 are:

- Enron Power Marketing (10,159,874 MWhr)
- Citizens Lehman Power, L.P. (2,479,862 MWhr)
- Electric Clearinghouse, Inc. (2,430,478 MWhr)
- LG&E Power Marketing, Inc. (2,186,245 MWhr)
- Louis Dreyfus Electric Power, Inc. (1,550,779 MWhr)
- Koch Power Services, Inc. (1,430,955 MWhr)
- Vitol Gas & Electric, L.L.C. (1,042,127 MWhr)
- CNG Energy Services Corp. (796,138 MWhr)
- AES Power Inc. (659,808 MWhr)
- Valero Power Services Co. (587,419 MWhr)

FUTURE PROJECTIONS FOR MARKETERS

According to Fitch, despite the numerous new entrants into the power and energy marketing business, market shares will gravitate to a limited number of major players. They will be able to operate on a large enough scale to diversify portfolio risks and establish the needed risk management systems.

This limited number of players will have good product development and marketing capabilities, a solid customer reputation, and a strong capital base relative to the risks undertaken by the enterprise and the risk limits and controls employed. Fitch predicts that smaller players will specialize in the future in retail market niches and act as aggregators and resellers of services. Fitch rates the major players based on a variety of credit guidelines, many of which are contained in this chapter.

OUTLOOK: MARKET OPPORTUNITIES

An R.J. Rudden report on the profitability of competitively marketed power developed projections of the volumes of power that will be sold in the power marketplace under three alternative scenarios: high-growth, reference, and low-growth cases. The consulting firm prepared the report for a major combination gas and electric company that was considering entering the power marketing business.

According to Rudden, the characteristics that distinguish each growth scenario from the others

primarily relate to differences in assumptions as to the speed with which open access is assumed to occur, the speed with which electric utilities will cut their rates in response to competition, and customer open access participation rates.

The reference case recognizes that competition has already begun in the wholesale market, and assumes that the participation rate in this market will move rapidly toward 100% between 1995 and 2000. In the retail market, the reference case assumes:

- the California schedule for open access will be met,

- all other states in the Western Systems Coordinating Council (WSCC) will follow with open access programs of their own within two years of California, and

- all other states will open their grids in a fashion similar to California within one year of WSCC doing so.

In addition, through its report, Rudden assumed that in response to competition from power marketers, utilities would reduce their rates in the competitive markets to levels approximating marginal costs within five years of the beginning of open access in their respective markets. Rudden also assumed for the purpose of its analysis that lost utility revenue margins and resulting stranded investment costs would be recovered in one or a combination of three ways: (1) reductions in utility equity, (2) utility cost reductions from improved efficiencies, and/or (3) higher rates to customers not participating in the competitive market.

Rudden's analysis showed that by 2010, the total combined wholesale and retail market would range from between $90 billion for the low-growth case and $150 billion annually for the

high-growth case. On a cumulative basis, competitive market revenues range between $2.6 trillion and $7.0 trillion by the year 2010, with the reference case estimate being $4.2 trillion.

The report estimated average annual profit margins would range from between $1.8 billion and $3.0 billion during the market maturing years 2000 through 2010.

The report noted, however, that the profitability of transactions in individual years could vary dramatically depending upon assumed customer participation patterns and the growth case selected for the analysis.

Cumulative profits, the report showed, through 2010 range between $23 billion for the low-growth case and $37 billion for the high-growth case.

The report stated that the aggregated national results belie the potential levels of profitability within the individual North American Electric Reliability Council regions (NERC). National aggregate profit margins per unit sold peak out at between approximately 1.6 and 6.7 mills per kilowatt-hour sold. These results vary due to the region, year, and growth scenario selected. However, Rudden pointed out that the maximum profit margins per kilowatt-hour in any given year for any individual NERC region range between a low of 0.7 mills to a high of 8.4 mills.

Rudden noted that profit levels within some NERC regions reach their maximum unit values early in the study's 15-year horizon, while others reach maximum levels much later—close to 2010.

The results of the Rudden report clearly indicate that there is a reasonable set of expectations about the future profitability of the power (and energy) marketing industry. The general findings of the report should prove useful to marketers as they strategize and plan their market activities for the future.

Chapter 22
Environmental Issues

HAIL FREDIANI
RAYTHEON ENGINEERS & CONSTRUCTORS

COMPETITION VERSUS THE ENVIRONMENT

Competition and environmental protection seem at first glance to be mutually incompatible. FERC has concluded that competition born from its open access Order 888 poses no environmental threat. EPA, on the other hand, believes that a significant increase in NO_x emissions will occur at the same time that reductions are required under both Title I and Title IV of the 1990 Clean Air Act Amendments (CAAA). Economists expect that competition will lower the price of electricity. The laws of Economics 101 dictate that these lower prices will stimulate more demand, which will in turn lead to more supply. The increase in supply will require more burning of fuels, leading to more pollution.

At the same time, environmentalists push for more stringent controls. EPA is mandated to update National Ambient Air Quality Standards and to define Maximum Achievable Control Technology (MACT) for air toxics. Deregulation of access to transmission facilities appears assured, but the attempt to dismantle environmental regulations under the banner of deregulation has run into a stone wall. Streamlining regulations, and shifting from the "Command and Control" type of historical regulation to new market-based approaches are high on EPA's priority list.

Determining whether competition as the result of deregulation can coexist with sustainable development, which requires economic policies to be compatible with environmental protection, requires that we look first at the recent history of environmental regulation.

271

RECENT AIR EXPERIENCE

NAAQS

Recent air experience includes Title I requirements to reevaluate National Ambient Air Quality Standards (NAAQS). NAAQS were originally established under the 1970 Clean Air Act for so-called "criteria pollutants": particulate matter (PM), sulfur oxides (SO$_x$), carbon monoxide (CO), nitrogen oxides (NO$_x$), lead, and ozone. All of these except lead are emitted in major quantities by fossil fuel-fired power plants. Primary standards were set, based on an assessment of the risks to human health, to what was perceived at the time as levels which included a reasonable safety factor. Secondary standards were set to prevent environmental and property damage. Title I of the 1990 CAAA includes requirements for EPA to reevaluate these standards and possibly revise them.

Air quality in the United States has improved under the Clean Air Act program. Figure 22–1 indicates that, if the program had not been instituted, emissions of criteria pollutants would have been significantly higher. Even based strictly on actual emissions, reductions have been accomplished during the past 10 years except for NO$_x$, which has increased 1%. Yet, EPA estimates that about 50 million Americans still breathe air that does not meet NAAQS. They report that the NAAQS for SO$_2$ do not need revision, but that standards for both ozone and PM do. They have missed several deadlines for review and revision of those standards, but hope to publish proposed new ones by the end of 1996.

Air Toxics

Air toxics emissions regulation has been expanded greatly by Title III of the CAAA, but steam, electric-generating units greater than 25 megawatts are presently excluded from new regulation. The EPA has been concentrating on other industries in which they expect to get the greatest reductions. However, they have been performing a human health study of air toxic emissions and potential controls for utilities. The outcome of that study will determine whether they decide to go ahead and promulgate new control strategy regulations for the power industry.

Reisman (*Power-Gen Americas,* December, 1995) reports that an air toxics evaluation was required for a 16-megawatt, biomass-fired unit proposed for Soledad, California. Results of that analysis are presented in Table 22–1.

Figure 22–1. Estimated reductions in emissions of criteria pollutants

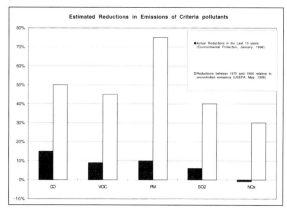

Table 22–1

Air toxic emissions from a 16-MW biomass-fired power plant

Compound	Emission Rate (lb/hr)	Offsite Concentration (ug/m³)
Antimony	0.120000000	0.080300000
Arsenic	0.000000299	0.000000200
Barium	0.000331000	0.000220000
Beryllium	0.000150000	0.000100000
Cadmium	0.001100000	0.000739000
Chromium (hex)	0.000299000	0.000200000
Cobalt	0.001500000	0.001000000
Fluorine	0.005950000	0.003990000
Mercury	0.002840000	0.001900000
Naphthalene	0.005950000	0.003990000
Nickel	0.000380000	0.000254000
Phenol	0.000004310	0.000002890
Selenium	0.120000000	0.080300000
Thallium	0.060000000	0.040200000
Zinc (as ZnCl fume)	0.006590000	0.004420000

Source: Joel I. Reisman, REA, 1995.

[Courtesy REA]

Acid Rain

Acid rain regulation has the goal of reducing SO_x and NO_x, the two main causative agents. It is estimated that 70% of the SO_x and 37% of the NO_x emissions in the United States are produced by the combustion of fossil fuels in electric power generating stations. Title VI of the CAAA intends to remove 10 million tons per year of sulfur dioxide. The SO_2 allowance trading program is in place and EPA estimates that reductions over the last five years have amounted to more than 1.7 million tons per year. These have been accomplished by utilities switching to low sulfur fuel, or installing flue-gas desulfurization systems (FGDS or scrubbers). They report that 23 million allowances have been transferred between private parties in more than 660 transactions. The vast majority of these transactions have been for the benefit of electric generating stations.

The implementation of NO_x reduction rules has been more difficult to accomplish. NO_x reduction of two million tons per year by the year 2000 is mandated under Title IV of the CAAA as part of the Acid Rain Deposition rule. Under Title I NO_x emissions reduction is required because NO_x is an ozone precursor, and reasonably available control technology (RACT) standards are to be set by state or local agencies. These are technology-based standards with the goal of reaching attainment for ozone in areas that are presently non-attainment. Under Title IV, EPA promulgated rules in Title 40, Part 76 of the Code of Federal Regulations (40 CFR 76) with the intention to "reduce the adverse effects of acidic deposition on natural resources, ecosystems, visibility, materials, and public health by reducing emissions of NO_x, a principal acidic deposition precursor."

The regulations essentially required most coal-fired plants to install low-NO_x burner (LNB) technology, a combustion control device. The original regulations were thrown out by a federal court after a suit was brought by Alabama Power Company. The rules were reissued, with the electric utility industry concurrence, in April 1995.

In spite of this rulemaking uncertainty, Woiwode (*Environmental Protection,* January, 1996) reports that out of total revenues for the air pollution control business in 1995 of $1.7 billion, $375 million or 22% of the expenditures were for NOx control.

Operating Permits

Operating permits are required under Title V of the CAAA. This program has been described as chaotic (*Pollution Engineering,* January, 1996). It is loosely modeled after the NPDES program from the water side. Instead of setting it up like the NPDES program, as a federal program administered by EPA to be taken over by individual states when they had the appropriate rules and agencies in place, the Title V program mandated that the states themselves had to set it up by a statutory deadline of November 15, 1993. EPA further compounded the problem by promulgating the 40 CFR 70 regulations governing the program eight months late. By the end of 1995, only 27 state programs had been approved by EPA.

The program requires that all major sources of air pollution must obtain a Title V permit to operate. This permit is intended to bring all of the Clean Air Act requirements for a facility into a single document. Each facility is required to perform a detailed emissions inventory, review all their existing permit requirements to make sure the new permit includes the most stringent ones, install continuous emissions monitoring systems (CEMS), include multiple operating scenarios, and certify at least once a year that they are in compliance with all of the applicable permit limits and other requirements.

At this time, virtually every power plant in the country should have submitted its application for a Title V permit. It is possible that state agencies (or local agencies where delegated) may not be able to review these documents for several years. The permits also expire in five years and thus have to be renewed, with the renewal application due at

least one year before permit expiration. Of course, the submission of each application also requires the payment of an application fee. For example, Georgia charges $25 a ton for each ton of PM, SO_x, NO_x, and VOC plus an additional $1000 for Hazardous Air Pollutants (HAPs or Air Toxics). The Soledad 16-megawatt, biomass-fired plant described in Table 22-1 would fall below the HAPs limit in Georgia. Its emissions of criteria pollutants were estimated as depicted in Table 22–2.

Table 22–2
Criteria pollutant emissions from a 16-MW biomass-fired power plant

Pollutant	Emission Rate (lbs/day)	Emission Rate (tons/year)
Particulate	76.2	13.9
NO_x	135.0	24.6
CO	337.0	61.5
ROC	20.0	3.7
SO_x	148.8	27.2
Total	717.0	130.9

Source: Joel I. Reisman, REA, 1995

[Courtesy REA]

Based on 130.9 tons per year of criteria pollutants for a period of five years, the Title V permit application fee in Georgia would be $16,362.50.

Global Warming

Global warming is a major potential environmental issue to power generators. Fully 70% of power generation in this country results from the combustion of fossil fuels. The dominant major ingredient of these fuels is carbon. Its oxidation, in the most efficient manner, produces carbon dioxide (CO_2). Scientists project an increase in CO_2 levels in the earth's atmosphere as a result of the present level of combustion, without even considering future increases. CO_2 is the one combustion by-product that cannot yet be minimized by good combustion practice, or removed by post-combustion controls.

Although scientific reports conflict about whether global warming is occurring and whether it is undesirable if it is occurring, voluntary

programs have already been started to reduce CO_2 production levels to those of 1990. The Clinton administration has committed the U.S. to this policy. A voluntary program called the Climate Challenge claims to have the participation of nearly 60% of U.S. electric utilities since its inception in 1994 (United States Energy Association, October, 1995).

A more realistic approach is being taken by the nation's largest user of coal, The Southern Company *(Atlanta Journal-Constitution,* June, 1996). Realizing that the solution to the problem is to balance CO_2 production by industry with its consumption by green plants (photosynthesis), they have funded the Smithsonian Institution's Tropical Research Institute to study the role of the tropical rain forest in removing CO_2 from the atmosphere. This is a sustainable approach, as opposed to arbitrary rollbacks which are not.

RECENT WATER EXPERIENCE

WQBELs

Recent water experience includes the implementation of water quality-based effluent limits (WQBELs). WQBELs are the water equivalent of air emission limits to achieve NAAQS. Every state has water quality limits for each water body within its territory. Much as NAAQS are based on human health and environmental protection, water quality standards are based on human and aquatic ecological health assessments. The Clean Water Act required that industrial wastewater discharges to surface water bodies be limited to achieve the desired water quality standards within those water bodies.

The permitting process was called the National Pollutant Discharge Elimination System (NPDES) and included technology-based effluent limits (TBELs) as well as WQBELs. Originally, TBELs

were published by EPA in 40 CFR 423 for the permitting agency (states if their program was approved by EPA, EPA if not) to use. At the time, there were insufficient data to document appropriate WQBELs. Therefore, the regulations called for the permitting agency to do a literature review each time they reviewed a permit application and set WQBELs on a case-by-case basis.

As research progressed, more and more constituents were documented to have lower and lower threshold levels at which organisms (aquatic inhabitants) would be adversely affected. Because each NPDES permit had to be renewed every five years, the permit writers could review the latest scientific research, and estimate new (and always lower) WQBELs. In this manner, the quality of the discharges improved over time as each facility renewed its permit to more stringent limits every five years. Today the general belief is that power plant industrial waste discharges are not a significant problem. In fact, the WQBELs have become low enough that most new power plants are proposed with so-called zero discharge systems which have no industrial wastewater discharges to surface waters.

Storm Water

Storm water discharges were perceived by EPA in the early 1990s to have become a worse problem than industrial waste discharges, as the latter were cleaned up. A massive program was initiated to issue storm water NPDES permits to municipalities and industries that were suspected of having significant quantities of pollutants in their storm water discharges. Due to the impact of EPA's National Expert on Thermal Discharges, Mr. Charles Kaplan, who was instrumental in including all potentially contaminated storm water streams from power plant sites within 40 CFR 423, the impact of storm water NPDES permitting on utilities was minimal. In most cases, it merely involved filing a Notice of Intent to be covered under a general permit, the preparation and

implementation of a Storm Water Pollution Prevention Plan (SWPPP), and the addition of a few extra NPDES sampling points. Coal and material pile runoff, and potentially oily runoff, had already been covered under the industrial NPDES permits.

Water Supply

Water supply also has been elevated to a prominent position. Although the federal government has overlooked covering this area, the occurrence of major droughts in Florida and California, and many other points between, coupled with the increasing demands for water associated with a growing population, have caused virtually every state, and many regions, to establish agencies to regulate the consumptive use of water. The virtual elimination of new once-through cooling systems by the Clean Water Act has caused most generating capacity built in the last 10 years to utilize some form of closed cycle cooling. The vast majority of these installations use wet evaporative cooling by either cooling towers or cooling ponds. The makeup requirements for these systems are significant in the scale of water supply permitting. Figure 22–2 illustrates how the consumptive use of water, on a per megawatt basis, has declined with the increasing difficulty of obtaining permits to consume water for the production of electricity.

Figure 22–2. Consumptive water use per MW

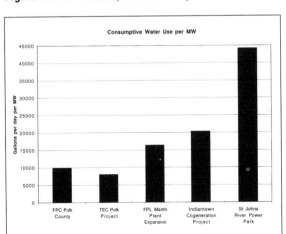

The FPC and TEC plants mentioned in the figure are under construction, the FPL and Indiantown plants have recently come on-line, and the St. Johns River Power Park came on-line in the mid-1980s.

Wetlands

Wetlands permitting has become slightly less onerous than it was in the recent past. In the late 1980s, there was a concerted effort by environmentalists to eliminate any possibility of impacting a wetland. Prior to that time, one could mitigate wetland impacts by creating or enhancing another wetland somewhere else. The idea was to make sure that there was no net loss of wetland habitat value.

The process now has evolved to where a utility actually could create a wetland ahead of time (called a wetland bank), or buy wetland credits from an external wetland bank created by someone else. They no longer must try to mitigate on-site by creating a small, isolated wetland which would have dubious ecological value even if it succeeded. Although the days are gone when one could fill in a large wetland area to create an industrial site, the days when the proposed filling of a few acres of wetlands on an existing industrial site was a fatal flaw in a project are also gone.

Solid Wastes

Other recent experience includes the handling of solid wastes produced by power generating stations. These are predominantly ash and scrubber sludge. The industry has been successful in maintaining the statutory exemption on the federal level from having to test these materials for hazardous waste characteristics under the Resource Conservation and Recovery Act (RCRA) rules. Some states have gone further and exempted ash monofills or reuse from nonhazardous portions of their solid waste regulations, while others have gone the other direction and required hazardous waste treatment of these materials even though they are exempt under the federal laws. Power plants also are still able to avoid classification of demineralizer regeneration wastes by self-neutralizing them in elementary neutralization units (ENUs) or totally enclosed treatment facilities (TETFs).

In a particularly disturbing ruling relative to RCRA, an Administrative Law Judge in Georgia decided that, even if a state incorporates a federal rule by reference, the exact same words can be interpreted differently by the state officials than by EPA. The potential ramifications of having states incorporate federal laws and then interpret the same words differently are almost limitless. None of them can be expected to be helpful to the regulated entity who, presumably, now has to meet the same rule under two different interpretations.

Storage Tank Rules

Storage tank rules also have evolved in the last few years. Originally, underground storage tank (UST) rules were designed to prevent the leakage of petroleum products into the groundwater. As UST rules became more onerous, utilities began replacing them (primarily vehicle refueling tanks) with aboveground storage tanks (ASTs). Of course, this resulted in new regulations to cover ASTs as well. Both older, oil-fired, conventional steam electric units and newer combined-cycle units are equipped with large ASTs. The latter are generally for backup fuel supplies (typically number 2 diesel). The regulation of ASTs then was expanded to cover other potentially hazardous substances stored in them. Among these substances were the acid and caustic which were present at almost every power plant for the regeneration of the ion exchange demineralizers used to prepare boiler makeup.

At about this same time, a legislative reaction to the tragic release in Bhopal, India, of methyl isocyanate (which killed approximately 4,000 people and injured an estimated 200,000) was

. . . .

E n v i r o n m e n t a l   I s s u e s

enacted. It was incorporated in the CAAA as a prevention program for releases of hazardous substances, in Section 112(r). Under this law, owners and operators of facilities regulated for hazardous substances are required to institute accidental release prevention programs. These programs involve release prevention, emergency planning, and risk management planning. The Title V permit will include a certification that a facility must comply with the rules, and the Risk Management Plan will be part of the Title V permit. These rules affect hazardous substances rather than hazardous wastes, which means a spill need not be covered; the material must be on-site. The rules are relatively onerous but don't fully go into effect at power plants until 1999. The most likely materials that will fall under these rules at a power plant are chlorine and ammonia.

EPCRA

EPCRA (Emergency Planning and Community Right-to-Know Act) has been in effect for about seven years. It requires industry to inform federal, state, and local agencies about OSHA hazardous materials that are used or stored on-site in quantities above a minimum threshold, and to provide them with material safety data sheets (MSDS) for each one. At a power plant, this includes such materials as gasoline, diesel fuel, and fuel oil.

Companies are required to file a Toxic Release Report for each chemical on-site, and notify the State Emergency Response Commission (SERC) and the Local Emergency Planning Committee (LEPC) whenever there has been a release of such materials in excess of a statutory reportable quantity (RQ) to the environment. Among the more obscure portions of the act are requirements that the facility notify the SERC that it is subject to the emergency planning requirements of EPCRA, and that it notify the LEPC of the designation of a person to be the facility emergency coordinator who will participate in their local planning.

Self-Auditing

Self-auditing has become a popular tool throughout industry to maintain compliance and to anticipate potential problem areas. As part of the recent worldwide trend toward deregulation of the power industry, the concept of an Environmental Management System (EMS) has arisen to enable international companies to demonstrate to governments that are unfamiliar with them that they are environmentally responsible. The institution and systematic accomplishment of internal environmental audits is a large part of such efforts, in particular ISO 14000. The problem arose in the litigious United States that, if an internal audit discovers a noncompliance, that information is required to be disclosed to the regulatory agency that has the power to fine the noncomplier. Even worse, the information is public knowledge which anyone who feels injured by the noncompliance can use to sue the reporting company. Companies are understandably reluctant to perform such self-audits if the results are to be used against them. That goes against our strong belief in the right to avoid self-incrimination.

Renewable Energy

Proponents of renewable energy sources such as wind, geothermal, solar, and biomass-fired generating stations have been trying to make these alternatives economical by pursuing technological advances that will reduce their costs enough to enable them to compete with the established generating technologies. Unfortunately for them, the price of electricity generated by the nuclear and fossil fuel-fired stations has been dropping faster than they can keep up. With deregulation and increased competition coming, renewables are unlikely to be able to compete without some form of government price support. Such support seems unlikely in the present atmosphere of market-based approaches.

THE FUTURE

Based on all the above information, what does the future hold for the power industry? As previously mentioned, competition requires economic optimization while sustainable development requires environmental protection. The assertions by EPA and FERC have actually assumed the wrong direction for the process. Instead of fearing that environmental protection will be reduced by the advent of economic competition, it is much more likely that economic competition will be limited by environmental protection. No one is proposing the slightest relaxation in environmental protection, only in the administration of that protection by cumbersome regulation. Anyone who has gone through a streamlining of environmental rules will have observed that none of the existing limitations were done away. If there are two limits for the same release, under two different rules, the streamlining will keep the more stringent of the two. If the rules are slightly different, the streamlined result will incorporate all of the special cases addressed by both rules. The same principle applies no matter how many rules affect the release. So the real question is not which economic optimization will damage the environment, but which environmental optimizations will allow the most economic benefit.

Gauntlett and Pierce (*Power-Gen Americas,* December, 1995) proposed the following areas of potential environmental optimization to be part of a utility's EMS:

Heat Rate Improvement. Reductions in heat rate (the number of Btus expended to generate each kilowatt-hour of electricity) improve both economic and environmental performance. They result in less consumption of fuel and less generation of air emissions and solid waste. Heat rate improvement is an area in which utilities will invest time and money.

Productive Utilization of Residuals.

Utilities generally promote utilization of ash and scrubber sludge for productive use in other industries. They will pursue more aggressive marketing in the future to eliminate disposal costs or convert them to revenue sources. They also will seek markets for other wastes such as water treatment sludges and wastewaters.

Environmental Process Optimization. Improvements in processes such as the FGDS will reduce the consumption of ingredients like limestone, and the production of waste products such as sludge. Past emphasis has been more in the area of assuring compliance with permitting requirements, with economic optimization as a secondary goal. As an example, dry scrubbing eliminates the need for scrubber blowdown, thereby reducing wastewater treatment costs.

Wastewater Recycle/Reuse. The cost of wastewater treatment increases as WQBELs are lowered, and the securing of water supplies becomes more difficult and expensive as competing water uses grow. The recycle of wastewater has already become the economic choice for new generation in some parts of the country. This trend will continue in the future. New technologies utilize waste heat from the steam or water side of the condenser, instead of expensive auxiliary power, to evaporate residual wastewaters left over from the recovery of usable water.

Market-Based Approaches

Market-based approaches will be the future direction of environmental protection. They will follow the precepts of the Plantwide Applicability Limit (PAL) concept included in the EPA's proposed remake of the New Source Review (NSR) program. Instead of EPA trying to command the exact concentration of each pollutant in each emission source, the PAL would set an overall emission limit for the facility, and leave it up to the owner to determine the best economic choice of how to control each source. The theory is that the free enterprise system will allow the owner to

optimize selection of control technologies, and the emission rates to the environment will still be acceptable. This concept has also been called the bubble concept.

The same approach has been proposed for the water side, in that a facility's releases to a watershed could meet an aggregate limit for each constituent of its wastewater discharges, without having to individually meet differing criteria for each individual waste stream before commingling (mixing) them. The watershed approach goes one step farther by proposing a credit system, similar to the sulfur dioxide credit system under the acid rain program. If another discharger to the same watershed can reduce its discharge more cheaply than you, it would be free to do so and accrue credits that you could then buy in lieu of treating your own discharge. The net result is that the river sees the same reduction in pollutants, but the industry sees lower costs.

EPA has also proposed a similar credit system to help reduce the emission rates of NOx and VOCs to try and reduce ground-level ozone concentrations. This market-based approach actually would reduce the concentrations below existing levels because it would retire 10% of the reduction credits whenever a purchase takes place. This program is also patterned after the sulfur dioxide credit system, and would be expected to help reduce acid rain deposition as well because of the NOx reduction portion.

Coal and Natural Gas

Coal and natural gas still will be the fuels of choice for the foreseeable future. How they will compare economically will be a function of how they compare environmentally. It comes down to the question of whether coal-fired plants can be economically controlled so that their emissions are as acceptable as those from gas-fired units. According to the Utility Data Institute (*Power Engineering,* June, 1996), the 10 lowest cost electricity producers in the United States for the period 1990-1994 were all coal-fired plants, with

the lowest having costs less than one cent per kilowatt-hour. This is a powerful incentive for the continued use of coal. The question that has to be answered is whether cheap coal can be cleaned to compete with natural gas environmentally without becoming too expensive.

Figures 22–3 and 22–4 were prepared from information supplied by Florida Power Corporation as part of their application to permit a new power plant site in 1993. The information included estimated emissions from pulverized coal-fired (PC) units with 95% sulfur removal by wet scrubbers and LNB, from synthetic coal gas-fired combined-cycle (CGCC) units with 98.5% sulfur removal in the gasification process, from fuel oil-fired combined-cycle (FOCC) units using fuel with sulfur content of .05%, and from natural gas-fired combined-cycle (NGCC) units.

Figure 22–3. NOx (lbs/MW-hr)

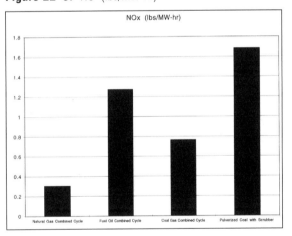

Figure 22–4. SO₂ (lbs/MW-hr)

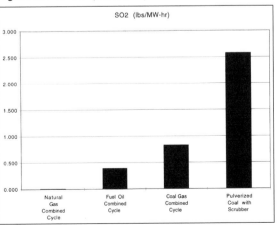

Figure 22–3 shows NO$_x$ emissions from the four types of units normalized to pounds emitted for each megawatt-hour of electricity generated. Assuming a utility needs to install capacity to generate a fixed number of megawatts, they will have to permit about five times the NO$_x$ emissions for conventional PC units with low NO$_x$ burners, about four times with FOCC units, and about three times with CGCC units, all relative to NGCC units. These numbers also indicate that, to lower their NO$_x$ emissions to compete with natural gas, the PC units need to add 80% more removal, the FOCC units about 75% removal, and the CGCC units about 67% removal. Since SCR has been demonstrated to achieve NO$_x$ removals in the 90% range in Japan and Germany, one concludes that coal-fired units can compete environmentally with gas on a NO$_x$ basis.

Assuming that regulations are restructured along the PAL idea previously presented, and a generator could avoid NSR by offsetting new generation by retiring older units, the information in Figure 22–3 can be interpreted from an offset standpoint. A new, natural gas-fired unit could be four times larger than a retired, fuel oil-fired unit, five times larger than a PC-fired unit, and three times larger than a coal gas-fired unit. Also, a new, coal gas-fired unit could be twice as large as a retired PC unit, and about 50% larger than an oil-fired one.

Figure 22–4 shows the pounds emitted per megawatt-hour of electricity generated for SO$_2$ assuming the same four types of generating unit. The advantage for natural gas is much larger than it was for the NO$_x$ case. For the same megawatts,

FOCC units emit about 100 times more SO$_2$ than NGCC units, CGCC units emit about 200 times more, and PC units about 650 times more. These estimates are for FOCC firing .05% sulfur fuel, and for PC units with 95% effective FGDS.

From the offset standpoint, a new 1000-megawatt NGCC unit would only require shutting down 1.6 megawatts of PC capacity, five megawatts of CGCC capacity, or 10 megawatts of FOCC capacity. Similarly, retiring 100 megawatts of PC capacity could provide offsets for 300 megawatts of CGCC capacity.

Based on the above analysis, it appears that unless a major breakthrough in sulfur removal from coal occurs, coal cannot compete environmentally with natural gas on an SO$_2$ basis. However, coal gasification can so compete with PC.

Self-Audit Immunity

Self-audit immunity has been sought and partially achieved by industry in several state jurisdictions, and with EPA on a policy basis. The arguments in favor of this policy all ignore the fact that the initial premise is that a facility is in violation of some environmental law, and that they realize that the violation is occurring before anyone else does. Look for environmental groups to challenge immunity in court and win on this basis.

The true analogy would be to a defendant who pleads guilty and throws himself on the mercy of the court. Although there may be extenuating circumstances, the point is that he is guilty.

Conclusion

BOB SMOCK
PUBLISHER
POWER GROUP MAGAZINES

The outlook for the global electric power industry is bright. Economies in many of the world's poorer nations are beginning to develop and electric power is at the heart of the infrastructure improvement that must be done first. Electric power industries in the developed western economies are being deregulated and privatized, opening new opportunities for improved efficiency, lower costs, and increased market penetration for electricity.

Electricity is already the most favored form of energy consumption. It will account for one-half of end-use energy consumption some time in the next century.

This *Electric Power Industry Outlook* has provided the reader with an overview of worldwide electric supply and demand by region, a review of fuels and technologies, and a look at regulatory developments.

Worldwide demand for new electric power generating capacity should average about 100 GW a year for the near future. Over the next 10 years,

the largest concentration of new capacity development will be in Asia, which will account for about 40% of the world total. Europe, east and west, and the Mideast will account for about 25% of new world capacity, and the Americas, north and south, for another 25%.

On a technology basis, new steam turbine capacity will account for about 40% of the new generating capacity; combined cycles, 25%; simple-cycle gas turbines, 10%; and hydro, 20%.

PRIVATIZATION STIMULATES DEMAND

Privatization of electric power generation is stimulating this demand for new capacity in both the developed and developing world. In the developing countries privatization unlocks the potential for outside investment and participation

by the world-class players in power project development to meet pent-up demand.

In the developed countries, privatization and increased competition are stimulating demand for new, low-cost, efficient, power generating facilities. For example, the United Kingdom is one of the most interesting countries in the world from the viewpoint of the electric power industry. Its privatization and competition-enhancing moves have served as a model for the rest of the world, specifically New Zealand, Australia, Canada, Argentina, and the United States. Six years ago the U.K. had a state-owned bulk power system built around its Central Electricity Generating Board. The U.K. electric system was privatized in 1990, virtually overnight. Two large, privately owned generating companies, Power Gen and National Power, were created. A privately owned electrical transmission system called the National Grid was also created, as were a group of privately owned electrical distribution companies.

The U.K. also created a wholesale bulk power pool that links the generating companies and distribution companies which must bid into the pool for supply or service for the next day. The supply side is open to any generators, including independent producers who can match or beat the market-clearing price. In addition, there is direct access between buyers and sellers of electricity, originally for buyers larger than one megawatt, now 100 kW, and by 1998 all consumers.

Since privatization, real (inflation-adjusted) industrial electricity prices in the U.K. have dropped 17%. Real retail prices are down 11%. Surveys of consumer reaction show complaints, but no one wants to go back. The U.K. privatization and competition experience has been a success.

It's turned the U.K., which has a relatively slow-growing economy, into a thriving market for new generating capacity. Old, high-cost capacity is being shut down, and new, low-cost, natural gas-fired combined-cycle capacity is being built. Independent generators are being attracted to the U.K. by the pool market-clearing price.

Privatization and competition have energized the U.K. electricity market and they promise to do the same on a larger scale as other electric systems move in the same direction.

PROBLEMS IN THE UNITED STATES

Focusing on the U.S. market, one realizes that trouble is brewing. The move to electric utility deregulation, restructuring, and competition has caused paralysis on the part of most companies. They eventually should energize the market, but at the moment they have paralyzed it because the new rules are not yet clear. The United States did not change overnight as did the U.K. As a result, virtually no new generating or power delivery capacity has been added to the U.S. system for the past two years. Planning has come to a standstill.

In July 1996, a dozen western states were hit by a cascading electrical system failure that started at one transmission entity and spread, uncontrolled, throughout the west. Almost exactly the same thing happened 18 months previously. The electrical system is being strained beyond its capacity. Electricity demand is growing steadily in the United States. Consumption of electrical energy and power has been increasing at an annual rate of 2–3%, right along with economic growth. With consumption growing and facilities stagnating, the United States is using up capacity margins and is heading for problems.

Electric power generating reserve margins in the United States are getting low. In the 1990s, U.S. utility, summer-peak demand climbed from 546 GW to more than 600 GW. Over that same period, generating capacity grew from 691 GW to only 705 GW. The reserve margin dropped from 21% to less than 15%. There is little new capacity in the U.S. construction pipeline. Simple-cycle gas turbines can be added quickly to handle short-term peaks, but that will not be enough.

The United States is asking for trouble. Utilities are cutting service to customers due to capacity shortages. The New England Power Pool warned of possible capacity shortfalls in the summer of 1996.

Some say the United States does not need a reserve margin of 15%. Some say 10% is plenty. At the current rate of demand and capacity growth, the United States will be at 10% reserve margin within a year or two. Zero reserve margin is not too far away.

U.S. utilities are not only ignoring new construction, but are ignoring existing capacity, too. For example, there have been no applications for extension of nuclear plant operating licenses which are issued for 40 years. The oldest nuclear plants are approaching the end of their licensed lives. In its latest Annual Energy Outlook, the U.S. Department of Energy assumes that no nuclear plants will operate past their 40-year licensed lives. If that happens, the U.S. will lose 37 GW of existing generating capacity by the year 2015. The situation is similar with fossil-fired capacity. Utilities are spending little to maintain, upgrade, or repower aging fossil-fired power plants.

DOE assumes that utilities will repower or extend the life of 268 GW of existing fossil-fired generating capacity at an average cost of $260 per kW. DOE says utilities must refurbish 770 coal-fired generating units, 172 gas-fired units, and 74 oil-fired units. So far, U.S. utilities have shown little inclination to spend that money. The need is clear for both new and existing capacity. Utilities surely will begin the capital improvement program soon, but at the moment there is no sign of it.

GLOBAL GROWTH MARKETS

Asia is the hot market for new capacity today, as is thoroughly discussed in the preceding pages. The two regions that promise to develop as the next growth markets are Eastern Europe and Latin America.

As mentioned in our review of electricity demand in Europe and Russia, there are a few bright spots in that region which lead to optimism. Four countries in Eastern Europe look particularly promising: the Czech Republic, Slovakia, Hungary, and Poland. These countries are doing the best job of shedding their controlled-economy heritage and are moving toward market economies. The picture is not as optimistic in most of the other countries formerly controlled by the Soviet Union, including Russia.

The market in these countries will probably first develop as a power facility upgrade market. Construction of significant amounts of new capacity will follow the upgrade trend. Old generating plants and power delivery facilities will be modernized and repowered using western technology and expertise.

Several nuclear power plants in Eastern Europe have already been upgraded with modern, electrical-process control systems. Old, coal-fired power plants have been repowered with new, fluidized-bed boilers and modern pollution control systems.

Latin America is less predictable. Argentina is one of the world leaders in privatization and adoption of competition in electrical markets. Brazil is one the largest, most populous, and resource-rich countries in the world. Mexico's growing economic ties to the United States through the North American Free Trade Agreement hold great promise for that country's economic growth.

Some new capacity construction has begun in South America, but only time will tell if this region develops to its full potential.

Other major regions of the world, notably Africa, still show little sign of major growth of their electrical industries.

ELECTRIC VEHICLES

One of the great unknowns for worldwide electricity demand growth is the future of electric

vehicles. There are signs of activity in the United States, but there have been signs of a takeoff before and nothing happened.

Interest in electric vehicles in the United States is focused on California and a few states in the northeast which have mandated that automobile producers supply a certain percentage of pollution-free vehicles by certain dates, as early as 1998. The only way manufacturers can meet these requirements, and protect their markets, is by selling a small, but growing, number of electric vehicles in those states.

Auto manufacturers in the United States say the requirements are unreasonable, that electric vehicles cost too much, that battery technology is not good enough. However, they are preparing to supply commercial electric vehicles in the United States in 1998. Electric utilities in California and other states are preparing infrastructure to support EVs, such as charging stations and off-peak price schedules.

As mentioned earlier, electricity penetration of end-use energy consumption is expected to reach 50% in the near future. Widespread adoption of electric vehicles would push that much higher, however. Transportation is the major energy consumption market that has not seen any significant penetration by electricity. (The only other significant one is space heating, where electricity has a foothold with heat pump technology.)

Significant penetration of the transportation market by electricity would change all the predictions and forecasts in this outlook. It is difficult to guess at the impact such a development would have.

FUEL SUPPLY OUTLOOK

Our chapter on fuels shows that the global power industry is headed toward a major increase in natural gas as a power generation fuel and a corresponding decrease in nuclear energy over the next 20 years. Coal, the fuel with the largest

market share at about 35%, is assumed to stay about the same level. Those forecasts are based on current fuel price relationships and environmental standards.

We should be prepared for the possibility of major shifts in those forecasts. The aftermath of the Arab Oil Boycott of 1973 and the huge increase in all fuel costs, even uranium, showed us how vulnerable fuel prices and supply are to disruptive, difficult-to-predict events.

The fuel situation is not stable. Prices could fluctuate tremendously. Availability assumptions could turn out to be wrong. Environmental factors could produce major changes. For example, a crackdown on carbon dioxide emissions in the name of preventing global warming could reduce coal's share of electrical energy. That would put tremendous pressure on all the other energy sources and probably result in major price increases for the other fossil fuels and uranium.

A revival of OPEC could upset the fuel marketplace. Can natural gas really meet the forecasted demand? The only effective way to deliver natural gas is by medium-length pipelines. Attempts to move it long distances (in a global perspective), such as liquefied natural gas in ocean-going tankers, have never been particularly successful. Will these transportation limits keep natural gas from meeting the forecasts?

NUCLEAR POWER

The assumption that nuclear power will play a diminished role is also open to question. Vulnerability of fossil fuels to environmental problems, real or imagined, such as acid rain and global warming make it difficult to predict the future of nuclear power with assurance.

Vulnerability of nuclear power to another Chernobyl-like disaster also makes it difficult. Nuclear power could go either way. At present and for the near future, Asian countries such as Japan, South Korea, Taiwan, and China are keeping the nuclear option alive for the rest of the world. They have decided to make nuclear power a part of their electrical energy mix and have aggressively moved to order and construct nuclear power plants.

Going even further, the Asians and particularly the Japanese have moved nuclear technology forward by encouraging the development of advanced designs and by ordering them. World power generators owe these Asian nations a debt for having the courage to move forward with nuclear power in the face of its problems in the West.

If global warming becomes a serious issue, we're going to need a lot more nuclear energy than we are currently planning.

RENEWABLES

The only renewable source of energy that can be relied on is the old standby, hydroelectricity. There are opportunities in many countries for significant hydroelectric development. That opportunity is not just in developing nations. Quebec, for example, has been eager to develop hydroelectric resources in the James Bay region for many years and export the energy to the United States.

Other renewables offer little promise for significant contribution to world electricity needs because costs are too high. Subsidies are the only hope for developing these technologies, and the trend toward competitive, low-cost-producer electricity is not favorable for subsidized renewables.

GAS TURBINE RELIABILITY

Natural gas is the fuel of the future for the world electricity generation industry and the gas turbine-based combined-cycle is the technology we're betting on to use that natural gas. Combined-cycle generating plants are approaching 60% thermal efficiency now and promise to go even higher. No other thermal power plant technology can approach that efficiency. Coupled with natural gas's low cost and environmental advantages, it's easy to see why this combination is a favorite for electricity suppliers.

However, a cloud has appeared on the gas turbine horizon. There were some failures of machines in 1995 that led some to doubt about the viability of the technology. The doubt was fueled by the rapid advances in gas turbine technology in the late 1980s and early 1990s. First-stage turbine inlet temperatures rose from less than 2000 F to 2350 F and are headed for 2500 F in the next generation, which manufacturers say will be available in a few years. These high temperatures require sophisticated jet engine technology such as cooled turbine blades.

The rash of failures in 1995 led some users and insurers to believe that gas turbine designers have gone too far. However, it has been the editorial position of *Power Engineering* magazine that there is no reason to lose faith. If power engineers take a close look at what is really happening with gas turbines, they will see the problems are within the norms for any rapidly advancing technology. Debugging is the price that must be paid for any significantly advanced design, and gas turbine manufacturers have taken the lead in advancing the design of commercially-available generation technologies.

Many of the recent gas turbine problems appeared to have little to do with the new technology, but some did. Some gas turbine types suffered more than others, but the problems were widespread. Suppliers and operators are working together closely to solve the problems. Solutions, for the most part, already have been put in place or are in hand. None of the problems appear to be showstoppers.

Gas turbines, in simple-cycle and combined-cycle form, have been the dominant form of new technology ordered in the world power generation market for at least the last five years. Simple-cycle gas turbines and combined-cycle

plant orders have been running at the rate of about 30 GW a year. That rate will increase if the predictions for new capacity are to be met. There's no real reason to think that gas turbine technology is not up to the challenge.

COAL GASIFICATION

One of the more interesting technical developments in recent years is the acceptance and commercial success of solid-fuel gasification. This is a key technology for linking solid fuels such as coal with the gas turbine and combined cycle, which can not burn fuels in solid form.

The petroleum industry started using gasification plants to burn solid waste fuels such as petroleum coke in combined-cycle plants showing significant numbers in recent years. This is the commercial breakthrough for gasification, at long last after decades of development work.

Prior attempts to gasify solid fuels have concentrated on coal, and that still seems to hold the most promise for the long term. Coal gasification will tie together our most abundant, lowest cost, and most easily transported fossil fuel with the highest-efficiency thermal power plant technology.

ENERGY MARKETING

The U.K. has shown the way for many national and regional power markets to open up to competition. The United States is moving in that direction and, at 10 times the size of the U.K. market, promises to pioneer competitive power production and trading on a large scale.

As described in our chapter on energy marketing changes, federal law opened the door for more electricity sales among utilities and the wholesale market. Changes in state regulation are opening the door for competition at the retail level.

Wholesale electricity trading in the United States is equal to about 25% of the retail market. The 1996 changes in federal rules opening up access to the high-voltage transmission system are expected to increase that level of wholesale trading significantly.

However, the U.S. transmission system was not built to support a much higher level of activity. Advocates of competitive electricity marketing claim there is substantial excess transfer capacity on most lines that can support the increased trading. However, there is no sound basis for that assumption.

It is likely that a small increase in trading can be accommodated with existing facilities, and then the limits will be reached: thermal limits, reliability limits, and safety limits.

A massive transmission system construction program will be needed in the United States to support the new, more competitive wholesale market that is unfolding. The same is true for the competitive retail market that is coming. Without significant new transmission capacity, retail buyers will be limited to local suppliers and will remain tied to local cost structures. The retail electricity price variation in the United States is approximately 10 to 1, so there is great incentive to reach distant, low-cost suppliers.

There must be other significant changes in the way the transmission system is designed and operated to support a massive increase in electric trading. For example, sophisticated control systems must be installed. Most of the high voltage systems in the United States feature free-flowing ties governed only by Kirchhoff's Laws. High-voltage, solid-state power control systems are being developed and must be adopted on a widespread basis. Much more sophisticated VAR, voltage, and frequency support must be installed. A massive transmission system upgrade and construction program is almost inevitable.

Another tricky issue is the unbundling of ancillary services such as spinning reserve and VAR support so that they can be procured competitively and priced separately. This is a completely new concept in the control and

operation of the U.S. power system and will be difficult to develop. These complexities will probably slow the headlong rush toward competitive power in the United States, but they will not stop it. As in the U.K., there undoubtedly will be a lot of problems and a lot of complaining, but no one will want to give up new choices and go back to the old system.

ENVIRONMENTAL REGULATIONS

The environmental movement has been somewhat on hold in the 1990s, particularly in the United States. Globally, the rush to develop economies in Asia and Eastern Europe has also pushed environmental concerns aside to some extent. That is going to change. Considerable pressure is building to deal with new environmental issues. Global warming is the main worldwide issue, and its potential impact on fuel consumption and power generation technology choices has been discussed earlier.

Another boundaryless environmental problem is the EMF issue, fear of electrical and magnetic fields near electrical facilities such as transmission lines. The EMF scare is largely caused by academic reports from investigators who link exposure to electric or magnetic fields, or simple proximity to transmission lines or electrical substations, to diseases such as cancer.

Lawsuits in litigious countries such as the United States are multiplying, using those academic studies as evidence. So far, the U.S. electrical industry has successfully defended itself, but the cost is rising. Lawmakers and regulators in most countries have not imposed regulations on electrical systems to prevent EMF that are more stringent than good engineering design practice, but that could easily change in coming years.

Other environmental issues are building up momentum, particularly in the United States. The U.S. Congress enacted a comprehensive federal environmental law in 1990 called the Clean Air Act Amendments that has had a profound effect on the power industry. Major impact was through the law's acid rain reduction provisions that call for power generators to reduce emissions of sulfur dioxide by approximately one-half by the year 2000, then cap the emissions at that level. The law required power generators to take an interim step in sulfur dioxide emission reduction in 1995. The law allowed generators to trade emission rights, and it set a legislative price level of $1500 per ton of sulfur dioxide emissions per year.

Power generators overachieved the 1995 emission reduction goal by a wide margin and at a cost of less than $100 a ton. The acid rain program has been such a success in the United States that the Environmental Protection Agency now says emissions should be cut in half again by the year 2010. Power generators feel they are being punished for doing well.

Other environmental issues facing U.S. power producers are hazardous air pollutants (particularly mercury), nitrogen oxide emission reductions to solve ground level ozone problems, and reductions in emissions of particulate matter smaller than 10 microns. All of these are likely to be the subject of new, strict regulations in the next few years.

The ozone issue is potentially the most severe. Most U.S. cities violate federal air quality standards for a class of pollutants collectively called ozone. According to the EPA, nitrogen oxide is one of the major precursors for ozone and the power generation industry is one of the major emitters of nitrogen oxides. Auto emissions are also a source of nitrogen oxide emissions, but EPA has made it clear that it plans to focus on the power industry. Tighter limits on these emissions are sure to come, and sure to come soon. Environmental regulation worldwide is likely to follow a similar trend toward tighter emission limits, although the level of regulation varies widely and the focus differs greatly.

We hope this overview of the world power industry has provided you with the information you need. We will be updating this publication

regularly, so please let us know if there are areas we missed or there are subjects on which you want more information.

Readers who would like to get a closer look at the worldwide electric power markets should consider attending PennWell Publishing Company's global family of power industry conferences. For 1997 we are planning:

- DistribuTECH in San Diego in January, covering utility automation technology and applications in the United States

- Arab Electricity in Manama, Bahrain in March

- Central and Eastern European Power Industry Forum in Warsaw in March

- American Power Conference in Chicago in April

- POWER-GEN Europe and Power Delivery Europe in Madrid in June

- POWER-GEN Asia, Power Delivery Asia, and DA/DSM Asia in Singapore in September

- EnergyMart Americas in Chicago in October

- Independent Energy Forum in New York in October

- POWER-GEN International and Power Delivery Americas in Dallas in November

- China Electric Power Industry Forum '97 TBA

- EnergyMart Asia, TBA

- EnergyMart Europe, TBA

- POWER-GEN Latin America, TBA.

For more information on these events call PennWell Conferences and Exhibitions, Houston, 713-621-8833.

Atlas

WSCC
Western Systems Coordinating Council

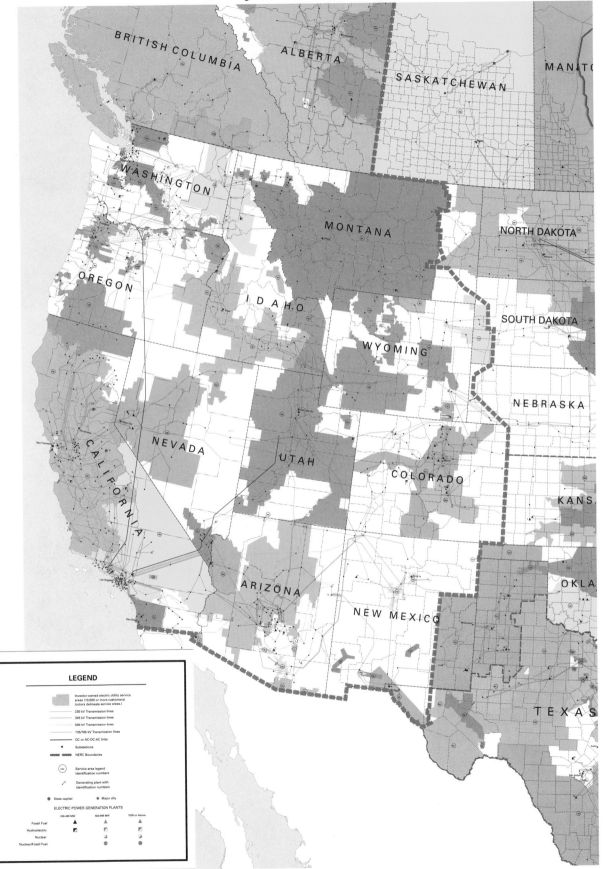

LEGEND

Investor-owned electric utility service areas (10,000 or more customers) (colors delineate service areas.)

230 kV Transmission lines
345 kV Transmission lines
500 kV Transmission lines
735/765 kV Transmission lines
DC or AC-DC-AC links
Substations
NERC Boundaries

Service area legend identification numbers

Generating plant with identification numbers

State capital   Major city

ELECTRIC POWER GENERATION PLANTS

	200-499 MW	500-999 MW	1000 or Above
Fossil Fuel			
Hydroelectric			
Nuclear			
Nuclear/Fossil Fuel			

ELECTRIC POWER INDUSTRY OUTLOOK AND ATLAS

SPP
Southwest Power Pool

/

ERCOT
Electric Reliability Council of Texas

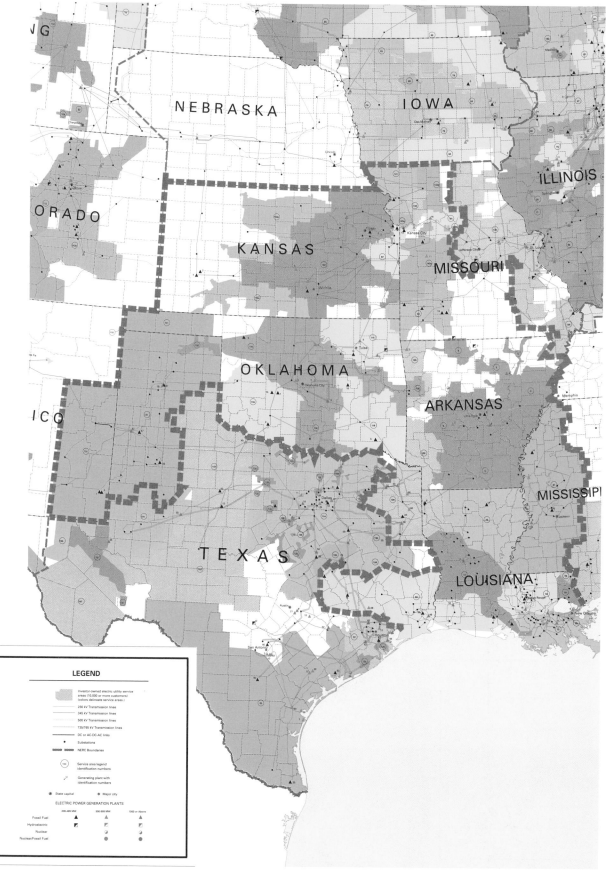

MAPP
Mid-Continent Area Power Pool

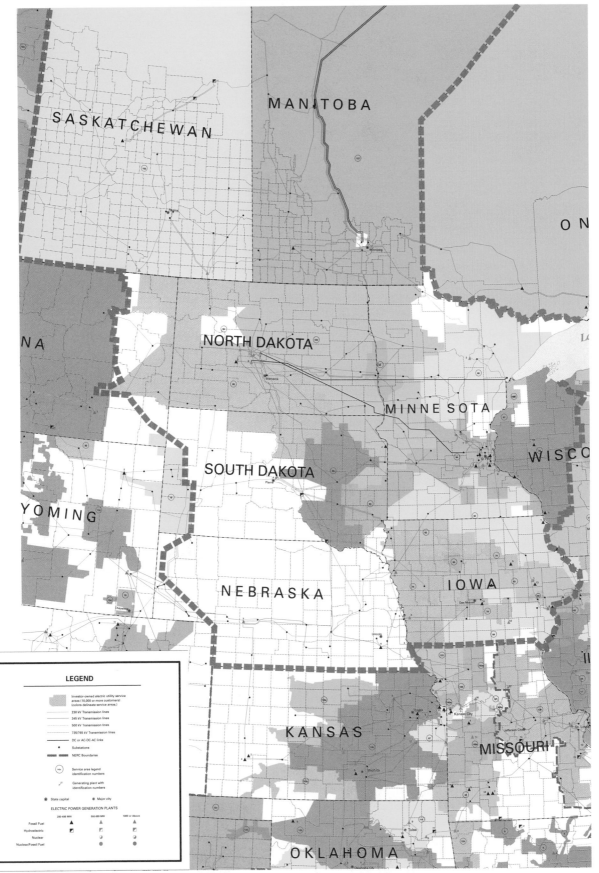

SASKATCHEWAN

MANITOBA

ONTARIO

NORTH DAKOTA

MINNESOTA

WISCONSIN

SOUTH DAKOTA

WYOMING

NEBRASKA

IOWA

ILLINOIS

KANSAS

MISSOURI

OKLAHOMA

LEGEND

Investor-owned electric utility service
areas (10,000 or more customers)
(colors delineate service areas.)

——— 230 kV Transmission lines

——— 345 kV Transmission lines

——— 500 kV Transmission lines

——— 735/765 kV Transmission lines

——— DC or AC-DC-AC links

• Substations

▬▬ NERC Boundaries

⬭ Service area legend
identification numbers

⤴ Generating plant with
identification numbers

⊛ State capital   ⊛ Major city

ELECTRIC POWER GENERATION PLANTS

	200-499 MW	500-999 MW	1000 or Above
Fossil Fuel	▲	▲	▲
Hydroelectric	◨	◨	◨
Nuclear		●	●
Nuclear/Fossil Fuel		●	●

MAIN
Mid-America Interconnected Network

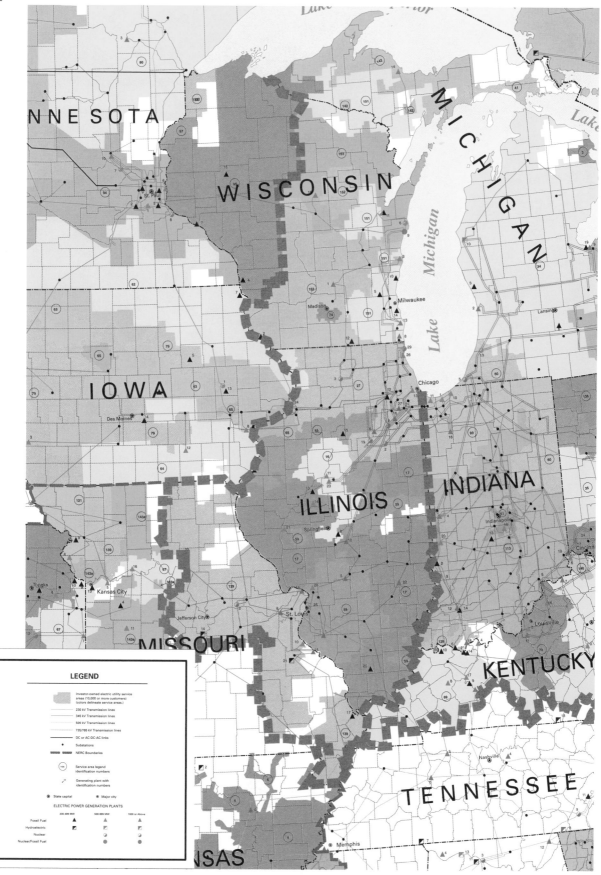

LEGEND

Investor-owned electric utility service
areas (10,000 or more customers)
(colors delineate service areas.)

230 kV Transmission lines
345 kV Transmission lines
500 kV Transmission lines
735/765 kV Transmission lines
DC or AC-DC-AC links
• Substations
NERC Boundaries

(14k) Service area legend
identification numbers

Generating plant with
identification numbers

● State capital ● Major city

ELECTRIC POWER GENERATION PLANTS

	200-499 MW	500-999 MW	1000 or Above
Fossil Fuel			
Hydroelectric			
Nuclear			
Nuclear/Fossil Fuel			

ECAR
East Central Area Reliability Coordination Agreement

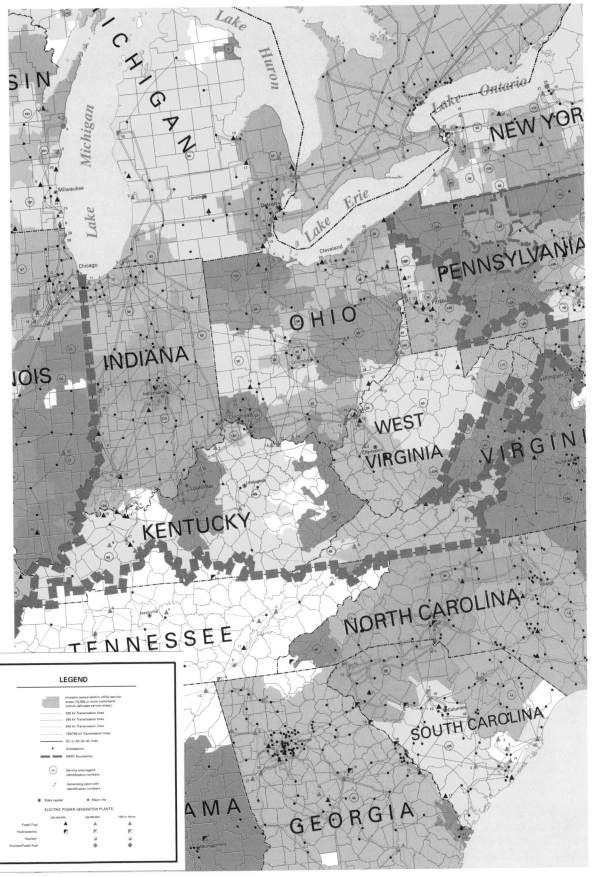

LEGEND

Investor-owned electric utility service areas (10,000 or more customers) (colors delineate service areas.)

230 kV Transmission lines

345 kV Transmission lines

500 kV Transmission lines

735/765 kV Transmission lines

DC or AC-DC-AC links

• Substations

NERC Boundaries

Service area legend identification numbers

Generating plant with identification numbers

◉ State capital   • Major city

ELECTRIC POWER GENERATION PLANTS

	200-499 MW	500-999 MW	1000 or Above
Fossil Fuel	▲	▲	▲
Hydroelectric			
Nuclear			
Nuclear/Fossil Fuel			

SERC
Southeastern Electric Reliability Council

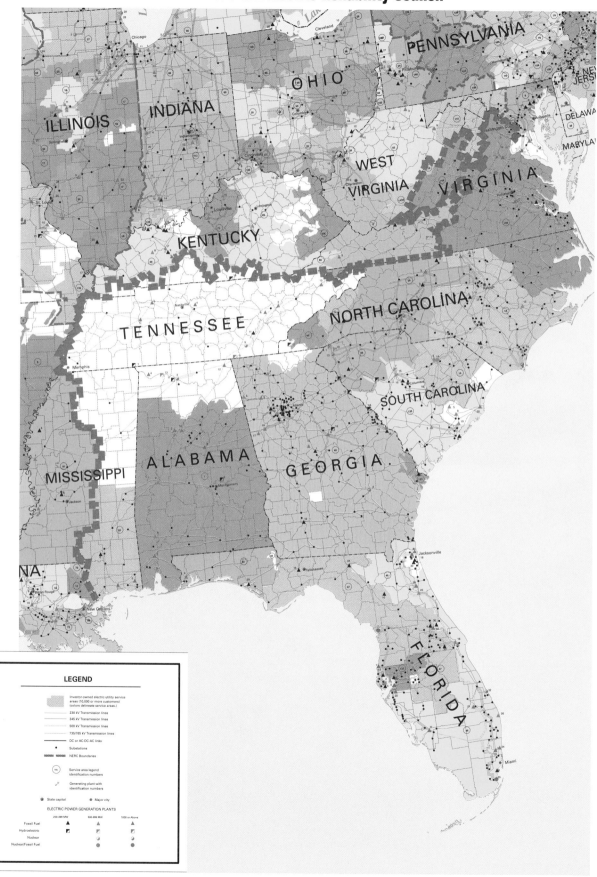

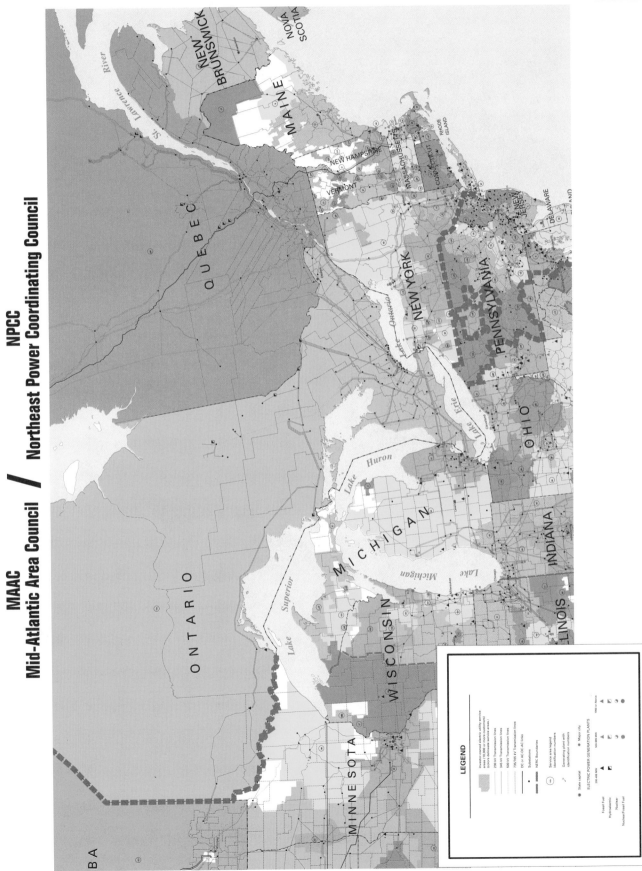

MAAC
Mid-Atlantic Area Council
NPCC
Northeast Power Coordinating Council

LEGEND

North America

LEGEND

Investor-owned electric utility service areas (10,000 or more customers) (colors delineate service areas.)

230 kV Transmission lines

345 kV Transmission lines

500 kV Transmission lines

735/765 kV Transmission lines

DC or AC-DC-AC links

Substations

NERC Boundaries

Service area legend identification numbers

Generating plant with identification numbers

State capital

Major city

ELECTRIC POWER GENERATION PLANTS

	200-499 MW	500-999 MW	1000 or Above
Fossil Fuel	▲	▲	▲
Hydroelectric	◢	◢	◢
Nuclear		◢	◢
Nuclear/Fossil Fuel		●	●

Canada

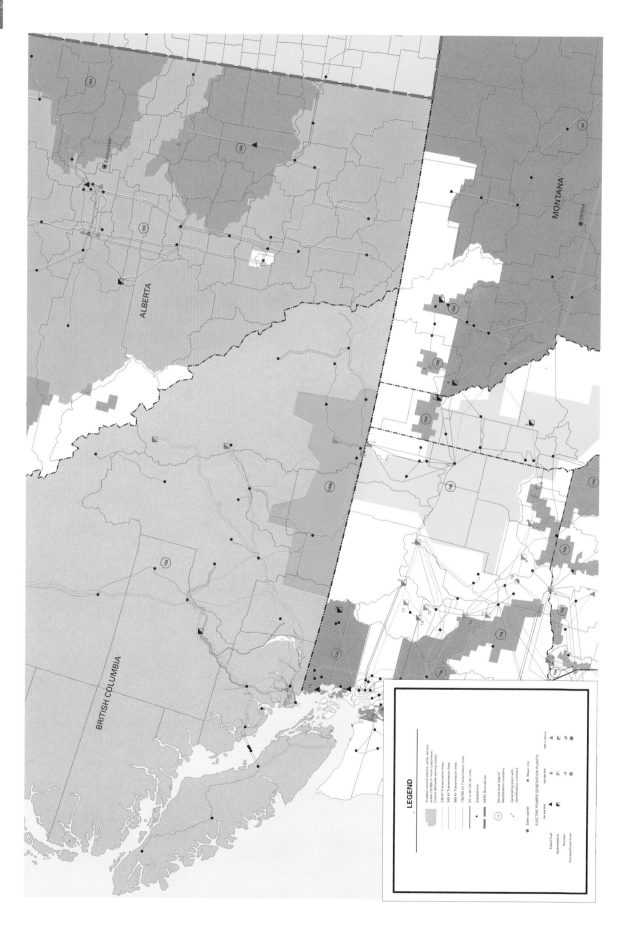

Canada

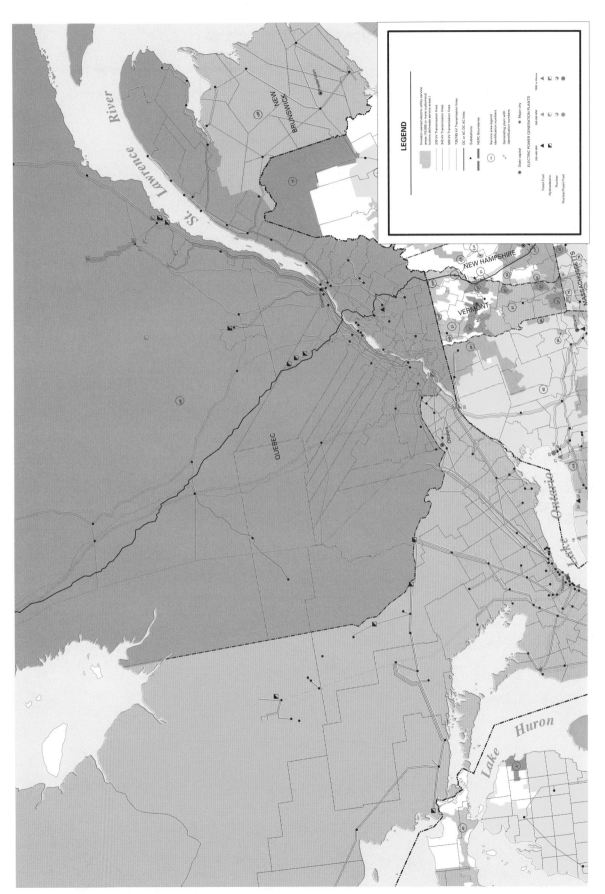

Mexico and Central America

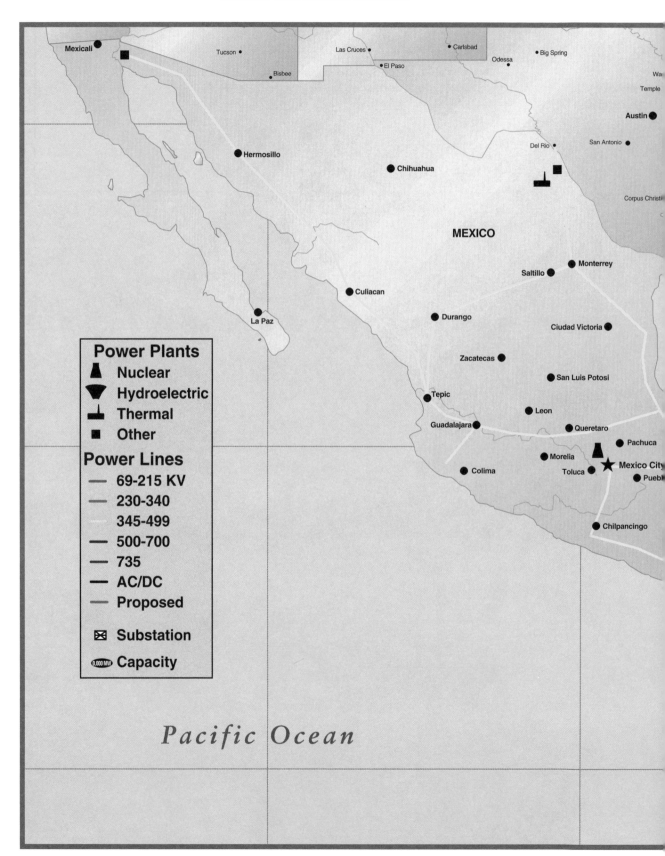

Power Plants
- ▲ Nuclear
- ▼ Hydroelectric
- ⊥ Thermal
- ■ Other

Power Lines
- — 69-215 KV
- — 230-340
- — 345-499
- — 500-700
- — 735
- — AC/DC
- — Proposed

- ⊠ Substation
- ⬭ Capacity

Pacific Ocean

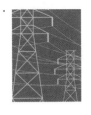

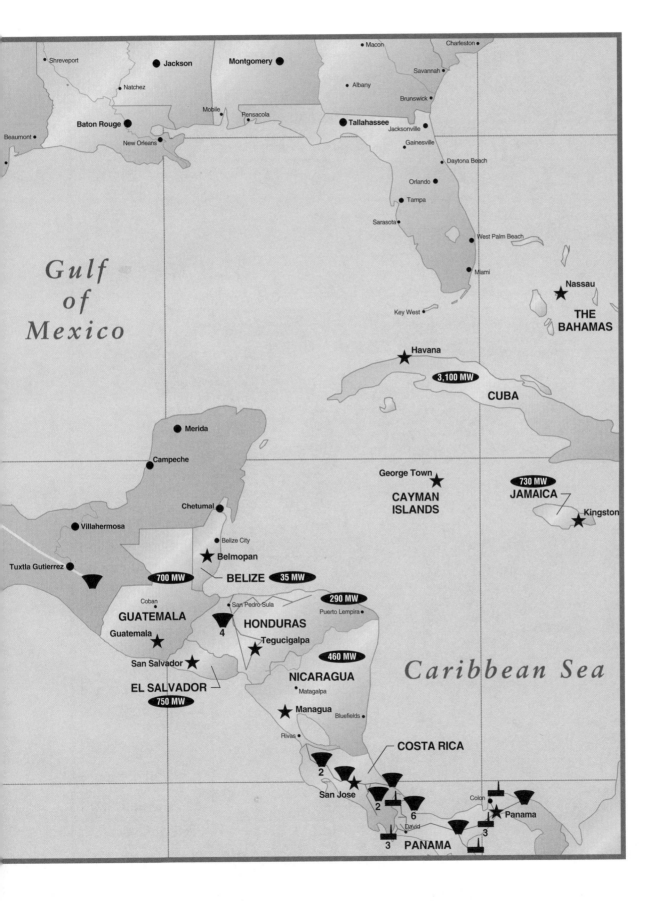

Gulf
of
Mexico

Caribbean Sea

Shreveport

Jackson

Montgomery

Macon

Charleston

Savannah

Natchez

Albany

Brunswick

Mobile

Pensacola

Baton Rouge

Tallahassee

Jacksonville

New Orleans

Gainesville

Beaumont

Daytona Beach

Orlando

Tampa

Sarasota

West Palm Beach

Miami

Key West

Nassau

**THE
BAHAMAS**

Havana

3,100 MW

CUBA

Merida

Campeche

George Town

**CAYMAN
ISLANDS**

730 MW

JAMAICA

Kingston

Chetumal

Villahermosa

Belize City

Belmopan

Tuxtla Gutierrez

700 MW

BELIZE

35 MW

Coban

San Pedro Sula

290 MW

GUATEMALA

Puerto Lempira

HONDURAS

Guatemala

4

San Salvador

Tegucigalpa

460 MW

EL SALVADOR

NICARAGUA

750 MW

Matagalpa

Managua

Bluefields

Rivas

COSTA RICA

2

San Jose

2

6

Colon

Panama

David

3

3

PANAMA

303

South America

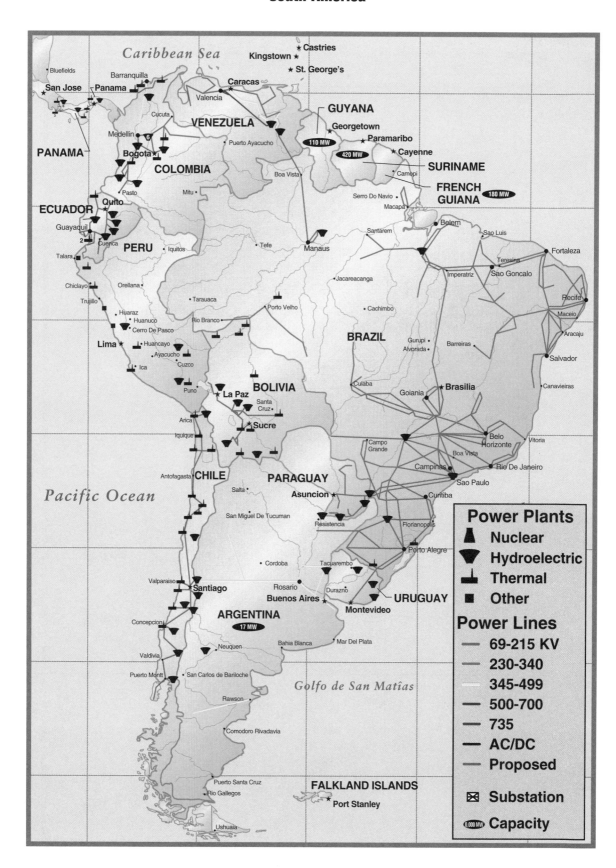

Europe

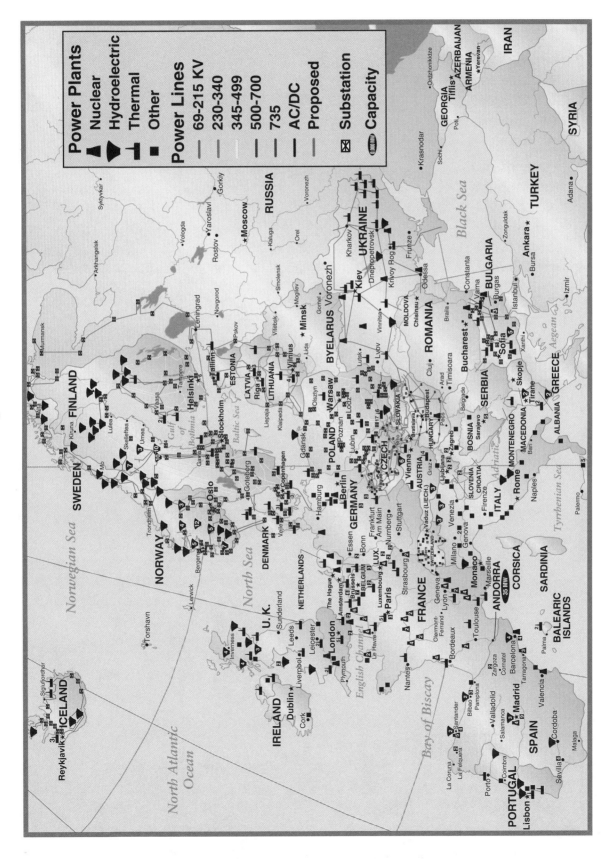

United Kingdom

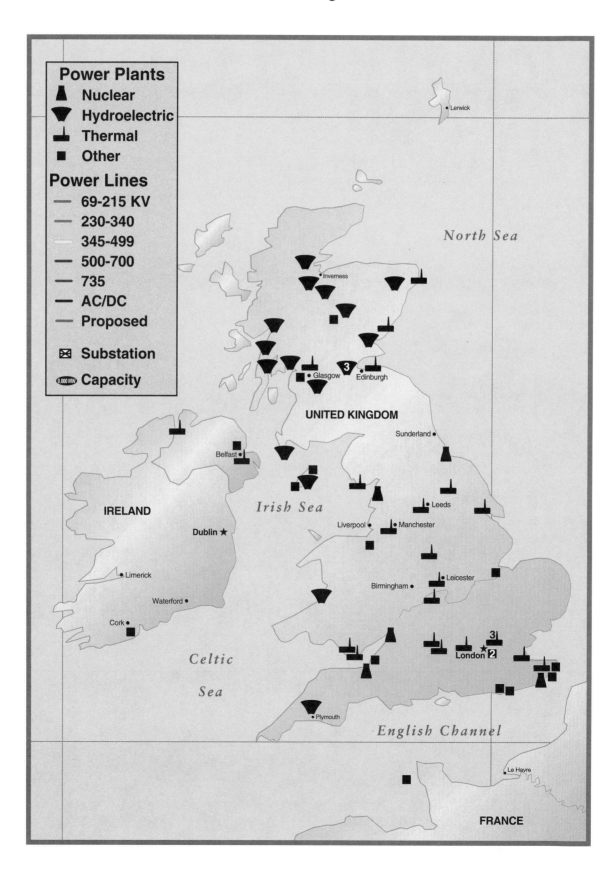

Northern Europe

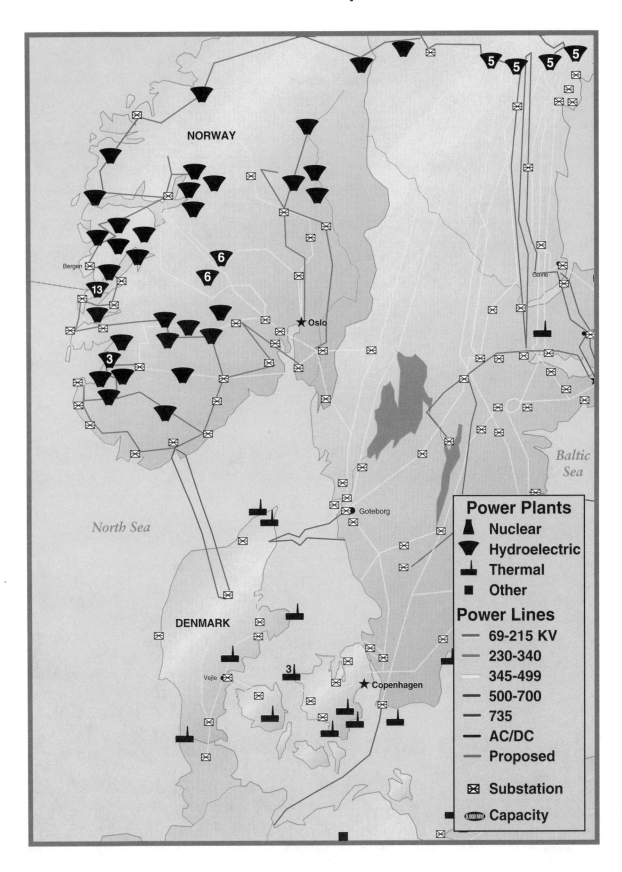

NORWAY

Bergen

13

6

6

3

3

Oslo

Gavle

North Sea

Baltic Sea

Goteborg

Power Plants
- **Nuclear**
- **Hydroelectric**
- **Thermal**
- **Other**

Power Lines
- 69-215 KV
- 230-340
- 345-499
- 500-700
- 735
- AC/DC
- Proposed

⊠ Substation

Capacity

DENMARK

Vejle

3

Copenhagen

307

Central Europe

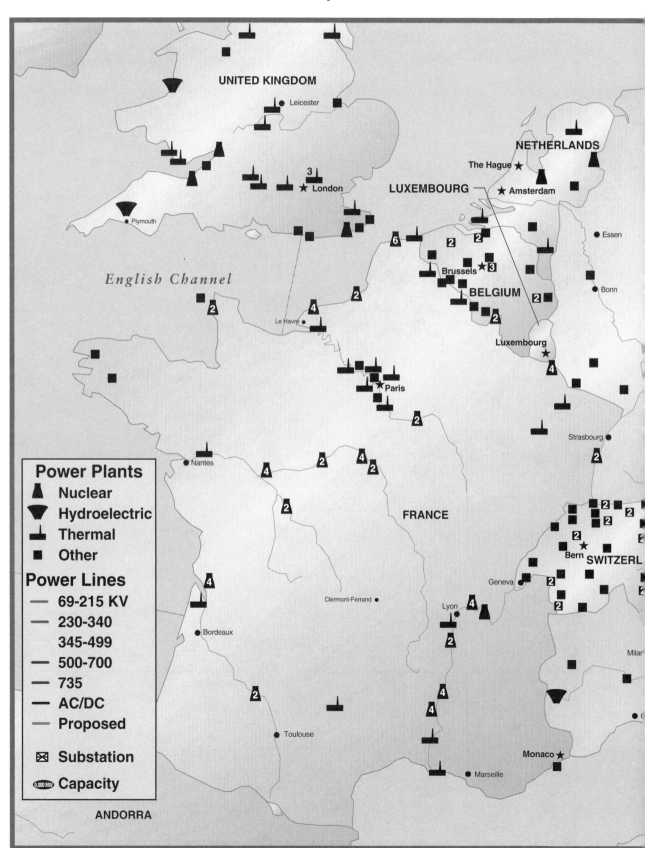

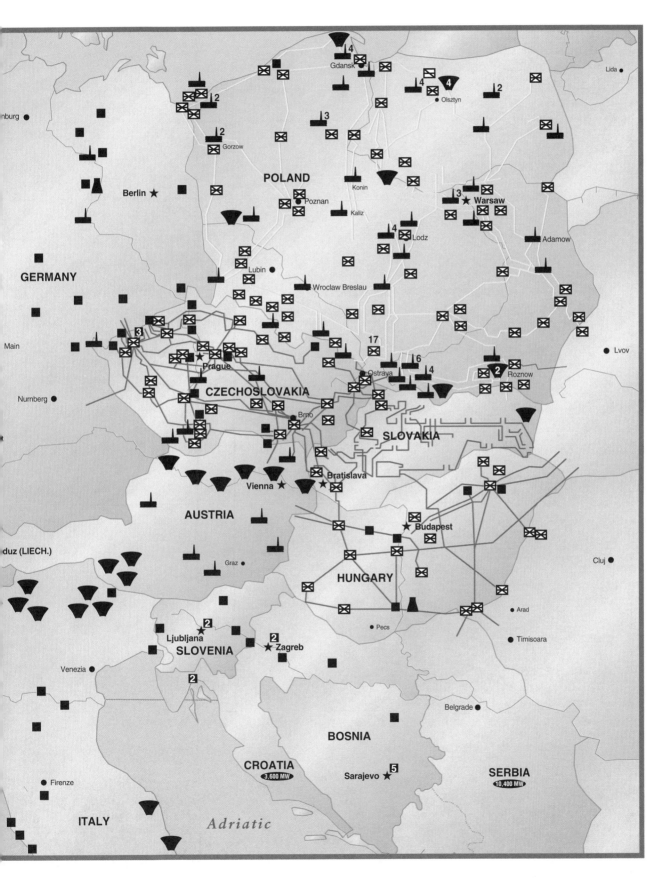

Commonwealth of Independent States

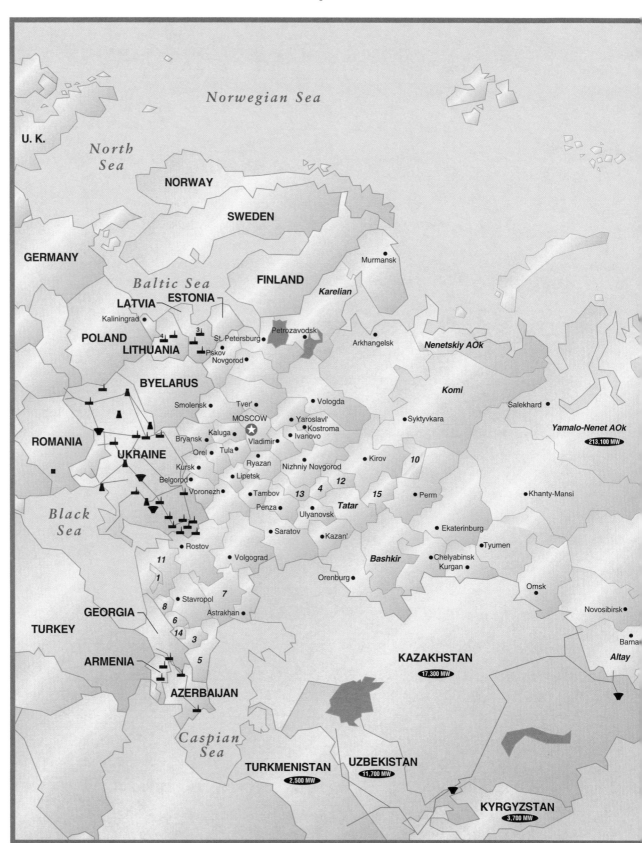

Norwegian Sea

U.K.

North Sea

GERMANY

NORWAY

SWEDEN

Baltic Sea

FINLAND

Murmansk

LATVIA

ESTONIA

Kaliningrad

Karelian

POLAND

LITHUANIA

St. Petersburg

Petrozavodsk

Arkhangelsk

Nenetskiy AOk

Pskov

Novgorod

BYELARUS

Smolensk

Tver'

Vologda

Komi

Salekhard

MOSCOW

Yaroslavl'

Syktyvkara

Yamalo-Nenet AOk

213,100 MW

Kostroma

ROMANIA

Kaluga

Vladimir

Ivanovo

Bryansk

Orel

Tula

Ryazan

Nizhniy Novgorod

Kirov

10

Perm

UKRAINE

Kursk

Lipetsk

12

15

Khanty-Mansi

Belgorod

Voronezh

13

4

Tatar

Black Sea

Tambov

Penza

Ulyanovsk

Saratov

Kazan'

Bashkir

Ekaterinburg

Tyumen

Rostov

Volgograd

Chelyabinsk

Kurgan

Orenburg

Omsk

11

1

Stavropol

7

Novosibirsk

8

Astrakhan

GEORGIA

6

Barna

14

3

Altay

TURKEY

5

KAZAKHSTAN

ARMENIA

17,300 MW

AZERBAIJAN

Caspian Sea

TURKMENISTAN

UZBEKISTAN

2,500 MW

11,700 MW

KYRGYZSTAN

3,700 MW

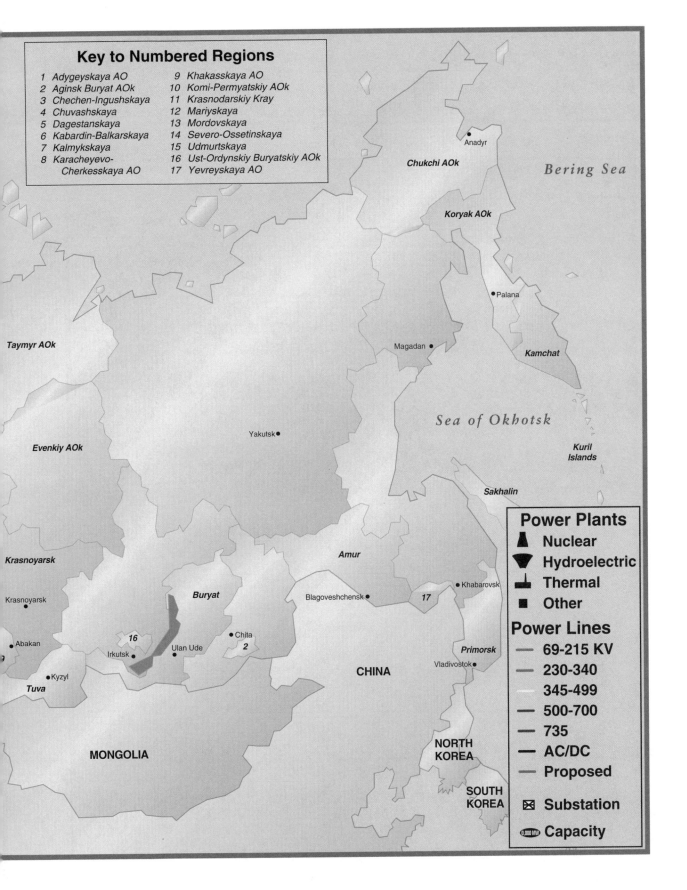

Key to Numbered Regions

1 Adygeyskaya AO
2 Aginsk Buryat AOk
3 Chechen-Ingushskaya
4 Chuvashskaya
5 Dagestanskaya
6 Kabardin-Balkarskaya
7 Kalmykskaya
8 Karacheyevo-
  Cherkesskaya AO
9 Khakasskaya AO
10 Komi-Permyatskiy AOk
11 Krasnodarskiy Kray
12 Mariyskaya
13 Mordovskaya
14 Severo-Ossetinskaya
15 Udmurtskaya
16 Ust-Ordynskiy Buryatskiy AOk
17 Yevreyskaya AO

Bering Sea

Chukchi AOk

Koryak AOk

Anadyr

Palana

Taymyr AOk

Magadan

Kamchat

Sea of Okhotsk

Evenkiy AOk

Yakutsk

Kuril Islands

Sakhalin

Krasnoyarsk

Krasnoyarsk

Amur

Buryat

Khabarovsk

Blagoveshchensk

17

Abakan

16

Chita

2

Irkutsk

Ulan Ude

Primorsk

Kyzyl

Vladivostok

Tuva

CHINA

MONGOLIA

NORTH KOREA

SOUTH KOREA

Power Plants
- Nuclear
- Hydroelectric
- Thermal
- Other

Power Lines
- 69-215 KV
- 230-340
- 345-499
- 500-700
- 735
- AC/DC
- Proposed

⊠ Substation

Capacity

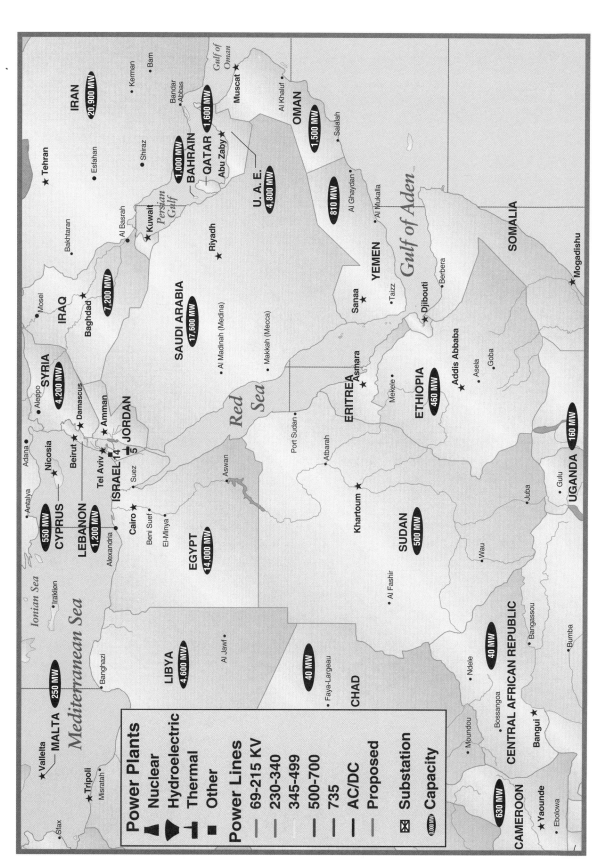

Northeast Africa

Power Plants
▲ Nuclear
◆ Hydroelectric
■ Thermal
■ Other

Power Lines
69-215 KV
230-340
345-499
500-700
735
AC/DC
Proposed

⊠ Substation

⬭ Capacity

IRAN 20,900 MW

• Kerman
• Bam
• Tehran
• Esfahan
• Shiraz
Bandar Abbas

Muscat ★ OMAN
• Al Khaluf
• Salalah
1,500 MW

Gulf of Oman

BAHRAIN 1,000 MW
QATAR 1,600 MW
Abu Zaby ★
U.A.E. 4,800 MW
810 MW
• Al Ghaydan
• Al Mukalla

• Al Basrah
Kuwait ★
Persian Gulf

• Bakhtaran
• Mosel
IRAQ
Baghdad ★ 7,200 MW

• Riyadh ★
SAUDI ARABIA 17,600 MW
• Al Madinah (Medina)
• Makkah (Mecca)

YEMEN
Sanaa ★
• Taizz
Djibouti •
• Berbera

Gulf of Aden

SOMALIA
Mogadishu ★

SYRIA 4,200 MW
• Aleppo
Damascus ★

• Adana
Nicosia ★
CYPRUS 550 MW
Beirut •
LEBANON 1,200 MW
Tel Aviv ■
ISRAEL 14
5
JORDAN
Amman ★

• Antalya
Iraklion •

Ionian Sea

Mediterranean Sea

MALTA 250 MW
★ Valletta

• Tripoli
Misratah •
• Sfax
• Banghazi

LIBYA 4,600 MW
• Al Jawf

Red Sea

ERITREA
Asmara ★
• Mekele
ETHIOPIA 460 MW
Addis Abbaba ★
• Asela
• Goba

• Port Sudan
• Atbarah

Khartoum ★
SUDAN 500 MW
• Wau
• Al Fashir

Cairo ★
• Beni Suef
• El-Minya
Alexandria •
Suez •
EGYPT 14,000 MW
Aswan •

UGANDA 160 MW
• Gulu
• Juba

CHAD 40 MW
• Faya-Largeau

CENTRAL AFRICAN REPUBLIC 40 MW
• Bangassou
• Bumba
• Ndele
• Bossangoa
Bangui ★
• Moundou

CAMEROON 630 MW
★ Yaounde
• Ebolowa

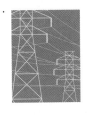

Northwest Africa

Power Plants

- ▲ Nuclear
- ◤ Hydroelectric
- ⊤ Thermal
- ■ Other

Power Lines

- 69-215 KV
- 230-340
- 345-499
- 500-700
- 735
- AC/DC
- Proposed
- ⊠ Substation
- ⬭ Capacity

Ionian Sea

Mediterranean Sea

• Alexandria

• Traklion

• Banghazi

MALTA ⬭ 250 MW

★ Valletta

• Tripoli

★ Misratah

LIBYA ⬭ 4,600 MW

• Banghazi

CHAD ⬭ 40 MW

• Bangassou

• Bumba

CENTRAL AFRICAN REPUBLIC ⬭ 40 MW

★ Bangui

★ Tunis

• Sfax

TUNISIA ⬭ 1,400 MW

• Gafsa

• Sabhah

• Marzuq

• Aozou

• Bilma

• Moundou

• Bossangoa

★ Tripoli

• Annaba

• Batna

• Ouargla

★ Algers

• Oran

ALGERIA ⬭ 5,800 MW

• Timimoun

• Reggane

NIGER ⬭ 60 MW

• Agades

• Tahoua

• Maiduguri

• Zinder

• Katsina

• Zaria

★ Abuja

• Kaduna

NIGERIA ⬭ 4,600 MW

★ N'Djamena

CAMEROON ⬭ 630 MW

★ Yaounde

• Ebolowa

★ Malabo

EQUATORIAL GUINEA ⬭ 40 MW

• Malaga

★ Gibraltar

• Tangier

★ Rabat

• Casablanca

★ Marrakech

MOROCCO ⬭ 2,600 MW

• Djanet

Canary Islands

WESTERN SAHARA ⬭ 60 MW

• Layoun

MAURITANIA ⬭ 110 MW

• Atar

★ Nouakchott

• Taoudenni

MALI ⬭ 90 MW

• Araouane

• Tessalit

• Tombouctou

• Gao

★ Niamey

BURKINA ⬭ 60 MW

★ Ouagadougou

• Tamale

• Korhogo

BENIN ⬭ 30 MW

TOGO ⬭ 30 MW

• Porto Novo

★ Accra

★ Lome

GHANA ⬭ 1,200 MW

⬭ 23 MW

• Ibadan

★ Dakar

★ Banjul

GAMBIA ⬭ 30 MW

SENEGAL ⬭ 230 MW

• Kayes

★ Bamako

GUINEA-BISSAU ⬭ 22 MW

★ Bissau

★ Conakry

GUINEA ⬭ 180 MW

• Kankan

★ Freetown

SIERRA LEONE ⬭ 130 MW

★ Monrovia

LIBERIA ⬭ 330 MW

IVORY COAST

★ Abidjan

• Man

⬭ 1,000 MW

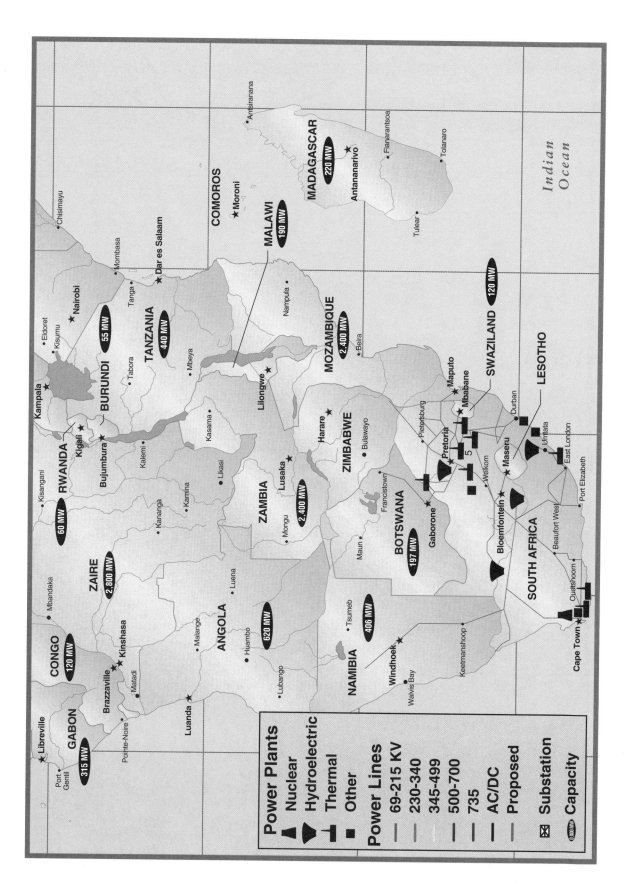

Southern Africa

Power Plants
- ▶ Nuclear
- ▶ Hydroelectric
- ┬ Thermal
- ■ Other

Power Lines
- | 69–215 KV
- | 230–340
- | 345–499
- | 500–700
- | 735
- | AC/DC
- | Proposed
- ⊠ Substation
- 0,000 MW Capacity

GABON — 315 MW
CONGO — 120 MW
ZAIRE — 2,800 MW
CONGO — 60 MW
ANGOLA — 620 MW
NAMIBIA — 406 MW
BOTSWANA — 197 MW
ZAMBIA — 2,400 MW
ZIMBABWE
MOZAMBIQUE — 2,400 MW
SWAZILAND — 120 MW
MALAWI — 190 MW
MADAGASCAR — 220 MW
TANZANIA — 440 MW
BURUNDI — 55 MW
RWANDA
COMOROS
LESOTHO
SOUTH AFRICA

Indian Ocean

Libreville
Port Gentil
Pointe-Noire
Brazzaville
Matadi
Kinshasa
Luanda
Lubango
Huambo
Malange
Luena
Mbandaka
Kisangani
Kamina
Kananga
Kalemi
Likasi
Kasama
Mbeya
Tabora
Kigali
Bujumbura
Kampala
Eldoret
Kisumu
Nairobi
Chisimayu
Mombasa
Tanga
Dar es Salaam
Lilongwe
Nampula
Beira
Harare
Bulawayo
Lusaka
Mongu
Maun
Francistown
Gaborone
Keetmanshoop
Walvis Bay
Windhoek
Tsumeb
Oudtshoorn
Beaufort West
Cape Town
Port Elizabeth
Beaufort West
East London
Umtata
Durban
Maseru
Bloemfontein
Welkom
Pretoria
Pietersburg
Maputo
Mbabane
Moroni
Antsiranana
Antananarivo
Fianarantsoa
Tulear
Tolanaro

India, Pakistan, and Sri Lanka

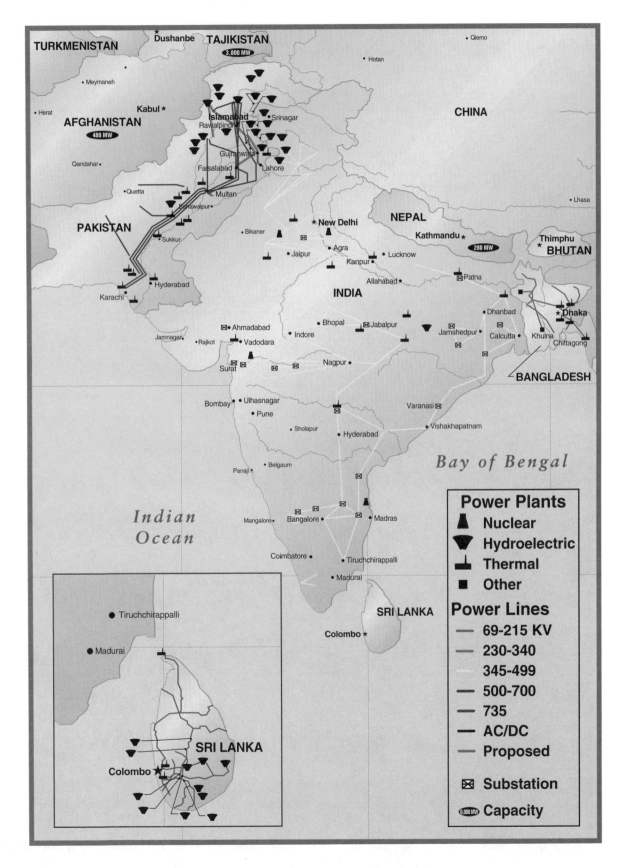

Power Plants
- ▲ Nuclear
- ▼ Hydroelectric
- Thermal
- ■ Other

Power Lines
- — 69-215 KV
- — 230-340
- — 345-499
- — 500-700
- — 735
- — AC/DC
- — Proposed

⊠ Substation

0,000 MW Capacity

China

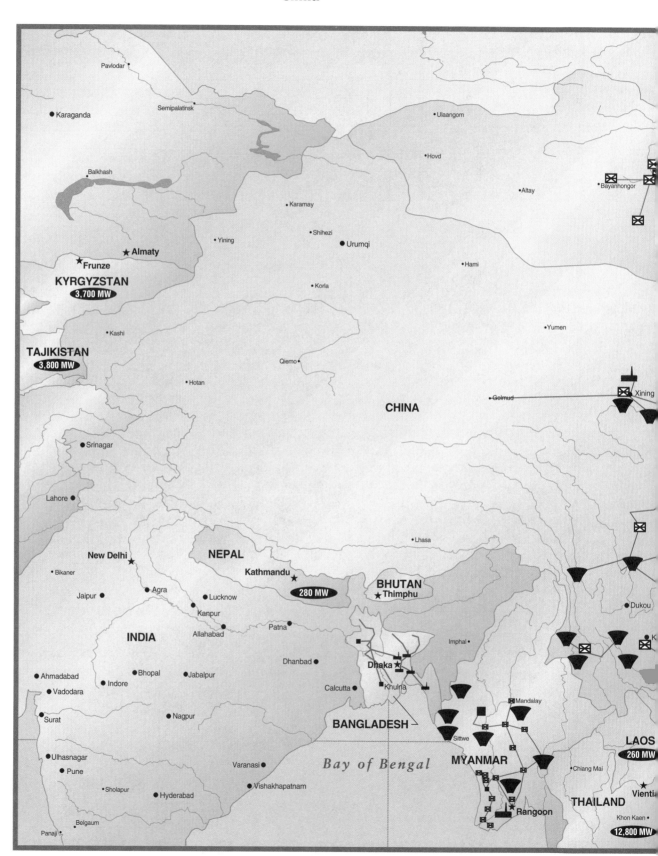

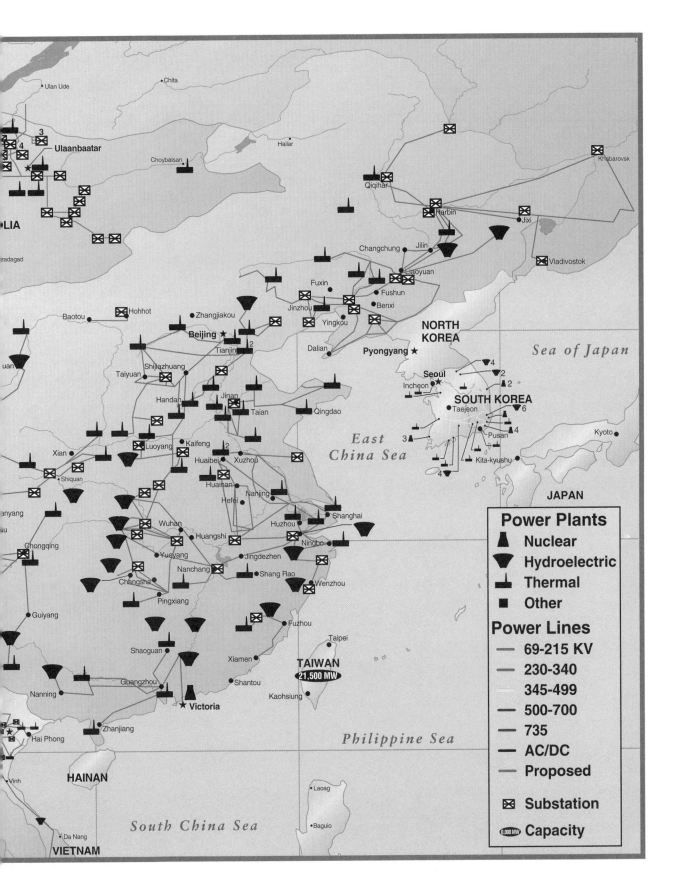

Ulan Ude
Chita
Hailar
Choybalsan
Qiqihar
Khabarovsk
Ulaanbaatar
Harbin
Jixi
Changchung
Jilin
Vladivostok
Liaoyuan
Fuxin
Fushun
Hohhot
Jinzhou
Benxi
Baotou
Zhangjiakou
Yingkou
NORTH KOREA
Beijing ★
Dalian
Pyongyang ★
Tianjin
2
Taiyuan
Shijiazhuang
Sea of Japan
Seoul ★
Incheon
SOUTH KOREA
Handan
Jinan
Taian
Qingdao
Taejeon
Xian
Luoyang
Kaifeng
2
Pusan
Kyoto
Shiquan
Huaibei
Xuzhou
East China Sea
Kita-kyushu
Huainan
Hefei
Nanjing
Chongqing
Wuhan
Huangshi
Shanghai
Huzhou
JAPAN
Yueyang
Jingdezhen
Ningbo
Guiyang
Changsha
Nanchang
Shang Rao
Pingxiang
Wenzhou
Fuzhou
Shaoguan
Xiamen
Taipei
TAIWAN
21,500 MW
Nanning
Guangzhou
Shantou
★ **Victoria**
Kaohsiung
Zhanjiang
Hai Phong
Philippine Sea
HAINAN
Laoag
Vinh
Da Nang
South China Sea
Baguio
VIETNAM

Power Plants
▲ Nuclear
▼ Hydroelectric
⊥ Thermal
■ Other

Power Lines
— 69-215 KV
— 230-340
— 345-499
— 500-700
— 735
— AC/DC
— Proposed

⊠ Substation
0,000 MW Capacity

Southeast Asia

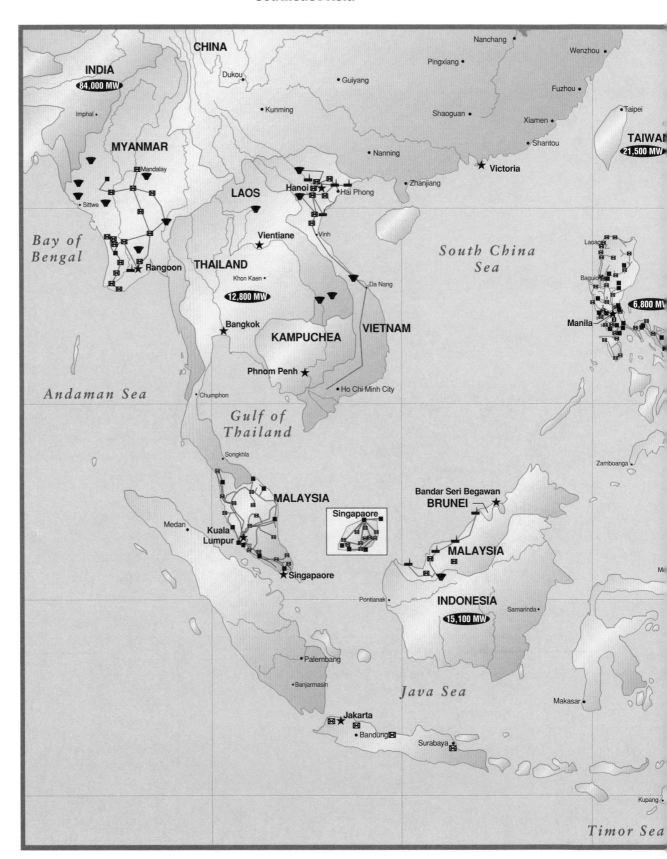

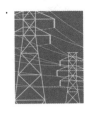

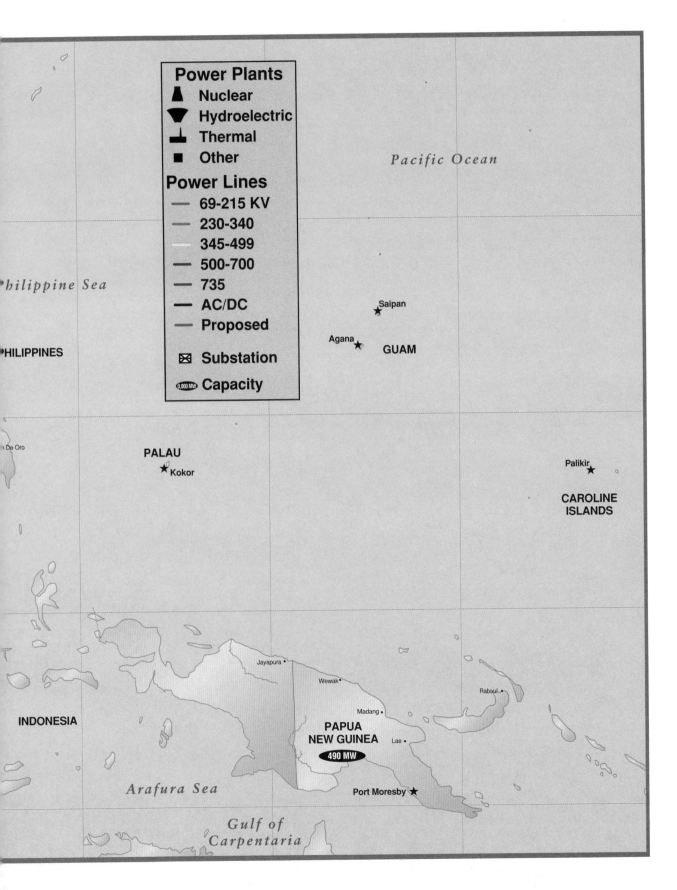

Power Plants
▲ Nuclear
▼ Hydroelectric
⊥ Thermal
■ Other

Power Lines
— 69-215 KV
— 230-340
— 345-499
— 500-700
— 735
— AC/DC
— Proposed

⊠ Substation

⬭ 0.000 MW Capacity

Pacific Ocean

Philippine Sea

PHILIPPINES

★ Saipan

Agana ★   GUAM

De Oro

PALAU
★ Kokor

Palikir ★

CAROLINE ISLANDS

Jayapura •

Wewak •

Rabaul •

Madang •

INDONESIA

PAPUA NEW GUINEA
⬭ 490 MW

Lae •

Arafura Sea

Port Moresby ★

Gulf of Carpentaria

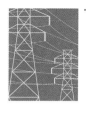

Australia and New Zealand

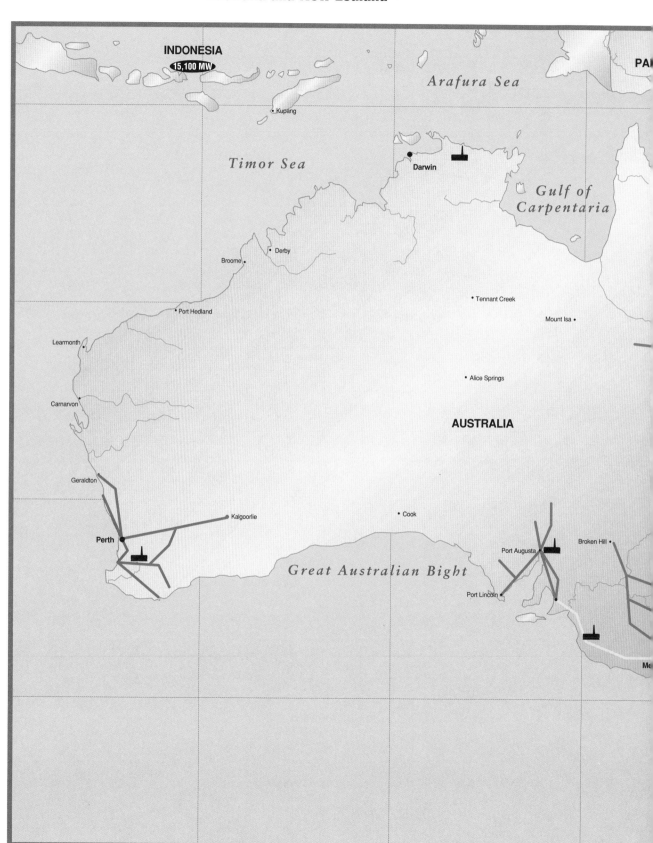

INDONESIA

15,100 MW

Kupang

Arafura Sea

PA

Timor Sea

Darwin

Gulf of Carpentaria

Derby

Broome

Tennant Creek

Port Hedland

Mount Isa

Learmonth

Alice Springs

Carnarvon

AUSTRALIA

Geraldton

Cook

Kalgoorlie

Port Augusta

Broken Hill

Perth

Great Australian Bight

Port Lincoln

Me

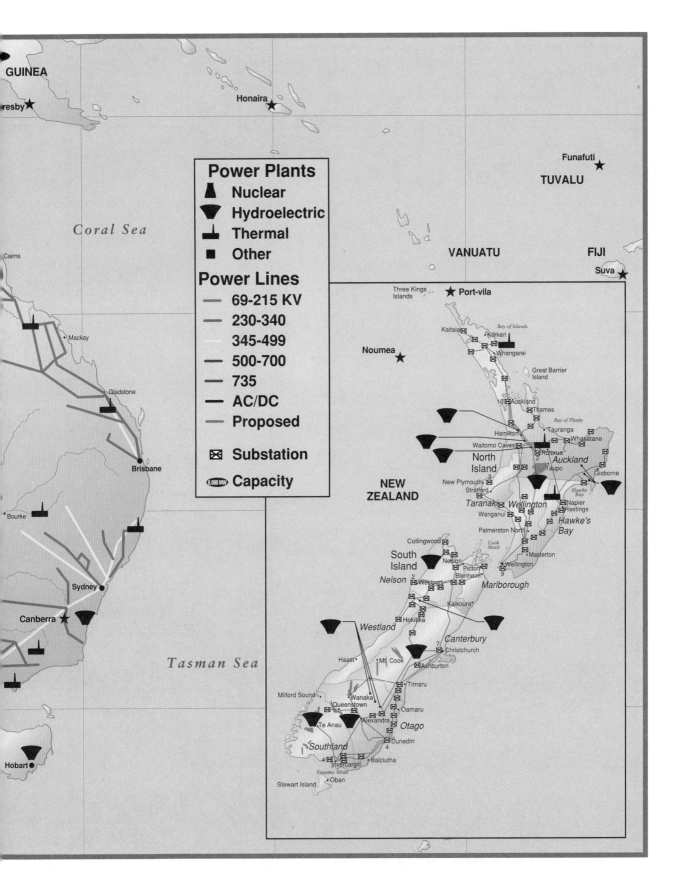

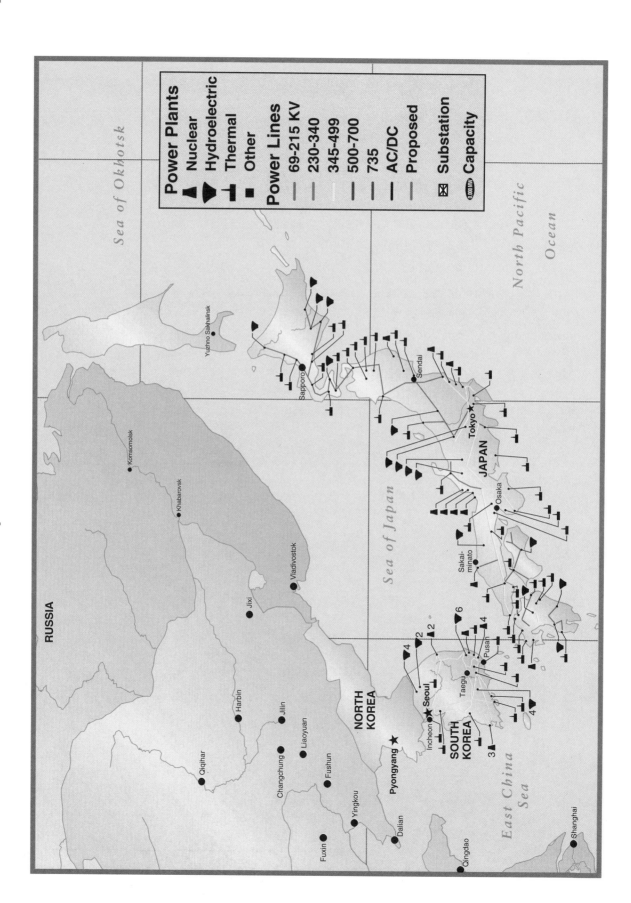

Japan and South Korea

Power Plants
Nuclear
Hydroelectric
Thermal
Other

Power Lines
69-215 KV
230-340
345-499
500-700
735
AC/DC
Proposed
Substation
Capacity

Sea of Okbotsk

North Pacific Ocean

Sea of Japan

East China Sea

RUSSIA

NORTH KOREA

SOUTH KOREA

JAPAN

Yuzhno Sakhalinsk
Sapporo
Sendai
Tokyo
Osaka
Sakai-minato
Komsomolsk
Khabarovsk
Vladivostok
Jixi
Harbin
Jilin
Liaoyuan
Changchung
Fushun
Yingkou
Dalian
Fuxin
Qiqihar
Qingdao
Shanghai
Pyongyang
Incheon
Seoul
Taegu
Pusan

Country	Population (millions)	Capacity (MW)	Generation (MkWh)	kWh per capita
Afghanistan	21.2	480	550	26
Albania	3.4	770	4,000	1,176
Algeria	28.5	5,800	18,400	646
Andorra	0.066	35	140	2,121
Angola	10.1	620	1,900	188
Argentina	34.3	17,330	54,800	1,598
Armenia	3.6	4,600	7,000	1,944
Australia	18.3	34,500	155,000	8,470
Austria	8	17,200	50,200	6,275
Azerbaijan	7.8	4,900	17,500	2,244
Bahrain	0.576	1,000	3,300	5,729
Bangladesh	1.3	2,700	9,200	7,077
Belarus	10.4	7,000	31,400	3,019
Belgium	10	14,000	66,000	6,600
Belize	0.214	35	110	514
Benin	5.5	30	10	2
Bhutan	1.8	360	1,700	944
Bolivia	7.9	0.75	2,400	304
Bosnia and Herzegovina	3.2	3,800	N/A	N/A
Botswana	1.4	197	900	643
Brazil	255,000	626	56,000	0.214
Brunei	0.292	380	1,200	4,110

Country	Population (millions)	Capacity (MW)	Generation (MkWh)	kWh per capita
Bulgaria	8.8	11,500	35,900	4,080
Burkina	10.4	60	190	18
Burma	45.1	1,100	2,600	58
Burundi	6.3	55	100	16
Cambodia	10.6	40	160	15
Cameroon	13.5	630	2,700	200
Canada	28.4	108,000	511,000	17,993
Central African Republic	3.2	40	100	31
Chad	5.6	40	80	14
Chile	14.2	4,810	24,400	1,718
China	1,200	162,000	746,000	622
Colombia	36.2	10,200	33,000	912
Congo	2.5	120	400	160
Costa Rica	3.4	1,000	4,100	1,206
Cote d'Ivoire	14.8	1,200	1,800	122
Croatia	4.7	3,600	N/A	N/A
Cuba	10.9	3,100	12,000	1,101
Cyprus	0.737	550	2,300	3,121
Czech Republic	10.4	14,500	56,300	5,413
Denmark	5.2	10,000	21,000	4,038
Djibouti	0.421	9	170	404
Dominican Republic	7.5	1,500	5,400	720

Country	Population (millions)	Capacity (MW)	Generation (MkWh)	kWh per capita
Ecuador	11.5	2,300	6,900	600
Egypt	62.8	14,000	45,400	723
El Salvador	5.9	750	2,400	407
Equatorial Guinea	0.42	23	20	48
Eritrea	3.6	N/A	N/A	N/A
Estonia	1.6	3,500	11,300	7,063
Ethiopia	56	460	1,300	23
Finland	5	13,400	58,000	11,600
France	58.1	105,300	447,000	7,694
French Guiana	0.145	180	450	3,103
Gabon	1.2	315	910	758
Gambia, The	1	30	70	70
Georgia	5.7	5,000	9,100	1,596
Germany	81.3	115,400	493,000	6,064
Ghana	17.8	1,200	6,100	343
Greece	10.6	9,000	35,800	3,377
Greenland	0.058	84	210	3,621
Guatemala	11	700	2,300	209
Guinea	6.6	180	520	79
Guinea-Bissau	1.1	22	40	36
Guyana	0.724	110	230	318
Honduras	5.5	290	2,300	418

Country	Population (millions)	Capacity (MW)	Generation (MkWh)	kWh per capita
Hungary	10.3	6,740	13,000	1,262
Iceland	0.266	1,000	4,700	17,669
India	937	84,000	314,000	335
Indonesia	203.5	15,100	44,000	216
Iran	64.6	20,900	50,800	786
Iraq	20.6	7,200	25,700	1,248
Ireland	3.6	3,900	14,900	4,139
Israel	5.4	6,400	25,000	4,630
Italy	58.3	63,000	220,000	3,774
Jamaica	2.6	730	2,600	1,000
Japan	125.5	205,100	840,000	6,693
Jordan	4.1	1,100	4,200	1,024
Kazakhstan	17.4	17,300	65,100	3,741
Kenya	28.9	810	3,300	114
Korea, Democratic People's Republic of	45.6	27,000	137,000	3,004
Korea, Republic of	23.5	9,500	50,000	2,128
Kuwait	1.8	7,200	11,000	6,111
Kyrgyzstan	4.7	3,700	12,700	2,702
Laos	4.8	260	870	181
Latvia	2.8	2,000	5,500	1,964
Lebanon	3.7	1,200	2,500	676

Country	Population (millions)	Capacity (MW)	Generation (MkWh)	kWh per capita
Lesotho	2	Supplied by South Africa	Supplied by South Africa	N/A
Liberia	3	330	440	147
Libya	5.2	4,600	16,100	3,096
Liechtenstein	0.031	23	150	4,839
Lithuania	3.9	6,200	18,900	4,846
Luxembourg	0.405	1,200	1,374	3,393
Macedonia, The Former Yugoslav Republic of	2.2	1,600	N/A	N/A
Madagascar	13.9	220	560	40
Malawi	10	190	820	84
Malaysia	19.7	6,700	31,000	1,574
Mali	9.4	90	310	33
Malta	0.37	250	1,100	2,973
Mauritania	2.3	110	135	59
Mauritius	1.1	340	920	836
Mexico	94	28,700	122,000	1,298
Moldova	4.5	3,000	8,200	1,822
Mongolia	2.5	900	3,100	1,240
Montenegro and Serbia	11.1	10,400	34,000	3,063
Morocco	29.2	2,600	9,900	339
Mozambique	18.1	2,400	1,700	94
Namibia	1.7	406	1,290	759

Country	Population (millions)	Capacity (MW)	Generation (MkWh)	kWh per capita
Nepal	21.6	280	920	43
Netherlands	15.5	17,500	72,400	4,671
New Zealand	3.4	7,500	30,500	8,971
Nicaragua	4.2	460	1,600	381
Niger	9.3	60	200	22
Nigeria	101.2	4,600	11,300	112
North Korea	23.5	9,500	44,000	1,872
Norway	4.3	27,300	118,000	27,442
Oman	2.1	1,500	7,000	3,333
Pakistan	131.5	10,800	52,400	398
Panama Canal	2.7	960	2,800	1,037
Papua New Guinea	4.3	490	1,800	419
Paraguay	5.4	6,500	26,500	4,907
Peru	24	4,200	11,200	467
Philippines	73.3	6,800	20,400	278
Poland	38.8	31,100	124	3
Portugal	11	8,200	29,500	2,783
Puerto Rico	3.8	4,200	15,600	4,105
Qatar	0.525	1,600	4,800	9,143
Romania	23.2	22,200	50,800	2,190
Russia	149.9	213,100	876,000	5,844
Rwanda	8.7	60	190	22

Country	Population (millions)	Capacity (MW)	Generation (MkWh)	kWh per capita
Saudi Arabia	18.8	17,600	46,000	2,447
Senegal	9	230	720	80
Serbia and Montenegro	11.1	10,400	34,000	3,063
Sierra Leone	4.8	130	220	46
Singapore	2.9	4,500	17,000	5,862
Slovak Republic	N/A	1,600	N/A	N/A
Slovakia	5.4	6,300	20,900	3,870
Slovenia	2	2,700	8,900	4,450
Somalia	7.3	N/A	N/A	N/A
South Africa	45	40,000	163,000	3,622
South Korea	45.6	30,500	155,900	3,419
Spain	39.4	43,800	148,000	3,756
Sri Lanka	18	1,400	3,200	175
Sudan	20	500	1,300	65
Suriname	0.43	420	1,400	3,256
Svalbard	0.003	21	45	15,000
Swaziland	0.967	120	410	424
Sweden	8.8	34,600	141,000	16,023
Switzerland	7	15,400	58,000	8,286
Syria	15.5	4,200	13,200	852
Taiwan	21.5	21,500	108,000	5,023
Tajikistan	6.2	3,800	17,000	2,742

Country	Population (millions)	Capacity (MW)	Generation (MkWh)	kWh per capita
Tanzania, United Republic of	28.7	440	880	31
Thailand	60.3	12,800	56,800	942
Togo	4.4	30	60	14
Tunisia	8.9	1,400	5,400	607
Turkey	63.4	18,700	71,000	1,120
Turkmenistan	4.1	2,500	10,500	2,561
Uganda	19.6	160	780	40
Ukraine	51.9	54,400	182,000	3,507
United Arab Emirates	3	4,800	16,500	5,500
United Kingdom	58.3	65,400	303,000	5,197
United States	263.8	695,100	3,100,000	11,751
Uruguay	3.2	2,000	9,000	2,813
Uzbekistan	23	11,700	47,500	2,065
Venezuela	21	21,000	72	3
Vietnam	74	3,300	9,700	130
Western Sahara	0.217	60	79	364
Western Samoa	0.209	29	50	239
Yemen	15	810	1,800	120
Zaire	44.1	2,800	6,200	141
Zambia	9.4	2,400	7,800	830
World	5,700	2,773,000	11,601,000	2,035